T0226220

Lecture Notes in Computer Science   10697

Commenced Publication in 1973
Founding and Former Series Editors:
Gerhard Goos, Juris Hartmanis, and Jan van Leeuwen

More information about this series at http://www.springer.com/series/7409

Christophe Debruyne · Hervé Panetto
Georg Weichhart · Peter Bollen
Ioana Ciuciu · Maria-Esther Vidal
Robert Meersman (Eds.)

On the Move to Meaningful Internet Systems

OTM 2017 Workshops

Confederated International Workshops
EI2N, FBM, ICSP, Meta4eS, OTMA 2017
and ODBASE Posters 2017
Rhodes, Greece, October 23–28, 2017
Revised Selected Papers

 Springer

Editors
Christophe Debruyne
Odisee University College
Brussels
Belgium

Hervé Panetto
University of Lorraine
Vandoeuvre-les-Nancy
France

Georg Weichhart
University Linz
Linz
Austria

Peter Bollen
Maastricht University
Maastricht
The Netherlands

Ioana Ciuciu
University Babes-Bolyai
Cluj-Napoca
Romania

Maria-Esther Vidal
Universidad Simón Bolívar
Caracas
Venezuela

Robert Meersman
TU Graz
Graz
Austria

ISSN 0302-9743   ISSN 1611-3349   (electronic)
Lecture Notes in Computer Science
ISBN 978-3-319-73804-8   ISBN 978-3-319-73805-5   (eBook)
https://doi.org/10.1007/978-3-319-73805-5

Library of Congress Control Number: 2017963771

LNCS Sublibrary: SL3 – Information Systems and Applications, incl. Internet/Web, and HCI

Printed on acid-free paper

This Springer imprint is published by Springer Nature
The registered company is Springer International Publishing AG
The registered company address is: Gewerbestrasse 11, 6330 Cham, Switzerland

General Co-chairs and Editors' Message for OnTheMove 2017

The OnTheMove 2017 event held October 23–27 in Rhodes, Greece, further consolidated the importance of the series of annual conferences that was started in 2002 in Irvine, California. It then moved to Catania, Sicily, in 2003, to Cyprus in 2004 and 2005, Montpellier in 2006, Vilamoura in 2007 and 2009, in 2008 to Monterrey, Mexico, to Heraklion, Crete in 2010 and 2011, to Rome in 2012, Graz in 2013, Amantea, Italy, in 2014 and lastly to Rhodes in 2015 and 2016 as well.

This prime event continues to attract a diverse and relevant selection of today's research worldwide on the scientific concepts underlying new computing paradigms, which of necessity must be distributed, heterogeneous, and supporting an environment of resources that are autonomous yet must meaningfully cooperate. Indeed, as such large, complex, and networked intelligent information systems become the focus and norm for computing, there continues to be an acute and even increasing need to address the implied software, system, and enterprise issues and discuss them face to face in an integrated forum that covers methodological, semantic, theoretical, and application issues too. As we all realize, e-mail, the Internet, and even video conferences are not by themselves optimal nor even sufficient for effective and efficient scientific exchange.

The OnTheMove (OTM) International Federated Conference series has been created precisely to cover the scientific exchange needs of the communities that work in the broad yet closely connected fundamental technological spectrum of Web-based distributed computing. The OTM program every year covers data and Web semantics, distributed objects, Web services, databases, information systems, enterprise workflow and collaboration, ubiquity, interoperability, mobility, as well as grid and high-performance computing.

OnTheMove is proud to give meaning to the "federated" aspect in its full title: It aspires to be a primary scientific meeting place where all aspects of research and development of Internet- and intranet-based systems in organizations and for e-business are discussed in a scientifically motivated way, in a forum of interconnected workshops and conferences. This year's 15th edition of the OTM Federated Conferences event therefore once more provided an opportunity for researchers and practitioners to understand, discuss, and publish these developments within the broader context of distributed, ubiquitous computing. To further promote synergy and coherence, the main conferences of OTM 2017 were conceived against a background of their three interlocking global themes:

- Trusted Cloud Computing Infrastructures Emphasizing Security and Privacy
- Technology and Methodology for Data and Knowledge Resources on the (Semantic) Web
- Deployment of Collaborative and Social Computing for and in an Enterprise Context

Originally the federative structure of OTM was formed by the co-location of three related, complementary, and successful main conference series: DOA (Distributed Objects and Applications, held since 1999), covering the relevant infrastructure-enabling technologies, ODBASE (Ontologies, Databases and Applications of Semantics, since 2002) covering Web semantics, XML databases and ontologies, and of course CoopIS (Cooperative Information Systems, held since 1993), which studies the application of these technologies in an enterprise context through, e.g., workflow systems and knowledge management. In the 2011 edition, security aspects, originally started as topics of the IS workshop in OTM 2006, became the focus of DOA as secure virtual infrastructures, further broadened to cover aspects of trust and privacy in so-called cloud-based systems. As this latter aspect came to dominate agendas in this and overlapping research communities, we decided in 2014 to rename the event as the Cloud and Trusted Computing (C&TC) Conference, and originally launched it in a workshop format.

These three main conferences specifically seek high-quality contributions of a more mature nature and encourage researchers to treat their respective topics within a framework that simultaneously incorporates (a) theory, (b) conceptual design and development, (c) methodology and pragmatics, and (d) application in particular case studies and industrial solutions.

As in previous years, we again solicited and selected additional quality workshop proposals to complement the more mature and "archival" nature of the main conferences. Our workshops are intended to serve as "incubators" for emergent research results in selected areas related, or becoming related, to the general domain of Web-based distributed computing. This year this difficult and time-consuming job of selecting and coordinating the workshops was brought to a successful end by Ioana Ciuciu, and we were very glad to see that our earlier successful workshops (EI2N, META4eS, FBM) re-appeared in 2017, in some cases in alliance with other older or newly emerging workshops. The Fact-Based Modeling (FBM) workshop in 2015 succeeded and expanded the scope of the successful earlier ORM workshop. The Industry Case Studies Program, started in 2011 under the leadership of Hervé Panetto and OMG's Richard Mark Soley, further gained momentum and visibility in its seventh edition this year.

The OTM registration format ("one workshop or conference buys all workshops or conferences") actively intends to promote synergy between related areas in the field of distributed computing and to stimulate workshop audiences to productively mingle with each other and, optionally, with those of the main conferences. In particular, EI2N continues to so create and exploit a visible cross-pollination with CoopIS.

We were very happy to see that in 2017 the number of quality submissions for the OnTheMove Academy (OTMA) noticeably increased. OTMA implements our unique, actively coached and therefore very time- and effort-intensive formula to bring PhD students together, and aims to carry our "vision for the future" in research in the areas covered by OTM. Its 2017 edition was organized and managed by a dedicated team of collaborators and faculty, Peter Spyns, Maria-Esther Vidal, inspired as always by the OTMA Dean, Erich Neuhold.

In the OTM Academy, PhD research proposals are submitted by students for peer review; selected submissions and their approaches are to be presented by the students in front of a wider audience at the conference, and are independently and extensively analyzed and discussed in front of this audience by a panel of senior professors. One may readily appreciate the time, effort, and funds invested in this by OnTheMove and especially by the OTMA Faculty.

As the three main conferences and the associated workshops all share the distributed aspects of modern computing systems, they experience the application pull created by the Internet and by the so-called Semantic Web, in particular the developments of big data, the increased importance of security issues, and the globalization of mobile-based technologies. For ODBASE 2017, the focus somewhat shifted from knowledge bases and methods required for enabling the use of formal semantics in Web-based databases and information systems to applications, especially those within IT-driven communities. For CoopIS 2017, the focus as before was on the interaction of such technologies and methods with business process issues, such as occur in networked organizations and enterprises. These subject areas overlap in a scientifically natural and fascinating fashion and many submissions in fact also covered and exploited the mutual impact among them. For our event C&TC 2017, the primary emphasis was again squarely put on the virtual and security aspects of Web-based computing in the broadest sense. As with the earlier OnTheMove editions, the organizers wanted to stimulate this cross-pollination by a program of engaging keynote speakers from academia and industry and shared by all OTM component events. We are quite proud to list for this year:

- Stephen Mellor, Industrial Internet Consortium, Needham, USA
- Markus Lanthaler, Google, Switzerland

The general downturn in submissions observed in recent years for almost all conferences in computer science and IT has also affected OnTheMove, but this year the harvest again stabilized at a total of 180 submissions for the three main conferences and 40 submissions in total for the workshops. Not only may we indeed again claim success in attracting a representative volume of scientific papers, many from the USA and Asia, but these numbers of course have allowed the respective Program Committees to again compose a high-quality cross-section of current research in the areas covered by OTM. Acceptance rates vary but the aim was to stay consistently at about one accepted full paper for three submitted, yet as always these rates are subject to professional peer assessment of proper scientific quality.

As usual, we separated the proceedings into two volumes with their own titles, one for the main conferences and one for the workshops and posters. But in a different approach to previous years, we decided the latter should appear after the event and thus allow workshop authors to eventually improve their peer-reviewed papers based on critiques by the Program Committees and on live interaction at OTM. The resulting additional complexity and effort of editing the proceedings were professionally shouldered by our leading editor, Christophe Debruyne, with the general chairs for the conference volume, and with Ioana Ciuciu and Hervé Panetto for the workshop volume. We are again most grateful to the Springer LNCS team in Heidelberg for their professional support, suggestions, and meticulous collaboration in producing the files and indexes ready for downloading on the USB sticks. It is a pleasure to work with staff that so deeply understands the scientific context at large, and the specific logistics of conference proceedings publication.

The reviewing process by the respective OTM Program Committees was performed to professional quality standards: Each paper review in the main conferences was assigned to at least three referees, with arbitrated e-mail discussions in the case of strongly diverging evaluations. It may be worthwhile to emphasize once more that it is an explicit OnTheMove policy that all conference Program Committees and chairs make their selections in a completely sovereign manner, autonomous and independent from any OTM organizational considerations. As in recent years, proceedings in paper form are now only available to be ordered separately.

The general chairs are once more especially grateful to the many people directly or indirectly involved in the set-up of these federated conferences. Not everyone realizes the large number of qualified persons that need to be involved, and the huge amount of work, commitment, and the financial risk in the uncertain economic and funding climate of 2017 that is entailed by the organization of an event like OTM. Apart from the persons in the aforementioned roles, we therefore wish to thank in particular explicitly our main conference PC chairs:

- CoopIS 2017: Mike Papazoglou, Walid Gaaloul, andLiang Zhang
- ODBASE 2017: Declan O'Sullivan, Joseph Davis and Satya Sahoo
- C&TC 2017: Adrian Paschke, Hans Weigand, and Nick Bassiliades

And similarly we thank the Program Committee (co-)chairs of the 2017 ICSP, OTMA, and Workshops (in their order of appearance on the website): Peter Spyns, Maria-Esther Vidal, Mario Lezoche, Wided Guédria, Qing Li, Georg Weichhart, Peter Bollen, Hans Mulder, Maurice Nijssen, Anna Fensel, and Ioana Ciuciu. Together with their many PC members, they performed a superb and professional job in managing the difficult yet existential process of peer review and selection of the best papers from the harvest of submissions. We all also owe a serious debt of gratitude to our supremely competent and experienced conference secretariat and technical admin staff in Guadalajara and Dublin, respectively, Daniel Meersman and Christophe Debruyne.

The general conference and workshop co-chairs also thankfully acknowledge the academic freedom, logistic support, and facilities they enjoy from their respective institutions, Technical University of Graz, Austria; Université de Lorraine, Nancy, France; Latrobe University, Melbourne, Australia; and Babes-Bolyai University, Cluj, Romania, and without which such a project quite simply would not be feasible. Reader, we do hope that the results of this federated scientific enterprise contribute to your research and your place in the scientific network... and we hope to welcome you at next year's event!

September 2017   Robert Meersman
                                                                 Hervé Panetto
                                                          Christophe Debruyne

Organization

OTM (On The Move) is a federated event involving a series of major international conferences and workshops. These proceedings contain the papers presented at the OTM 2017 Federated conferences, consisting of CoopIS 2017 (Cooperative Information Systems), C&TC 2017 (Cloud and Trusted Computing), and ODBASE 2017 (Ontologies, Databases, and Applications of Semantics).

Executive Committee

General Co-chairs

Robert Meersman	TU Graz, Austria
Tharam Dillon	La Trobe University, Melbourne, Australia
Hervé Panetto	University of Lorraine, France
Ernesto Damiani	Politecnico di Milano, Italy

EI2N 2017 PC Chairs

Mario Lezoche	University of Lorraine, France
Wided Guédria	Luxembourg Institute of Science and Technology, Luxembourg
Qing Li	Tsinghua University, China
Georg Weichhart	Profactor GmbH and Johannes Kepler University Linz, Austria

Meta4eS 2017 PC Chairs

Anna Fensel	STI Innsbruck, University of Innsbruck, Austria
Ioana Ciuciu	Babes-Bolyai University, Romania

FBM PC Chairs

Robert Meersman	T.U. Graz, Austria
Peter Bollen	University of Maastricht, The Netherlands
Hans Mulder	University of Antwerp, Belgium
Maurice Nijssen	PNA, The Netherlands

Industry Case Studies Program Chair

Hervé Panetto	University of Lorraine, France

OnTheMove Academy Dean

Erich Neuhold	University of Vienna, Austria

ODBASE 2017 PC Co-chairs

Adrian Paschke   Freie Universität Berlin and Fraunhofer FOKUS, Germany
Nick Bassiliades   Aristotle University of Thessaloniki, Greece
Hans Weigand   Tilburg School of Economics and Management, The
                       Netherlands

Local Organization Chair

Stefanos Gritzalis   University of the Aegean, Greece

Publication Chair

Christophe Debruyne   Odisee University College, Belgium

Logistics Team

Daniel Meersman

EI2N 2017 Program Committee

Agostino Villa
Alexis Aubry
Andres Garcia Higuera
Angel Ortiz Bas
Antonio Gionannini
Cesare Fantuzzi
Charlotta Johnsson
David Chen
David Romero Diaz
Dimitris Askounis
Eduardo Rocha Loures
Erik Proper
Esma Yahia
Fenareti Lampathaki
François B. Vernadat
Georg Grossmann
Georg Weichhart
Hamideh Afsarmanesh
Hervé Panetto
Istvan Mezgár
Ivan Lukovic
Janusz Szpytko
Juan-Carlos Mendez
Julio Nardi
Lea Kutvonen
Luis Camarinha-Matos

Marek Wegrzyn
Mario Lezoche
Martin Zelm
Michele Dassisti
Milan Zdravkovic
Miroslav Trajanovic
Nacer Boudjlida
Nenad Stefanovic
Ovidiu Noran
Peter Bernus
Qing Li
Qing-Shan Jia
Radu Emil Precup
Rafael Batres
Raul Poler
Ricardo Jardim Goncalves
Richard Soley
Ted Goranson
Udo Kannengiesser
Ulrich Jumar
Ulrike Lechner
Vincent Chapurlat
Xiaofan Wang
Yannick Naudet
Yannis Charalabidis

Meta4eS 2017 Program Committee

Adrian M. P. Brasoveanu
Alina Dia Trambitas
Ana Roxin
AndreaKo
Anna Fensel
Camelia-M. Pintea
Christophe Roche
Constantin Orasan
Doina Tatar
Efstratios (Stratos) Kontopoulos
Erik Mannens
Fouad Zablith
Georgios Meditskos

Ioana Ciuciu
Jorge Martinez-Gil
Liliana Ibanescu
Lorenzo Bigagli
Luz-Maria Priego-Roche
Magali Séguran
Maria Poveda Villalón
Mike Matton
Peter Spyns
Thanos G. Stavropoulos
Vikash Kumar
Vladimir Alexiev

FBM 2017 Program Committee

Adrian Walker
Baba Piprani
Clifford Heath
Cory Casanave
David Cuyler
David Newman
Dirk van der Linden
Ed Barkmeyer
Ellen Munthe-Kaas
Erik Proper
Gordon Everest
Hans Mulder
Hans van Bommel
Harald Eisenmann
Herman Balsters
Inge Lemmens
Jan Vanthienen
John Sowa
Jos Rozendaal
Jos Vos
Leo Obrst
Mariette Lokin

Mark von Rosing
Matthew Curland
Maurice Nijssen
Mustafa Jarrar
Pat Hallock
Paul Iske
Peter Bollen
Peter Spyns
Peter Straatsma
Pierre Schlag
Robert Meersman
Robert Schmaal
Robert van Doesburg
Roel Baardman
Serge Valera
Sjir Nijssen
Stijn Hoppenbrouwers
Terry Halpin
Tom van Engers
Tony Morgan
William Frank

ICSP 2017 Program Committee

Antoine Lonjon
Arturo Molina
Ayelet Sapir
Ben Calloni
Christoph Bussler
Christoph Niedermeier
Daniel Sáez Domingo
David Cohen
Detlef Zühlke
Dimitri Varoutas
Dirk Slama
Dominique Ernadote
Ed Parsons
Eduardo Loures
Eva Coscia
Fabrizio Gagliardi
Francesco Danza
François B. Vernadat
Gash Bhullar
Georg Weichhart
Giancarlo Fortino
Giuseppe Di Fatta
Gottfried Luef
Hans Vandheluwe
Hervé Panetto
Ian Bayley
Jacques Durand
Jean Simao
Jean-Luc Garnier
Joe Salvo
Juan-Carlos Mendez
Kurt Fessl
Lawrence Whitman
Luis Camarinha-Matos
Marc Delbaere

Mark Schulte
Martin Zelm
Mathias Kohler
Mattew Hause
Maximiliano Vargas
Michael Alexander
Michael Ditze
Michele Dassisti
Milan Zdravkovic
Nicolas Figay
Pascal Gendre
Paulo Whitman
Peter Benson
Peter Gorm Larsen
Peter Loos
Piero De Sabbata
Qing-Shan Jia
Ricardo Goncalves
Richard Martin
Richard Soley
Serge Boverie
Sergio F. Ochoa
Sheron Koshy
Silvana Muscella
Sinuhe Arroyo
Sobah Abbas Pertersen
Stan Schneider
Ted Goranson
Tuan Dang
Vasco Amaral
Vincent Chapurlat
Wenchao Li
Yannick Naudet
Yasuyuki Nishioka

OTMA 2017 Program Committee

Galia Angelova
Christoph Bussler
Paolo Ceravolo
Claudia d'Amato

Manu De Backer
Rik Eshuis
Claudia Jiménez
Frédéric Le Mouël

Erich J. Neuhold
Hervé Panetto
Erik Proper
Rudi Studer

Peter Spyns
Maria-Esther Vidal
Georg Weichhart

ODBASE 2017 Program Committee

Adrian Paschke
Alessandra Mileo
Alexander Artikis
Anastasios Gounaris
Anna Fensel
Annika Hinze
Asuncion Gomez Perez
Athanasios Tsadiras
Bernd Neumayr
Charalampos Bratsas
Christian Kop
Christophe Debruyne
Costin Badica
Danh Le Phuoc
Dietrich Rebholz
Dimitris Plexousakis
Dumitru Roman
Efstratios Kontopoulos
Fotios Kokkoras
Georg Rehm
George Vouros
Georgios Meditskos
Gines Moreno
Giorgos Giannopoulos
Giorgos Stamou
Giorgos Stoilos
Gokhan Coskun

Grigoris Antoniou
Grzegorz J. Nalepa
Hans Weigand
Harald Sack
Harry Halpin
Heiko Paulheim
Ioannis Katakis
Irlán Grangel-González
Kalliopi Kravari
Kia Teymourian
Manolis Koubarakis
Marcin Wylot
Markus Luczak-Roesch
Naouel Karam
Nick Bassiliades
Olga Streibel
Oscar Corcho
Ralph Schäfermeier
Rolf Fricke
Ruben Verborgh
Soren Auer
Sotiris Batsakis
Stefania Costantini
Vadim Ermolayev
Vassilios Peristeras
Witold Abramowicz

OnTheMove 2017 Keynotes

Pragmatic Semantics at Web Scale

Markus Lanthaler

Google, Switzerland

Short Bio

Dr. Markus Lanthaler is a software engineer and tech lead at Google where he currently works on YouTube. He received his Ph.D. in Computer Science from the Graz University of Technology in 2014 for his research on Web APIs and Linked Data. Dr. Lanthaler is one of the core designers of JSON-LD and the inventor of Hydra. He has published several scientific articles, is a frequent speaker at conferences, and chairs the Hydra W3C Community Group.

Talk

Despite huge investments, the traditional Semantic Web stack failed to gain widespread adoption and deliver on its promises. The proposed solutions focused almost exclusively on theoretical purity at the expense of their usability. Both academia and industry ignored for a long time the fact that the Web is more a social creation than a technical one. After a long period of disillusionment, we see a renewed interest in the problems the Semantic Web set out to solve and first practical approaches delivering promising results. More than 30% of all websites contain structured information now. Initiatives such as Schema.org allow, e.g., search engines to extract and understand such data, integrate it, and create knowledge graphs to improve their services.

This talk analyzes the problems that hindered the adoption of the Semantic Web, present new, promising technologies and shows how they might be used to build the foundation of the longstanding vision of a Semantic Web of Services.

Evolution of the Industrial Internet of Things: Preparing for Change

Stephen Mellor

Industrial Internet Consortium, Needham, MA 02492, USA

Short Bio

Stephen Mellor is the Chief Technical Officer for the Industrial Internet Consortium, where he directs the standards requirements and technology & security priorities for the Industrial Internet. In that role, he coordinates the activities of the several engineering, architecture, security and testbed working groups and teams. He also co-chairs both the Definitions, Taxonomy and Reference Architecture workgroup and the Use Cases workgroup for the NIST CPS PWG (National Institute for Standards and Technology Cyberphysical System Public Working Group).

He is a well-known technology consultant on methods for the construction of real-time and embedded systems, a signatory to the Agile Manifesto, and adjunct professor at the Australian National University in Canberra, ACT, Australia. Stephen is the author of Structured Development for Real-Time Systems, Object Lifecycles, Executable UML, and MDA Distilled.

Until recently, he was Chief Scientist of the Embedded Software Division at Mentor Graphics, and founder and past president of Project Technology, Inc., before its acquisition. He participated in multiple UML/modeling-related activities at the Object Management Group (OMG), and was a member of the OMG Architecture Board, which is the final technical gateway for all OMG standards. Stephen was the Chairman of the Advisory Board to IEEE Software for ten years and a two-time Guest Editor of the magazine, most recently for an issue on Model-Driven Development.

Talk

The fundamental technological trends presently are more connectivity and more capability to analyze large quantities of data cheaply. But no one knows where those technological trends will take us, so we need to prepare for change.

Prediction is difficult, especially about the future, as several people are reputed to have said. But this keynote will peer ahead into several areas that we can see need attention, such as:

- Security for everything.
- Innovation and funding
- Learning, deployment and competitiveness

We need strategies to prepare for evolution in these areas, and we also need to understand longer term trends. Already we see improvements in operational efficiency, and changes in the economy from pay-per-asset to pay-per-use. More changes are likely, towards pay-per-outcome and direct consumer access to "pull" products autonomously.

These changes will fundamentally change the economy and drive technological innovation. The industrial internet is only at the beginning of perhaps forty more years of change.

On Data, the World's Most Valuable Resource, and Data Science

Michael Brodie

MIT, Cambridge, MA 02139, USA

Short Bio

Dr. Michael L. Brodie is a research scientist in the Computer Science and Artificial Intelligence Lab at MIT. As Chief Scientist of Verizon, the 2nd largest Telco in the world, for 25 years, he has a keen interest in advanced technology and its applications in the real world. His responsibility on the Scientific Advisory Board of two of the world's 60+ Data Science Research Institutes [Insight Center for Data Analytics, Ireland, (2015-), and Swinburne Data Science Research Institute (2017-)] is to understand the opportunities, state of the art, and research challenges for the emerging discipline of Data Science. This lecture presents the Big Picture of Big Data and of Data Science and the consequent revolutions in science and industry.

Talk

Data is being conceived as having potential for transforming all human endeavors for which adequate data is available. While data analytics has been used since before Pharaonic Egypt, it is now becoming a powerful force in discovery and prediction, notwithstanding domain expertise, e.g., in economics, that economic trends are inherently unpredictable. On the other hand, data science has led to accelerating discovery in many domains, e.g., cancer cures, exoplanets, paleontology, FinTech, and retail optimization. Equally powerful threats abound, e.g., influencing the 2016 US election.

Seven of the world's largest ten enterprises are data-driven companies, mere startups two decades ago. To compete, corporations are transforming themselves to be data-driven. Based on Big Data and Data Science, science, engineering, and the humanities are entering the 5th paradigm of discovery. Every major university has developed a Data Science Research Institute (DSRI) most within the last two years. Yet, Data Science is in its infancy without adequate principles to distinguish correlation from causation.

This keynote explores the emergence of Big Data and Data Science by looking at the state of the art, industrial use cases, and research conducted in DSRIs.

Semiotics and BREXIT

Ronald Stamper

Short Bio

- 1953 Army – modelled short career on the Good Soldier Svejk
- 1955 University College, Oxford – mathematics (and opera).
- 1958 NHS-Statistician at Oxford Regional Hospitals working on organisational problems;
- 1961 UK Steel industry – Operational Research; then, at the staff college, he created the first courses on information systems analysis and design outside the computer industry. Discovered semiotics and, as a result, and wrote his book "Information in Business and Administrative Systems"
- 1968 his syllabus became the basis for the UK's national programme for which he wrote a book of case studies and moved to the London School of Economics to teach and research.
- 1970s Principal Investigator on LEGOL-MEASUR programme funded by IBM, Digital two UK Research Councils (physical and social sciences).
- 1979 Semantics paper at IFIP DB Architecture conference: chair said "too philosophical".
- 1988 Prof. of Information Management at U. Twente, research continued.
- 1999 'Retired' (joke) continued the research and attempted to transfer the technology to industry against the evident wishes of the UK's Department of Business, Innovation and Skills, which presides over the worst productivity in the OECD. As our Semantic Normal Form makes huge improvements in productivity, the DBIS's record was threatened.

Talk

"When did you stop beating your wife/husband?" Answer with 'Yes' or 'No'...

Semiotics: Called by John Locke (1690) the "doctrine of signs", dates back to ancient Greek philosophy. Signs stand for other things; Stamper reviewed their properties: three technical ones are handled by hardware, telecoms and software industries, but those central to business and this meeting (semantic, pragmatic and social properties) have been neglected until recently.

Port Clearance Rules in PSOA RuleML:
From Controlled-English Regulation
to Object-Relational Logic
(Tutorial)

Gen Zou and Harold Boley

University of New Brunswick, Canada

Short Bios

Gen Zou is a PhD candidate at the Faculty of Computer Science at the University of New Brunswick, Canada. His research interests include the overlapping areas of data & knowledge modeling, graph-relational interoperation, rule-based querying, as well as machine learning. His recent work is the foundation, implementation, and evaluation of the translation and execution framework PSOATransRun for Positional-Slotted Object-Applicative (PSOA) RuleML. In PSOA RuleML, knowledge bases integrate relational data as positional facts, graph data as object-centered attribute-value facts, and object-classification facts, as well as class subsumptions and rules for query-subquery reduction to facts. The instantiations of his PSOATransRun framework translate a PSOA knowledge base to intermediate languages, TPTP and ISO Prolog, executed via translated queries. The translators designed and implemented by him consist of transformation modules reusable across all instantiations and a conversion module specific to the targeted execution environment such as Prolog. He also evaluated PSOATransRun with a test suite and use cases including PortClearanceRules.

Dr. Harold Boley is adjunct professor at the Faculty of Computer Science, University of New Brunswick, Canada, and chair of RuleML Inc. His work on Declarative Specification, Programming, and AI includes leading the development of the RuleML 1.02 system of families of languages. RuleML has been combined with OWL to SWRL, has become the main input to the W3C Recommendation RIF, and has provided the foundation for OASIS LegalRuleML Core Specification Version 1.0. Two of his projects in data-plus-knowledge representation are the object-relational PSOA RuleML and the visualization framework Grailog. He recently contributed to related efforts at the Stanford Logic Group, CSLI, and SRI.

Tutorial

The Decision Management (DM) Community Challenge of March 2016 consisted of creating decision models from ten English Port Clearance Rules inspired by the

International Ship and Port Facility Security Code. Based on an analysis of the moderately controlled English rules and current online solutions, we formalized the rules in Positional-Slotted, Object-Applicative (PSOA) RuleML. This resulted in: (1) a reordering, subgrouping, and explanation of the original rules on the specialized decision-model expressiveness level of (deontically contextualized) near-Datalog, non-recursive, near-deterministic, ground-queried, and non-subpredicating rules; (2) an object-relational PSOA RuleML rulebase which was complemented by facts to form a knowledge base queried in PSOATransRun for decision-making. Thus, the DM and logical formalizations get connected, which leads to generalized decision models with Hornlog, recursive, non-deterministic, non-ground-queried, and subpredicating rules.

The tutorial will:

- Bridge between the Decision Management, RuleML, and OTM Communities
- Explain rules for a harbor security use case, leading to Cyber Physical Systems
- Exemplify the Pragmatic Semantic Web by prohibiting certain ship types to enter a harbor
- Provide a hands-on demo with audience-driven queries of the Object-Relational Decision Model
- Recommend models using generalized rule (and ontology) expressivity in PSOA RuleML

Contents

OTM/IFIP International Workshop on Enterprise Integration, Interoperability and Networking (EI2N) 2017

Hybrid Production-System Control-Architecture for Smart Manufacturing . . .   5
Michele Dassisti, Antonio Giovannini, Pasquale Merla,
Michela Chimienti, and Hervé Panetto

Model Based, Modular Configuration of Cyber Physical Systems
for the Information Management on Shop-Floor   16
Frank-Walter Jaekel, Jan Torka, Martin Eppelein,
Wolf Schliephack, and Thomas Knothe

Interoperable Process Design in Production Systems   26
Georg Weichhart and Christian Stary

Ontology-Based Decision Support System for Enterprise Interoperability   36
Mahdi Zouch, Wided Guedria, and Riadh Ben Halima

Rethinking of Framework and Constructs of Enterprise Architecture
and Enterprise Modelling Standardized by ISO 15704, 19439 and 19440   46
Qing Li, Iotong Chan, Qianlin Tang, Hailong Wei, and Yudi Pu

Digital Connected Production: Wearable Manufacturing
Information Systems   56
Stefan Schönig, Stefan Jablonski, Andreas Ermer,
and Ana Paula Aires

A User-Centered Perspective on Interoperability: Capturing Stakeholder
Interaction for Mediating Design   66
Christian Stary and Claudia Kaar

Interoperability for Human-Centered Manufacturing   76
Magnus Åkerman and Åsa Fast-Berglund

International Workshop on Methods, Evaluation, Tools and Applications for the Creation and Consumption of Structured Data for the e-Society (Meta4eS) 2017

Medical Monkeys: A Crowdsourcing Approach to Medical Big Data   87
Lorenzo Servadei, Rainer Schmidt, Christina Eidelloth,
and Andreas Maier

Superstore Sales Reporting: A Comparative Analysis of Relational
and Non-relational Databases: Short Paper   98
Gheorghe Coşofreţ and Ioana Ciuciu

Integrating Product Classification Standards into Schema.org:
eCl@ss and UNSPSC on the Web of Data   103
Alex Stolz and Martin Hepp

Ontology-Based Personalized Resource Efficiency Management for
Residential Users of Smart Homes: Short Paper   114
Mihaela Teoca and Ioana Ciuciu

Towards Linking DBpedia's Bibliographic References
to Bibliographic Repositories   120
David Nazarian and Nick Bassiliades

International Workshop on Fact Based Modeling (FBM) 2017

Fact Based Modeling as Mandatory Subject in the First Year
of a Knowledge Engineering Program   133
Peter Bollen

Towards Grounded Enterprise Modelling   141
Henderik A. Proper, Marija Bjeković, Bas van Gils,
and Stijn J. B. A. Hoppenbrouwers

An FBM Model of ISO Cloud Computing Architecture   152
Baba Piprani

Analyzing the New 2019 Dutch Environment and Planning Act   163
John Bulles, Bas Cartigny, and Peter Bollen

An IT-Independent Reference Model for IT-Supported, Interactive,
Regulation Based Services   173
Sjir Nijssen, Diederik Dulfer, Peter Bollen, and Jos Rozendaal

The Role of States and Transitions in IT-Supported, Interactive,
Regulation Based Services   183
Sjir Nijssen, Diederik Dulfer, Peter Bollen, and Jos Rozendaal

Meaning Based Structured Legal Code   193
Sjir Nijssen, Diederik Dulfer, Peter Bollen, and Jos Rozendaal

How to Fulfil Regulatory Requirements Consistently:
A Semantic-Based Approach   202
Inge Lemmens, Bas van de Laar, Johan Saton, and John Bulles

An Evaluation of a Design Science Research Artefact in the Field
of Agile Enterprise Design   212
   Klaas Meijer, Maurice Nijssen, and John Bulles

Industry Case Studies Program (ICSP) 2017

The Recent AIPLA Meeting's New Trend as to Nationwide §101-
Guidelines and the "Invention Description Language, IDL" —
Trivializing Using ETCIs' FSTP-Tests   223
   Sigram Schindler

User Experience and Agile Software Practices – An Industry Perspective   232
   Prabal Mahanta and Bhavneet Kaur

Optimization Approaches for the Physical Internet   236
   Viktoria A. Hauder, Erik Pitzer, and Michael Affenzeller

Manufacturing Intelligence in Furniture Product-Service Design   246
   *Evmorfia Biliri, Fenareti Lampathaki, Angelos Arvanitakis,
   Ariadni Michalitsi-Psarrou, Javier Martin, Fernando Gigante,
   Vicente Sales, and Maria Jose Nunez*

DESDEVOPS - A New Paradigm for Dev-Ops: Rethinking
Transition of Quality from Dev to Production   251
   Prabal Mahanta, Pavendra Maurya, and Akhilesh Kumar

OnTheMove Academy (OTMA) 2017

Developing a Modelling and Mining Framework for Integrated
Processes and Decisions   259
   Faruk Hasić, Johannes De Smedt, and Jan Vanthienen

An Overview of Challenges and Research Avenues for Green Business
Process Management: Exploring the Concept of a Circular Economy   270
   Dries Couckuyt

Real-Time Business Process Model Tailoring: The Effect of Domain
Knowledge on Reading Strategy   280
   Sven Vermeulen

**International Conference on Ontologies, DataBases,
and Applications of Semantics (ODBASE) 2017 – Posters**

District-Scale Data Integration by Leveraging Semantic
Web Technologies: A Case in Smart Cities   289
   *Kiril Tonev, Simon Kappe, Preslava Krahtova,
   Hendro Wicaksono, and Jivka Ovtcharova*

Digital Assistance Based on an Ontology Driven Model
of the IT-Systems Along the Product Lifecycle...................... 293
   Klemens Haas, Simon Kappe, Martin Siebert,
   Hendro Wicaksono, and Jivka Ovtcharova

Systematical Representation of RDF-to-Relational Mappings
for Ontology-Based Data Access.............................. 297
   Lars Runge, Sebastian Schrage, and Wolfgang May

Towards a Core Ontology for Financial Reporting Information
Systems (COFRIS) 302
   Ivars Blums and Hans Weigand

Author Index 307

OTM/IFIP International Workshop on Enterprise Integration, Interoperability and Networking (EI2N) 2017

EI2N 2017 PC Chair's Message

In 2017 the 12th edition of the Enterprise Integration, Interoperability and Networking workshop (EI2N'2017) has been organised as part of the On The Move Federated Conferences (OTM'2017) in Rhodes, Greece. The workshop has established itself as a major interactive event for researchers exchanging ideas in the context of organisations and information technologies. This is shown by the long list of groups and committees that support this event.

This year, the workshop is supported by IFIP. IFIP Work Groups TC 5 WG 5.12 on Architectures for Enterprise Integration and TC 5 WG 5.8 on Enterprise Interoperability support this year's workshop. EI2N received support from IFAC's Technical Committee 5.3 "Enterprise Integration and Networking" (main sponsor) and IFAC TC 3.1 (Computers for Control). Additionally, the SIG INTEROP Grande-Région on "Enterprise Systems Interoperability", the French CNRS National Research Group GDR MACS, and the industrial internet consortium have shown their continuing interest in EI2N.

Flexibility to meet customer demands requires adaptable organisational structures. Instant access to information about the enterprise system state and the possibility to adapt processes are required. To reach this business goal, enterprises will connect everything. Enterprise integration, interoperability and networking are major disciplines studying collaborative, communicative enterprise systems. Enterprise Modelling Techniques, Next Generation Computing Architectures and Socio-technical Platforms along with Semantic Interoperability approaches are essential pillars supporting the networked and adaptive enterprise system.

For EI2N'2017 14 papers have been received. After a rigorous review process 8 papers have been accepted. At least three members of the program committee evaluated every submitted paper. Due to the quality, we have decided to include all accepted papers as long papers in the proceedings. Accepted papers will be made available in pre-proceedings. After the OTM workshops authors are able to revise their papers and include feedback from the interactive sessions in their work. This improves the quality of the scientific work, and places emphasis on importance of the interaction in scientific workshops.

With respect to interactivity, EI2N will host a highly interactive session called "Workshop Café". This special session is now an integral part of EI2N since many years. The outcomes of these discussions will be reported during a plenary session jointly organized with the CoopIS and the OTM Industry Case Studies Program, in order to share topics and issues for future research with a larger group of experts and scientists.

In this year's Workshop Café we are discussing the topic "Interoperable Cyber Physical Enterprise System: from a singular system to the enterprise system of systems, a convergence". Results will be made available at the IFAC TC 5.3 webpage: http://tc.ifac-control.org/5/3.

We would like to thank the authors, international program committee, sponsors, supporters and our colleagues from the OTM organising team who have together contributed to the continuing success of this workshop. We welcome all attendees and participants and look forward to an enthusiastic exchange of ideas and thoughts for the progress of science at the workshop.

The EI2N'2017 Workshop Co-chairs

October 2017

Mario Lezoche
Wided Guédria
Qing Li
Georg Weichhart

Hybrid Production-System
Control-Architecture for Smart Manufacturing

Michele Dassisti[1(✉)], Antonio Giovannini[2], Pasquale Merla[3],
Michela Chimienti[2], and Hervé Panetto[4]

[1] DMMM, Politecnico di Bari, Bari, Italy
michele.dassisti@poliba.it
[2] InResLab Scarl, Monopoli, BA, Italy
{a.giovannini,m.chimienti}@inreslab.org
[3] Ali6 SRL, Monopoli, BA, Italy
merla@ali6.it
[4] CRAN, University of Lorraine, CNRS, Vandoeuvre-les-Nancy, France
Herve.Panetto@univ-lorraine.fr

Abstract. Highly customized products with shorter life cycles characterize the market today: the smart manufacturing paradigm can answer these needs. In this latter production system context, the interaction between production resources (PRs) can be swiftly adapted to meet both the variety of customers' needs and the optimization goals. In the scientific literature, several architectural configurations have been devised so far to this aim, namely: hierarchical, heterarchical or hybrid. Whether the hierarchical and heterarchical architectures provide respectively low reactivity and a reduced vision of the optimization opportunities at production system level, the hybrid architectures can mitigate the limit of both the previous architectures. However, no hybrid architecture can ensure all PRs are aware of how orienting their behavior to achieve the optimization goal of the manufacturing system with a minimal computational effort. In this paper, a new "hybrid architecture" is proposed to meet this goal. At each order entry, this architecture allows the PRs to be dynamically grouped. Each group has a supervisor, i.e. the optimizer, that has the responsibility: (1) to monitor the tasks on all the resources, (2) to compute the optimal manufacturing parameters and (3) to provide the optimization results to the resources of the group. A software prototype was developed to test the new architecture design in a simulated flow-shop and in a simplified job shop production.

Keywords: Cyber physical production system · Factory automation
Hybrid control architecture · Intelligent manufacturing system
Reconfigurable manufacturing system

1 Introduction

Market mutations from a local to a global economy are urging production systems to face new challenges. Recent years have witnessed the switch from mass production to mass customization, with customers requiring product even more customized, maintaining high quality and low prices [1, 2]. Manufacturing companies, to remain competitive, should improve their ability to swiftly adapt their production capacities to this demand for variety. In a smart manufacturing scenario [3, 4], the production control-system architectures are strategical as a orchestrating system of manufacturing parameters at each production resource (PR).

Several scientific papers in recent years proposed solution to these challenges by devising distinct types of control architectures (CA). There are three main approaches that correspond to three main architecture of production system control classes [5]: Fully HIerarchical architectures (FHI), Fully HEterarchical architectures (FHE) and Hybrid Control Architectures (HCA). The centralization of the FHI reduces the reactivity to unpredictable events. The decentralization of the FHE reduces the optimization opportunities.

The current HCA do not ensure all the production resources are always aware of the operating parameters to meet the optima conditions. In this paper, we propose a new HCA to provide a "global view", i.e. the resources involved in the manufacturing process should have information about how to behave to achieve the optimization goal of the manufacturing system. Moreover, to deal with complex manufacturing systems characterized by a high production variety, attention is paid to the computational effort required to ensure the global view in the proposed CA.

In our proposal, each production resource (PR, made by a physical part, e.g. the operating machine, and a logical part, e.g. control logic) is aware of the optimal behavior (i.e. set of manufacturing parameters) that PR can apply when no unpredictable events should be managed locally, e.g. a delay of the supplier PRs.

The paper is organized as follow. Section 2 states the problem and the operating scenario for the proposed architecture and shows as the existing CAs would face the problem. Section 3 details the proposed architecture and explains how it face the stated problem. Section 4 shows the software prototype. Section 5 explains the tests and the validation of the architecture. In the Sect. 6, the conclusions and the future perspectives are discussed.

2 Literature Review

2.1 Problem Statement

As identified above, this paper aims to design and develop a CA for production systems, characterized by a high production variety, therefore this CA, also considering the challenges proposed in [6] by IFAC TC 5.3, should meet the following requirements:

- all PRs must have a constant availability (i.e. with a high refresh rate) of the global view, i.e. each PR should have the availability of the optimal parameters setting related to the best available optimization goal;
- the CA must be reactive with a low computational effort.

2.2 Control Architectures

This section presents a review of the production CAs in the scientific literature.

The papers are discussed according to the classification in [5] that identifies three main classes of CAs:

- FHI: the PRs presents in the production system have master/slave interactions;
- FHE: the PRs have the maximum decisional autonomy;
- HCA: this class includes this architectures combine the advantages of both the previous classes, switching from hierarchical to non-hierarchical and vice versa.

2.3 Architecture Type

The FHI architectures can partially satisfy the problem statement but, due to their structural characteristics, these are rigid and do not guarantee the reactivity required to control a high production variability. If we apply this architecture type to the problem proposed, it results that all knowledge and decisional ability it will be given to the Central Unit (Fig. 1(a)). Since all the computational effort resides on the Central Unit, it is not possible to guarantee the required reactivity: the time necessary to estimate the optimal parameters settings for all devices (according to global optimization rule) as well as the central-unit effort required to transfer all the information to all the devices under its control increases the basis of the number of resources. If one add intermediate units to control each cell (understood as a group of PRs i.e. a production department) that do not interact with each other (e.g. [7]), the computational burden to get higher refresh rates lowers, but there is a less complete global view (Fig. 1(b)).

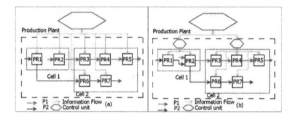

Fig. 1. Scheme of a Hierarchical architecture

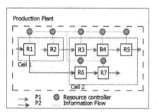

Fig. 2. Scheme of an Heterarchical architecture

On the opposite, the FHE architectures (e.g. [8]) ensure the continuous reconfiguration of the PRs that have learning and decisional abilities. These architectures are not able to guarantee always the global view, since they are affected by "short-sightedness" due to the lack of a central authority that suggests the best behavior to achieve the global optimization. This latter is often in conflict with the local objective of the machines. If one adopts a heterarchical architecture (Fig. 2), each PRs (physical part or software component) can take decisions and act behaviors to reach a local goal and to interact with each other. In this way, no resource controller can provide the global view to each other because each try to achieve its local goal.

The following sections analyze the HCA, that aim to combines the advantages of both the other two classes.

2.4   Hybrid Control Architectures

The HCA [9–19] can be classified according to the degree of evolution of the control structure during the execution of production [11]: architectures can be dynamic (D-HCA) or static (S-HCA). They differ because of the evolution of the control system, which evolves in D-HCA and remains the same in S-HCA. As described in Sect. 2, it is mandatory that in all operating situations, the global view of the system and their optimal manufacturing parameter settings (e.g. temperature, velocity) is available for all the production resources to achieve the global optimization.

2.5   S-HCA

In S-HCA [14–18] the control does not evolve, i.e. the configuration is the same all of time. They are very close to the FHI architectures, but in this case, the lower levels are always can refuse the guidelines to the upper level, e.g. they can ask to upper level make a new reconfiguration. Apparently, these architectures can meet completely the problem statement and for this, each of them has been analyzed in detail.

In [17] a monolithic structure is adopted which does not allows flexibility (see case in Fig. 1(b)): here only one controller for each production cell is adopted that do not interact with the others. Product P1 must pass in both the cells and since the interaction between cells is lacking, the optimization will concern only cell 1.

When resource R2 releases P1 the optimization will concern only cell 2 and so on. In [18] the requests to merge the individual interests is triggered directly from the PRs that as in case of FHE do not have the global view of the system. In [15] instead a dynamic group definition is proposed, although how it forms the cluster is unclear. The major issue is that the PRs communicates only with the mediators and there may be bottlenecks if the number of resources increases, as in FHI. In [14] two different agents have been used to improve the production: Order (OA) that contains the production plan for a single production order and Resource (RA) that corresponds to a single production resource. When a new order arrives, the OA verifies its feasibility and after questioning the RA, according to their responses, the OA inserts the new activities in the Gantt of each RA. The OA monitors the production advancement. The RA managed their own Gantt. They react to little perturbation changing slightly and if a major perturbation occurs, the RA that has detected the perturbation, asks to corresponding OA to reschedule. In this case, each OA limits to allocate the resources and it make a re-scheduling only if a RA so requests. In this way is not possible ensure the global view because the RAs managed their Gantt and the re-orchestration request trigger from themselves. Only if the OA is continuously to the research of the best possible solution, rather than to be only in wait, this architecture could be completely satisfy the problem statement. In [16] defined hierarchy is adopted based on the assumption that changes in production plans are infrequent. In this way, the intermediate controllers are defined during the design of the system and they do not interact with them. For example, let us apply this architecture to the scenario shown in Fig. 3 where there are

9resources, 3 products and 3 production Cells. The result will be an upper level that monitor all production resources and an intermediate control level composed by a control unit for each production cell. Each intermediate control unit tries to achieve the optimum for its own cell, based on its own goals, which can be in contrast with each other.

2.6   D-HCA

The D-HCA [9–13] cannot satisfy completely the sustainability of production control. These in fact start with a hierarchical configuration, but under a disruption, the PRs do not respect the "authority" of their control unit: the control system thus evolves from hierarchical to heterarchical. Some situations are possible in which the production resources operate as fully independent entities (heterarchical configuration), and thus the constraint posed in the problem statement will be only partially fulfilled, since in the heterarchical configuration is not possible to ensure the global view.

Finally, a comparison is required with PROSA [19], where exists a software supervisor (Staff Holon (SH)) that represents an external expert that suggests advices to PR (PRs can refuse advices). However, the amount of SHs and their knowledge should be fixed a priori. In a high production variety scenario, this constraint and the unpredictability of the production can result in an under- or over-estimation of the amount of the required computational effort and knowledge resources to implement the SHs.

The next section proposes a new architecture, where groups and supervisors are dynamically defined and dynamic is also the knowledge assignment to the supervisor.

3   The New "Hybrid Architecture"

From the analysis of these works emerges that the existing CAs only partially fulfill the requirements to solve the proposed problem statement. The architecture here proposed belongs to the HCA class that fulfils the requirement of the smart manufacturing paradigm.

A central unit configures groups of PRs based on each order entry. Each group is independent, i.e. each product (P) requires the resources of only one group of PRs to be finalized. The central unit defines an optimizer O for each group of PRs. This O (1) gathers periodically the states of the PRs in the groups (2) compute the optimal process parameters for all the PRs in the group and (3) provide to the PRs the results of the optimization.

To preserve the global view with minimal effort, and thus assure adequate flexibility, our architecture tries to solve the following problems:

- to dynamically create (re-orchestration) the intermediate control units (Optimizer O) when the production plan change (a new order is provided), to decide, case by case, the PRs under their control (Optimization Group OG) and to create dynamically the communication channels between the PRs belonging to the same OG;

- to provide only to Os, dynamically defined by the CU, only the necessary knowledge according to the optimization goal of the manufacturing system. Doing so, the computational effort is dynamically transferred from the CU to the Os.

Both these features make the proposed architecture prone to be implemented in a smart manufacturing context. The next sections detail the behavior of the proposed architecture both in re-configuration and in execution phase.

3.1   Re-configuration Phase

The CU starts from a waiting state for an introduction of a new order (PO).

- Step 1: the CU receives a PO composed by products set that are characterized from their working sequence (operations, e.g. lamination, cooking etc. and PRs linked to them);
- Step 2: the CU sends a stop signal to all available PRs and asks them their advancement state (the completed operations until that moment without the ongoing operations);
- Step 3: the PRs sends the answer to the CU. If they are running a process they continue it, otherwise stop;
- Step 4: the CU when receives all answers creates the new production plan merging the new PO with the operations of the old production plan that the PRs must still perform, if they exist;
- Step 5: the CU starting from the new production plan, identifies the independent paths (a path is defined as the machines sequence that allows passing from raw material to finished product and two paths are independents if they not cross i.e. if they do not share no PR). Each path corresponds to an OG;
- Step 6: for each OG, a PR (that for as they were defined paths, the PRs can belong to only one OG at a time) is chosen to assume the role of O. It will have under its control and will able to interact only with the PRs (slaves) belonging to its OG. The difference between the slaves and the Os resides in an executable software that the CU compiles and sends to each PRs in this step, according to their role;
- Step 7: the CU sends to each PR its own new production plan (agenda) and it relies on the Os the task to manage their own OG;
- Step 8: the CU returns to waiting for a new PO to make a new re-orchestration.

The Fig. 4(a) shows the condition of a production plant during the execution phase (three OG have already been defined), instead the Fig. 4(b) shows the result of a re-configuration when a new PO (it contains P5 and P6) is introduced. After the re-configuration, the OG (and then the O's) have become two and they are different from those in the above condition.

After the re-configuration, the production can restart. Step 2 highlights how the PRs send only the finalized operations without considering the ones in progress. The ongoing operations are considered in the new agenda: when the production resume, their duration is updated based on the percentage of work done during the re-configuration stage.

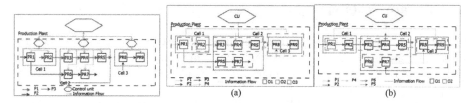

Fig. 3. Application of [16]   **Fig. 4.** Re-configuration phase

3.2 Execution Phase

The execution phase starts after each PR receives its executable software and its updated agenda that contain all products that it must perform in a defined sequence. During execution phase (the fluxes between PRs are shown in Fig. 5):

1. each O reads the state (the value of the controllable manufacturing parameters to achieve an optimization result, e.g. velocity) of each PRs under its control;
2. each O sends to all PRs belonging its OG the best manufacturing parameters setting to achieve a global goal according to an optimization rule (e.g. energy saving);
3. each PRs, including Os, carry on the production expected from their agenda, setting their manufacturing parameters as suggested from their O, if it is feasible and they can react quickly to unpredictable events.

As described above, a fundamental characteristic of this architecture is that thanks to the dynamic creation of the OG, any global optimization problem is divided in more small problems, allowing to maintain the global view and minimize the computational effort. In this way, an intermediate control unit manages fewer PRs than those managed by the CU, with a consequent performance boost that affect the time required to have an appropriate solution by an optimization algorithm (Heuristic, Genetic Algorithm etc.) as well as the reaction time.

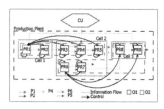

Fig. 5. Execution phase

This work does not consider the PRs' breakdown, allocation or re-allocation.

In the next sections, an example to validate this architecture is proposed. It will be demonstrated how this architecture can satisfy completely the problem statement.

4 Software Prototype

To test if the dynamic re-configuration of the intermediate control level is possible with the architecture proposed, a software prototype was implemented. The focus was on the global view. To test the dynamic grouping, the reference scenario adopted for the test is composed by 4 PRs (PR1, PR2, PR3, PR4).

To simulate the CU and the PRs it has been used a Linux Debian terminal for each entity. As described in Sect. 3, the POs contain the products set with their working sequence characterized from operations and PRs linked to them and we assume that the PO is correct, i.e. there is not the possibility that a PO cannot be performed. The PRs presentation board and the PO was implemented in XML (eXtensible Markup Language).

The behavior of the CU and those of the PRs (the code to generate the executable program in Sect. 3) have been implemented in C++. The PRs' production plans (agendas) are text files. The optimization goal is the energy saving and the algorithm to find the best manufacturing parameter setting is a heuristic. To allow the communication between CU and PRs, TCP/IP protocol has been used.

5 Tests

This section describes the tests that allow to show how the proposed architecture fulfill the problem statement. Two PO have been inserted. The first PO has two products, P1 (to be machined on PR1, PR2, PR4) and P2 (to be machined on PR4). The second one has two products, P3 (to be machined on PR2, PR4) and P4 (to be machined on PR2, PR3, PR4).

When PO1 is sent, the CU defines an OG formed only by PR1, PR2, and PR4, since there are not products that involve PR3. Then, the CU assigns to PR1 the O role.

The Fig. 6(a) shows the agenda of all PRs involved in the optimization. It is possible to notice that: (1) only the PR1 agenda contains information related to all products and all PRs belonging to its OG (in red circle); (2) PR2 and PR4 agendas

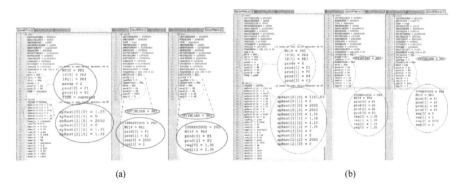

(a)   (b)

Fig. 6. (a) Agenda of PRs belonging to OG after PO1 insertion (b) Agenda of PRs belonging to OG after PO2 insertion (Color figure online)

contain information related to O IP (blue circle), IP of their previous PR, and operations that they must perform (green circle).

PR1 completed all planned operations and then PO2 starts working. The CU performs a re-configuration: as shown in Fig. 6(b), the OG dynamically changes (now is composed only by PR2; PR4; PR3) and PR2 is chosen as O.

Figure 7 shows on left side an example of an agenda that Os sends to a PR belonging to its own OG. Each row in Fig. 7 is structured as follows: on left side <starting time>; <ending time>; <parameter to apply> and on right side <reading time>; <value read>. Moreover, Fig. 7 shows on right side the lectures of the same PR in the same period and shows the PRs refusing the suggested parameters if a product is on delay: PR readings are 0 on the highlighted area, despite the values in the plan, since a product is on delay.

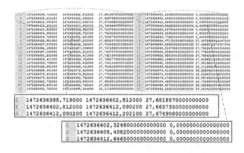

Fig. 7. Predicted (left) and real (right) production plan

6   Conclusions: Limits and Future Perspectives

In this work, a new hybrid control-system architecture is presented. As discussed in Sect. 2, no-architecture in the literature could meet the requirements in the problem statement, since the FHI architectures cannot ensure the necessary reactivity, the FHE architectures cannot ensure the global optimum, and HCA cannot ensure both the requirements of global view with the required reactivity. By means of the tests described in Sect. 5, it is possible to show that the new proposed HCA fulfill the problem statement:

- All PRs have the constant (i.e. with a high refresh rate) availability of their own best manufacturing parameters, necessary to ensure the global view;
- By means of the dynamic grouping and of the dynamic assignment of the knowledge, the computational effort is re-allocated at each order entry.

The limits of the proposed architecture concern the limit in sharing products between different PR groups: this point makes the proposal less effective in a general job-shop scenario. Consequently, a future perspective can be the extension of the application domain to all job shop cases, assembly systems and the handling of the resource allocation.

Acknowledgement. This research was partially supported by Gestal 2000 Srl which committed to InResLab Scarl the project "GEM - Gestal Energy Management".

References

1. Dassisti, M., De Nicolò, M.: Enterprise integration and economical crisis for mass craftsmanship: a case study of an Italian furniture company. In: Herrero, P., Panetto, H., Meersman, R., Dillon, T. (eds.) OTM 2012. LNCS, vol. 7567, pp. 113–123. Springer, Heidelberg (2012). https://doi.org/10.1007/978-3-642-33618-8_19
2. Brettel, M., Friederichsen, N., Keller, M., Rosenberg, M.: How virtualization, decentralization and network building change the manufacturing landscape: an Industry 4.0 perspective. Int. J. Mech. Ind. Sci. Eng. **8**(1), 37–44 (2014)
3. Kagermann, H., et al.: Recommendations for implementing the strategic initiative Industrie 4.0: securing the future of German manufacturing industry; final report of the Industrie 4.0 working group (2013)
4. Dassisti, M., et al.: Industry 4.0 paradigm: the viewpoint of the small and medium enterprises. In: 7th International Conference on Information Society and Technology, ICIST 2017, Kopaonik, Serbia, vol. 1, pp. 50–54 (2017)
5. Trentesaux, D.: Distributed control of production systems. Eng. Appl. Artif. Intell. **22**(7), 971–978 (2009)
6. Panetto, H., Zdravković, M., Jardim-Goncalves, R., Romero, D., Cecil, J., Mezgár, I.: New perspectives for the future interoperable enterprise systems. Comput. Ind. **79**, 47–63 (2016)
7. Pfrommer, J., Stogl, D., Aleksandrov, K., Escaida, N.S., Hein, B., Beyerer, J.: Plug & produce by modelling skills and service-oriented orchestration of reconfigurable manufacturing systems. At-Automatisierungstechnik **63**(10), 790–800 (2015)
8. Weyer, S., Schmitt, M., Ohmer, M., Gorecky, D.: Towards Industry 4.0 standardization as the crucial challenge for highly modular, multi-vendor production systems. IFAC-PapersOnLine **48**(3), 579–584 (2015)
9. Leitão, P., Restivo, F.: ADACOR: a holonic architecture for agile and adaptive manufacturing control. Comput. Ind. **57**(2), 121–130 (2006)
10. Barbosa, J., Leitão, P., Adam, E., Trentesaux, D.: Dynamic self-organization in holonic multi-agent manufacturing systems: the ADACOR evolution. Comput. Ind. **66**, 99–111 (2015)
11. Pach, C., Berger, T., Bonte, T., Trentesaux, D.: ORCA-FMS: a dynamic architecture for the optimized and reactive control of flexible manufacturing scheduling. Comput. Ind. **65**(4), 706–720 (2014)
12. Jimenez, J.-F., Bekrar, A., Zambrano-Rey, G., Trentesaux, D., Leitão, P.: Pollux: a dynamic hybrid control architecture for flexible job shop systems. Int. J. Prod. Res., 1–19 (2016)
13. Zambrano Rey, G., Pach, C., Aissani, N., Bekrar, A., Berger, T., Trentesaux, D.: The control of myopic behavior in semi-heterarchical production systems: a holonic framework. Eng. Appl. Artif. Intell. **26**(2), 800–817 (2013)
14. Rolón, M., Martínez, E.: Agent-based modeling and simulation of an autonomic manufacturing execution system. Comput. Ind. **63**(1), 53–78 (2012)
15. Maturana, F., Shen, W., Norrie, D.H.: MetaMorph: an adaptive agent-based architecture for intelligent manufacturing. Int. J. Prod. Res. **37**(10), 2159–2173 (1999)
16. Heragu, S.S., Graves, R.J., Kim, B.-I., St Onge, A.: Intelligent agent based framework for manufacturing systems control. IEEE Trans. Syst. Man Cybern. Part Syst. Hum. **32**(5), 560–573 (2002)

17. Ou-Yang, C., Lin, J.S.: The development of a hybrid hierarchical/heterarchical shop floor control system applying bidding method in job dispatching. Robot. Comput. Integr. Manuf. **14**(3), 199–217 (1998)
18. Cox, J.S., Durfee, E.H.: Discovering and exploiting synergy between hierarchical planning agents. In: Proceedings of the Second International Joint Conference on Autonomous Agents and Multiagent Systems, New York, NY, USA, pp. 281–288 (2003)
19. Van Brussel, H., Wyns, J., Valckenaers, P., Bongaerts, L., Peeters, P.: Reference architecture for holonic manufacturing systems: PROSA. Comput. Ind. **37**(3), 255–274 (1998)

Model Based, Modular Configuration of Cyber Physical Systems for the Information Management on Shop-Floor

Frank-Walter Jaekel[✉], Jan Torka, Martin Eppelein,
Wolf Schliephack, and Thomas Knothe

Fraunhofer Institute for Production Systems and Design Technology,
Pascalstr. 8-9, 10587 Berlin, Germany
frank-walter.jaekel@ipk.fraunhofer.de

Abstract. Many of the current manufacturing systems are still implemented as sequential inflexible production lines. This creates difficulties to fulfil the customer request for customized products. The production of customized products is accompanied by major changes in the production infrastructure. To support more flexible production, the sequential production lines nowadays start to change to workshop production. In that case all production systems will be grouped by their tasks, e.g. all drilling machines are located in the same place. A manufacturing system stands for the different involved hardware and software components at the manufacturing process. Each manufacturing system is connected with the help of the shop-floor IT. The term shop-floor indicates the productive area of a factory and includes the operative work. Shop-floor IT includes the information processes and IT solutions that control, secure and record product activities. Therefore the shop-floor IT supports directly the execution on field level. The model based view of a production process simplifies the understanding of the product lifecycle and planning. To optimize and speed up building and changing of product processes, the modular shop-floor IT has been developed by technologies derived from cyber physical systems and internet of things. However, interoperability issues such as different implementation of controls and process variations are a major challenge.

Keywords: Internet of things · Cyber physical systems and industry 4.0
Interoperability challenges

1 Motivation and Challenge

Information technology (IT) aspects are addressed still quite late in the design and planning process of manufacturing systems in industry. Usually the IT infrastructure for manufacturing systems is implemented in a permanent way for a specific production line or factory. It creates difficulties regarding setup-time and flexibility.

Flexible and resilient manufacturing systems require a dynamic adaptability of the IT configurations along with the dynamic reconfiguration of the shop-floor related to demands such as:

© IFIP International Federation for Information Processing 2018
Published by Springer International Publishing AG 2018. All Rights Reserved
C. Debruyne et al. (Eds.): OTM 2017 Workshops, LNCS 10697, pp. 16–25, 2018.
https://doi.org/10.1007/978-3-319-73805-5_2

- New products or services.
- Events of failure and change.
- Robust and secure IT realizations.
- Management of customer orientation.

This requirement even already arises in "mass production". Thereby a large number of new variants appear and the repetition number of the same product can be easily lower than 1.4 products per year. This has been identified from different industry sectors during several projects in the last 5 years. Therefore, approaches are required to increase the flexibility as well as to move the development of the information management for the shop-floor into earlier planning phases. This information management is also called shop-floor IT.

The shop-floor IT is directly involved in the production. It is responsible for the control, management and monitor of the production facilities in real time. Shop-floor IT functions (IEC62264) are for example "specification management", "execution management", "data acquisition" and tracing.

The approach for the development and maintenance of the shop-floor IT is at the moment usually sequential. The shop-floor architecture and infrastructure is developed after the final definition of the machinery. This final step connects the embedded IT of the machinery with the shop-floor IT by adaptation of the communication and the implementation of the manufacturing processes. This approach creates a close dependency between the machinery and the shop-floor IT.

New manufacturing approaches arise and the number of product variances increases and becomes more complex. These would lead to an increase of manufacturing functions. It goes along with continues automation processes within industrial digitalization and industry 4.0. Currently the high number of manufacturing steps results in a high number of IT-functions for control, management and monitor of the machinery. This easily extends the complexity and resource costs for the shop-floor IT planning. Furthermore, the high number of functions and devices increase the risk of failures.

At the same time, the demand of rapid changes in the production is growing and additional to that the information management during the manufacturing execution needs to be adapted in short term.

To insure continuous production, new configurations needs to be applied during the manufacturing process online without stopping the process. But also if failures appear alternative machinery should easily be put in place. This is currently very difficult and challenging to realize within the current shop-floor IT setups because of interoperability issues such as:

- Control devices are different with different communication mechanism and openness.
- The plug-in of new devices or services into a network of manufacturing systems requires effort in adaptation of the communication mechanism. This relates to the diversity of controllers for physical devices as well as different implementation on top of the controllers.
- Differences between shop-floor IT relations even within the same organization [1].

Within the current automation pyramid the shop-floor IT is located between the machinery and low level Manufacturing Execution System (MES) functions [2, 3]. This covers Programmable Logic Controller (PLC) [4], Supervisory Control and Data Acquisition (SCADA) [3] and the production data acquisition and monitoring of the MES.

Currently, setup and work sequences are derived from the product structure and the structure of the manufacturing system. The shop-floor IT is not considered here. In future, predefined services should be used which already contain interfaces in a standardized form.

The approach developed in cooperation with industrial stakeholders focuses on a modular solution and the representation of IT functions of manufacturing facilities in terms of services provided by cyber physical systems so called "modular shop-floor IT". Indeed modular concepts are developed since decades also for manufacturing. The paper focuses on the use of such concepts to improve the reusability of the design of the information management for manufacturing.

The assumption is that the IT functions required by the shop-floor are quite often similar. Therefore, manufacturing functions can be represented by a small set of normalized services which can be grouped into modules. This has been analyzed, specified, grouped and categorized in previous industrial research projects. It can reduce the effort for development, implementation and maintenance by using these generic functions for the shop-floor IT architecture. It also forces a harmonization of functions across factories and interfaces to the machinery [5]. Details of the approach and the technical concept are described in Sect. 3.

2   Related Technologies

With industry 4.0 the focus on cyber physical systems and internet of things in industry becomes more prominent. Technologies such as OPC-UA [6], DDS [7], IIRA [8], RAMI4.0 [9], CoAP [10] and MQTT [11] support the connection of physical components with the cyber world. They also provide frameworks to create smart networks via intranet and internet.

Taken OPC-UA it provides a standardized architecture and protocols to access physical systems. However, the specific interface still needs to be developed. This covers the functionalities as well as the security level [12, 13]. Furthermore, OPC-UA is only one possibility for a standardized access to the physical world. Currently, each machinery provider developed their own control software. Therefore, the problem of the plug and produce into the shop-floor IT without programming effort is still a challenge.

Ontology approaches exist, such as the "method for connecting automatic functional unit in hierarchically structured manufacturing system, involves providing connecting functional unit with readable data, and transforming and enriching data with semantic information" [14]. It does not address explicitly modularity and a model based approach. It also focuses especially on OPC-UA whereas the shop-floor IT concept presented in the paper addresses openness for protocols and architectures. It proposes a normalized service interface for each physical component which hides the used access to the physical system.

In the described reference, architecture parts and ideas are implemented related to RAMI4.0 and industrial internet reference architecture (IIRA) [8]. This simplifies compliance to RAMI4.0 and IIRA in the future.

3   Architecture

For the modular shop-floor IT, three layers has been identified from a physical system to the network of systems to a representation layer (see Fig. 1):

- **Cyber Physical System:** The "shop-floor IT enablers" provide a set of services related to a cyber physical system. It delivers for each physical component in the shop-floor related services to establish a common service interface for each of these components.
- **Network:** The execution engine benefits from the services are provided by the shop-floor IT enabler and establish the workflow between the different cyber physical systems. Using the provided services, it can start and stop the manufacturing process on the cyber physical system as well as stepwise progress and manage the feedback from the cyber physical system. The information is sent to the information management monitor "IM monitor" in terms of user interface.
- **Representation/Event detecting and debugging:** The "IM monitor" provides a view on the actual progress on orders in the shop-floor. It also allows a kind of debugging within the shop-floor process.

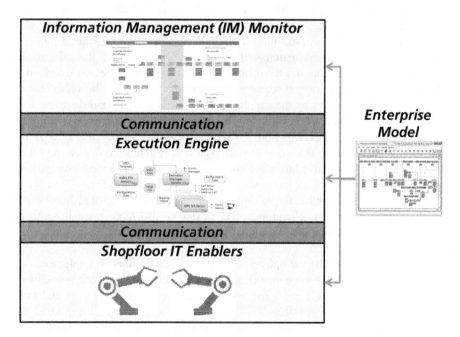

Fig. 1. Components of IoT infrastructures for flexible manufacturing systems

An enterprise model of the shop-floor processes and related data provides common information for the configuration of the shop-floor IT. It is built by applying a library of modules. The modules consist of service descriptions relevant for the shop-floor IT execution. The service descriptions are based on the "Unified Service Description Language" (USDL) [16] and the "Web Services Description Language" (WSDL) [15]. USDL is used to carry data such costs of the service, responsibilities etc. whereas the executable service is described by WSDL. The model includes the relation between the shop-floor IT enablers and the manufacturing processes. The shop-floor IT enablers represents a virtualization of a machinery in terms of services to control the machinery.

The main objective of the "shop-floor-IT enablers" is the harmonization of the interface to the devices on the shop-floor. The assumption is that it is possible to define a set of services which provides a common interface to manage the devices. Currently each device has its own specific interface. Standardized interfaces are sometimes provided but they differ in terms of specific semantics such as possibilities to start and stop a device or to get feedback.

Therefore, an adapter is proposed to provide a minimum set of services for each device. The initial set is just start, stop and step forward. Each of these services is parameterized with information about the expected work of the device such as for the start service. In fact, the adapter does an abstraction of the real functionality of the device and transfers the specific work as well as order and product information directly to the device.

This is possible because the realization of the information management does not take care of the specific service of the device. But it is required to get feedbacks such as status information e.g. ready, stopped, error, shutdown, and alive as well as potential service data. The data which provided from the device for other services is also managed like a black box. An example could be a camera which provides a figure to identify a product. This information will be directly forwarded by the information management of the shop-floor to identification services which provides the information to the next device. Each device requires its own adapter and in the future theses adapters should be provided by the suppliers of industrial services and devices.

To know which services are available, they are grouped into a service registry. The execution engine uses the services from the service registry to process and manage the information about the shop-floor (see Fig. 2). The details about the devices and their possible connections are derived from the same enterprise model which contains process information and also data about the services, products and orders (see also Sect. 4).

The shop-floor IT enablers target the development of a harmonised interface to access devices and services. Therefore, every device is also represented in terms of services. This provides a unique strategy independent from if it is a physical device or a service.

The diversity of controllers for physical devices as well as different implementation on top of the controllers are the major challenge. Therefore, the approach proposes an adaptor which hides the real implementation of the controllers, protocols and even architectures to access the physical devises or sensors because even using OPC-UA different implementations are possible. The initial implementation of the "shop-floor IT enablers" uses OPC-UA but it is not mandatory and other architectures are also possible.

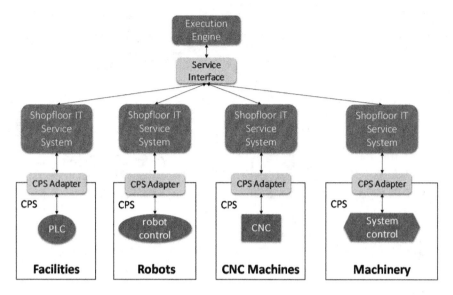

Fig. 2. Shop-floor IT enablers and execution engine service interfaces

In detail, the shop-floor IT enablers are implemented as Shopfloor IT Service Systems. Together they build an IoT infrastructure, in which every Shopfloor IT Service System represents a CPS and publishes its services. A Shopfloor IT Service System controls the execution of a service, ensures safety measures and handles behavior in case of errors. Access to the Shopfloor IT Service Systems is realized through service interfaces.

4 System Network and Service Execution

The overall objective of the Execution Engine is the realisation of a path within a network of CPSs. The network together with the related date is stored within an enterprise model. The Execution Engine consists of different services and files. The Index File Service and the Execution Manager Service are the main software components. These components are supported by different templates and configuration files. Each component is represented at Fig. 3.

The enterprise modelling system MO^2GO [17] has been used to design required information model as well as the process descriptions. The method used is the integrated enterprise modelling (IEM) [18]. It provides input/output relation and actions to model object transformations as well as the related resources required for the transformation. The resources are connected by a dotted line to the action. Within MO^2GO NG the user has the possibility to create a process model. This process model has to consist of the modules of the modular Shop-floor IT stored in a MO^2GO model library.

The model based view of a production process simplifies the understanding of the product lifecycle and planning. The production process is divided into modules similar

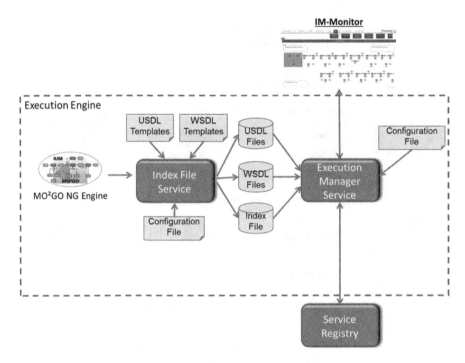

Fig. 3. Execution engine architecture

to building blocks. Every module represents a single production step and consists of three parts, such as:

- standardized interaction function
- standardized basic information function
- generic operation module

Generic operation modules combine execution functions on the field level. The standardized interaction functions are IT modules which are used for the in- and output parameters from the module. Standardized basic information functions are used for other data processing, e.g. data synchronization.

In Fig. 4 "signal setting" and "handle feedback" are standardized interaction functions. The part "data processing" is a standardized basic information function. An example for a generic operation module is "mating". By combining and rearranging modular shop-floor IT modules, different production processes are enabled. This enables a flexible reconfiguration for customized products and variants as well as a faster setup of new production processes.

In order to be able to produce a product later, a process model must be created first. This process model has to consist of predefined modules of the modular shop-floor IT. Next the Index file service has to evaluate the process model. With the information of the evaluation the execution engine can control the connected components. Every of these components have to send a feedback to the execution engine. On the basis of the

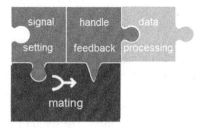

Fig. 4. Module of the modular shop-floor IT

feedback, the execution engine stops the whole production process or can start the next module to complete the production.

The second step is the connection between the execution engine and the shop-floor. To control all machines and measure related production data, the IoT technology can be used here. It means all production objects should be (building) up as IoT components in a virtual network as an infrastructure. Those production objects could be physical things like a machine with its controller or virtual things like a software component. To transform the physical production objects into IoT components cyber physical systems (CPS) concepts are used.

Finally, Fig. 5 illustrates the components involved in the realization of the approach. The execution engine works with the stored model information. The execution engine uses a range of messages to communicate with the connected components. These components are on the one hand the IM monitor and on the other hand various OPC UA servers.

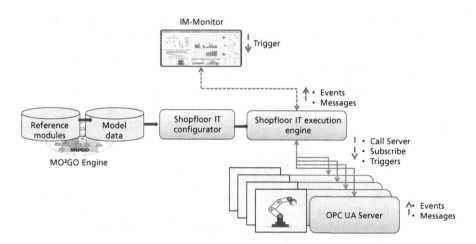

Fig. 5. Main components for the execution of the shop-floor information management

5 Conclusion

Tests of the concept and related prototypes have been applied. The initial tests were on an artificial manufacturing line and illustrated the potentials in terms of modularity and flexibility. Now two industrial related cases are established. Whereas the first uses a traditional intranet implementation, the second uses a cloud infrastructure and has a little modified setup. It shows already the flexibility in terms of infrastructure as in both cases the previous described IT system is used. The setup of the demonstrator consists basically of two incorporating commercial robots, a visual detection for the availability of various parts as well as hard- and software components, which is an usual configuration in industry. A visualisation and interface for user offers a Monitor next to the robot cage.

A current case is where the two robots assemble three gears into a planetary gear. The demonstrators are an important indicator of the feasibility of the approach. It was possible to show that different devices could be networked via different network protocols in order to produce a product. Therefore, modular approach allows users a quick and easy change of the process model. Next steps are the implementation of the concept and prototypes within productive environments. But a major objective for the future is test concepts to ensure security, robustness and interoperability. This is currently under development as part of a national project called IoT-T (http://www.iot-t. de/en/).

References

1. http://www.iot-t.de/wp-content/uploads/sites/11/2017/06/IoT-T_R1.1.pdf. Accessed 31 July 2017
2. Bajric, A., Mertins, K., Rabe, M., Jaekel, F.-W.: A success story: manufacturing execution system implementation. In: Popplewell, K., Harding, J., Poler, R., Chalmeta, R. (eds.) Proceeding of the 6th International Conference on Interoperability for Enterprise Software and Applications (IESA 2010), Coventry, UK, April 13–15, pp. 357–366. Springer, London (2010). https://doi.org/10.1007/978-1-84996-257-5_33
3. ISA95, Enterprise-Control System Integration. https://www.isa.org/isa95/. Accessed 31 July 2017
4. Heinrich, B., Linke, P., Glöckler, M.: Grundlagen Automatisierung Sensorik, Regelung, Steuerung. Springer Fachmedien, Wiesbaden (2015). ISBN 978-3-658-05960-6
5. Riedel, O., Margraf, T., Stölzle, S., Knothe, T., Eggers, A., Wintrich, N.: Modellbasierte modulare Shopfloor IT - Integration in die Werkzeuge der Digitalen Fabrik. Study, Electronic Publication (2014). http://publica.fraunhofer.de/eprints/urn_nbn_de_0011-n-3162488.pdf. Accessed 31 July 2017
6. OPC-UA. https://opcfoundation.org/about/opc-technologies/opc-ua/. Accessed 1 Aug 2017
7. Data Distribution Service (DDS) Version 1.4. Object Management Group (2015). www.omg.org/spec/DDS/1.4/PDF/. Accessed 1 Aug 2017
8. Industrial Internet Reference Architecture (IIRA). www.iiconsortium.org/IIRA.htm. Accessed 1 Aug 2017

9. RAMI4.0. https://www.vdi.de/fileadmin/vdi_de/redakteur_dateien/gma_dateien/5305_Publikation_GMA_Status_Report_ZVEI_Reference_Architecture_Model.pdf. Accessed 1 Aug 2017
10. The Constrained Application Protocol (CoAP). https://tools.ietf.org/html/rfc7252. Accessed 1 Aug 2017
11. MQTT Version 3.1.1 OASIS Standard, 29 October 2014. http://docs.oasis-open.org/mqtt/mqtt/v3.1.1/os/mqtt-v3.1.1-os.html. Accessed 1 Aug 2017
12. Common Criteria Protection Profile vom Bundesamt für Sicherheit in der Informationstechnik (BSI). https://www.bsi.bund.de/SharedDocs/Downloads/DE/BSI/Zertifizierung/Reporte/ReportePP/pp0047ma1b_pdf.pdf?__blob=publicationFile&v=2. Accessed 1 Aug 2017
13. https://www.bsi.bund.de/EN/TheBSI/thebsi_node.html. Accessed 1 Aug 2017
14. Sauer, O.: Verfahren zur Anbindung einer technischen Funktionseinheit in ein hierarchisches Fertigungssystem. Patent DE102008017997A1 2009.01.22
15. Web Services Description Language (WSDL). https://www.w3.org/TR/wsdl20/. Accessed 1 Aug 2017
16. Unified Service Description Language XG Final Report. https://www.w3.org/2005/Incubator/usdl/XGR-usdl-20111027/. Accessed 1 Aug 2017
17. Fraunhofer IPK. www.moogo.de. Accessed 1 Aug 2017
18. Spur, G., Mertins, K., Jochem, R.: Integrierte Unternehmensmodellierung. Beuth, Berlin (1993)

Interoperable Process Design
in Production Systems

Georg Weichhart[1,2(✉)] and Christian Stary[2]

[1] PROFACTOR GmbH, Steyr-Gleink, Austria
Georg.Weichhart@PROFACTOR.at
[2] Department of Communications Engineering – Business Informatics,
Johannes Kepler University, Linz, Austria
Christian.Stary@jku.at

Abstract. In Sensing, Smart, and Sustainable (S^3) Enterprises information is not only gathered from an internet of production things supporting smart decision making, but this information also allows execute processes automatically. These processes need to be interoperable for sustainable operation while enabling dynamic adaptation. In this paper we present a development framework successfully tested in a European project demonstrating key features of subject-orientation for production process support across the IEC 62264 control hierarchy layers. It aligns business planning and logistics with manufacturing operations and production management, utilizing a communication protocol choreography, message passing and data exchange between production-relevant behavior encapsulations. The overall system is modular and adaptive, where interoperability is supported through process models.

Keywords: Enterprise interoperability
Subject-oriented Business Process Management · Internet of Things

1 Introduction

The vision of the Sensing, Smart and Sustainable Enterprise (S^3 Enterprise) builds around a layer of abstraction (the enterprise operating system) that allows to make use of data from heterogeneous sources. Sensing technologies, like the Internet of Things (IoT) are targeting low-power, wireless sensor networks which are connected to the cloud. Collected data is stored context free, information about concrete sources is hidden. The data is analyzed and processed, for supporting decision makers. Sub-symbolic AI algorithms (deep learning) support classification of events using high volume data. To become sustainable, the enterprise system must then adapt to these smart decision. A pragmatic approach to interpretability is needed. This implies changing the way processes are executed reacting to environmental changes. However, planning and executing production processes is not executing simple chains of service calls where semantically unified data is used to trigger one service after the other. Production steps implemented by different human and artificial actors need to be orchestrated. Adaptation in the enterprise implies maintaining interoperability of processes. Advanced process support for actors is required from the global production process point of view. Interoperability is not sufficient on the technological and data semantics layer but is also required on organizational process and pragmatics layer.

For understanding the needed process interoperability support, a simple process where a human and a robot collaborate, is used to pinpoint the direction of future work.

In Sect. 2 we present interoperability research with a focus on adaptive, modular systems and organizational interoperability. Section 3 presents an initial approach developed in the So-Pc-Pro project for interoperability of processes. This is then summarized in the conclusions at the end of this article.

2 Interoperability

The production *process* is the most important integrating aspect of a production system. Subsystems like machine and human actors need to align their activities with resource availabilities and part flows. When going into details, execution of process parts is dependent on the concrete machines executing these segments.

On a higher level of abstraction, a similar situation exists. The execution of processes along the supply chain is decentralized, where suppliers determine their own production schedule, partially executed concurrently, taking decisions independently. However, at the end of the day, a globally synchronized production plan is required which links machines across multiple supply chain participants.

Therefore, in a production system both, parallel and independent executed sub-systems with their specific behavior, as well as their output and behavior being interoperable with the rest of the system is need.

In the following, we review our view on Enterprise Integration and Interoperability in general, and discuss then process-related approaches to enterprise interoperability.

2.1 Enterprise Integration/Interoperability

Enterprise Integration [1] has its roots in Computer Integrated Manufacturing (CIM) approaches developed in the 80's and 90's. Its aim is to support the alignment of the enterprise's information sub-systems. The enterprise information system includes artificial and human agents that share and exchange information [2].

Integration is an activity, which is necessary to bring together independently created systems in order to realize a larger function that requires all involved systems. Integration activities are researched in the fields of enterprise integration (EI) [1], enterprise interoperability [3], enterprise application integration (EAI) [4]. EAI focuses on the technical aspects of distributed applications and middleware.

It is of importance to understand, that all these research fields are model-driven approaches. The exchanged information and the interfaces between systems is explicit [5]. Enterprise Modelling (EM) and Enterprise Architecture (EA) have strong connections to the problems discussed in enterprise integration and interoperability [6]. Interoperability builds on research on integration, but places emphasis on loosely coupled systems, and stresses the independence and decentralized aspects of the involved systems.

The to-be integrated, independent systems have interfaces across which it is necessary to exchange information to realize the overarching function. This implies that there is a technical interface, which is used by the other system to exchange information. Such interfaces include human machine interfaces (HMI) when one of the two systems is a human.

These pieces of information must not only have the correct technical data format, but also the semantics of the conveyed information must be clear and synchronized (also in the HMI case). The semantic interoperability barrier (aka conceptual interoperability barrier) refers to the representation of a real-world element and problems with the interpretation of its structure and meaning by different systems.

In addition to syntactical and semantical interoperability, there is an organizational aspect of information exchange. In the case of machine-to-machine communication for example the APIs (application programming interface) must be called in the correct sequence. In the case of considering a production system on supply chain level, (business) processes of the organizational systems need to be aligned. The use of information within a process provides the specific context in which information is used. This aspect incorporates pragmatics and addresses the use of data beyond its context free interpretation.

The European Interoperability Framework discusses three essential levels or dimensions of interoperability [1]. On the bottom, the syntactic level is concerned with technical interoperability between two systems. In the middle, there is the semantic level concerned with the interpretation of data. On top, there is the pragmatic level concerned with the use of information in a concrete context.

Besides the different levels of concern, there is also the degree to which multiple systems are interoperable. This quality is described on a continuum.

To be *fully integrated* implies that there is a common (concrete) model, which is implemented, in full detail, in all involved systems. This is an extreme position on the discussed spectrum, because, as a consequence, the interfaces between the systems get blurred. All systems are dependent, and any change needs to be addressed in all systems.

At the other end of the spectrum are *incompatible* systems. These systems are not able to exchange information or interact (technical aspect), required information is not understood or interpreted in the wrong way (semantic aspect), or the behavior of one system has negative impact on other systems (e.g., incompatible processes: organizational aspect).

In the continuum between *incompatible* and *fully integrated* systems are interoperable systems. The research field of Enterprise Interoperability, in contrast to Enterprise Integration, places emphasis on the loosely coupled (loosely integrated) systems and discusses unified and federated interoperability [7]. It is not implied that the integration end of the continuum provides higher quality. On the contrary, loosely coupled systems are more adaptive and are much harder to engineer.

2.2   Approaches Supporting Interoperability in Production

In a stable system interoperability is less often disturbed once reached. In a system which is dynamic and facing a lot of changes, more sophisticated support for sustainable interoperability is needed.

In the following we review selected approaches supporting interoperability, giving attention to their support for process interoperability and modular, adaptive systems. Due to space constraints, we have to focus on a limited list of approaches.

Technology Approaches

One example for a technological approach is the *Cilia Middleware* service oriented, integration environment. It is based on mediators, supporting the monitoring and dynamical adaption of mediator chains during execution [8]. While the possibility to adapt is a core aspect of the cilia middleware, this adaptation is triggered from the outside. Missing is the possibility to do a process re-planning beyond the exchange of services, if a better candidate is available and requires a changed interaction.

Semantic Approaches

A combination of middleware and ontology is implemented in the Ontology of Enterprise Interoperability extended for Complex Adaptive Systems (OoEI^{CAS}) [9]. It implements middleware aspects using an actor-based system, where the actors encapsulate the external systems to be made interoperable. The realized Domain Specific Language (DSL) implements the systemic aspects of the Ontology of Enterprise Interoperability [10]. This DSL supports the implementation of actors as a core concept for representing systems. This allows to implement interoperability on process level, as the actors may map the behavior of external systems to interoperable behavior.

The Liquid Sensing Enterprise (LSE) approach [11] also assumes that the enterprise is a complex adaptive system. This approach provides the infrastructure that the enterprise evolves over time. Fundamentally, this approach is a model driven engineering approach. Independent agents communicate with others using models. This implies that used models (e.g., for decision making or communication) change and need to be transformed. A model morphism agent is responsible for proposing model mappings. Simulation is used to estimate the impact of change on the existing system. Models may also describe behavior of systems.

Organizational Approaches

The multi-agent-system based SUddEN environment supports organizational interoperability through the use of performance indicators [12]. A core team of supply chain participants designs the performance measurement system for the planned chain. Supporting the collaborative design activity supports alignment of business goals and due to the need to make indicators explicit, organizational interoperability is indirectly required and measured in the following.

In CrossWork, an agent based systems approach is used to provide a modular infrastructure for supply chain planning [13]. In this approach, process interoperability, requires explicit process models at the external level. An ontology is provided that allows to capture goals, capabilities as well as roles of supply chain partners [14]. Here local workflows (represented by agents) contribute to global workflows.

The Mediation Information System approach (MIS) [15] is a methodological framework for supporting knowledge management and continuous interoperability management for the supply chain. It supports alignment of information systems and collaborative behavior. Adapting MIS needs to be performed manually.

S-BPM (Subject Oriented Business Process Management) can be used to support interoperability [16] and implement production processes [17]. By extending the business process features and directly interfacing machines S-BPM allows to implement a level of abstraction where subjects (roles of agents) exchange information objects, but internal behavior is hidden. Yet the semantics of the information objects has to be defined externally (i.e. full integration is needed). The interface between subjects needs to be determined *ex ante*.

3   Adaptive Processes and Interoperability

In the S^3 Enterprise vision, information is gathered from an internet of production things to enable smart decisions for the enterprise system which are turned into actions to maintain sustainability. Taking a simple scenario from collaborative robotics, in assembly processes show the need for ad-hoc & local re-planning of processes. However, local process changes have impact on the global level as well. The scenario below will serve as an initial case to highlight requirements and needs for an interoperability support infrastructure capable to re-plan processes.

We are considering a collaborative robotic system, where robots work with humans assembling small parts (following [18]). Both sub-systems, the human and the artificial, need to have appropriate tools for their tasks available. It is not possible, that the tools are passed from humans to robots (tools need to be mounted to the robot arm). Not only because of this, for rescheduling a task from a human to a robot, logistic, and preparatory steps have to be taken. Task-relocation happens due to external and also internal events. A GPS sensor is capable of reporting that the delivery of parts is delayed. That information needs to be connected to the right-order schedule, and the overall schedule needs to be redone, where different task processing times of the robot and the human need to be taken into account. Internal rescheduling events will trigger task re-location when a sensor signals physical or cognitive overload of the worker. This will happen on the spot, making ad-hoc changes may be necessary. Task-reallocation to the other direction happens when a sensor identifies a worn-out tool of the robot.

This scenario reveals interoperability issues on all three levels of interoperability, which will be used in the following to structure the discussion.

3.1   General Organizational Interoperability Requirements

On technical level, all components have to be connected and a standard for machine-to-machine communication have to be in place. Assembly is, in principle, a flexible process. It is required, that the hardware components have to be modular in order to re-arrange the overall assembly system over time.

Descriptions of tasks (i.e. models) have to be available in machine and human readable form. The semantics of the tasks depends on the application domain. It captures active resources (artificial and human agents, including their skills), passive resources (e.g. materials), and activities.

Agents are the main elements that execute a certain task. Different agents have different skills allowing to execute different tasks. Agents may be able to execute a task in different qualities. Agents may be organized in teams, projects, and organizational units.

For executing tasks, resources like raw materials, knowledge are needed, and semi-finished parts are produced. Flows of parts and materials (passive resources) between agents are one kind of flows that needed to be addressed. Not only physical flows but also activity flows need to be captured and controlled. Some activities have to be executed in parallel (synchronous, asynchronous), some in sequence. The possibility to use coordination patterns is needed for planning (see the following).

Skills are concepts that allow to do initial planning and select agents capable to certain tasks. Skills are realized by coordinated activities called processes.

All these model elements need to be understood by all agents. The semantics needs to be clear and the syntax needs to be machine and human readable as well.

Given the scenario above, re-planning/redesign takes place in case of events when processes can not be executed as planned/designed.

3.2 Process Design and Execution

In the following, we present a Business & Production Process Management approach, which allows to orchestrate different human and artificial agents on the shop floor. This partially fulfils the above presented requirements.

Subject-oriented Business Process Management (S-BPM) represents a generic approach to modelling, execution and improvement of business processes. It has been applied in production companies, expanding the scope of process management to planning, logistics, and shop floor activities [17]. The different levels of abstraction and granularity of the IEC 62264 control hierarchy have been seamlessly integrated on the process level using the S-BPM approach in the EU-funded project "Subject-Orientation for People-Centred Production"[1]. As shown in Fig. 1, the vertical integration for modularisation is based on using subject-oriented process models as a uniform representation layer. In S-BPM, processes at all levels of the IEC 62264 control hierarchy, including High Level Control (HLC) and Low Level Control (LLC), can be represented. Processes on the LLC levels (i.e. Levels 1 and 2) execute them in real time. Processes on HLC levels (i.e. Levels 3 and 4) operate not on in real time. Data exchange between processes at the different levels can be based on existing automation standards, including OPC UA (IEC 62541) and B2MML (IEC 62264). OPC UA as a communication protocol is implemented in most modern PLC environments. It allows exchanging semantic data models also via web services or binary protocols.

---

[1] www.SO-PC-Pro.eu.

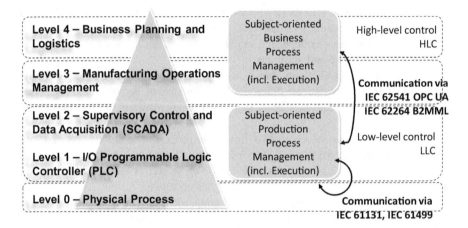

Fig. 1. Vertical integration of processes based on S-BPM and existing data standards including OPC UA extended based on (cf. [19])

Vertical integration allows modularisation of operating processes in mutual dependency with respect to planning, executing and monitoring requirements. The SO-PC-Pro project has led to an S-BPM based process integration framework. Technically SO-PC-Pro is based on recent developments using the Metasonic Suite (www. metasonic.de) with a B2MML interface, an OPC UA interface, an extension for transforming S-BPM behaviours to executable IEC 61131-3 conform PLC code. As a standard for vendor- and platform-independent communication, we have been using OPC UA (cf. IEC 62541) to interface LLC processes executed by Programmable Logic Controllers (PLCs).

The S-BPM approach provides an abstraction that supports process descriptions and designs for human and artificial actors. In the following, we sketch process communication via OPC UA to show how humans and robots are coordinated in a single process. Runtime communication between level 3 and level 2 processes has been enabled including data exchanged (according to the OPC UA standard) [17], p. 33ff.

The OPC UA standard (IEC 2008) supports specification of the interface of the address space of OPC UA servers', to define content that is visible/editable for clients. Clients can monitor and subscribe to attributes and events on the server. Figure 2 shows the schema for the interplay between the behaviour of the "Robot" subject (in the Metasonic Suite) and a PLC addressable via an OPC UA client/server. It enables the configuration of the endpoint of the server and the relevant node (e.g. variable, method, and event). It also allows reading/writing variables from/to information objects carrying data to be exchanged, invoking methods on the server, and subscribing to server events.

The OPC UA S-BPM connector enables (i) reading values from a Robot or any PLC and storing them in a business object, and (ii) writing concrete values of an information object to variables of a PLC or Robot. In this way, the concrete OPC UA server endpoint providing desired variables can be implemented. When an action and a relevant information object needs to be selected before mapping variables onto each

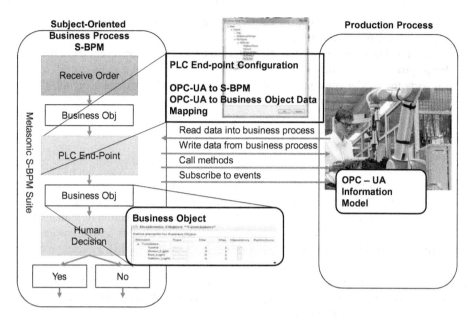

Fig. 2. Schematic interface description (cf. [19])

other, the connection mechanism supports mapping multiple PLC variables to different fields of information objects.

Currently, semantics in the exchanged information objects is not represented, albeit the lack of automated re-planning support.

3.3   Towards Automated Planning

Preparation steps need to be executed by all agents prior to any collaborative activity. Consequently, in order to maintain interoperability in case of events triggering change, either automated re-planning or manual re-design has to be performed [20].

To automate process planning in production, both is needed, a local detailed resource-centric/agent-centric point of view and a collaboration/production-process point of view. Distinguishing between these two layers allows to project the particu-larities of the concrete hardware and resources to a middleware.

The resource point of view is needed to encapsulate hardware specific aspects. The network point of view is needed to align all process steps/segments with a common (global) product process.

To allow local autonomy and global synchronization in a *process-centric auto-mated control environment* with automated re-planning, there is a need for a framework that (cf. [17, 21]):

- provides a middleware and abstract data-model for adaptability
- provides services supporting automated re-planning (e.g. directory of skills; logging for quality assurance, etc.)

- supports human and artificial production resources on the one hand side and the network layer for connectivity
- allows for decentralized specification and execution of process segments for different production resources
- supports the model concepts and their semantics (tasks, processes, agents, skills, resources, … see above)

4 Conclusions

The initial work in the SO-PC-Pro project shows a running environment for executing processes partly by humans, partially on machines. This work reveals that the abstraction using a paradigm similar to agents supports the coordination of humans and machines in a single process. This is an important aspect towards a middleware that supports automated control of production processes executed by IoT systems, robots, and humans. Still much more research has to be done, to support an abstract production process description to be automatically planned and deployed in such an environment. This does not only involve the organizational interoperability levels, but also the semantic and technical interoperability levels.

Acknowledgement. The research described in this paper has been partially funded by the European Commission and the State of Upper Austria in the projects "Smart Factory Lab" and "DigiManu", and the European Commission within the project SO-PC-Pro (Subject Orientation for People-Centred Production - grant agreement n° 609190).

References

1. Vernadat, F.B.: Technical, semantic and organizational issues of enterprise interoperability and networking. Ann. Rev. Control **34**, 139–144 (2010)
2. Romero, D., Vernadat, F.B.: Enterprise information systems state of the art: past, present and future trends. Comput. Ind. **80**, 3–13 (2016)
3. Ducq, Y., Chen, D., Doumeingts, G.: A contribution of system theory to sustainable enterprise interoperability science base. Comput. Ind. **63**, 844–857 (2012)
4. He, W., Xu, L.D.: Integration of distributed enterprise applications: a survey. IEEE Trans. Ind. Inform. **10**, 35–42 (2014)
5. Zacharewicz, G., Diallo, S.Y., Ducq, Y., Agostinho, C., Jardim-Goncalves, R., Bazoun, H., Wang, Z., Doumeingts, G.: Model-based approaches for interoperability of next generation enterprise information systems: state of the art and future challenges. IseB **15**, 1–28 (2016)
6. Chen, D., Doumeingts, G., Vernadat, F.B.: Architectures for enterprise integration and interoperability: past, present and future. Comput. Ind. **59**, 647–659 (2008)
7. Tu, Z., Zacharewicz, G., Chen, D.: A federated approach to develop enterprise interoperability. J. Intell. Manufact. **27**, 11–31 (2014)
8. Lalanda, P., Morand, D., Chollet, S.: Autonomic mediation middleware for smart manufacturing. IEEE Internet Comput. **21**, 32–39 (2017)

9. Weichhart, G., Guédria, W., Naudet, Y.: Supporting interoperability in complex adaptive enterprise systems: a domain specific language approach. Data Knowl. Eng. **105**, 90–100 (2016)
10. Naudet, Y., Latour, T., Guédria, W., Chen, D.: Towards a systemic formalisation of interoperability. Comput. Ind. **61**, 176–185 (2010)
11. Agostinho, C., Jardim-Goncalves, R.: Sustaining interoperability of networked liquid-sensing enterprises: a complex systems perspective. Ann. Rev. Control **39**, 128–143 (2015)
12. Weichhart, G., Feiner, T., Stary, C.: Implementing organisational interoperability – the SUddEN approach. Comput. Ind. **61**, 152–160 (2010)
13. Mehandjiev, N., Grefen, P. (eds.): Dynamic Business Process Formation for Instant Virtual Enterprises. Springer, London (2010)
14. Grefen, P., Mehandjiev, N., Kouvas, G., Weichhart, G., Eshuis, R.: Dynamic business network process management in instant virtual enterprises. Comput. Ind. **60**, 86–103 (2009)
15. Bénaben, F., Mu, W., Boissel-Dallier, N., Barthe-Delanoe, A.-M., Zribi, S., Pingaud, H.: Supporting interoperability of collaborative networks through engineering of a service-based Mediation Information System (MISE 2.0). Enterp. Inf. Syst. **9**, 556–582 (2015)
16. Weichhart, G., Wachholder, D.: On the interoperability contributions of S-BPM. In: Nanopoulos, A., Schmidt, W. (eds.) S-BPM ONE 2014. LNBIP, vol. 170, pp. 3–19. Springer, Cham (2014). https://doi.org/10.1007/978-3-319-06065-1_1
17. Neubauer, M., Krenn, F., Majoe, D., Stary, C.: Subject-orientation as design language for integration across organisational control layers. Int. J. Prod. Res. **55**(13), 3644–3656 (2017)
18. Fast-Berglund, Å., Palmkvist, F., Nyqvist, P., Ekered, S., Åkerman, M.: Evaluating Cobots for Final Assembly Procedia. CIRP **44**, 175–180 (2016)
19. Neubauer, M., Stary, C. (eds.): S-BPM in the Production Industry. Springer International Publishing, Heidelberg (2017)
20. Åkerman, M., Fast-Berglund, A., Ekered, S.: Interoperability for a dynamic assembly system procedia. CIRP **44**, 407–411 (2016)
21. Dar, K., Taherkordi, A., Baraki, H., Eliassen, F., Geihs, K.A.: A resource oriented integration architecture for the Internet of Things: a business process perspective. Pervasive Mobile Comput. **20**, 145–159 (2015)

Ontology-Based Decision Support System for Enterprise Interoperability

Mahdi Zouch[1,2], Wided Guedria[1(✉)], and Riadh Ben Halima[2]

[1] ITIS, Luxembourg Institute of Science and Technology (LIST),
5 avenue des Hauts-Fourneaux, 4362 Esch-sur-Alzette, Luxembourg
{mahdi.zouch,wided.guedria}@list.lu
[2] National Engineering School of Sfax ENIS,
University of Sfax, 3038 Sfax, Tunisia
{mahdi.zouch,riadh.benhalima}@enis.tn

Abstract. With the increased globalization of the economy, the competitiveness has become ubiquitous and enterprises need to be reactive and to collaborate with different stakeholders to survive in its environment. Within this context, the choice of suitable collaborators and partners with whom collaboration may happen without problems is a key factor of success. In this paper, an ontology-based approach to support interoperability and help enterprises to solve interoperability problems before they occur is proposed.

Keywords: Ontology · Decision support system
Enterprise interoperability · Interoperability problem · Knowledge

1 Introduction

There are a lot of success stories about enterprise collaboration. However, it should not be denied that collaboration is sometimes synonymously with problems and that there are also stories of collaborations that have been a failure. By having a close look, one's may clearly see that solving collaboration problems or preventing them from appearing by choosing the suitable partners, can help enterprises avoid failed business stories. When such a choice is available, decision makers need to take into account different criteria including the impact of a given collaboration in terms of potential problems. Making a decision is a tough task that has enormous impacts on the enterprise future and more likely the success or the failure of a business. According to Forbes[1], nine startups out of ten fails in making "good" decisions. Making "bad" decisions could lead to serious consequences, especially when these decisions are related to collaboration. This explains the growth of collaboration tool software. In fact, seven CEOs out of ten planned to increase their spending on collaboration tools in 2003 while the rate of growth of such software reached 38% in 2014. This shows the need for this kind of tools.

Since there is no decision support tool that prevents potential interoperability problems before occurring and proposes solutions to the identified problems to help

---

[1] American business magazine.

C. Debruyne et al. (Eds.): OTM 2017 Workshops, LNCS 10697, pp. 36–45, 2018.
https://doi.org/10.1007/978-3-319-73805-5_4

organizations planning their interoperability from an AS-IS situation to a TO-BE one, this work focuses on implementing such system.

The remainder of this paper is structured as follows: Sect. 2 presents some related work, while Sect. 3 presents the proposed approach and the architecture of the system. Section 4 shows a real use case scenario using the proposed system and finally Sect. 5 concludes the paper and highlights some future work.

2 Related Work

In this section, we introduce the ontology of enterprise interoperability which constitutes the basis of this work, and give an overview of some existing decision support systems.

2.1 The Ontology of Enterprise Interoperability (OoEI)

Interoperability is ubiquitous but not easy to understand due to its numerous definitions and interpretations [1]. Ford et al. point out that according to their survey, thirty-four definitions of interoperability were proposed since 1977 [2]. Some definitions can be found in [3–7]. Within this context the Ontology of Interoperability (OoI) [8] was proposed to give a common understanding about interoperability. It considers the Interoperability as a problem to solve: "*An interoperability problem appears when two or more incompatible systems are put in relation. Interoperability per se is the paradigm where an interoperability problem occurs*" [9].

Based on that, the Ontology of Enterprise Interoperability (OoEI) [1] was proposed as an extension of the OoI in the enterprise field. The OoEI is composed of three main parts which are:

- The Systemic model where the enterprises are instantiated and defined in the ontology. Definitions are found in [1, 9, 10].
- The Decisional model where the analysis is performed to identify problems and related solutions. Definitions are found in [10].
- The Knowledge model where the expert's knowledge is stored [10].

2.2 Existing Decision Support Systems

A decision support system (DSS) is a "*set of related computer programs and data required to assist with analysis and decision making within an organization*". Many decision support systems have been proposed in the literature. Some of them adopt an ontology-based approach. The main relevant works that we have found are:

- In the health field, the PESCaDO project exploits environmental data, weather forecasts as well as user's health profile and activities to determine if the desired activity could cause potential health issues due to the weather [11]. Another relevant research work in the same field proposes a diagnosis and treatment recommendation system for diabetes [12].

- In [13], the authors propose an ontology based decision support system to help nontechnical consumers to select the "right" domestic solar hot water system (i.e. that is tailored to their needs), with updated information on installation costs, components and interrelationships [13].
- A research work has also been conducted in the field of self-driving and autonomous vehicles. It focuses on making fast driving decisions at cross-roads by representing the data collected from sensors in a machine understandable format to help vehicles understanding traffic situations and making decisions [14].

The research works cited above have a number of common components which are: The Ontology, the reasoner, the inference rules, the knowledge base and the query engine. The ontology is defined as an "explicit specification of a conceptualization" [15]. It allows to define standardized concept, notions and relationships that can be used by every individual involved in a specific domain. There are several types of ontologies, the most common types are upper-ontologies and domain ontologies [16]. But other works suggest other types such as task and application ontologies [17]. Ontology is composed of concepts, relations and instances [18]. The reasoner is an important element in any ontology-based system. It is a tell/ask interface [16] that uses inference rules to perform the reasoning. Inference rules used to derive new knowledge from existing knowledge in the ontology [16]. Knowledge bases are the combination of an ontology with associated instances [18]. The components cited above will be considered to establish a proof of concept of a DSS for enterprise interoperability.

3 The Ontology-Based Decision Support System for Enterprise Interoperability

In order to implement the decision support system, some additions and changes have been done to the OoEI. We start by redefining the knowledge model. In fact, in the literature, the knowledge base definition is often linked to TBOX and ABOX pair only [13]. So, it is a set of instances around the concepts. Since the knowledge model in the ontology does not interfere with the reasoning process, we can split the OoEI into two parts. The first part includes the Systemic model and the Decisional Model where the reasoning happens. The second part is the knowledge graph that contains the knowledge model and other concepts from the decisional model. This is done for performance reasons because the system loads the ontology for each request. Thus, it seems reasonable to put only the part where the reasoning will take place in order to minimize the loading time.

3.1 The Knowledge Graph

The knowledge graph (Fig. 1) is composed of two parts: (a) The knowledge base which contains the problems and solutions as depicted in the left part of the Fig. 1, (b) The enterprise and user's database where all users and enterprises information are stored as shown in the right part of Fig. 1.

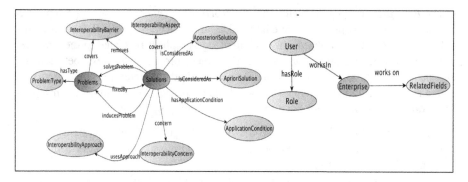

Fig. 1. The knowledge graph and enterprise nodes

3.2 The Systemic and Decisional Model

In this section, we give an overview of the systemic and decisional model, as defined in [1] as well as the added concepts and properties. For the sake of space, some concepts are omitted and some other concepts are removed because they can be represented as data properties. Figure 2 shows the main concepts of the ontology. Added concepts and properties are presented with green color while the orange ellipses represent concepts of the systemic model. The blue ellipses are concepts of the decisional model and the yellow ones are concepts linking the decisional model with the systemic model.

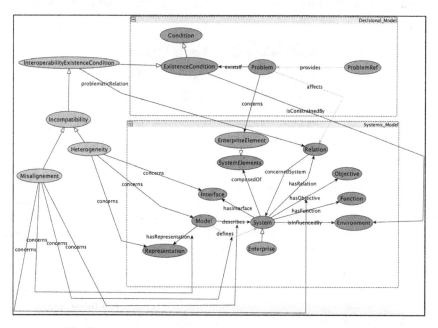

Fig. 2. Decisional and the systemic model (Color figure online)

The *Enterprise* concept as well as the *EnterpriseElement* concept are represented as subclasses of the concept *System*. We have added the concept *ProblemRef* that contains all the references of the problems in the knowledge graph. It is related to the *Problem* concept with a new relation *"provides"*. The object property *"affects"* between the *Problem* and the *Relation* is also added to help us find the enterprises involved in a particular problem. We have also added new Data properties. For example, all instances of the *Representation* concept have the following data properties:

- Speaks: xsd:string, it is used to add the official language of an enterprise.
- isClient: xsd:Boolean, it is used indicate if the enterprise is the client or is a part of the networked enterprise.
- useOfficeTool: xsd:string, it is used to indicate what office suite the enterprise is using.

3.3   Inference Rules

Inference rules are crucial in a decision support system. They are interpreted and used by the reasoner to achieve the problem detection process. In order to detect interoperability problems, three inference rules have been defined for almost each problem as depicted in Fig. 3. These rules are incremental and dependent:

- First rule is used to detect the existence of an incompatibility between enterprises.
- Second rule is used to locate the source of incompatibility by finding the concerned enterprises.
- Third rule is mainly used to find the problem; it summarizes all the previous rules.

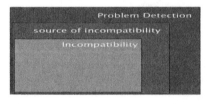

Fig. 3. Incremental rules in the problem detection process

It is worth noting that these rules are dynamic. This means that they change every time we add new constraints. One example to mention is the internal language barrier problem: Suppose that we have an interoperability problem due to the language barrier between two enterprises s1 and s2 that speak different languages *a* and *b*, respectively. The corresponding rules are written as follows:

- Incompatibility detection rule:
  Entreprise(?s1) ∧ Entreprise(?s2) ∧ Model(?m1) ∧ Model(?m2) ∧ Representation(?sr1) ∧ Representation(?sr2) ∧ describes(?m1, ?s1) ∧ describes(?m2, ?s2) ∧ hasRepresentation(?m1, ?sr1) ∧ hasRepresentation(?m2, ?sr2) ∧ speaks(?sr1, ?a) ∧ speaks(?sr2, ?b) ∧ swrlb:notEqual(?a, ?b) -> Incompatibility(heterogeneity) ∧ concerns(heterogeneity, ?sr1) ∧ concerns(heterogeneity, ?sr2)

– Locating the source of incompatibility:

Entreprise(?s1) ^ Entreprise(?s2) ^ Model(?m1) ^ Model(?m2) ^ Relation(?r) ^ Representation(?sr1) ^ Representation(?sr2) ^ composedOf(?s1, ?r) ^ composedOf (?s2, ?r) ^ concerns(heterogeneity, ?sr1) ^ concerns(heterogeneity, ?sr2) ^ describes(?m1, ?s1) ^ describes(?m2, ?s2) ^ hasRepresentation(?m1, ?sr1) ^ hasRepresentation(?m2, ?sr2) ^ speaks(?sr1, ?a) ^ speaks(?sr2, ?b) ^ swrlb: notEqual(?a, ?b) ^ Incompatibility(heterogeneity) ^ concerns(heterogeneity, ?sr1) ^ concerns(heterogeneity, ?sr2) -> problematicRelation(existenceCondition, ?r)

– Problem detection rule:

Entreprise(?s1) ^ Entreprise(?s2) ^ Model(?m1) ^ Model(?m2) ^ Relation(?r) ^ Representation(?sr1) ^ Representation(?sr2) ^ composedOf(?s1, ?r) ^ composedOf (?s2, ?r) ^ concerns(heterogeneity, ?sr1) ^ concerns(heterogeneity, ?sr2) ^ describes (?m1, ?s1) ^ describes(?m2, ?s2) ^ hasRepresentation(?m1, ?sr1) ^ hasRepresentation(?m2, ?sr2) ^ problematicRelation(existenceCondition, ?r) ^ speaks (?sr1, ?a) ^ speaks(?sr2, ?b) ^ swrlb:notEqual(?a, ?b) ^ isClient(?sr1, false) ^ isClient(?sr2, false) - > Problem(LanguageBarrierInternal) ^ affects(LanguageBarrierInternal, ?r)

3.4 System Architecture

The proposed system is designed for enterprises. It is mainly dedicated to decision makers who need to have a clear view about interoperability problems and related possible solutions regarding a potential collaboration or to improve a current one. The needed information is found in the knowledge base that has to be updated regularly by the knowledge expert. The system has also an administrator to configure it and to be contacted in case of technical problems. It was developed as a web application using Spring boot framework, apache tomcat as the web server as depicted in Fig. 4. Screenshots can be found at this link: https://goo.gl/QCpnDX.

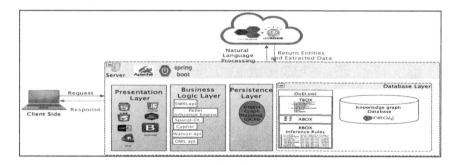

Fig. 4. System architecture

Three principal parts can be distinguished: (1) **The client side:** It represents the operations performed by the client using a web browser. In this case, the client can be the administrator, the knowledge expert or the user. (2) **The server side:** It receives all the requests from the client to process them and send the result back to the client. In the server, we distinguish four layers: (a) Presentation layer: it is the layer responsible for the user interface. It translates tasks and results to a user-understandable form using jsp, html, css, javascript, jquery, bootstrap and visjs. (b) Business logic layer: it is the layer containing all the application functionalities. This layer uses a number of APIs and technologies namely OWLapi, SWRLapi, Pellet inference engine, watson api, Cypher and sparql-DL, etc. (c) Persistence layer: also known as Data Access Layer, it makes the access to the database easier for the Business Logic Layer by providing an API that exposes methods for managing the database. This layer uses OGM (Object graph mapping) which is a fast object-graph mapping library for Neo4j database that uses Cypher query language, it is like JPA and uses annotations on simple POJO domain objects. (d) Database layer: it contains the Knowledge base stored in Neo4j and the Ontology file. This is where information is stored and retrieved. (3) **The cloud services:** They are used for natural language processing to extract relevant entities from the enterprise description text. To achieve this, two cloud services are used: (a) IBM Watson Knowledge Studio: This service allows to build a dedicated and personalized machine learning model for the enterprise domain. (b) IBM Bluemix: This platform allows to run, build, deploy and manage applications on the cloud.

3.5   The Decision Support System Workflow

The proposed decision support system works as follows: (1) Enterprise data are instantiated as ABOX in the ontology file, the data comes either from database or a text description. (2) The reasoner uses the SWRL rules to infer new information and detect the possible problem by finding the problem reference. (3) Once the problem references are detected, the system launches the query module which uses sparql and Cypher to retrieve the result from the Knowledge graph. Figure 5 gives an overview of the system workflow.

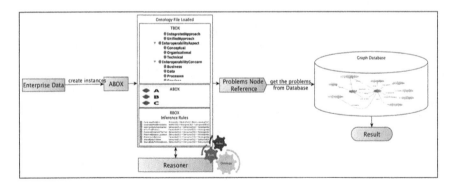

Fig. 5. Overview of the decision support workflow

4   Use Case Description

In order to establish the proof of concept of our decision support system, we have defined our system based on interviews with real enterprises located in Luxembourg. For privacy reasons, we will omit the names of the enterprises and use fake names instead of the real ones.

CL is the client in this scenario. (It offers to print companies a variety of innovative software services for managing and orchestrating printers.) It is willing to settle up a new business in Luxembourg. **CL** contacted **Innovation Company (Innov)** (an innovation and strategy consulting agency and a member of **Innov-hub** and the **Marketing Group (MG)**) for its consulting services. After checking its profile and needs in terms of innovation, **Innov** oriented **CL** to **Innov-hub** network (a soft-landing platform and accelerator for national and international start-ups.). For the purpose of this study, no details about **Innov-hub** network are given and it is considered as a black box entity that has as input a startup that needs help and output a growing startup. After doing the project with **Innov-hub**, our client wanted to promote the project, **Innov** oriented **CL** to **Offline Marketing Company (OMC)** (a full-service communication consulting company and member of the MG).

The first problem encountered by **OMC** and **CL** is the language Barrier. In fact, **CL** has German as official language while **OMC** has French as official language.

It is worth saying that this kind of problem is frequent in Luxembourg where there exist three official languages: Luxembourgish, French and German.

To overcome this problem, **OMC** which is a part of **MG**, needed a mediator, in our case **Digital Marketing (DG)** (a digital marketing agency) which is also a part of the **MG**. **DG** plays the role of the mediator between the two enterprises. A meeting was organized between **OMC** (i.e. the service provider), **DG** (i.e. the mediator) and **CL** (i.e. the client) to gather the client's needs.

After removing the language barriers, **OMC** is still having problems in understanding the client's needs due to its lack of expertise regarding innovation projects. To overcome this problem, **OMC** contacted **Innov** which is also member of the **MG**. Experienced in innovation, **Innov** played the role of the mediator and helped **OMC** understanding the client's needs. **OMC** then proposed an offer. After some negotiations, **CL** accepted the service offer and signed the contract. As soon as the contract signed, **OMC** defined the main tasks and related deadlines and assign tasks to the concerned actors.

Taking the fact that in the contract, the client has only three propositions, if none of them was satisfying the client should pay for the next propositions. Due to the misunderstanding between the **CL** and **OMC** and to the tight budget of the client, **CL** was not satisfied and ended the contract.

For the sake of space and clarity, we represent an extract of the instantiated systemic model for the language barrier problem as depicted in Fig. 6. The orange and green ellipses represent the concepts in the ontology while the pink ellipses are the instances. The blue color represents the data properties with the corresponding data.

The data properties can be assimilated to attributes in a java class. They carry all the needed information. These information as well as inference rules, are processed via the

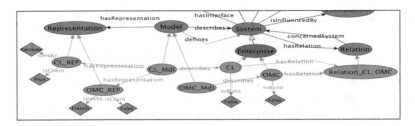

Fig. 6. Extract of the instantiated systemic model (Color figure online)

reasoner to discover the existence of a language barrier. The DSS workflow is described in Sect. 3. Figure 6 shows the knowledge that is needed to detect the external language barrier. CL speaks German and is the client, that's why we see the *speaks* property and *isClient* data property in the *CL_REP* instance. The same thing for OMC that speaks French. The applied rules are the ones presented in Sect. 3. For our case, we use the following rule:

Entreprise(?s1) ∧ Entreprise(?s2) ∧ Model(?m1) ∧ Model(?m2) ∧ Relation(?r) ∧ Representation(?sr1) ∧ Representation(?sr2) ∧ composedOf(?s1, ?r) ∧ composedOf(?s2, ?r) ∧ concerns(heterogeneity, ?sr1) ∧ concerns(heterogeneity, ?sr2) ∧ describes(?m1, ?s1) ∧ describes(?m2, ?s2) ∧ hasRepresentation(?m1, ?sr1) ∧ hasRepresentation(?m2, ?sr2) ∧ problematicRelation(existenceCondition, ?r) ∧ speaks(?sr1, ?a) ∧ speaks(?sr2, ?b) ∧ swrlb:notEqual(?a, ?b) ∧ isClient(?sr1, true) ∧ isClient(?sr2, false) -> Problem (LanguageBarrierExternall) ∧ affects(LanguageBarrierExternal, ?r).

5   Conclusion

In this paper, we have proposed a decision support system for enterprise interoperability. In order to build the system, we have used a real use case scenario. We have also made changes and adaptations to the existing Ontology of Enterprise Interoperability which was developed in a previous research work. We then designed and built the prototype. The developed system will constitute the basis for further improvements which can be categorized into short-term, mid-term and long-term goals. The mid-term goals are more oriented to the quality of the use case. In order to improve the prototype, there is a need to define a much more complex use case with a large amount of constraints. Long-term consist on developing new machine learning based mechanisms to find the relevant knowledge and feed the knowledge graph without the intervention of knowledge experts in the feeding process of the knowledge base.

Acknowledgements. This work has been conducted in the context of the PLATINE project (PLAnning Transformation Interoperability in Networked Enterprises), financed by the national fund of research of the Grand Duchy of Luxembourg (FNR), under the grant C14/IS/8329172.

References

1. Guedria, W.: A contribution to enterprise interoperability maturity assessment (Doctoral dissertation, Bordeaux 1) (2012)
2. Ford, T., et al.: Measuring system interoperability: an i-score improvement. In:Proceedings of the 6th Annual Conference on Systems Engineering Research, Los Angeles, CA, 4–5 April (2008)
3. Institute of Electrical and Electronics Engineers. IEEE standard computer dictionary: a compilation of IEEE standard computer glossaries (1990)
4. Department of Defense, Washington. Joint Pub 1-02, DoD Dictionary of Military and Associated Terms, 2001 (INTEROP, 2003) Interoperability Research for Networked Enterprises Applications and Software, Network of Excellence, Annex 1 – Description of Work (2003)
5. IDEAS project deliverables (wp1–wp7). Technical report (2003)
6. Chen, D., Dassisti, M., Elvester, B.: Di.3: enterprise interoperability framework and knowledge corpus - final report. Technical report, INTEROP Network of Excellence, IST-Contract no. IST-508 011 (2007)
7. Morris, E., Levine, L., Meyers, C., Place, P., Plakosh, D.: System of systems interoperability (SOSI). Final report. Software Engineering Institute, Carnegie Mellon University, Pittsburgh (2004)
8. Rosener, V., Naudet, Y., Latour, T.: A model proposal of the interoperability problem. In: CAISE05 workshops, EMOI 2005, vol. 2, pp. 395–400 (2005)
9. Naudet, Y., Latour, T., Hausmann, K., Abels, S., Hahn, A., Johannesson, P.: Describing interoperability: the OoI ontology. In: EMOI-INTEROP (2006)
10. Naudet, Y., Latour, T., Guedria, W., Chen, D.: Towards a systemic formalisation of interoperability. Comput. Ind. **61**(2), 176–185 (2010)
11. Rospocher, M., Serafini, L.: Ontology-centric decision support. In: Proceedings of the 2012 International Conference on Semantic Technologies Meet Recommender Systems & Big Data, vol. 919, pp. 61–72. CEUR-WS.org (2012)
12. Alharbi, R.F., Berri, J., El-Masri, S.: Ontology based clinical decision support system for diabetes diagnostic. In: Science and Information Conference (SAI), pp. 597–602. IEEE (2015)
13. Kontopoulos, E., Martinopoulos, G., Lazarou, D., Bassiliades, N.: An ontology-based decision support tool for optimizing domestic solar hot water system selection. J. Cleaner Production **112**, 4636–4646 (2016)
14. Zhao, L., Ichise, R., Sasaki, Y., Liu, Z., Yoshikawa, T.: Fast decision making using ontology-based knowledge base. In: 2016 IEEE Intelligent Vehicles Symposium (IV), pp. 173–178. IEEE (2016)
15. Gruber, T.R.: A translation approach to portable ontology specifications. Knowl. Acquis. **5**(2), 199–220 (1993)
16. Gomez-Perez, A., Fernández-López, M., Corcho, O.: Ontological Engineering: with Examples from the Areas of Knowledge Management, e-Commerce and the Semantic Web. Springer Science & Business Media (2006)
17. Guarino, N.: Formal ontology and information systems. In: Proceedings of FOIS, vol. 98, no. 1998, pp. 81–97 (1998)
18. Stevens, R., Goble, C.A., Bechhofer, S.: Ontology-based knowledge representation for bioinformatics. Brief. Bioinform. **1**, 398–414 (2000)

Rethinking of Framework and Constructs of Enterprise Architecture and Enterprise Modelling Standardized by ISO 15704, 19439 and 19440

Qing Li$^{(\boxtimes)}$, Iotong Chan, Qianlin Tang, Hailong Wei, and Yudi Pu

Department of Automation, Tsinghua University,
Beijing 100084, People's Republic of China
liqing@tsinghua.edu.cn

Abstract. Enterprise Architecture (EA) and Enterprise Modelling (EM) are systems engineering tools to understand, design, develop, implement and integrate complex enterprise and information systems. ISO 15704, 19439 and 19440 define fundamental concepts and principles of EAs and EMs, which are emphasized as the top standards of smart manufacturing by NIST's smart manufacturing ecosystem and relative standardization roadmap. Since the three international standards will soon be subject to revision, this paper rethinks the basic principles of EAs and EMs, and presents a General Enterprise Modelling (GEM) framework and a relative EA (GEM-EA). GEM-EA provides tools and methodology of model-based systems engineering (MBSE) to enterprise and automation systems integration. GEM involves a set of models and methods to describes different aspects of a system and covers its lifecycle. GEM and GEM-EA can greatly facilitate the process of enterprise diagnosis, business process reengineering and information system implementation.

Keywords: Enterprise Architecture · Enterprise Modelling · Framework
Construct

1 Introduction

Enterprise Architecture (EA) and Enterprise Modelling (EM) are effective ways to analyse the system integration issues of information and communication technology (ICT) systems, especially in the face of increasingly complex industrial automation systems. In the past forty years, experts from different professional domains committed themselves in the study of EAs, and produced a set of significant works, including Zachman Framework, CIM-OSA (computer integrated manufacturing open system architecture), PERA (Purdue enterprise reference architecture), ARIS (architecture of integrated information system), GERAM (generalised enterprise reference architecture and methodology), FEAF (federal enterprise architecture framework), DoDAF (department of defence architecture framework), TOGAF (the open group architecture framework), etc. At the meanwhile, international standards such as ISO 15704 [1], 19439 [2] and 19440 [3] were published to underpin the identification of requirements for enterprise reference models, the establishment of enterprise modelling framework and the formation of enterprise modelling methodology respectively. It is worth noting that the National Institute of Standards and Technology(NIST) stated that the three standards are the cornerstones of its proposed smart manufacturing eco-system, implying that those standards are of importance in the revolution of smart manufacturing [4].

In additional to enterprise architecture, enterprise modelling methods and languages have undergone rapid evolutions in order to satisfy the demanding analysis requirements for complex systems. Enterprise modelling languages such as IDEF (integration definition) series modelling languages (including IDEF0, IDEF1x, IDEF3, IDEF5, et al.), UML (unified modelling language, which includes multiple views and diagrams), DFD (data flow diagram), ERD (entity relationship diagram), EPC (event process chain), BPMN (business process modelling notation), BPEL (business process execution language), Petri net and the newly developed SysML are gaining increasing popularity in the field of enterprise modelling.

Emerging technologies, including mobile internet, cloud computing, internet of things (IoT), big data, CPS (cyber-physical system) and artificial intelligence (AI), have posed great challenges to both areas of enterprise infrastructure and operation. In response to the substantial technological changes within the global industries, many countries have initiated some domain-specified architectures for the sake of the high-level understanding of enterprise integration amid the new technology era. For example, Germany has proposed a Reference Architecture Model for industry 4.0 [5]; NIST has presented a Smart Manufacturing Eco-system to identify smart-manufacturing-related standards [4]; Industrial Internet Consortium (IIC) has published an Industrial Internet Reference Model to guide to development of industrial internet systems [6]; The framework of IoT and the framework of CPS are also developed [7–9]. On the whole, EAs are widely used to solve systems engineering issues of complex ICT-based industrial systems.

Since ISO 15704, 19439, 19440 have been published for more than 10 years, they will be subject to revision based on the new development of EAs, EMs, as well as emerging technologies. This paper rethinks the basic principles of existing EAs and its corresponding modelling methods at first, and then proposes the General Enterprise Modelling (GEM) framework and the GEM Enterprise Architecture (GEM-EA) based on the result of the discussion.

2 Enterprise Architecture and Enterprise Modelling Review

An EA is a set of models and methods describing different aspects of the system and covering its whole lifecycle of an enterprise-integration project from its initial concept through definition, functional design or specification, detailed design, physical implementation or construction, operation to decommission or obsolescence [1].

Based on systematic literature review of existing enterprise architectures, a set of basic elements of architecture are identified as follows:

- Division of views: it simplifies an enterprise/system into various aspects to help stakeholders review an enterprise or an integrated system from different perspectives.
- Relationship among views: it describes the relationship of different views and finally realizes the synthetic description and analysis of an enterprise or a system.
- Components of integrated system: hardware, software, human resources units/elements and so forth that form a real system.
- Lifecycle: it defines the phases and succession of system development and integration. It also provides a project management baseline for each phase.
- Guidance or methodology: it gives a structured approach for the integrated system design, implementation and operation.
- Mechanism of models reusing: it provides how to form reference models and create the enterprise knowledge based on models.

In accordance to ISO 15704 [1] and ISO 19439 [2], the minimal set of enterprise models is identified as function view, organization view, resource view and information (Data) view, along with additional view including decision view and economic view. ARIS [11] instead specifies function view, organization view, data view, product/service view and process view as the pillars of its architecture. Although different architectures adopt different methods of view divisions, it is commonly accepted that organization, function, resource and information aspects of an enterprise should be considered during the implementation of enterprise/system integration. The relationships among views in these architectures remained different as well. Usually there are three types of relationships as follows:

- Views are independent from each other and they have equal status. Each view can be described and analysed separately and need not be closely related to each other. However, because of the emphasis on independent analysis of each view, the relationship and convergence between views are weak.
- Views are ordered according to modelling sequence. This kind of relationship provides a guideline to develop synthetically enterprise models, but it does not show how to converge information between views.
- The relationships among views are both associated and combined. This kind of relationship simplifies the content of every view and realizes a synthetic analysis through combined analysis among different views.

The lifecycle presented by an architecture not only reflects the phase division of enterprise engineering or system integration project management, but also provides stage division after the project implementation phase, such as operation, maintenance and re-configuration stage.

The comparison of some widely used EAs is shown in Table 1.

Enterprise modelling is the abstract representation, description and definition of the structure, processes, information and resources of an enterprise [2]. While an enterprise architecture is primarily used to define key concepts, identify views and their relationships on an organization, enterprise modelling offers an explicit representation of

Table 1. Comparison of EAs

EAs	Comparison
CIM-OSA	Views: organization, resource, function, information
	Relationships between views: start from function view, then generate organization and resource view, and finally get the information View of the enterprise
	Lifecycle: requirements definition→design specification→implementation description
	Methodology: generic building block→partial building block→particular building block
PERA	Lifecycle: enterprise definition→conceptual engineering → preliminary engineering → detailed engineering → construction → operations → decommissioning → enterprise dissolution
	Methodology: tasks and focuses in the process of system construction
	System components: facilities, people, control and information systems
IMPACS	Views: resource, information, function, decision
	Relationships between views: start from function view, then generate decision and physical view, and finally get the information view
	Lifecycle: analysis→design→technical design→development
	Methodology: conceptual(analysis→design) → structural (design → technical design) → realization (technical design→development)
	System components: Information Techniques, Manufacturing Techniques, Organization
ARIS	Views: organization, data, function, output, process/control
	Relationships between views: the control/process view combines organization, data, function and output views together
	Lifecycle: requirements definition→design specification→implementation description
Zachman	Views: data, function, network, people, time, motivation
	Lifecycle: business goal/scope→enterprise model→system model→technique model→detailed description→enterprise operation
GERAM	Views: function, information, organization, resource
	Lifecycle: identification→concept→requirements→preliminary design → detailed design→implementation→operation→decommission
	Methodology: generic building block→partial building block→particular building block
	System components: customer service, management and control, software, hardware, machine, human
FEAF	Sub architectures: business, data, application, technology
	Viewpoints: planner/scope (contextual) → owner/business model (conceptual) → designer/system model (logical) → builder/technology model (physical) → sub-contractor/detailed representations (out of context)
DoDAF	Views: operational, systems, technical standards
TOGAF	Sub-architectures: business, applications, data, technology
	Lifecycle: preliminary → architecture vision → business architecture → information systems architecture → technology architecture → opportunities and solutions → migration planning → implementation governance → architecture change management
UAF	Grid style frame work with blocks for views, artifacts, and sequence

different views on an enterprise with the use of semantics or diagrams. In response to the increasing complexity of enterprise organizations, a set of enterprise modelling methods or languages, aiming at depicting different aspects of enterprises, have been developed by industry and academia.

Enterprise modelling methods enable the understanding of the structure, behaviour and performance aspects of an enterprise, and they can also be categorized into views of EAs. The comparison of widely used enterprise modelling methods is presented in Table 2.

Table 2. Comparison of EMs

Methods	Description	Types		
		Structure	Behaviour	Performance
DFD	Function model of data transformation	x		
IDEF0	Function model		x	
ER	Data model	x		
IDEF1x	Data model	x		
IDEF3	Process model and object transformation model		x	
IDEF5	Ontology capture method	x		
EPC	Event-driven process model		x	
GRAI grid and net	Decision model	x	x	
UML class diagram	Static view of the system	x		
UML use case diagram	Function model	x		
UML activity diagram	Process model		x	
UML sequence diagram	Process model		x	
UML state machine diagram	Process model		x	
AHP (analytic hierarchy process)/ANP (analytic network process)	Decision model/evaluation model			x
System dynamics	Evaluation model			x
SysML	Structure, behavior, Requirements, parametric models	x	x	x
ArchiMate	Structure and behavior models with some extension	x	x	

Based on the above discussion, the basic methodology of an architecture is to describe a complicated system separately and respectively through different views. Since each view only provides particular information on certain aspect of the system, the recognition of the whole system can be acquired through synthesizing descriptions of various views from different angles and all views in EAs are related to certain kind of enterprise modelling methods.

3 General Enterprise Modelling Framework and Constructs

Based on the discussion from the previous section, a General Enterprise Modelling (GEM) framework is proposed, as shown in Fig. 1. The GEM framework is organized into three layers, from top to down that is, system evaluation and economic analysing

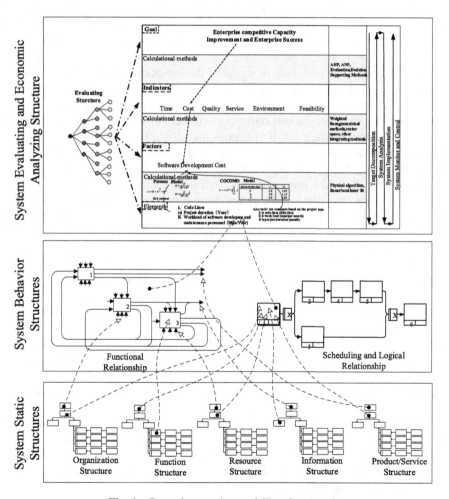

Fig. 1. General enterprise modelling framework

structure layer, system behaviour/dynamic structure layer and system static structure layer. Models at each layer reflect a particular aspect of an enterprise, and the description of each layer of the framework is given as follows:

- System static structure layer: models at which define the static structures of an enterprise including the organizational structure, resource structure, data/information structure, product/service structure and function structure, which define the existence of an enterprise and answer the question of what is the system.
- System behaviour/dynamic structure layer: models at which describe logical, sequential and correlative characteristics of the whole system and combine elements defined at the static structure layer together and define the operation mechanism of the enterprise.
- System performance structure layer: model at which define the target of the system, the related performance indicators and measurement methods.

Models at system static and behaviour layer describe the system structures and operation mechanism subject to the constraint of the system objective, forming the basis for economic/performance analysis. Built on the foundation of system structure and behaviour layer, system performance structure layer provides a modelling formalism to the economic/performance aspect of the integrated system, draws upon the existing model content and establishes analytical methods to inform decision makers. Since performance evaluation is critical for decision makes and stakeholders in the early stage of a system integration project, performance-related modelling becomes one of the key divisions in the field of enterprise modelling. For instance, ISO 22400 is developed for Automation systems and integration – Key performance indicators (KPIs) for manufacturing operations management [10]; ISO/IEC 42030 is developed for Systems and Software Engineering – Architecture Evaluation. Evaluation modelling and analysis can point out the optimization direction of enterprise development [1]. In ISO 15704 Amd 2005, AHP/ANP (Analytical Hierarchy/Network Process) method and Activity Based Costing (ABC) are proposed to facilitate the decision-making process on the multiple criteria's aspect of system integration justification.

In fact, various structures have mutual correlation, therefore, structured units at every aspect of architecture can all be used as the focus to associate with other units, reflecting that views are the embodiment of a certain aspect of the enterprise system. For instance, the product structure cannot reflect the panorama of the product without the description of the producing process; the organizational structure cannot reflect well the operation of enterprise without the constraint of operating mechanism in the organization; the resource structure only reflects existence and quantity, but it is the dynamic resource configuration and utilization that really influences the enterprise operation.

With the guidance of enterprise strategy and performance evaluation mechanism, the reticular description with structure components comes into being according to mutual correlation (input, output, control, mechanism) or sequential and logical relationship; and the functional relationship diagram and process network diagram can both describe operation mechanism.

4   General Enterprise Modelling - Enterprise Architecture

Based on the enterprise modelling framework derived from the previous section, a new enterprise architecture titled GEM-EA is constructed, as shown in Fig. 2. GEM-EA includes three axes: view, lifecycle and realization.

- View: According to the above discussion, GEM includes seven views: Function View, Organization View, Resource View, Information View, Product View, Process View and Economic/Performance Evaluation View.
- Lifecycle: Project lifecycle starts from project definition and ends up with implementation. The sole difference between lifecycle of GEM-EA and project lifecycle is that the lifecycle of GEM includes operation and maintenance of the system. That is because architecture can also benefit the operation of an integrated system about tremendous track, modification and optimization, and the modelling methods of architecture are equally important for system operation.
- Realization: This axis reflects the major methodology of the architecture, namely, how to accomplish system analysis, design, operation and maintenance by means of modelling methods. Firstly, according to the division of views, the description of current system is formed with the methods of describing views, and then other enterprise modelling methods are introduced to mutually form AS-IS models with coherence based on the description of views. Secondly, the AS-IS models shall be analysed to find the problems and contradictions. Next, the problems are arranged in terms of their significance and then resolved step by step. Afterwards TO-BE models are developed, providing a solution on the principle and abstract layer to meet the requirement, which is the content of preliminary design (or in the beginning of detailed design). Thirdly, in the phase of detailed design, according to the verified requirement embodied by various models (or views), the requirement is transferred into design specification in three concrete domains (or called subsystems) by constructing tools and then the real system is built. What should be emphasized is that there is "multi-to-multi" mapping between the design specification and the description of models (or views). At present, many developing tools or tool sets can benefit the mapping such as CASE tool, Workflow Management Technique, etc.

One of the important ideas of this architecture is that the system recognition and construction are evolved step by step. In the phase of conceptual definition, it is necessary to define the strategic goal of the enterprise and then confirm the target of the integrated system. Sequentially according to these purposes, we can describe the actuality of an enterprise from the aspects of organization, resource, information, product, function and operating process and then infrastructure and operation mechanism. Under constraints of these descriptions, the system can be analysed with suitable modelling and analysis methods to find its problems and then improve it. Then the target system is constructed and its various views can be formed. This is a specifying and optimizing process. When describing the target system, we can apply other modelling methods besides the method of view description to characterize the system comprehensively. When model-based design is accomplished, it will be translated into

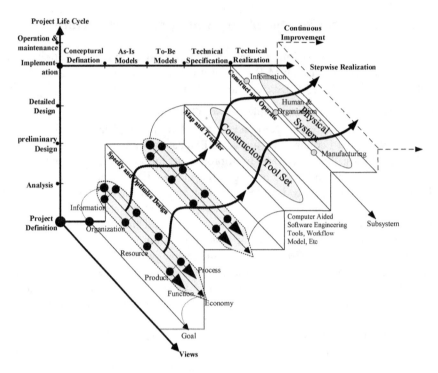

Fig. 2. GEM Enterprise Architecture

technique instruction for constructing system with the help of constructing tool sets and then a real system will be formed. Because the description of the system will still work on while the system operation, it can be used as the operating reference of the real system and then modifies and optimizes the real system.

5 Summary and Conclusion

This paper attempts to point out the revising direction for ISO 15704, 19439 and 19440 based on literature reviews and systematic comparisons of both existing EAs and EMs. Moreover, the GEM framework and GEM-EA are proposed to condense the key concepts and ideas gleaned from our previous research of enterprise architecture and modelling. In summary, some recommendations for the refinement of ISO 15704, 19439 and 19440 are listed as follows:

- The division and relationships of views: GEM framework includes three layers and seven views, which presents a new consideration to the organization of enterprise model views.
- Performance evaluation view: performance evaluation view identifies the development and optimization direction of enterprise/system integration, and its corresponding modelling and analysing methods support enterprise re-engineering and continuous improvement.

- Model-based systems engineering (MBSE): continuous system evolvement from the As-Is model to the To-Be model is the key methodology of GEM-EA, which is an important MBSE approach for system integration.

Acknowledgements. This work is sponsored by the China High-Tech 863 Program, No. 2001AA415340 and No. 2007AA04Z1A6, the China Natural Science Foundation, No. 61174168 and 61771281, the Aviation Science Foundation of China, No. 20100758002 and 20128058006.

References

1. ISO TC 184 SC5. ISO 15704:2000/Amd 1:2005. Industrial automation systems – Requirements for enterprise-reference architectures and methodologies
2. ISO TC 184 SC5. ISO 19439:2006. Enterprise integration – Framework for enterprise modelling
3. ISO TC 184 SC5. ISO 19440:2007. Enterprise integration – Constructs for enterprise modelling
4. Lu, Y., Morris, K.C., Frechette, S.: Current Standards Landscape for Smart Manufacturing Systems. https://doi.org/10.6028/NIST.IR.8107
5. Adolphs, P., Bedenbender, H., Dirzus, D., et al.: Reference architecture model Industrie 4.0 (RAMI 4.0). VDI/VDE Society Measurement and Automatic Control (GMA) (2015)
6. Lin, S.W., Miller, B., Durand, J., et al.: Industrial Internet reference architecture. Technical report, Industrial Internet Consortium (IIC) (2015)
7. Lin, S.W., Miller, B., Durand, J., et al.: The Industrial Internet of Things. Reference Architecture, vol. G1. Technical report, Industrial Internet Consortium (IIC) (2017)
8. Bauer, M., Boussard, M., Bui, N., et al.: Internet of Things–Architecture IoT-A Deliverable D1. 5–Final architectural reference model for the IoT v3.0 (2013)
9. MJB, KAS, ERG. Framework for Cyber-Physical Systems - Release 1.0. Cyber Physical Systems Public Working Group (2016)
10. ISO TC184 SC5. ISO 22400-2:2014. Automation systems and integration – Key performance indicators (KPIs) for manufacturing operations management – Part 2: Definitions and descriptions
11. Li, Q., Chen, Y.: Modelling and Analysis of Enterprise and Information Systems – From Requirements to Realization. Springer and High Education Press, Beijing and New York (2007)

Digital Connected Production: Wearable Manufacturing Information Systems

Stefan Schönig[1,2](✉), Stefan Jablonski[1], Andreas Ermer[2],
and Ana Paula Aires[2]

[1] Institute for Computer Science, University of Bayreuth, Bayreuth, Germany
{stefan.schoenig,stefan.jablonski}@uni-bayreuth.de
[2] Maxsyma GmbH & Co. KG, Floß, Germany
{sschoenig,aermer,aaires}@maxsyma.de

Abstract. A manufacturing information system is targeted for use anywhere production is taking place. Modern manufacturing information systems are generally computerized and are designed to collect and present the data which production operators need in order to plan and direct operations within the production. The application of mobile and wearable devices can support operators' tasks without distracting them from their core duties. In this paper, we present an approach towards a wearable manufacturing information system that is able to implement decentralized production monitoring and control and supports users in their core tasks. Building upon acquired and digitally stored production data, these devices provide different user-specific information and services when required. A practical example from corrugation industry highlights advantages of mobile devices compared to conventional centralized systems in the field of manufacturing.

Keywords: Production information systems · Process monitoring
Smart devices · Wearables · Industry 4.0

1 Introduction

The term *Industry 4.0* describes the support of manufacturing processes by means of information technology [1]. A manufacturing information system is targeted for use anywhere production is taking place. Modern manufacturing information systems are generally computerized and are designed to collect and present the data which production operators need in order to plan and direct operations within the production [1,2]. The growing interest and further development of concepts and systems that use digital information in industrial environments opens up several possibilities to optimize information processing and therefore to increase efficiency in production processes [3]. Furthermore, *Industry 4.0* concepts frequently imply a turning away of fully centralized equipment control towards a more flexible, decentralized production control [4].

C. Debruyne et al. (Eds.): OTM 2017 Workshops, LNCS 10697, pp. 56–65, 2018.
https://doi.org/10.1007/978-3-319-73805-5_6

The connection between production and information technology leads to an ubiquity of digitally supported information processing systems in production environments. This situation can generally be summarized under the term *Ubiquitous Computing* [5,6]. In the field of manufacturing this term comprises the digital integration of production equipment and subordinated information systems. This way, all participating production objects and entities, i.e., machinery as well as human production operators are able to communicate and interact with each other based on a digital, potentially mobile infrastructure. Thus, such a manufacturing system represents a typical *cyber-physical system* where computer based controlling and monitoring facilities are tightly integrated with its users, e.g. human operators. In such a system environment, relevant information can be tracked and made available in realtime whereby processes alongside the whole value added chain can be designed efficiently [7].

One way of integrating human users into a cyber-physical system seamlessly is to equip them with *Wearable Computing Systems (Wearables)* like smartphones or smartwatches [7]. These *mobile* and *smart* devices support users in their operative tasks by directly proving them - ubiquitously, independent from their physical location - with most recent information about the production process and production equipment. Additionally, this information can be highly personalized.

In this paper, we present an applied approach towards a wearable manufacturing information system that is able to implement decentralized production monitoring and control and supports users in their core tasks. First, we give an overview of related work (Sect. 2). Section 3 discusses a conceptual approach how to efficiently and effectively identify tasks that can optimally be supported and enacted through a cyber-physical system approach, here based on wearables. Subsequently, Sect. 4 introduces a general applicable technical architecture of a digitally connected production site supported by mobile devices based on the protocol MQTT. Section 5 describes the evaluation and application of our approach in corrugation industries that highlights the advantages of mobile devices in the field of manufacturing. The paper is finally concluded in Sect. 6.

2 Enabling Technologies and Related Work

Within a digitally connected production, different devices such as sensors, actuators and controllers can record the current status and values of objects [8]. Different heterogeneous devices can communicate with each other and server gateways by means of Service-Oriented Architecture (SOA) protocols like the web-service oriented Hypertext Transfer Protocol (HTTP) or the local network oriented MQ Telemetry Transport (MQTT)[1] protocol enabling interconnectivity at an object level. Sensors have the capability of measuring a multitude of parameters frequently and collecting plenty of data. Analysis of Big Data, both historical and real-time, can facilitate predictions on the basis of which proactive

---

[1] OASIS, http://docs.oasis-open.org/mqtt/mqtt/v3.1.1/mqtt-v3.1.1.html.

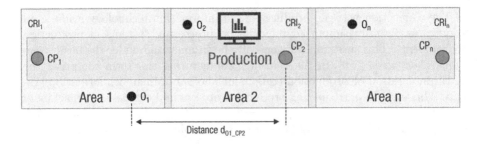

Fig. 1. Conceptual modelling of a production hall

maintenance decision making can be performed [9,10]. The e-maintenance concept can significantly address these challenges. There are several research works that introduce intelligent agents that are directly implemented at the shop floor level [11]. Furthermore, there is research about web-based production maintenance services and architectures that include wireless sensing of process data and identification technologies, data and services integration and interoperability [8].

Portable computing devices have been used for production monitoring for many years. Though initially offered as an integrated instrumentation solution, mobile devices such as PDAs and tablets have been programmed with a mobile capacity to analyze and present data, disconnected from the actual sensing components [5,12]. These solutions introduce concepts, architectures and prototypical implementations for configuring the sensing infrastructure and for presenting certain process and equipment data on mobile devices.

The work at hand extends current solutions by introducing an architecture for context relevant information provision and actively influencing and controlling production processes and equipment by means of mobile devices. Furthermore, we present a full-fledged implementation of a wearable manufacturing information system by means of smartphones and smartwatches.

3   Process Monitoring and Control Using Mobile Devices

Inspired by the promising prospects of ubiquitous computing and its combination with wearables we investigated how these new technologies could be utilized best in our applications.

3.1   Problem Description and Conceptual Solution

We focus on shop floor applications where products are manufactured in automatized production lines. Typically, such a production line is divided into several production areas (cf. Fig. 1). Each area is independent from the others with well-defined interfaces between them. Each part of the production line has a couple of so-called control panels (CP). A CP is needed for different operators O to intervene the production processes, sometimes due to errors, but mostly due to maintenance tasks. It is also typical that error and maintenance information as well as other context relevant information (CRI) is depicted on one (or a few) central information devices. There is a simple rule of thumb saying that the longer the reaction time of an operator to take care of the intervention is, the worse it is for the production process.

When we were looking for a good deployment site for wearables, we were recapitulating their main benefits. One of the major advantages of wearables is immediate notification of operators independent of where the operator is located and where the information stems from as long as it is part of the information system. This fast notification enhances the situational awareness of the operators on the shop floor. A second major benefit is the ability to actively intervene production through a wearable device, i.e., that a production line could be controlled remotely.

Combining the need for intervention and the chance of immediate notification and remote control through wearables leads to the idea of using wearables as fast information medium and control panel for operators. The gain of time fostered by the usage of wearables can easily be calculated. In the former setting, the time an operator O_i in a certain area i needed to operate a control panel CP_j is composed of three parts:

- **(i)** the time to find out whether at all and what control panel intervention is required, i.e., the time to go from the operators current position to the information devices (t_{noti})
- **(ii)** the time to select the relevant information CPI_i from the information device (t_{read})
- **(iii)** the time to go from the information device to the control panel (t_{cont}), i.e., to walk a certain distance d_{O-CP}.

In sum, $t_{intervene} = t_{noti} + t_{read} + t_{cont}$ is a timespan which is heavily determined by physical work, i.e., the time elapsed since operators have to walk from a current position to the information device and then from this information device to the control panel. A third time component is the time operators need to select and filter relevant information on the information device since often those devices are heavily overloaded with status information from a whole production line.

Figure 1 illustrates the solution idea by depicting a situation in a corrugation plant where we deployed the proposed solution. In this plant, a production area is about 140 m long. An operator stands somewhere in that production area. To be informed about potential intervention, the operator has to go to the local information device (t_{not}); after having found relevant status information (t_{read}), he has to go to a control panel for intervention (t_{cont}). Through observations we found out that filtering status information takes on average about 20 s and that an operator on average covers a distance of 40 m per intervention. In total, it takes about 2 min for a necessary intervention. Within this reaction time, e.g., deficient products are produced.

To cope with the observed issues we are introducing innovative technology, here in the form of wearables. These concepts change fully centralized information and equipment control towards flexible, decentralized production monitoring and control. In particular, we deploy mobile concepts for *(i) process monitoring*, i.e., the provisioning of up-to-date and individual production process and equipment information, and *(ii) process control*, i.e., actively impacting production processes from potentially arbitrary locations within the plant. We detail these two issues further within the next two sub-sections.

3.2 Process Monitoring with Mobile Devices

A complete digital interconnection of the production site offers the possibility to record and store relevant process and equipment data in a structured reusable form. Using industrial M2M communication protocols, e.g., HTTP or MQTT, and interfaces, recorded process and machine data is accessible worldwide. Mobile devices enact these standardized and web-based interfaces for accessing the recorded data. Based on that, wearables provide a multiplicity of monitoring functions to users: *(i)* visualization and confirmation of alarm and error messages; *(ii)* observation of current status information and process parameters of different production modules; *(iii)* graphical visualization of recorded process data and based on that statistic process control mechanisms (e.g., *Nelson Rules*) and *(iv)* communication between different operating users.

Thus, responsible operating and maintenance staff is pointed to current alarm messages or instructions of machinery in real time on smartphones or smartwatches on their wrist. Here, messages and instructions are transmitted to responsible users through visual, acoustic and, in case of noisy environments through haptic signals like vibration alarms. By means of configurable user roles or user priority groups, production or shift supervisors, equipment operators or maintenance staff are able to react to disturbances and changes situations immediately.

3.3 Process Control with Mobile Devices

Alongside to observation and visualization of process data, it is also possible to actively influence production processes by means of mobile devices. This way, users are able to control functionality that is necessary to operate machinery by means of wearable devices directly on site as well as off site via internet connection. For example, production speed can be adjusted by a corresponding operation on a smartwatch on the operators' wrist.

Note that both for process monitoring as well as for process control, functionality and visualized information can depend on the current position of the device (i.e., GPS signal of the device) or on the users' role that is currently logged in to the device. Hence, application specific services and information is only accessible and shown where they are necessary and needed. This is fundamental for goal-oriented work and protects users from information overload.

4   Technical Implementation and Architecture

Figure 2 visualizes an holistic architecture of a digitalized production hall. It contains the different layers that are necessary to implement the different concepts and functionalities mentioned in Sect. 2. The whole architecture is based on the communication protocol MQTT.

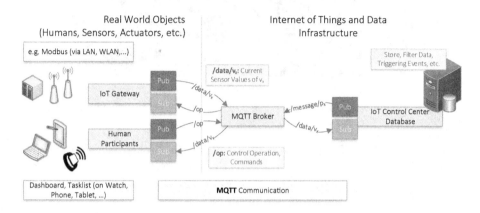

Fig. 2. Architecture of a digital production hall that uses mobile devices

In this architecture, real worlds objects, i.e., humans, sensors or actuators, represent both publishers and subscribers. Devices located on the production line (e.g., programmable logic controllers or sensors) are connected to an IoT gateway using specific architectures such as Profibus, LAN, WLAN or Bluetooth. Manufacturing data of a specific device v_x is acquired and afterwards published on a specific MQTT topic $/data/v_x$. Through a MQTT Broker the acquired data is sent to interested monitoring and controlling devices such as mobile devices of human operators. Therefore, mobile devices of interested operators have to subscribe to the topic $/data/v_x$. For data storage and alarm and info messaging, an IoT Control Center always subscribes to all MQTT topics. This way, current sensor values are continuously recorded and compared to defined thresholds and, in case of violations, certain messages are fired. These messages are then published on an operator p_x specific topic $/message/p_x$.

On the device end, which could be web browser, a smartphone or a smartwatch application the received MQTT messages are converted back to data. Therefore, the MQTT service becomes the data source, that can be accessed for different types of applications simultaneously. Note that current smartwatch technique doesn't allow to communicate directly with external services. A smartphone is currently still required that manages service communication.

The other flow direction can also be implemented, in other words the same application used for monitoring can interact with the production line and perform controlling. When the user interacts with the application, these interactions

Fig. 3. Remaining time of current job and stack size modules on smartphone

are sent via the MQTT topic */op* to the Broker. The Broker delivers the command to the subscribed actuator gateway. Here, the message is processed, i.e., converted to machine specific commands, which are processed and executed on the devices located on the production field.

5   Evaluation and Industrial Application

In this section, we describe the evaluation of the proposed concepts and techniques by means of an extensive application in industry. The described concepts have been implemented in a corrugation plant. Due to increasing automation and staff reduction, less operators are available to control such a production line. Hence, interactions between users and machinery in case of this up to 140 m long facility requires several location changes of users between control panels that result in delayed information flows. These delayed reaction times are frequently the reason for increased deficient products.

The concepts where implemented by additionally defining a user role model. Here, available operators were assigned to a specific area of production that depicts their area of responsibility. Additionally, neighbouring areas can partially overlap and therefore users can share tasks or execute them alternating. The concepts allows for dynamic changes of areas and assignments, e.g., by incorporating dynamic GPS signals of users' smartphones. This way, shift supervisors or reserve pool employees can be added on demand. Display elements can be ordered and configured individually to provide the greatest possible flexibility of information provision.

For example wearable devices offer diverse functionality to operators at the *Dry-End* (the area where produced corrugated paper leaves the plant), e.g., *(i)* remaining time of current production job; *(ii)* remaining time to next stack transport; or *(iii)* current production speed. Information modules that implement function *(i)* and *(ii)* are shown in Fig. 3. The module that shows the

Fig. 4. Warp control service and current production speed on smartphone

Fig. 5. Error and warning message service on smartphone application

current production speed, e.g., is visualized in Fig. 4 on the right hand side. Furthermore, users can influence current process and equipment parameters in realtime via certain scroll bars, e.g., adjusting the current warp of the corrugated paper. This functionality is visualized in Fig. 4 on the left hand side. Users at the *Wet-End* (the area where original paper is inducted to the plant) receive continuously information w.r.t. *(i)* the next necessary roll change or *(ii)* occurring error and defects of machinery modules.

Alongside to process data operators receive error messages and instructions from the different plant modules. This way, concrete and goal-oriented instructions in error cases or warning messages for supply shortfalls can be transmitted to users. The implemented message service is visualized on the left hand side in Fig. 5.

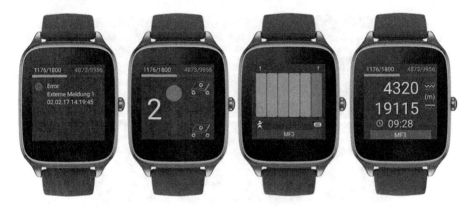

Fig. 6. Different monitoring and control services on the smartwatch

Another important aspect of the implemented concept is depicted by the involvement of maintenance staff, since the greatest part of errors only occurs during actual production service. For example, a decreasing value of a specific pressure sensor or an increasing temperature value of a propulsion engine results in an instruction message that summons the maintenance staff to clean filters of a corresponding equipment assembly.

All the different information and control services on the smartphone have a corresponding interface for smartwatches that can be worn on the users' wrist. An exemplary set of services is visualized in Fig. 6. Through the described implementation of a wearable production information system it was possible to significantly reduce reaction time intervals. Furthermore, the amount of deficient products could be decreased and the overall quality of the produced corrugated paper has been improved. The overall equipment downtime was significantly decreased, since problems have been prohibited or recognized in advance and were solved proactively. As a result, the overall equipment efficiency could be increased effectively.

6   Conclusion

In this paper, we presented an applied approach towards a wearable manufacturing information system that is able to implement decentralized production monitoring and control and supports users in their core tasks. Building upon acquired and digitally stored production data, these devices provide different user-specific information and services exactly when required. A practical example from corrugation industry highlighted advantages of mobile devices in the field of manufacturing.

The implementation of the described concepts are given by example applications on smartphones and smartwatches. By means of visual controls users are able to adjust specific equipment parameters in realtime and receive corresponding warning messages or work instructions.

For future conceptual extensions we plan to further standardize the described concepts so that the approach is applicable in a diverse set of production industries without substantial adjustments of the core product.

References

1. Tao, F., Cheng, Y., Zhang, L., Nee, A.: Advanced manufacturing systems: socialization characteristics and trends. J. Intell. Manuf. 1–16 (2015)
2. Lee, J., Bagheri, B., Kao, H.-A.: A cyber-physical systems architecture for industry 4.0-based manufacturing systems. Manuf. Lett. **3**, 18–23 (2015)
3. Westkamp, M.: Einsatz und Nutzenpotenziale von Data Mining in Produktionsunternehmen. Studie Fraunhofer-Institut für Produktionstechnik und Automatisierung IPA, Stuttgart (2014)
4. Spath, D., Ganschar, O., Gerlach, S., Hämmerle, M., Krause, T., Schlund, S.: Produktionsarbeit der Zukunft-Industrie 4.0. Fraunhofer Verlag Stuttgart (2013)
5. Arnaiz Irigaray, A., Gilabert, E., Jantunen, E., Adgar, A.: Ubiquitous computing for dynamic condition-based maintenance. J. Qual. Maint. Eng. **15**(2), 151–166 (2009)
6. Poslad, S.: Ubiquitous Computing: Smart Devices, Environments and Interactions. Wiley, Chichester (2011)
7. Günthner, W.A., Wölfle, M., Fischer, R., Potthast, J.-M., Baumgarten, S., Schneider, O., Hohenstein, F.: Wearable Computing und RFID in Produktion und Logistik-Ansätze zur bereichsübergreifenden Nutzung digitaler Informationen. Log. J. 10–2011 (2011)
8. Pistofidis, P., Emmanouilidis, C., Koulamas, C., Karampatzakis, D., Papathanassiou, N.: A layered e-maintenance architecture powered by smart wireless monitoring components. In: Industrial Technology (ICIT), pp. 390–395. IEEE (2012)
9. Bousdekis, A., Papageorgiou, N., Magoutas, B., Apostolou, D., Mentzas, G.: A real-time architecture for proactive decision making in manufacturing enterprises. In: Ciuciu, I., et al. (eds.) OTM 2015. LNCS, vol. 9416, pp. 137–146. Springer, Cham (2015). https://doi.org/10.1007/978-3-319-26138-6_17
10. Li, Q., Jiang, H., Tang, Q., Chen, Y., Li, J., Zhou, J.: Smart manufacturing standardization: reference model and standards framework. In: Ciuciu, I., Debruyne, C., Panetto, H., Weichhart, G., Bollen, P., Fensel, A., Vidal, M.-E. (eds.) OTM 2016. LNCS, vol. 10034, pp. 16–25. Springer, Cham (2017). https://doi.org/10.1007/978-3-319-55961-2_2
11. Muller, A., Marquez, A.C., Iung, B.: On the concept of e-maintenance: review and current research. Reliab. Eng. Syst. Saf. **93**(8), 1165–1187 (2008)
12. Campos, J., Jantunen, E., Prakash, O.: A web and mobile device architecture for mobile e-maintenance. Int. J. Adv. Manuf. Technol. **45**(1), 71–80 (2009)

A User-Centered Perspective on Interoperability: Capturing Stakeholder Interaction for Mediating Design

Christian Stary[(✉)] and Claudia Kaar

Johannes Kepler University, Linz, Austria
{Christian.Stary,Claudia.Kaar}@jku.at

Abstract. When recognizing the need of involving stakeholders for mapping role-specific requirements to system behavior, semantic interoperability is becoming a crucial issue in development. Elicitation, analysis, and specification need to go beyond a purely functional perspective on system development and integrate interactions relevant for stakeholders. We discuss a behavior perspective to mutually adjust role-specific elements, and in this way design organization-relevant support systems. Since interacting role element specifications can be automatically executed, designs can be evaluated interactively, and digital support systems can be developed incrementally.

Keywords: Semantic interoperability · Communication analysis
Stakeholder perception · Interaction · Behavior encapsulation
Subject-orientation

1 Introduction

The development of interactive systems has shifted continuously to dynamic adaptation of technological artifacts and end user computing (cf. [1–3]). Thereby, not only the modular structure and thus functional decomposition plays a crucial role, but also dynamic communication and interaction processes between different stakeholders (cf. [4]), in particular when taking into account existing expertise and different mental models on organizing work and technologies (cf. [5]). The latter is becoming increasingly important in digital ecosystems (cf. [6, 7]). In order to recognize user needs, stakeholders should get involved at the beginning of a project (cf. [8]), and engage in articulating and refining design- and implementation-relevant information [9–11]. This kind of development influences the acceptance of digital support systems [12, 13]. Hence, the design of interoperable systems could benefit from user-validated design specifications. Subject-orientation [14] has been introduced as a paradigm and IT-supported methodology in the field of Business Process Management (BPM) to enable stakeholders not only to express their knowledge of work but also to design interactive systems by mapping interactions to message exchanges (cf. [15, 16]). The approach has been applied effectively in the field featuring functional design of digital systems [17, 18], rather than taking into account stakeholder-specific vocabularies and their anticipated digital feature chains (cf. [19]).

© IFIP International Federation for Information Processing 2018
Published by Springer International Publishing AG 2018. All Rights Reserved
C. Debruyne et al. (Eds.): OTM 2017 Workshops, LNCS 10697, pp. 66–75, 2018.
https://doi.org/10.1007/978-3-319-73805-5_7

Aiming for interoperable system design we want to make use of semantically coherent specifications stemming from potential users of those systems. We continue an approach engaging stakeholders guided by their epistemological connection to digital systems and their development process [20, 21]. We follow findings [22] getting people engaged in design through personal and epistemological connection. They allow drawing on stakeholders' previous knowledge, and encourage design thinking. The incremental approach to semantic alignment of behavior representations builds upon diagrammatic representations, inspired by recent initiatives [23]. In Sect. 2 we discuss semantic interoperability from a stakeholder perspective reviewing related work. Section 3 introduces the semi-structured support for subject-oriented behavior encapsulations and checking semantic interoperability of interacting role elements. In Sect. 4 we summarize the results and interpret them in terms of achieving organizational interoperability continuing this type of research.

2   Stakeholders and Semantic Interoperability

If we want stakeholders to actively get involved in design it requires systems' thinking, as well as multiple perspectives on emergent properties of systems beyond engineering an isolated system [24]. Several constellations may occur [25], ranging from integration (mutual dependencies of systems) to federation allowing for stand-alone operation while being interconnected to other systems. Semantic interoperability of systems does not only concern concepts and structures, as captured through ontologies (cf. [26]), but also the dynamic of system development [27, 28]. It needs to go beyond Domain Specific Languages (DSL) (cf. [29]) allowing for agility and proactivity. Interoperability is required to recognize autonomous behavior of interacting system elements and at the same time enable integrated or network behavior due to their connectivity to other system elements [30]. When keeping autonomous system elements isolated, neither connectivity nor diversification of behavior is enabled. Such kind of systems cannot be aligned explicitly according to a common goal, as required for designing semantically interoperable systems [31]. Hence, system elements need to have the ability to cooperate with each other, in particular agreeing upon a common way of interaction in order to collaborate and share information (cf. [32]).

Changes may occur on the level of individual system elements, as well as on the level of interaction, affecting the overall system behavior (cf. [33, 34]). The integrated representation of the structure and behavior of systems including their environmental conditions can either take into account tasks and related processes (cf. [21, 35]). In case of mapping interaction sequences to workflow specifications, e.g., [36], deviations between modeled and actual behavior can be identified, triggering the re-design of systems. In any case, semantic interoperability requires context-sensitive understanding and representations (cf. [37, 38]). Mediation systems, such as proposed by Benaben et al. [39] help initiating and supporting the interoperability of collaborative situations among potential partners of a network. Individual and collaborative knowledge needs to be collected referring to collaborative business behavior. In addition, previously deduced collaborative processes need to be graspable for stakeholders through the automated generation of collaborative workflows, which keeps the process agile for managing continuous change.

3 Behavior Alignment Through Reflective Design

In this section we provide some conceptual background on the proposed approach from the field of reflective design before introducing the procedure and the subject-oriented representation scheme supporting semantic interoperability of syntactically unified systems. Reflective design has been promoted for contextual representation capturing static and dynamic affinities, and facilitating participatory design [40, 41]. Developed further to critical design (cf. [42]), it attempts to challenge existing structures and assumptions in the course of designing artifacts, and thus, innovate through design. Artifacts developed along critical design processes provoke in-depth reflection on structural issues. Reflective design of this kind does not only manifest its ideas through taking into account implementation, e.g., allowing for interactive experience through prototyping artifacts, but also brings playfulness to design due to its research perspective on design (cf. [43]). Artifacts can be digital, physical, or a combination of these, depending on the designers' intention [44]. As shown in [45], so-called first-level abstractions should be taken into account for design. First-level abstraction is the initial way individuals view their perceived reality. Hence, first-level abstractions allow individuals to find their entry points for developing a meaningful understanding, since first-level abstractions act as building blocks of sense- and meaning-making, and thus of shared knowledge repertoires.

Role-specific understanding helps stakeholders to adopt the perspective of another person. However, system design and development projects typically discourage this type of perspective-taking. Instead of a normative process including observation and analysis of phenomena, active participation 'within phenomena' should be triggered (cf. [46]). Then, design can become an exploratory and participatory endeavor, in particular for complex processes that arise from simple interactions (*ibid.*). Consequently, reflecting role-specific behavior while creating models is the core driver in the proposed approach. The development procedure allow addressing individual or domain-specific practices constructively in the course of design. The objective is to create a coherent set of encapsulated behavior descriptions satisfying the needs of a stakeholder group involved in some task setting. The first group of activities contains *preparation activities* facilitating the setup of a (subject-oriented) design space and setting the scope. Subsequently, concerned stakeholders perform interaction-specific *specification* taking particular roles. The third set of activities leads to *consolidation and refinement for prototypical execution*, and can be performed by each of the stakeholders involved in the addressed setting or third parties responsible for development.

Stakeholder contributions may vary not only in terms encapsulating behaviors, but also in providing a complete interaction picture. Interaction patterns can be checked for correspondence of sending and receiving message, ensuring a continuous flow of information and control. Keeping track of this progress allows the construction of Subject Interaction Diagrams based on the encapsulated behavior specifications, as they contain all interfaces to be checked for interoperability. Once stakeholders have provides the attributes for each business (data) objects exchanged between stakeholders, they can run the process as specified, in order to get feedback on behavior sequences. A facilitator could help keeping track of the design progress and provides methodological support, if required, as each role specification needs to be detailed in terms of its task-specific functions and interaction activities before executing task-relevant behavior.

Subject-oriented Business Process Management (S-BPM) is used as enabler, since it support encapsulating behavior and refinement according to services to be processed for accomplishing tasks [14, 15]. These services either refer to directly performed action (system functions or manually accomplished tasks), or sending/receiving messages. Hence, behavior is constituted by performing an activity, sending a message (after preparing its content), and receiving a message (by analyzing its content). According to this type of representation, validated models can be executed.

We exemplify the approach considering the development of a sales support system. The goal is to integrate and share work practices among sales persons while providing access to underlying concepts of products and services. The case has been tested involving an Austrian service company providing method expertise in eliciting implicit knowledge for various purposes, including human resource development, market behavior studies, and product tests.

Creating a design space is based on identifying role elements denoting task- or situation-specific behavior encapsulations. In our case, five stakeholders took part in various functional roles relevant for the organization's work practice: CEO, operation management, method expert, sales representative, and marketing. Each of them was asked to represent their perspective. In the following we will exemplify interoperability checks based on design specifications, starting with the operation manager, as this role has also been assigned to set up the sales support system.

The role elements specified by the operation manager are shown in Fig. 1 and exemplify specific communication network partners for sales support. Each role element finally will represent a subject according to subject-oriented representation principles, but needs to be refined for checking its interoperability. *Incoming information* distinguishes trigger from input (data) for a role-specific behavior. Both provide relevant context for invoking a specific behavior sequence. *Role-specific behavior encapsulation* specifies relevant activities to be set by a role carrier. In this way, the context of actions can be represented. As *deliverables* we distinguish outcome, i.e., the effect of some behavior, from output data.

Figure 2 shows sample entries for role element specifications from the perspective of Content Management, Sales Expert, and Sales Representative. According to the structure of the representation scheme, one type of semantic interoperability issues can be addressed from a communication perspective. For instance, implementing the role of the Sales Expert would lead to a gap in quality control, as the message sent by Content Management is not processed according to the role understanding of Sales Expert. The same holds for other outgoing data, such as for advice for Sales Representative.

In the sales support field test it turned out to be beneficial to elaborate on the recognized issues concerning semantic interoperability in the group of involved stakeholders before detailing their respective behavior. It is this first-level abstraction of

Fig. 1. Relevant role elements for sales support

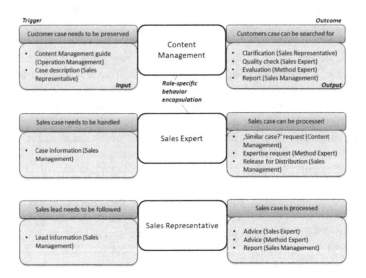

Fig. 2. Sampe role element specifications

interaction that sets the stage for refining the encapsulated behavior – what is not communicated along interaction paths is not processed by role carriers. As such it scopes a role. Vice versa, it allows identifying operational gaps from a business-relevant perspective. In the case at hand, this kind of semantic interoperability issue has been resolved by adding all missing messages the group of stakeholders could agree on, either on the incoming or outgoing side of the role element specification.

In case different objectives need to be met by processing various incoming messages or data, the 'trigger'-part of the role element reprentation and the 'input' part are numbered, in order to identify corresponding trigger – input (data) pairs. This notational handle facilitates behavior specifications, as it provides required context when describing the processing the incoming data. For semantic interoperability all required data attributes to be transmitted in either way need to be specified, in order to enable task-complete processing. Once all issues on the interactional level are resolved, a Subject Interaction Diagram (SID) can be generated, as the interaction pairs are complete from a stakeholder perspective for the case at hand.

Interoperability may also need to be discussed on the role behavior level. This level is represented by Subject Behavior Diagrams (SBDs) that need to be created for each of the previously specified role elements. They can either be adjusted according to reference patterns (cf. [47]) or created from scratch. SBDs encapsulate the procedural steps of each role behavior by aligning functional and interactional activities. Figure 3 shows part of the behavior specification of Content Management and Method Expert. It represents the situation when a Content Manager needs to decide whether a work practice including the application of the method can be included into the sales support system.

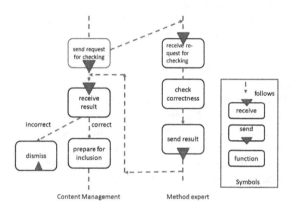

Fig. 3. Sample interaction between the two role elements Content Management and Method Expert on the SBD level

The Content Manager (left part of the Fig. 3) sends a request for evaluation and waits for a result. In case the result confirms the correctness of method application the case can be included into the sales support system. In case the method has not been applied properly, the workflow ends and the work practice is not included. The Method Expert receives the request, and evaluates whether the method has been applied correctly. Then, he/she delivers the results.

In case of novel requirements of or a lack of semantic behavior correspondence the respective SBD can be enriched utilizing Fleischmann et al.'s [48] message guard concept for alternative behavior specifications. The message guard embodies alternative behavior. A role element, e.g., Content Management, could request a certified statement for a business case (i.e., a method application), e.g., when required for a quality audit. The Method Expert is the message guard extending behavior capabilities.

It receives such a request as an event and processes it. It could lead to involving additional advice and nested procedures, i.e., interactions.

In order to identify those constellations, the elements of a SBD allowing for behavior alternatives or extensions, are marked with special symbols. Since the message guards can be executed during runtime, stakeholders can experiment when resolving interoperability issues on the individual behavior level. According to the S-BPM notation, message guards can be positioned at any point in the business logic, since the interaction pattern is identical - it is decided on the semantic layer whether normative behavior is going to be implemented or exception handling has to be included.

4 Conclusion

Once stakeholders are involved in system development their perception of situations, their needs and expectations become an essential design ingredient. Utilizing the subject-oriented paradigm elicitation and specification can be performed from a functional *and* interactional perspective, actively engaging stakeholders or potential users in the development process. The technique allows checking semantic interoperability through behavior alignment the way stakeholders perceive their work practice. It also lays ground sharing an individual perspective on the overall organization of work for an organization.

Since the field test of the approach revealed the capability of stakeholders to achieve semantically coherent and consistent specifications, subject-oriented diagrams could serve as scaffolds and executable entities to experience workflow support interactively. However, future applications will reveal the impact on organizational interoperability, as the implementation of consolidated stakeholder representations finally reveal the practicality of aligned role model behaviors.

References

1. Leonhard, G., Kospoth, C.-A.G.: Exponential technology versus linear humanity: designing a sustainable future. In: Osburg, T., Lohrmann, C. (eds.) Sustainability in a Digital World, pp. 77–83. Springer, Cham (2017). https://doi.org/10.1007/978-3-319-54603-2_6
2. Jia, Y.J., Chen, Q.A., Wang, S., et al.: ContexIoT: towards providing contextual integrity to appified IoT platforms. In: Juels, A. (ed.) Proceedings 2017 Network and Distributed System Security Symposium. Internet Society, Reston (2017)
3. Shelley, C.: Social agendas. In: Shelley, C. (ed.) Design and Society: Social Issues in Technological Design. SAPERE, vol. 36, pp. 105–124. Springer, Cham (2017). https://doi.org/10.1007/978-3-319-52515-0_7
4. Dyba, T., Cruzes, D.S.: Process research in requirements elicitation. In: 3rd International Workshop on Empirical Requirements Engineering (EmpiRE), pp. 36–39. IEEE (2013)
5. Rosenkranz, C., Vranesic, H., Holten, R.: Boundary interactions and motors of change in requirements elicitation: a dynamic perspective on knowledge sharing. J. Assoc. Inf. Syst. **15** (6), 306–345 (2014)

6. Accenture: Trend reports (2017). https://www.accenture.com/de-de/insight-disruptive-technology-trends-2017?c=ad_gigermanyFY17_10002002&n=bac_0317, https://www.accenture.com/de-de/company-news-release-fjord-trends-2017?c=ad_gigermanyFY17_10002009&n=bac_0317. Accessed 23 Jul 2017

7. Ames, M.G., Bardzell, J., Bardzell, S., et al.: Making cultures. In: Jones, M., Palanque, P., Schmidt, A., et al. (eds.) Proceedings of the Extended Abstracts of the 32nd Annual ACM Conference on Human Factors in Computing Systems (CHI EA 2014), pp. 1087–1092. ACM Press, New York (2014)

8. Hess, J., Randall, D., Pipek, V., et al.: Involving users in the wild—participatory product development in and with online communities. Int. J. Hum Comput Stud. 71(5), 570–589 (2013). https://doi.org/10.1016/j.ijhcs.2013.01.003

9. Miller, T., Lu, B., Sterling, L., et al.: Requirements elicitation and specification using the agent paradigm: the case study of an aircraft turnaround simulator. IEEE Trans. Softw. Eng. 40(10), 1007–1024 (2014). https://doi.org/10.1109/tse.2014.2339827

10. Oppl, S.: Towards scaffolding collaborative articulation and alignment of mental models. Procedia Comput. Sci. 99, 125–145 (2016). https://doi.org/10.1016/j.procs.2016.09.106

11. Schneider, F., Bruegge, B., Berenbach, B.: The unified requirements modeling language: shifting the focus to early requirements elicitation. In: 3rd International Workshop on Comparing Requirements Modeling Approaches (CMA@RE), pp. 31–36. IEEE (2013)

12. Seyff, N., Todoran, I., Caluser, K., et al.: Using popular social network sites to support requirements elicitation, prioritization and negotiation. J. Internet Serv. Appl. 6(1), 75 (2015). https://doi.org/10.1186/s13174-015-0021-9

13. Vitharana, P., Zahedi, F., Jain, H.K.: Enhancing analysts' mental models for improving requirements elicitation: a two-stage theoretical framework and empirical results. J. Assoc. Inf. Syst. 17(12), 804–840 (2016)

14. Fleischmann, A., Schmidt, W., Stary, C., et al.: Subject-Oriented Business Process Management. Springer, Heidelberg (2012). https://doi.org/10.1007/978-3-642-32392-8

15. Fleischmann, A., Stary, C.: Whom to talk to? A stakeholder perspective on business process development. Univers. Access Inf. Soc. 11(2), 125–150 (2012). https://doi.org/10.1007/s10209-011-0236-x

16. Fleischmann, A., Schmidt, W., Stary, C.: Subject-oriented BPM = socially executable BPM. In: IEEE 15th Conference on Business Informatics, pp. 399–407. IEEE (2013)

17. Fleischmann, A., Schmidt, W., Stary, C.: S-BPM in the Wild: Practical Value Creation. Springer, Cham (2015). https://doi.org/10.1007/978-3-319-17542-3

18. Neubauer, M., Stary, C.: S-BPM in the Production Industry: A Stakeholder Approach. Springer, Cham (2017). https://doi.org/10.1007/978-3-319-48466-2

19. Eberle, P., Schwarzinger, C., Stary, C.: User modelling and cognitive user support: towards structured development. Univers. Access Inf. Soc. 10(3), 275–293 (2011). https://doi.org/10.1007/s10209-010-0210-z

20. Stary, C., Stary, E.: Creating meaningful representations. J. Inf. Knowl. Manage. 12(04), 13 (2013). https://doi.org/10.1142/s021964921350041x

21. Stary, C., Krenn, F., Lerchner, H., et al.: Towards stakeholder-centered design of open systems. In: de Greef, T., Marasek, K., Dittmar, A., et al. (eds.) Proceedings of the European Conference on Cognitive Ergonomics 2015 (ECCE 2015). ACM Press, New York (2015)

22. Resnick, M., Bruckman, A., Martin, F.: Pianos not stereos: creating computational construction kits. Interactions 3(5), 40–50 (1996). https://doi.org/10.1145/234757.234762

23. Slavin, R., Lehker, J.-M., Niu, J., et al.: Managing security requirements patterns using feature diagram hierarchies. In: IEEE 22nd International Requirements Engineering Conference (RE), pp. 193–202. IEEE (2014)

24. Frank, M.: Engineering systems thinking: cognitive competencies of successful systems engineers. Procedia Comput. Sci. **8**, 273–278 (2012). https://doi.org/10.1016/j.procs.2012.01.057

25. Weichhart, G., Stary, C.: Traceable pedagogical design rationales for personalized learning technologies. Int. J. People Oriented Program. **3**(2), 25–55 (2014). https://doi.org/10.4018/ijpop.2014070102

26. Weichhart, G., Stary, C., Vernadat, F.B.: Enterprise modeling for the interoperable and knowledge-based enterprise. Int. J. Prod. Res. **55**, 1–23 (2017)

27. Raz, A.K., DeLaurentis, D.A.: A system-of-systems perspective on information fusion systems: architecture representation and evaluation. In: AIAA Infotech @ Aerospace, AIAA SciTech Forum (AIAA 2015-0644) (2015). https://doi.org/10.2514/6.2015-0644

28. Zacharewicz, G., Diallo, S., Ducq, Y., et al.: Model-based approaches for interoperability of next generation enterprise information systems: State of the art and future challenges. Inf. Syst. e-Bus. Manage. https://doi.org/10.1007/s10257-016-0317-8

29. Weichhart, G., Stary, C.: A domain specific language for organisational interoperability. In: Ciuciu, I., et al. (eds.) OTM 2015. LNCS, vol. 9416, pp. 117–126. Springer, Cham (2015). https://doi.org/10.1007/978-3-319-26138-6_15

30. Bezerianos, A., McEwan, G.: Presence disparity in mixed presence collaboration. In: Czerwinski, M., Lund, A., Tan, D. (eds.) Proceeding of the Twenty-Sixth Annual CHI Conference Extended Abstracts on Human Factors in Computing Systems (CHI 2008), pp. 3285–3290. ACM Press, New York (2008)

31. Jamshidi, M. (ed.): System of Systems Engineering: Innovations for the Twenty-First Century. Wiley, New York (2011)

32. Curry, E.: System of systems information interoperability using a linked dataspace. In: 7th International Conference on System of Systems Engineering (SoSE), pp. 101–106. IEEE (2012)

33. Baldwin, W., Sauser, B.: Modeling the characteristics of system of systems. In: IEEE International Conference on System of Systems Engineering (SoSE 2009), pp. 1–6. IEEE, Piscataway (2009)

34. Stary, C., Wachholder, D.: System-of-systems support – a bigraph approach to interoperability and emergent behavior. Data Knowl. Eng. **105**, 155–172 (2016). https://doi.org/10.1016/j.datak.2015.12.001

35. Kolb, J., Hübner, P., Reichert, M.: Automatically generating and updating user interface components in process-aware information systems. In: Meersman, R., et al. (eds.) OTM 2012. LNCS, vol. 7565, pp. 444–454. Springer, Heidelberg (2012). https://doi.org/10.1007/978-3-642-33606-5_28

36. Franke, J., Charoy, F., El Khoury, P.: Framework for coordination of activities in dynamic situations. Enterpr. Inf. Syst. **7**(1), 33–60 (2013). https://doi.org/10.1080/17517575.2012.690891

37. Panetto, H., Cecil, J.: Information systems for enterprise integration, interoperability and networking: theory and applications. Enterpr. Inf. Syst. **7**(1), 1–6 (2013). https://doi.org/10.1080/17517575.2012.684802

38. Vernadat, F.B.: Technical, semantic and organizational issues of enterprise interoperability and networking. Annu. Rev. Control **34**(1), 139–144 (2010). https://doi.org/10.1016/j.arcontrol.2010.02.009

39. Benaben, F., Mu, W., Boissel-Dallier, N., et al.: Supporting interoperability of collaborative networks through engineering of a service-based mediation information system (MISE 2.0). Enterp. Inf. Syst. **9**(5–6), 556–582 (2015). https://doi.org/10.1080/17517575.2014.928949

40. Louridas, P., Loucopoulos, P.: A generic model for reflective design. ACM Trans. Softw. Eng. Methodol. **9**(2), 199–237 (2000). https://doi.org/10.1145/350887.350895

41. Sengers, P., Boehner, K., David, S., et al.: Reflective design. In: Bertelsen, O.W., Bouvin, N.O., Krogh, P.G., et al. (eds.) Proceedings of the 4th Decennial Conference on Critical Computing Between Sense and Sensibility (CC 2005), pp. 49–58. ACM Press, New York (2005)
42. Bardzell, S., Bardzell, J., Forlizzi, J., et al.: Critical design and critical theory. In: Proceedings of the Designing Interactive Systems Conference on (DIS 2012), pp. 288–297. ACM Press, New York (2012)
43. Bardzell, J., Bardzell, S.: What is "critical" about critical design? In: Mackay, W.E., Brewster, S., Bødker, S. (eds.) Proceedings of the SIGCHI Conference on Human Factors in Computing Systems (CHI 2013), pp. 3297–3306. ACM Press, New York (2013)
44. Menendez-Blanco, M., Bjorn, P., de Angeli, A.: Fostering cooperative activism through critical design. In: Lee, C.P., Poltrock, S., Barkhuus, L., et al. (eds.) Proceedings of the 2017 ACM Conference on Computer Supported Cooperative Work and Social Computing (CSCW 2017), pp. 618–629. ACM Press, New York (2017)
45. Hornidge, A.K.: Mid-range concepts–the lego bricks of meaning-making: an example from Khorezm, Uzbekistan. In: Mielke, K., Hornidge, A.K. (eds.) Area Studies at the Crossroads, pp. 213–230. Palgrave Macmillan, New York (2017)
46. Resnick, M., Wilensky, U.: Diving into complexity: developing probabilistic decentralized thinking through role-playing activities. J. Learn. Sci. 7(2), 153–172 (1998). https://doi.org/10.1207/s15327809jls0702_1
47. Stary, C.: System-of-systems design thinking on behavior. Systems 5(1), 3 (2017). https://doi.org/10.3390/systems5010003
48. Fleischmann, A., Schmidt, W., Stary, C., et al.: Nondeterministic events in business processes. In: La Rosa, M., Soffer, P., et al. (eds.) Business Process Management Workshops. LNBIP, vol. 132, pp. 364–377. Springer, Heidelberg (2013). https://doi.org/10.1007/978-3-642-36285-9_40

Interoperability for Human-Centered Manufacturing

Magnus Åkerman[(⊠)] ⓘ and Åsa Fast-Berglund ⓘ

Chalmers University of Technology, Gothenburgh, Sweden
magnus.akerman@chalmers.se

Abstract. Interoperability is of high focus for the manufacturing industry that is currently undergoing a transformation into the fourth industrial revolution. Factories are adopting smart technologies and implementing decentralized and human-centered manufacturing systems. To use ICT for cognitive automation and information sharing is becoming more common and increasingly important for factory workers. To implement these ICT solutions, it is important to consider their interoperability with the entire manufacturing system. This study suggests a framework that combines the context of human-centered manufacturing with areas of concerns in enterprise systems. The framework is presented and discussed regarding its usefulness to assess and/or improve system interoperability.

Keywords: Interoperability · Human-centered manufacturing · ICT

1 Introduction

Interoperability is a broad term that many people associate with the technical issues of computer interactions but it also includes a soft side of human communications and organizational aspects. Interoperability is of high focus for the manufacturing industry that is currently undergoing a transformation into Industry 4.0, the fourth industrial revolution. On a general level this is achieved by implementing the concepts of Cyber Physical Systems (CPS), Internet of Things (IoT), Internet of Services, and Smart Factory [1]. As new technologies are adopted, new dynamics will be introduced opening doors to external service providers, increasing the relevance of interoperability [2]. Interoperability has been thoroughly researched and several reference frameworks and evaluation models have been presented over the years. These models [3–7] have been mostly focused on the technical issues that disregards the human perspective [8]. The focus towards more dynamic and flexible manufacturing systems have also increased the focus of humans role in the system [9]. Today, the Industry 4.0 framework has the potential to include also humans into its highly innovative processes. When the physical and cognitive level of automation and complexity within manufacturing increases, the importance of support to the remaining workers are vital [9]. With the recent advances of information and communication technologies (ICT), it is a tempting proposition to increase the utilization of ICT as cognitive automation to enable context aware information and information sharing for manufacturing operators [10]. The development will continue and the competences needed from manufacturing

C. Debruyne et al. (Eds.): OTM 2017 Workshops, LNCS 10697, pp. 76–83, 2018.
https://doi.org/10.1007/978-3-319-73805-5_8

operators is bound to change when the industry adapts to more smart solutions [11–13]. This shift puts more emphasis on collaboration between information systems and operators [14]. Context-aware information requires a system that acknowledges the need of individuals and can provide the right information at the right place in the right time [12]. A powerful technical infrastructure is needed to facilitate this bottom up engineering of interoperable solutions. The infrastructure needs to allow and support the creation of interoperability solutions within and between technical systems, exchanging data and organizational systems that are part of a common business process.

This paper aims to present an interoperability framework that can be used to evaluate system strengths and weaknesses, which enables flexibility and adoptability between Information Technologies (IT) and Information Systems (IS) and thereby creates a more human-centered manufacturing system.

2   Interoperability Framework

According to the classic IEEE definition, interoperability is "the ability of two or more systems or elements to exchange information and to use the information that has been exchanged" [15]. By this definition, interoperable systems need to be able to both communicate and to be able to interpret what is being communicated. These abilities are often represented in four separate interoperability levels: technical, syntactical, semantic, and organizational [8]. These levels can be used as a maturity measure of interoperability where interoperability barriers prevent reaching to higher levels. Interoperability models usually divide these barriers into different areas where they can occur. In the interoperability maturity model, LISI [3], the areas are procedures, applications, infrastructure, and data. This is similar to the Framework of Enterprise Interoperability (FEI) that use business, process, service, and data [7]. Without connecting them to interoperability barriers or levels in an explicit framework, Koussouris et al. [6] presented twelve different research areas, divided into four granularity levels, that can connect interoperability with the enterprise system. The first granularity level is based on a description of the basic components of an enterprise: infrastructures, data, processes, policies, and people. From those five components, they suggest six fundamental areas: data, process, rules, objects, software systems, and cultural. These areas are chosen to represent different enterprise interoperability aspects. Unlike other frameworks the interoperability areas are not directly mapped against levels or barriers, instead the focus is towards the human perspective.

Interoperability is strongly linked to the concept of collaboration, which is the sharing of information, resources, and responsibilities between distributed entities of humans or machines [16]. Since the framework focus on human-centered manufacturing, it underlines the usage of ICT as a tool for collaboration, which from a human perspective concerns other humans and machines.

Table 1 shows the framework which is a matrix of 24 different areas of interoperability solutions and/or concerns. The vertical axis are the six fundamental interoperability areas and the horizontal axis represents human operators' collaboration with humans and computers using ICT. The table is partly populated with color-coded data.

Text with a blue background represents an industrial use case to exemplify how the framework can be populated (described in the next chapter). A green background highlights shorter examples that are used in the discussion below.

Table 1. Interoperability framework for human-centered manufacturing.

Interoperability areas for enterprise systems [6]	Manufacturing operators use of ICT			
	Human-Human collaboration		Human-Computer collaboration	
	Internal (Manufacturing Operations)	**External** (Outside MO)	**Monitor and control**	**Cognitive automation** [17]
Data		AML [18-20]	IO-Link [21]	
Process	Preventive maintenance [22]		Production overview with alarm info [22]	Adapts timing and content of checklist [22]
	Disturbance reporting [18, 19]	Engineers and operators view of the automation equipment [18, 19]		Instructions [18, 19]
Rules	Disturbance reporting [22]			
Objects				QR codes [22]
				RFID [18]
Software	RESTful web service [19, 23]		OPC UA [18, 24]	
			ISA 95 / B2MML [25]	
Cultural		Translation aid		

2.1 Data - Accessibility of Relevant Data

The data interoperability area is about ensuring the access of all the relevant data needed for a specific ICT implementation. Many **human-computer** implementations in the manufacturing industry rely on sensor **data** to trigger events in the system. One way to improve accessibility of this sensor data is to support, or even force, a specific system standard for sensor connections e.g. I/O link [21].

2.2 Process - Alignment with the Manufacturing Process

Process interoperability is the easiest to imagine and exemplify. In a previous study by the authors a customized mobile application was introduced to manufacturing operators [22]. This mobile tool included many functions that fits well in this area. First of is a digital preventive maintenance checklist. This checklist helped the operators to perform the preventive maintenance, an important part of the manufacturing **process**. This tool also helped others, like maintenance engineers, to trust the results. Therefore, it can relate to both **internal** and **external** collaboration. Two other functions can exemplify **human-computer** collaboration. One is an overview of the manufacturing systems with current alarm info, which is a typical **monitor and control** function. The other is an automatic reminder and dynamic content of the maintenance checklist, which is an example of **cognitive automation**.

2.3 Rules - Inclusion of Relevant Rules and Regulations

Another function from the mobile application mentioned above was a digital disturbance report tool. Anyone could input information about things that was out of the ordinary, which was then accessible to other operators regardless of where they were or what shift they belong to. This tool improves the **internal** communication and it helped them keep the production area free from problems, which is necessary from a safety viewpoint and is highly regulated (**rules**).

2.4 Objects - Identification and Interconnection with Relevant Objects

With increased focus on Cyber Physical Systems (CPS) and demand for traceability, being able to identify and interconnect with relevant objects are crucial in the manufacturing context. Let's go back to the example of the preventive checklist in the mobile application [22]. Each checkpoint provided some instruction on how and what to inspect (**cognitive automation**). These instructions could be started by scanning a QR code next to the checkpoint, connecting the right instruction to the correct station (**object**).

2.5 Software - Interconnectivity with Relevant Software Systems

Interconnecting software is perhaps what most people naturally connect to interoperability. This can be aided by utilizing a sound model, e.g. service oriented architecture (SOA), or by committing to well documented standards. For example, if you wanted to connect to an existing enterprise resource planning (ERP) system (**software**) to gain access to e.g. production KPI's (**monitor and control**), it would be easier if it already followed the ISA 95 [25] standard and implemented B2MML to transfer the data.

2.6 Cultural - Different Traditions, Languages, Social Norms etc.

The last interoperability area, cultural, refers to the fact that people that collaborate have different traditions, languages, social norms etc. To accommodate this in ICT implementations for human-centered manufacturing can sometimes be very relevant in a global context. One example could be to include translation aid for human-human collaboration over organizational borders (**external**).

3 Exemplifying the Framework

This section exemplifies how the interoperability framework could be utilized in an industrial case example. The case refers to a mobile dynamic assembly system developed in a research project [18].

3.1 Human-Human Collaboration

Part of the assembly system, an automation management platform, mogas [19], was developed as a Web application built with the Play Framework [23]. Play framework automatically build web applications that are accessible with a RESTful API, which improves system integration (**software**). The application consists of a database that represents an automation system and its components. For each component, users can add, edit, and use issue reports and instructions. The system allows several different organizations and users. Each organization can have one or several manufacturing systems and each system have an automation equipment hierarchical structure.

An interesting feature of this system is how the database (**data**) is originally populated, which is through automatic generation from an Automation ML file [26]. If this file is updated, it is possible to regenerate the structure with maintained system information. Automation ML files can be generated from other systems with such support or created with the specialized editor that can be downloaded from the official AML website. Figure 1 shows the assembly system represented in the Automation ML editor and in the automation management platform respectively.

The Automation ML (AML) data format is built on the CAEX (Computer-Aided Engineering eXchange) model, which is an internationally standardized file format, which provides an object-oriented structured meta-model [27]. AML aims to simplify information exchange between tools used during the automation engineering process. It supports storage of plant topology, geometry and kinematic (COLLADA), behavior description (PLCopen), references, and relations. Automation ML consists of class libraries and a concrete instance hierarchy [20].

From an interoperability perspective, this platform aligns the view of the automation system (**process**) between manufacturing operators and maintenance engineers (**external**) that also can be extended to automation developers. This is made

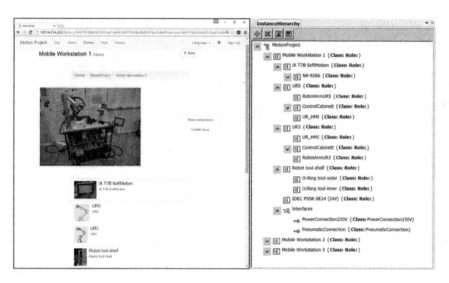

Fig. 1. To the left: The platform mogas (Management of Generic Automation Systems) exemplified with an assembly system from the research project MOTION. To the right: The same structure in Automation ML Editor.

possible by sharing the same semantic structure derived from the automation design tool (AML). AML also allow for an automatic population and structure of the database, which is relevant from data interoperability point of view.

3.2 Human-Computer Collaboration

Each mobile station has an HMI and a PLC to control various automation equipment. A purposeful limitation within the project was that each HMI/PLC combination came from different suppliers. This hindered copy pasting code to control common automation equipment, which in this case was the RFID system to identify different pallets. To remedy this problem, a separate RFID system was implemented using a Raspberry Pi connected to a RC522 RFID reader. OPC UA was supported by all the suppliers so it was chosen for top level communication. Thanks to the fact that OPC UA is open and platform independent [24], it was relatively easy to use this standard to also connect the Raspberry Pi and the RFID solution to the HMI's.

When populating the framework regarding human-computer collaboration there are three important features. Dynamic instructions (**cognitive automation**) were implemented to better aid the assembly tasks (**process**). The dynamic feature was possible by connecting the RFID system, that identified the pallets (objects). In general, human-computer collaboration was also made possible by OPC UA that enabled interconnection between different systems (**software**), such as a traditional PLC/HMI implementations and a RFID system built on a Raspberry Pi.

4 Conclusion

This paper provides an interoperability framework that aims to create a common language between decision makers in manufacturing industry and ICT/IS developers. According to Rezaei et al. [8] it is important that an interoperability evaluation model is easy to use and that it considers every aspects of interoperability. The result matrix can be a step towards such a model for the human-centered manufacturing context.

Acknowledgements. This paper is adapted from a licentiate thesis written by Åkerman [28], available online. The work has been carried out within the Production Area of Advance at Chalmers University of Technology and has been funded by VINNOVA (Swedish Agency for Innovation Systems). Their support is gratefully acknowledged.

References

1. Hermann, M., Pentek, T., Otto, B.: Design principles for industrie 4.0 scenarios. In: 49th Hawaii International Conference on System Sciences (HICSS), Hawaii (2016)
2. Agostinho, C., Ducq, Y., Zacharewicz, G., Sarraipa, J., Lampathaki, F., Poler, R., et al.: Towards a sustainable interoperability in networked enterprise information systems: trends of knowledge and model-driven technology. Comput. Ind. **79**, 64–76 (2016)
3. C4ISR: Levels of information systems interoperability (LISI) (1998)
4. Clark, T., Jones, R.: Organisational interoperability maturity model for C2 (1999)
5. Guédria, W., Naudet, Y., Chen, D.: A maturity model assessing interoperability potential. In: Halpin, T., Nurcan, S., Krogstie, J., Soffer, P., Proper, E., Schmidt, R., Bider, I. (eds.) BPMDS/EMMSAD-2011. LNBIP, vol. 81, pp. 276–283. Springer, Heidelberg (2011). https://doi.org/10.1007/978-3-642-21759-3_20
6. Koussouris, S., Lampathaki, F., Mouzakitis, S.: Digging into real-life enterprise interoperability areas: definition and overview of the main research areas. In: Proceedings of CENT (2011)
7. Chen, D., Daclin, N.: Framework for enterprise interoperability. In: Proceedings of IFAC Workshop EI2N, pp. 77–88 (2006)
8. Rezaei, R., Chiew, T.K., Lee, S.P., Aliee, Z.S.: Interoperability evaluation models: a systematic review. Comput. Ind. **65**, 1–23 (2014)
9. ElMaraghy, H.A.: Flexible and reconfigurable manufacturing systems paradigms. Int. J. Flex. Manuf. Syst. **17**, 261–276 (2006)
10. Karlsson, M., Mattsson, S., Fast-Berglund, Å., Stahre, J.: Could the use of ICT tools be the way to increase competitiveness in Swedish industry? IFAC Proc. Volumes **46**, 179–186 (2013)
11. Bauernhansl, P.D.T., Diegner, D.B., Diemer, J., Dümmler, D.M., Eckert, P.D.C., Herfs, D.W., et al.: Industrie 4.0 - Whitepaper FuE-Themen (2014)
12. Kagermann, H., Wahlster, W., Johannes, H.: Recommendations for implementing the strategic initiative industrie 4.0 (2013)
13. Lorenz, M., Rüßmann, M., Strack, R., Lueth, K.L., Bolle, M.: Man and machine in industry 4.0 (2015)
14. Schuh, G., Potente, T., Varandani, R., Hausberg, C., Fränken, B.: Collaboration moves productivity to the next level (2014)

15. Breitfelder, K., Messina, D. (eds.): The Authoritative Dictionary of IEEE Standards Terms, 7th edn., p. 582. Standards Information Network. IEEE Press (2000)
16. Moghaddam, M., Nof, S.Y.: The collaborative factory of the future. Int. J. Comput. Integr. Manuf. **30**, 23–43 (2017)
17. Frohm, J., Lindström, V., Stahre, J., Winroth, M.: Levels of automation in manufacturing. Ergonomia Int. J. Ergonomics Hum. Factors **30** (2008)
18. Åkerman, M., Fast-Berglund, Å., Ekered, S.: Interoperability for a dynamic assembly system. Procedia CIRP **44**, 407–411 (2016)
19. Åkerman, M.: mogas - Management of Generic Automation Systems (2016)
20. Drath, R., Lüder, A., Peschke, J., Hundt, L.: AutomationML - the glue for seamless automation engineering. In: IEEE International Conference on Emerging Technologies and Factory Automation (ETFA), pp. 616–623 (2008)
21. What is IO-Link? (2017). http://www.io-link.com/en/Technology/what_is_IO-Link.php?thisID=76
22. Åkerman, M., Fast-Berglund, Å., Karlsson, M., Stahre, J.: Introducing customized ICT for operators in manufacturing. Procedia CIRP **41**, 490–495 (2016)
23. Play Framework. https://www.playframework.com/
24. Opc Foundation. https://opcfoundation.org/
25. ANSI/ISA: Enterprise Control System Integration Part 3: Activity Models of Manufacturing Operations Management (2005)
26. AutomationML. https://www.automationml.org/o.red.c/home.html
27. Vyatkin, V.: Software engineering in industrial automation: state-of-the-art review. IEEE Trans. Ind. Inform. **9**, 1234–1249 (2013)
28. Åkerman, M.: Towards interoperable information and communication systems for manufacturing operations. Institutionen för produkt- och produktionsutveckling, Produktionssystem, Chalmers tekniska högskola, Göteborg (2016)

International Workshop on Methods, Evaluation, Tools and Applications for the Creation and Consumption of Structured Data for the e-Society (Meta4eS) 2017

Meta4eS 2017 PC Chair's Message

The future eSociety, addressed with our workshop, is an e-inclusive society based on the extensive use of digital technologies at all levels of interaction between its members. It is a society that evolves based on knowledge and that empowers individuals by creating virtual communities that benefit from social inclusion, access to information, enhanced interaction, participation and freedom of expression, among other.

In this context, the role of the ICT in the way people and organizations exchange information and interact in the social cyberspace is crucial. Large amounts of structured data – Big Data and Linked (Open) Data – are being generated, published and shared on the Web and a growing number of services and applications emerge from it. These initiatives take into account methods for the creation, storage and consumption of increasing amounts of structured data and tools that make possible their application by end-users to real-life situations, as well as their evaluation. The final aim is to lower the barrier between end-users and information and communication technologies via a number of techniques stemming from the fields of semantic knowledge processing, multilingual information, information visualization, privacy and trust, etc.

To discuss, demonstrate and share best practices, ideas and results, the 6th International IFIP Workshop on Methods, Evaluation, Tools and Applications for the Creation and Consumption of Structured Data for the eSociety (Meta4eS 2017), an event supported by IFIP TC 12 WG 12.7, The Big data roadmap and cross-disciplinarY community for addressing socieTal Externalities (BYTE) project and Data Licenses Clearance Center (DALICC), with a special focus on cross-disciplinary communities and applications associated with Big Data and their impact on the eSociety, brings together researchers, professionals and experts interested to present original research results in this area.

We are happy to announce that, for its sixth edition, the workshop raised interest and good participation in the research community. After a thorough review process, with each submission refereed by at least three members of the workshop Program Committee, we accepted 3 full papers and 3 short papers covering topics such as ontology engineering, Big Data, smart knowledge processing and extraction, social semantics, decision making, data management, user interfaces, and applied to the fields of e-Health, ambient assisted living, e-Tourism and e-Commerce.

We thank the Program Committee members for their time and effort in ensuring the quality during the review process, as well as all the authors and the workshop attendees for the original ideas and the inspiring discussions. We also thank the OTM 2017 Organizing Committee members for their continuous support. We are confident that Meta4eS will bring an important contribution towards the future eSociety.

October 2017

Anna Fensel
Ioana Ciuciu

Medical Monkeys: A Crowdsourcing Approach to Medical Big Data

Lorenzo Servadei[1(✉)], Rainer Schmidt[1(✉)], Christina Eidelloth[1(✉)],
and Andreas Maier[2(✉)]

[1] University of Applied Sciences, Lothstraße 64, 80335 Munich, Germany
{lorenzo.servadei,rainer.schmidt,c.eidelloth}@hm.edu
[2] University of Erlangen-Nuremberg, Schloßplatz 4, 91054 Erlangen, Germany
andreas.maier@fau.edu

Abstract. Big data play a central role in eHealth and have been crucial for designing and implementing clinical decisions support systems. Those applications can avail on data analysis and response capabilities, often empowered by Machine Learning algorithms, which can help clinician in diagnostic as well as therapeutic decisions. On the other hand, in the context of eSociety, eCommunities can be essential actors for managing and structuring medical data. In fact, they can support in gathering, providing and labeling data. This last task is highly relevant for medical Big Data, as it is a key point for supervised Machine Learning algorithms, which need an extensive data annotation process. This improves prediction and analysis capabilities of the algorithms on large datasets. Our approach on the medical Big Data labeling problem is the design and prototyping of a crowdsourcing collaborative Web Application, used for the annotation of medical images, that we named Medical Monkeys. Under the principles of mutual advantage and collaboration researchers, online gamers, medical students and patients will be involved, within this platform, in a virtual and mutually beneficial cooperation for improving Machine Learning algorithms. Using our application on large scale data analysis, algorithms for image segmentation will become useful for clinical decisions support systems. Our application is the result of a collaboration of several universities and research institutes and has, as principal aim, the integration, in form of gaming tasks, of eCommunities for the implementation of a more accurate analysis and diagnostic on MRI or CT images.

Keywords: Free innovation · Medical Big Data · Medical innovation · eHealth
Gamification · Open innovation · Medical images segmentation

1 Introduction

An exponential amount of sensors, monitoring, data storage systems, multimedia and devices has been generating what we identify as the Big Data phenomenon [1]. Big Data are large sets of data not merely outlined by their amount, but also by a higher degree of complexity as well as a larger value derived by the application of innovative analysis techniques [2]. Further than that, Big Data are characterized, in comparison to traditional Small Data, by a higher *velocity* and *variety* [3]. This means that they are often generated

© Springer International Publishing AG 2018
C. Debruyne et al. (Eds.): OTM 2017 Workshops, LNCS 10697, pp. 87–97, 2018.
https://doi.org/10.1007/978-3-319-73805-5_9

on real time (velocity) and composed by different sorts of data as images, audio, texts, etc. (variety) [3]. Due to their relevance for the business, such as the statistical trends forecasting and key indicators obtained, currently companies set more and more effort than ever in their gathering, storage and evaluation [4].

On the other hand, Machine Learning (ML) methods can extract meaning from Big Data as such [5]. Today this is already being applied in very different fields by all different kind of private companies [6]. But the establishment of own free data stocks for ML analysis is failing due to the high costs and the comparably low benefit for society. This complicates the role of research in universities, and take them out of a strategical role in the Big Data research [7].

With medical data such a data collection is not possible today, as the transfer of medical data is protected by law and usually complicated. Without explicit consent of the users, this would be highly unethical [8]. However, this is not seen in all countries, and there are also efforts all around the world to loosen these regulations [9].

In order to unify efforts of different actors and institutions for academic data gathering and annotation, we designed and prototyped a Web Application which avail of two pieces of collaborative software. A collaborative software is defined as an application whose intent is to realize a shared purpose, dividing the effort among users [10]. This approach can generate solutions to common problems and thus create a solid base for innovation, generating a common innovation model [11]. The power of a collaborative software, if it is not directed towards economical compensation and comes from unpaid development, can be an essential part of a free innovation model - a project where the innovation designs are not being protected by the developers [12]. These constraints are motivated by the self-reward, which is based on benefits excluding compensated transactions, and is sometimes motivated by altruistic purposes [12]. Based on this path, we got inspired by two medical projects that have been created with the goal of a free sharing of innovations design and ideas, named *Patient-Innovation.com*[1] and *Nightscout*[2].

At this moment, to our knowledge, it does not exist any platform for extensive labeling of different medical images, which maintains their statistical analysis and results free and available for research scopes. Our paper presents an approach to develop such a platform and maintain labeled images within the academic community. Therefore, we propose requirements, research design and prototypes for a crowdsourcing Web Application, based upon the free innovation and collaborative paradigm, for labeling medical images. We explore the free cooperation among Web users, researchers and image donors as a gateway for enhancing the performance of ML algorithms on medical images. This will lead to better automatic segmentation and detection algorithms, improving clinical decisions support systems and reducing the human-based error on diagnostic and therapeutic evaluation [13].

In the following chapter of this paper, we will analyze first the literature sources which helped us to explore the main scientific areas of the project: medical Big Data

---

[1] https://patient-innovation.com/.
[2] http://www.nightscout.info/.

and their analysis, free innovation patterns and collaborative innovation, crowdsourcing, crowdsourcing for medical images segmentation and its gamification.

In the third chapter, the core of our paper, we will proceed then enucleating our research design. We will first outline, through a use case scenario, the interaction among actors and the requirements for our medical images segmentation application.

After that we will enter the areas of data gathering and storage requirements of the system, where we will describe the functionalities of our distributed file system prototype. At last, we will briefly introduce the data analysis and algorithm evaluation step. In the fourth chapter we will then state the conclusions of the paper and the next steps for our project and research.

2   Literature

In Table 1 we summarized all the important pieces of literature for our research design.

Table 1. Selection of literature, categorized by main topic of interest.

Medical Big Data	Free and collaborative innovation	Crowdsourcing innovation	Crowdsourcing for medical images segmentation	Crowdsourcing, gamification and segmentation
[14–18]	[12, 19–21]	[22–24]	[25–28]	[29–32]

2.1   Medical Big Data

As a first step into our literature research, we deepened our knowledge on Medical Big Data. We first focused on their potential for medical analysis, gaining an overview over their importance for clinical diagnosis and research [14]. In particular, we looked towards the fundaments for the collection of medical imaging online, which is a sought-after topic in the scientific research [15]. On the side of data collection, the Internet of Things (IoT) and diffused sensors have been shown to be an important and pioneering step in the direction of data gathering for a multi-sources analysis [16]. But concerning the more related topic of Big Data in form of medical imaging, we evaluated some papers that introduce to their collection and analysis, which is the final purpose of the project [17, 18].

2.2   Free and Collaborative Innovation

On free innovation, the kind of innovation the project aims at, the research of Eric von Hippel provides a theoretical framework and pattern analysis [12]. In this work it is analyzed the motivation behind free innovators and, through a quantitative analysis on surveys over free innovators projects in Finland and Canada, it is provided an insight on motivation for free innovators [12, 19]. On the other hand, collaborative innovation relates to a cooperation in the prototyping and implementation of our project. Collaborative innovation is a very effective method to get a better contribution for different tasks from other individuals, enhancing the chances of excelling in a larger amount of assignments [21]. At the same time, a collaborative innovation tends to have a broader diffusion, reaching a larger share of potential users [20]. As a result, a collaborative work on the free innovation pattern can lead to an even better result, sharing the effort and the costs of the design and development and introducing new and effective ideas [12].

2.3 Crowdsourcing Innovation

For enhancing our perspective on performing the images segmentation, we deepened into the crowdsourcing innovation. For the development of free innovations, crowdsourcing gives the possibility of conveying additional expertise to the project: This could help to find better and more creative solutions to existing problems and features [22, 23]. The practical contribution of crowdsourcing in problem solving tasks comes from the vast experience and different background that a multitude of individuals takes along [22]. This mechanism explains the rising of crowdsourcing in solving specific tasks and long-term projects [24].

2.4 Crowdsourcing for Medical Images Segmentation

A general review of crowdsourcing for health-related tasks has been useful for a first orienteering within the technical aspects of this topic [26]. The first important fundament of our research is the effectiveness of crowdsourcing for medical image segmentation. The result of scientific works shows that a large crowd of non-expert can reach a high accuracy on image labelling for particular medical tasks, resulting comparable to the accuracy of expert medical doctors [27]. Crowdsourcing has shown its effectiveness for segmentation of medical images in tasks where the detection of particular entities has been required on large numbers of images. In specific tasks as cell mitosis in breast-cancer, Convolutional Neural Networks based on ground truth data generated by a crowd of non-experts has reached outstanding performance on diseased cells mitosis detection [25]. In order to collect a large number of data and collaborators, a Web Application based workflow has been previously proposed: Its online availability would increase the amount of people contributing to the tasks [28].

2.5 Crowdsourcing, Gamification and Segmentation

For attracting a crowd of users to accomplish medical tasks, gamification has been proven to be a very effective strategy. This has been shown for medical students [29] as well as for crowds of non-experts [31]. This technique is a gateway to gain better motivation for users even for non-trivial tasks [30]. Regarding objects segmentation, a statistical analysis over the crowd contribution and the filtering out of inconsistent segmentations dramatically improves the result of a non-expert crowd. This leads to the status where the performance of non-experts moves very close to the performance of professionals [27]. Through semi-supervised objects segmentation, it is possible to keep track of the algorithm performances and adapt the algorithms to the proposed task. A precise quantification of time involved and difficulty level of the task helps furthermore to elaborate a better gaming interface and attract a larger crowd to the proposed online project [32].

3   Research Design

The research design has been structured in four steps, corresponding to the main points of the research. In order to conduct a structured research, we will borrow concepts and guidelines from the design science [33]. In particular, we will refer to the design science in the Information Systems Research. The artifacts that we are going to develop present in fact an innovative solution to an existing problem, and its utility is going to be evaluated on our specific domain, from a technical and business related point of view [33].

3.1   Step I: Design and Planning

After an accurate review on literature and the achievement of a structured theoretical background, the first step of the research is the design and planning of an evolutionary prototype for a Web Application [34], which is used to accomplish the goal expressed for the free innovation development: Create better automatic segmentation algorithms for medical organs images. As the evolutionary prototype pattern implies, the prototype will be robust and will constitute a reliable basis for a final version of the application [34].

In order to explain the functionalities of the software proposed, we will borrow the concept of use cases. Use cases are defined as a succession of events generated by actors, which point out dependencies and functional structure of the software [35].

The three main actors identified in the Medical Monkeys Application are the *Image Donor*, the *Solver – Gamer* and the *Researcher*.

The Image Donor provides own medical images for the Web Application. He donates his images for medical purposes and manages them, editing or even excluding them from the game.

The *Solver – Gamer* participates to the segmentation game on the medical images. His performance will be tested by the system and, in case of enough accuracy, his result will be submitted and the data collected and stored, for further statistical evaluation.

The *Researcher* has the role of analyzing and interacting with the data submitted by Image Donors and Solvers. In the first case, the researcher will be in charge of an evaluation over the uploaded images (so that they can be relevant for the research). In the second case, the researcher will be collecting and analyzing data results from the segmentation game.

Given these actors, we can build up a scenario for the use cases. A scenario is defined as an ordered amount of interactions among partners, who are mostly represented by external actors and a given system [36]. In the use case scenario, the succession of events (e.g. the work steps and interactions) is pointed out. The diagram in Fig. 1 is representing graphically our use case scenario.

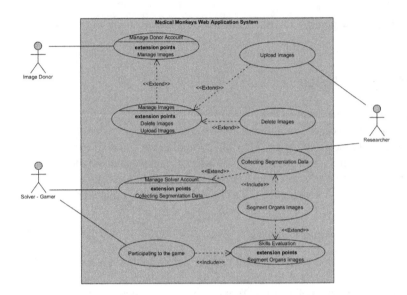

Fig. 1. Use case scenario diagram.

The medical images received from the image donors are collected and categorized following the organ representing. These images will be inserted, as a 3D model representation, in the Web Application, which will offer a game interface, where a crowd of users can participate to segment the donated organs images.

The gaming interface will be organized in levels and will motivate users with scoring and competition mechanisms. Through that, users will be triggered in keeping focused on the task and improve their performance. The levels will be structured by increasing difficulty, in order to stimulate solvers to get more accurate. The results of the game labelling task will be taken and analyzed by the researchers. A continuous improvement of the algorithms will be ensured by an increasing amount of gamers and donors. The larger the amount of images and the more the segmentation gamers, the more accurate will be the algorithms for organs images segmentation [27].

3.2   Step II: Web Application Implementation

As a second step, the tool will be implemented on a Web Platform. From this point, the Web Application will be available, and data of patients and game-solver will be collected. During the initial part of the data collection, the gamer will play against automatic segmentation algorithms, in order to obtain an own score. The Web Application will be gradually implemented and deployed for mobile devices as well, enhancing the chance of increasing participation by game-solvers. For each annotated layer the user gets points, which he can then post on social media. A public high-score list should then also allow the formation of groups, which then allows a competition between institutions. Currently, the Web prototype is to be found online, together the informative webpage. Image Donors and Gamers can register and manage their own profile, images and account[3]. The segmentation game is still in development. We have as well a public repository for our Web Application[4].

3.3 Step III: Data Collection and Storage

In the current step of our project, we request patients for data donations after medical investigations. Image data are particularly suitable for that, since these are often available as a DVD for the patients. Images of patients will be sent to us together with an agreement certificate. Once provided, we will store the images in a private cloud service. Before dispatching, the donor taps a TAN on the envelope, with which he then accesses his data online and can revoke the user authorization. Furthermore, the donor will get access to all research results obtained with his data. All the scientific work based on these data will be therefore published as open access.

For a first implementation of the storage, we realized a fault-tolerant and scalable distributed file system [37] based on Hadoop and managed by a local application. This is used mainly for uploading administering the medical images. Apache Hadoop enables Big Data to be stored, accessed and processed in a distributed way across clusters of commodity servers [38]. In order to provide an appropriate Hadoop based architecture for the storage and uploading of the medical images, we outlined first the requirements for our architecture, as shown in Fig. 2.

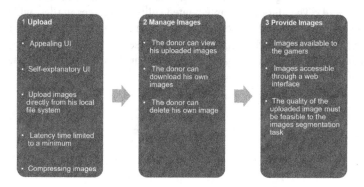

Fig. 2. Distributed file system requirements

The local application we prototyped for fulfilling these requirements has a lightweight frontend-solution which directly interacts with the distributed file system. Therefore, the system consists of three major components which implement all necessary interactions with the data storage mechanism. The diagram in Fig. 3 shows the components together with their utilized interfaces.

---

[3] http://medicalmonkeys.ddns.de.

[4] https://github.com/Lorenzo1985/Monkey_BackBone.git.

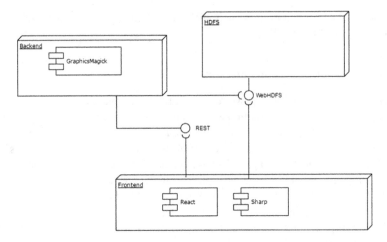

Fig. 3. Local application connected to the distributed file system

Both, frontend and backend of the application interact with HDFS using WebHDFS [37]. To initialize the backend processes, the frontend uses a REST interface. The architecture is implemented with JavaScript, and we show with the following flowcharts, the necessary steps for storing and administering images in accordance to the given requirements (see Fig. 4). The algorithm implemented splits the images in tiles, which will be separately compressed in order to enhance the speed for reading the images and show them online for gaming and administration purposes. The introduction of Hadoop consent data as well as algorithm parallelism in our artifact. This means, faster writing

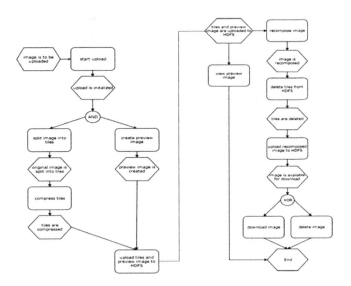

Fig. 4. Local application flow chart – administering images

as well as reading operations. For a deeper look into the implementation, it is possible to refer to this repository[5].

3.4   Step IV: Data Analysis and Algorithm Evaluation

The last step will focus on the evaluation of the data obtained and the derived machine learning algorithms. Through statistical analysis, data coming from anomalous or not focused player will be ignored in the processing. This will lead to an improvement in the data collection and analysis [27]. In this step, a ground truth for the segmentation algorithm will be formed from the the valid values obtained by gamers. Given the ground truth created, ML algorithms will be measured and their accuracy will be evaluated against the state-of-the-art performances.

4   Conclusions and Future Work

ML algorithms for medical images segmentation are sensitive to the lack of large labelled training sets [39]. The reasons for that are mainly to be found in the privacy policies [39] and in the missing labelling which, differently from public internet images, cannot easily be performed by a non-expert crowd [40]. For solving this problem, we propose through Medical Monkeys a collaborative free innovation pattern that, using crowdsourcing to increase diffusion, enhances the amount of medical images and the segmentation accuracy of the algorithms, through a copious labeling. This paper presented the research design, requirements and prototype of our crowdsourcing Web Application, developed over a free innovation pattern, for medical images segmentation. We explored the possibility of free cooperation from Web users, researchers and images donors for improving the application, as a gateway for enhancing the performance of machine learning algorithms on medical images. This will lead to better automatic segmentation and detection algorithms, improving clinical decisions support systems and reducing the human-based error on anomalies evaluation [13]. The next steps of our research will lead to exploring effective way for designing our segmentation game and increasing the participation of the crowd. At the same time, we will continue with the data collection from hospitals and cooperation with institutions, in order to create a larger dataset of images.

References

1. Cai, L., Zhu, Y.: The challenges of data quality and data quality assessment in the big data era. Data Sci. J. **14**, 2 (2015)
2. Ward, J.S., Barker, A.: Undefined By Data: A Survey of Big Data Definitions. arXiv: 1309.5821 Cs. (2013)
3. De Mauro, A., Greco, M., Grimaldi, M.: A formal definition of big data based on its essential features. Libr. Rev. **65**, 122–135 (2016)

---

[5] https://github.com/chrissike/saveimages.git.

4. LaValle, S., Lesser, E., Shockley, R., Hopkins, M.S., Kruschwitz, N.: Big data, analytics and the path from insights to value. MIT Sloan Manag. Rev. **52**, 21–32 (2011)
5. Qiu, J., Wu, Q., Ding, G., Xu, Y., Feng, S.: A survey of machine learning for big data processing. EURASIP J. Adv. Signal Process. **2016** (2016)
6. Einav, L., Levin, J.: The data revolution and economic analysis. Innov. Policy Econ. **14**, 1–24 (2014)
7. O'Neil, C., Schutt, R.: Doing Data Science (2013)
8. Cios, K.J., William Moore, G.: Uniqueness of medical data mining. Artif. Intell. Med. **26**, 1–24 (2002)
9. Aicardi, C., Del Savio, L., Dove, E.S., Lucivero, F., Tempini, N., Prainsack, B.: Emerging ethical issues regarding digital health data. On the World Medical Association Draft Declaration on Ethical Considerations Regarding Health Databases and Biobanks. Croat. Med. J. **57**, 207–213 (2016)
10. Johnson-Lenz, P., Johnson-Lenz, T.: Post-mechanistic groupware primitives: rhythms, boundaries and containers. Int. J. Man Mach. Stud. **34**, 395–417 (1991)
11. West, J., Gallagher, S.: Challenges of open innovation: the paradox of firm investment in open-source software. R Manag. **36**, 319–331 (2006)
12. von Hippel, E.: Free innovation (2017)
13. Zhou, S.K., Greenspan, H., Shen, D.: Deep Learning for Medical Image Analysis. Academic Press, Cambridge (2017)
14. Raghupathi, W., Raghupathi, V.: Big data analytics in healthcare: promise and potential. Health Inf. Sci. Syst. **2**, 1–10 (2014)
15. Steinbrook, R.: Personally controlled online health data–the next big thing in medical care? N. Engl. J. Med. **358**, 1653–1656 (2008)
16. Dimitrov, D.V.: Medical Internet of Things and big data in healthcare. Healthc. Inform. Res. **22**, 156 (2016)
17. Aji, A., Wang, F., Saltz, J.H.: Towards building a high performance spatial query system for large scale medical imaging data. In: Proceedings of the 20th International Conference on Advances in Geographic Information Systems (2012)
18. Van Horn, J.D., Toga, A.W.: Human neuroimaging as a "Big Data" science. Brain Imaging Behav. **8**, 323–331 (2014)
19. de Jong, J.P.J., von Hippel, E., Gault, F., Kuusisto, J., Raasch, C.: Market failure in the diffusion of consumer-developed innovations: patterns in Finland. Res. Policy **44**, 1856–1865 (2015)
20. Ogawa, S., Pongtanalert, K.: Exploring characteristics and motives of consumer innovators: community innovators vs. independent innovators. Res. Technol. Manag. **56**, 41–48 (2013)
21. Akgün, A.E., Keskin, H., Byrne, J.C.: Procedural justice climate in new product development teams: antecedents and consequences. J. Prod. Innov. Manag. **27**, 1096–1111 (2010)
22. Jeppesen, L.B., Lakhani, K.R.: Marginality and problem-solving effectiveness in broadcast search. Organ. Sci. **21**, 1016–1033 (2010)
23. Afuah, A., Tucci, C.L.: Crowdsourcing as a solution to distant search. Acad. Manage. Rev. **37**, 355–375 (2012)
24. The Rise of Crowdsourcing|WIRED. https://www.wired.com/2006/06/crowds/
25. Albarqouni, S., Baur, C., Achilles, F., Belagiannis, V., Demirci, S., Navab, N.: AggNet: deep learning from crowds for mitosis detection in breast cancer histology images. IEEE Trans. Med. Imaging **35**, 1313–1321 (2016)
26. Ranard, B.L., Ha, Y.P., Meisel, Z.F., Asch, D.A., Hill, S.S., Becker, L.B., Seymour, A.K., Merchant, R.M.: Crowdsourcing—harnessing the masses to advance health and medicine, a systematic review. J. Gen. Intern. Med. **29**, 187–203 (2014)

27. Maier-Hein, L., et al.: Can masses of non-experts train highly accurate image classifiers? In: Golland, P., Hata, N., Barillot, C., Hornegger, J., Howe, R. (eds.) Medical Image Computing and Computer-Assisted Intervention – MICCAI 2014, MICCAI 2014, Lecture Notes in Computer Science, vol. 8674, pp. 438–445. Springer, Cham (2014). https://doi.org/10.1007/978-3-319-10470-6_55

28. Chávez-Aragón, A., Lee, W.-S., Vyas, A.: A crowdsourcing web platform-hip joint segmentation by non-expert contributors. In: IEEE International Symposium on Medical Measurements and Applications Proceedings (MeMeA), 2013, pp. 350–354. IEEE (2013)

29. Leba, M., Ionică, A., Apostu, D.: Educational software based on gamification techniques for medical students. Wseas Us., pp. 225–230 (2013)

30. Spampinato, C., Palazzo, S., Giordano, D.: Gamifying video object segmentation. IEEE Trans. Pattern Anal. Mach. Intell. 1 (2016)

31. Carlier, A., Salvador, A., Cabezas, F., Giro-i-Nieto, X., Charvillat, V., Marques, O.: Assessment of crowdsourcing and gamification loss in user-assisted object segmentation. Multimed. Tools Appl. **75**, 15901–15928 (2016)

32. Salvador, A., Carlier, A., Giro-i-Nieto, X., Marques, O., Charvillat, V.: Crowdsourced object segmentation with a game. In: Proceedings of the 2nd ACM international workshop on Crowdsourcing for multimedia, pp. 15–20. ACM (2013)

33. Hevner, A.R., March, S.T., Park, J., Ram, S.: Design science in information systems research. MIS Q. **28**, 75–105 (2004)

34. Overmyer, S.: Revolutionary vs. evolutionary rapid prototyping: balancing software productivity and HCI design concerns. In: Proceedings of the 4th International Conference on Human-Computer Interaction (1991)

35. Jacobson, I.: Object Oriented Software Engineering: A Use Case Driven Approach. http://www.citeulike.org/group/8357/article/348273

36. Seybold, C., Meier, S., Glinz, M.: Scenario-driven modeling and validation of requirements models (2006)

37. An introduction to Apache Hadoop|Opensource.com. https://opensource.com/life/14/8/intro-apache-hadoop-big-data

38. Ishwarappa, K., Anuradha, J.: A brief introduction on big data 5Vs characteristics and hadoop technology. Procedia Comput. Sci. **48**, 319–324 (2015)

39. Cho, J., Lee, K., Shin, E., Choy, G., Do, S.: How much data is needed to train a medical image deep learning system to achieve necessary high accuracy? arXiv:1511.06348 Cs. (2015)

40. Startups, R. for: Deep Learning in Healthcare: Challenges and Opportunities (2016). https://medium.com/the-mission/deep-learning-in-healthcare-challenges-and-opportunities-d2eee7e2545

Superstore Sales Reporting: A Comparative Analysis of Relational and Non-relational Databases

Short Paper

Gheorghe Coşofreţ and Ioana Ciuciu[✉]

Universitatea Babes-Bolyai, Cluj-Napoca, Romania
cosofret.geo@gmail.com, ioana.ciuciu@cs.ubbcluj.ro

Abstract. The purpose of this paper is to realize a comparative analysis of relational and non-relational database management systems. Both conceptual and technical characteristics are introduced, presenting the benefits and disadvantages of each model, using a hybrid application. The application, named Superstore-SalesReporting, generates comparative reports which describe the technical characteristics of both SQL and NoSQL databases based on the executed operations. The application constitutes the contribution of this study, together with the creation of the SQL Server internal processes for migrating data from a flat file into a star schema.

Keywords: Relational databases · Non-relational databases · SQL
Comparative report · Comparative analysis · NoSQL · E-commerce application

1 Introduction

The work in this paper has been done in the context of the university degree thesis of Gheorghe Coşofreţ [1]. The theoretical concepts described were used in order to build an application with the aim of highlighting the characteristics, benefits and disadvantages of relational and non-relational databases.

The actual database management systems collate with a huge variety and diversity of data. More and more applications demand the use of data without too many constraints of model management in order to be more flexible and easier to maintain. On the other hand, the classical data management, the relational model, is still present. It sustains organizations that use data warehouses to store their business data. When trying to design an application or a business software solution, an essential aspect consists in choosing the right database management system. Each application has its own specificity and it's hard to say which one of the relational and non-relational is better. In this paper, we try to show concisely what relational and non-relational databases represent, hoping that this presentation will constitute a guide towards the right choice.

© Springer International Publishing AG 2018
C. Debruyne et al. (Eds.): OTM 2017 Workshops, LNCS 10697, pp. 98–102, 2018.
https://doi.org/10.1007/978-3-319-73805-5_10

2 Relational vs Non-relational Database Models

2.1 The Relational Model

The relational data model was defined in June 1970 by Dr. Edgar F. Codd [2]. Codd introduced concepts like data independence, data stored in tabular form for an easier retrieval, and data manipulation and administration using a query language called SQL (Structured Query Language). It is based on the relational model, actually being the world's most widely-used relational database query language. Every operation executed in the relational model must respect the ACID properties: Atomicity, Consistency, Isolation, and Durability [3]. The relational model is very much used in production and is still a strong data model; however, it has some technical limitations: (*i*) Each relation (table) has a fixed schema; (*ii*) Integration of data which are dependent on other data (from other databases) is difficult because they must be interconnected afterwards; (*iii*) To scale a relational database means to distribute it to more servers, table maintainability becoming a chaos in this case.

2.2 The Non-relational Model and Description of NoSQL Databases

The non-relational term is often associated with NoSQL (*not only SQL*). A NoSQL database management system is a non-relational database system, more often distributed, with a rapid data access; it allows ad-hoc organization of data with variable data types and also facilitates the analysis of large volumes of data. NoSQL is associated with cloud databases, non-relational databases, Big Data databases, etc. NoSQL databases became the first alternative for relational ones, the main reasons being scalability, availability of data and error tolerance[1]. Every NoSQL solution has its own data memory model. NoSQL database types are classified as follows: Key-Value Store Databases, Column-Oriented Databases, Document Store Databases and Graph Databases. In the non-relational model, the ACID properties are not present, being replaced by the BASE model (Basic Availability, Soft State, Eventual Consistency)[2]: (*i*) *Basic Availability*: data collection is replicated and distributed instead of using one single data source and somewhere in the network the data surely exists so that clients receive an answer to their queries; (*ii*) *Soft State*: the database management system doesn't guarantee database consistency, the application must be responsible of that. (*iii*) *Eventual Consistency*: the database can be inconsistent a moment in time, but it is supposed that the data will become consistent in the future.

In 2000 Eric Brewer formulated a conjecture based on experience with Inktomi search engine. The conjecture was demonstrated some years after and now it is known as the CAP Theorem (Consistency, Availability, Partition-tolerance) [4]:

Theorem 1 (CAP Theorem): It is impossible for a web service to provide simultaneously Consistency, Availability and Partition tolerance.

---

[1] https://academy.datastax.com/planet-cassandra/what-is-nosql, accessed on 30 Aug 2017.
[2] https://en.wikipedia.org/wiki/Eventual_consistency, accessed on 30 Aug 2017.

2.3 SQL vs NoSQL Comparative Analysis

In the following, we present a synthetic view of the advantages and disadvantages of SQL and NoSQL (Table 1). The main SQL advantages are: (i) data access from relational databases and the creation and deletion of databases and tables; (ii) data structure description and the process of data manipulation; and (iii) users can set permissions to database objects (stored procedures, views, tables). On the other hand, the NoSQL family presents the following advantages: (i) generally, NoSQL databases are faster than relational databases thanks to the data model, which is more simple and flexible; and (ii) users can create applications in the way they really need. At the same time, NoSQL presents some noticeable drawbacks, namely: (i) the lack of standards (such as, e.g., tables in SQL); (ii) database consistency is not guaranteed; and (iii) there are limited query possibilities and underperforming data modeling methods.

Table 1. Comparative analysis of SQL and NoSQL databases

Characteristics	NoSQL	SQL	Show cased
Data storage	–Flexible JSON documents –Not every record needs to store the same properties –New properties added dynamically –Suitable for semi-structured and unstructured data	–Tables –Less flexible, imposes that all records have the same properties; not always the case in our app –Suitable for structured data	Add new order, update order
Schema	–Allows for dynamic or flexible schemas –The application dictates the schema	–Only allows strict schema –Schema must be maintained and kept in sync between the application and the database	Get feedback to order
Transactions	–ACID transactions support varies per solution	–ACID transactions supported	
Consistency & availability	–Depending on solution	–Strong consistency enforced	
	–Consistency, availability and performance can be traded to meet the needs of the application	–Consistency is prioritized over availability and performance	All case studies
Performance	–All information about an entity is typically in a single record, so an update can happen in one operation	–Information about an entity may be spread across many tables, requiring many joins to complete an update	Update order, view orders

3   Application

The purpose of the Superstore Sales Reporting application is to generate comparative reports to describe the technical characteristics of SQL and NoSQL databases based on executed operations (such as, insert and update). The application manages the sales data of a supermarket, the main feature being the order management.

The application is hybrid, and it uses two databases: Microsoft SQL Server for structured data and MongoDB for unstructured data. of using both of them is both didactic, in order to distinguish the topic, and technical for using the corresponding storage technology. It allows access with two user types: (1) *Customer*: who can have multiple account types (Small Business, Consumer, Corporate) and can also buy new products, show his own sales history and get feedback; and (2) *Retailer*: which is the supermarket administrator and which establishes the delivery details (shipping mode, shipping date, shipping cost). The application is designed for the Windows platform and it was developed in .NET Framework 4.6.1 using Microsoft Visual Studio Professional 2015.

3.1   Case Studies

1. Adding a new order
   This is a customer feature. After the customer submits an order, this one is stored either using SQL Server or MongoDB for distinguishing the CRUD characteristics of both databases. In SQL Server data are stored in tables and transactions are used for storing an order (a complex object). In MongoDB an order is a document with nested JSON fields, so that we can eliminate consistency and referential integrity difficulties. This case study distinguishes technical storage characteristics.
2. Get feedback for an order
   This is also a customer feature. Feedback data is basically text, therefore unstructured data. The reviews data are stored simultaneously in SQL Server and MongoDB, and what is important here is that MongoDB stores only non-empty fields. In SQL Server, where data have a strict schema, the fields which have not been completed remain in the database with NULL values. This case study distinguishes the dynamic way we can manipulate this kind of data.
3. Order delivery
   This is a retailer feature. After the new order is submitted, the retailer must establish the delivery date, delivery mode, and the delivery cost. This implies an update operation in both databases. In case of SQL Server, an update means to set some attributes which already exists but have NULL values, and in the case of MongoDB an update means to change the document structure by adding new fields. This case study distinguishes the flexibility of both databases.

3.2   Example of Comparative Report on the 'Get Feedback for an Order' Case Study

Feedback data are basically unstructured data, containing a lot of text. In the main customer window there is a button named Order History. By pressing it, the customer arrives to another window where s/he can select one of his own orders and can share a feedback about it. The customer can check several boxes and optionally write suggestions as free text.

In order to successfully generate the comparative report, the customer must submit the review using both databases and then press the Show Operation Report button. The report presents the data structures used, the operations executed and the data format either using SQL Server or MongoDB. In the relational case, the schema is fixed; therefore, review attributes that correspond to unchecked boxes have the value NULL; this can generate many NULL attributes, which tanslates into a waste of disk space; this is because, in the relational case, we are constrained by the schema. In MongoDB, JSON documents are more flexible and only the necessary information is stored. By showing all this technical characteristics we can see clearly what is happening in relational and non-relational environment at the execution of an operation (submit review, in this case).

4   Results and Conclusion

Relational and non-relational databases are solving the same things in different ways, and choosing one model depends on the application's requirements, the migration from one system to another being a good solution sometimes. In Table 2 below we present several comparative metrics, based on the three case studies: the *time* needed to perform an operation, the *disk space* used for data storage and the *storage entity* involved.

Table 2. Comparative metrics SQL vs NoSQL

	SQL (SQL Server)			NoSQL (MongoDB)		
	Time	Disk space	Entity storage	Time	Disk space	Entity storage
Add a new order	282 ms	0.0498 kb	1 table	168 ms	0.24707 kb	1 collection
View all orders	916 ms	3624 kb	11 tables	3 ms	11.20313 kb	1 collection
Update an order	32 ms *Before* *After*	0.03418 kb 0.05078 kb	1 table	2 ms *Before* *After*	0.23145 kb 0.23633 kb	1 collection
Order Review	47 ms	0.65918 kb	1 table	26 ms	0.46973 kb	1 collection

As a conclusion, for some operations like add (in this case a shopping cart), or select, a NoSQL DBMS is better due to the way of storage. While an update operation is more suitable for a relational DBMS (the structure is already done, data only need to be added in those columns that were empty before the update operation time).

Future work will focus on the comparative metrics in order to highlight situations where one or the other of the models is better suited.

References

1. Coşofreţ, G.: Analiză comparativă a bazelor de date relationale şi non-relaţionale. Studiu de caz pe interacţiunea Customer-Retailer, Universitatea Babeş-Bolyai (2017)
2. Codd, E.: A relational model of data for large shared data banks. Commun. ACM **13**(6), 377–387 (1970). IBM Research Laboratory
3. Chamberlin, D.: SQL. In: Liu, L., Özsu, M.T. (eds.) Encyclopedia of Database Systems, p. 4355. Springer, Boston (2009). https://doi.org/10.1007/978-0-387-39940-9_1091
4. Gilbert, S., Lynch, N.: Brewer's conjecture and the feasibility of consistent, available, partition-tolerant web services. ACM SIGACT News **33**(2), 51–59 (2002)

Integrating Product Classification Standards into Schema.org: eCl@ss and UNSPSC on the Web of Data

Alex Stolz[✉] and Martin Hepp

Universität der Bundeswehr München, 85579 Neubiberg, Germany
{alex.stolz,martin.hepp}@unibw.de

Abstract. Product classification standards like eCl@ss and UNSPSC define tens of thousands of product categories, and some standards additionally provide specific product property definitions and enumerated values. Many organizations hold respective meta-data for their products readily available in back-end databases. While many approaches have been presented for using such standards for more granular product information on the Web of Data, none has so far received mainstream adoption. This can be partly explained by legal, technical, and administrative barriers for adoption. In this paper, we describe a novel approach for using product classification standards in Web data markup in Microdata and JSON-LD syntax that does not require the availability of proper Web ontology variants of the underlying standards. We can show that the approach can provide the very same effect for the consumption and interpretation of the resulting mark-up in a Linked Data and Semantic Web context. Our proposal has already been integrated into the official version of schema.org and can be readily used for research and business applications.

Keywords: Schema.org · Microdata · JSON-LD · eClass · UNSPSC
GPC · additionalType · additionalProperty · B2B · e-commerce
Product ontologies · Product classification standards · Linked Data
Semantic Web · Conceptual modeling

1 Introduction

Product classification standards (PCS) are very common in B2B scenarios, so that many companies already use them for classifying their products and services in order to facilitate information exchange. However, several back-end systems of manufacturers and vendors only provide property-value pairs to the Web applications, and data is often not sufficiently granular or incomplete and thus not suitable for populating the target data structure as specified in a product ontology.

Standard product classification systems, like the UNSPSC[1], eCl@ss[2], etc., are in fact rich languages for representing information about products and services. They provide tens of thousands of specific types for characterizing products and services, and

---

[1] https://www.unspsc.org/.
[2] https://www.eclass.eu/.

© Springer International Publishing AG 2018
C. Debruyne et al. (Eds.): OTM 2017 Workshops, LNCS 10697, pp. 103–113, 2018.
https://doi.org/10.1007/978-3-319-73805-5_11

some (like eCl@ss) even define properties and enumerated values for describing products and services at a high level of detail. Table 1 highlights the sizes of the most recent releases of three popular PCS, namely eCl@ss, UNSPSC, and the GS1 global product classification (GPC)[3]. While UNSPSC is mainly a product taxonomy for spend analysis and procurement with hierarchically organized categories for products, the eCl@ss and GPC standards additionally feature rich properties and enumerated values.

Table 1. Total number of classes, properties, and enumerated values of three popular product classification standards

Classification standard	# of classes	# of properties	# of values
eCl@ss 10.0.1	41,647	17,342	15,708
UNSPSC v19.0501	83,229	None	None
GPC (June 2017)	4,861	1,965	12,336

From the beginning of the Semantic Web activity, researchers and practitioners have tried to make use of product categorization systems as the basis for e-commerce applications on the Semantic Web (e.g. [1–3]). In 2005, a first correct and practically useful OWL version of eCl@ss has been presented (cf. [4, 5]).

The main direction of using product categorization systems for the Semantic Web has been to derive OWL or RDFS standards from these product classification standards [1, 2, 4]. This is conceptually not as simple as creating one class for each type in the standard, because product categorization systems are not designed as ontologies; for an overview of problems see [5–7]. Deriving and publishing OWL ontologies from product categorization systems, however, creates additional problems (cf. [8]):

1. Legal problems: Product categorization systems are intellectual property rights (IPR) and subject to copyright in many cases. In fact, eClassOWL [4] was only possible because we were able to negotiate a license with eCl@ss e.V. However, for many PCS we have been unable to clarify the legal status and could thus not release OWL variants for the public.
2. Evolution and change: Product categorization systems evolve; new entries are added, old ones are changed, deprecated ones are deleted, etc. E.g., eCl@ss has now reached version 10, UNSPSC version 19, and GPC is updated every six months. Hence, it can easily happen that the OWL ontology is not in sync with the standard, unless it is an official version released by the PCS owner in parallel to other formats. The latter would be desirable, but has not materialized despite a decade of efforts.
3. Access control: Besides the legal issues, many standards are not fully accessible on the Web as bulk downloads, but only offer an online search portal. For instance, the full eCl@ss downloads are available only at a substantial annual fee (e.g. EUR 5,000 for companies up to 1,000 employees)[4], while small businesses can find the proper codes for their products and services in an online portal free of charge.

---

[3] https://www.gs1.org/gpc.
[4] http://www.eclassdownload.com/catalog/pub/german/eclass_prices.pdf.

Similar licensing fees apply to UNSPSC, where a license for up to 40 users costs USD 6,600[5].

4. Also, implementing markup is difficult, if there exist differences between PCS and OWL versions that cannot be easily bridged automatically.

As an approach to mitigate the problems, we presented PCS2OWL [6], which is a set of scripts that allow the local generation of OWL ontologies for most PCS. By standardizing name space prefixes and transformation rules, the resulting ontologies are compatible. So, people with access to PCS dump files could locally generate OWL ontologies, and two such OWL ontologies generated at two different places would be compatible, i.e. using identical identifiers for conceptual elements and equivalent axioms in OWL. Yet, while PCS2OWL is able to solve problem 2 to a large extent by easing the creation of new OWL ontologies, it cannot solve problem number 1 and only partially problems 3 and 4. Although we were able to provide OWL ontologies of a number of product classification standards[6], we mostly published only those that are available for free (e.g. GPC and the common procurement vocabulary, CPV). In summary, the whole process is still very complicated, requires access to bulk versions of PCS and is thus a severe bottleneck towards the wide use of eCl@ss and UNSPSC and other PCS for a richer representation of products and services on the Web.

In this paper, we describe a novel way of using PCS in combination with schema.org in order to (1) utilize the full level of detail of the classification standards and catalog group systems (2) without the need to access the full PCS technically or legally, and (3) without deriving and materializing an OWL ontology therefrom. This will make adoption of PCS for the Semantic Web and Linked Open Data much simpler. It will also allow PCS owners to promote the use of their standards for the Semantic Web, Linked Open Data, and semantic SEO without giving up control over their assets.

2   Background

Product classification standards (PCS) are frequently used in B2B scenarios to help organize products and services for improving information retrieval, procurement, or spend analysis. They describe product types using unique class identifiers that allow to describe products in a consistent and uniform way. Popular standards like UNSPSC or eCl@ss typically arrange concepts in a hierarchical order. E.g., UNSPSC is an international classification standard that defines classes organized hierarchically, such as Food Beverage and Tobacco Products > Beverages > Raw milk products > Raw buffalo milk. The eCl@ss standard, developed and maintained by eCl@ss e.V. in Germany, is also hierarchically structured, but besides classes it defines properties and enumerated values too. The latest version is 10.0.1, which comprises over 41.6 k classes, more than 17.3 k properties, and at least 15.7 k values [9].

---

[5] https://www.unspsc.org/membership.

[6] http://www.ebusiness-unibw.org/ontologies/pcs2owl/.

Schema.org[7] is a joint initiative of the market-leading search engines Google, Yahoo!, Bing, and Yandex. The project was initiated in 2011 and it strives to compile a collection of commonly understood Web schemas (or vocabularies) under a single, consolidated namespace (i.e. http://schema.org/). These vocabularies cover various domains and allow to embed structured data into Web pages that can be found by search engines and novel data-consuming applications. Schema.org markup is usually encoded as Microdata or JSON-LD data formats in Web pages.

3 Product Classification and Description with Schema.org

Instead of deriving an ontology for a product classification standard (PCS) and then referring to the ontology, we develop a meta-model for embedding detailed references to PCS elements in schema.org markup. This markup can then be used by the consumer of the data

1. to reconstruct triples matching an OWL version of the ontology, so for the consumer, the data will remain as useful as if modeled with an ontology, and
2. to directly query the data in the same way as in an OWL version.

The main idea is to defer the creating of an OWL model of the PCS from the time before marking up and publishing data to the consumer, taking the burden from the many operators of Web content to the few consumers.

3.1 URN Schema for Conceptual Entities

We define a URN schema [10] for PCS and their versions (we are planning to register a "pcs" namespace identifier) and relate it to the URI schema proposed in [6].

    urn:pcs: <id>:<version>:[c|p|v]: <element-id-in-standard>

This URN pattern reflects name and version of the PCS, the kind of entity (c = class, p = property, and v = value), and its identifier.

```
CONSTRUCT {?product a ?uri} WHERE {
?product a ?urn .
BIND(IRI(CONCAT("http://eclass.eu/", SUBSTR(?urn, 16,
6), "/", UCASE(SUBSTR(?urn, 23, 1)), "_", SUBSTR(?urn,
25, 9), "-gen")) AS ?uri)
FILTER(STRSTARTS(?urn, "urn:pcs:eclass:10.0.1"))
}
```

Fig. 1. urn:pcs:eclass:10.0.1:c:AEI956006 to http://eclass.eu/10.0.1/C_AEI956006-gen

---

[7] http://schema.org/.

In principle, we could in place of a URN schema also define a URI schema, but one would then expect resources to be retrievable, which is not always the case, especially if no corresponding OWL representation exists. If an OWL version of a standard became available later on (e.g. via PCS2OWL [6]), then a mapping would be trivial, e.g. using a SPARQL CONSTRUCT query (cf. [11]) (Fig. 1).

In here, we are using the substring feature of SPARQL (cf. [11]) to extract the components from the URN pattern of the eCl@ss standard. A more robust solution based on regular expressions would be necessary in order to rewrite different URNs of multiple classification standards.

3.2   Additional Product Types

As schema.org has no inherent mechanism to list extra types from external vocabularies to an entity (cf. "itemtype" definition within Microdata specification [12]), we propose a dedicated property as a solution for that. The `additionalType` property is basically a fix within schema.org for the limited typing mechanism in Microdata syntax (Table 2).

Table 2. Schema.org additionalType property definition

additionalType [subproperty of rdf:type]	
Domain	Range
Thing	URL

http://schema.org/additionalType

```
{
  "@context": "http://schema.org/",
  "@id": "#notebook",
  "@type": "Product",
  "additionalType": "urn:pcs:eclass:10.0.1:c:AEI956006",
  "name": "ACME Notebook",
  "sku": "1234"
}
```

Fig. 2. JSON-LD example for additional product types

From an RDF perspective, the `additionalType` property is considered semantically equivalent to the RDF property *rdf:type*: It is conceptually defined as a subproperty of *rdf:type*. Consequently, secondary types are applicable to any concept (*schema:Thing*) in schema.org. The addition of secondary types does not confuse the scope of local properties, i.e. a product instance with an additional type *foo:Salt* will only expect properties defined by the class *schema:Product*.

In the following, we give a simple example of modeling a secondary type for a product using `additionalType` in JSON-LD syntax. We use a product category ("Notebook") from eCl@ss, as it can be found via the online search portal[8] of eCl@ss (Fig. 2).

3.3 Property-Value Mechanism

This section proposes a light-weight, generic modeling pattern for exposing arbitrary property-value pairs to schema.org. The property-value mechanism consists of an `additionalProperty` property and a corresponding `PropertyValue` class. In the context of products and services, it allows to attach product features that otherwise could not be mapped to schema.org properties. E.g., the eCl@ss standard version 10.0.1 defines more than 17 k precise product properties and almost 16 k enumerated values, which to incorporate as property-value pairs into schema.org is neither desirable nor feasible (Table 3).

With the addition of this mechanism to schema.org, it is essentially possible to describe property-value pairs that are often rendered as tables on Web pages, such as product features. We can even point these features and values to standardized entities defined by product classification standards (Table 4).

Table 3. Schema.org additionalProperty property definition

additionalProperty [subproperty of Property]	
Domain	Range
Place, Product, QualitativeValue, QuantitativeValue	PropertyValue

http://schema.org/additionalProperty

Table 4. Schema.org PropertyValue class definition

PropertyValue [subclass of StructuredValue]	
Property	Range
Value	Boolean, Number, StructuredValue, Text
minValue	Number
maxValue	Number
unitCode	Text, URL
unitText	Text
propertyID	Text, URL
valueReference	Enumeration, PropertyValue, QualitativeValue, QuantitativeValue, StructuredValue

http://schema.org/PropertyValue

---

[8] http://www.eclasscontent.com/.

Assuming that we use the online search portal (see footnote 8) of eCl@ss, we can easily find a proper class along with corresponding standardized properties (Fig. 3).

```
{
  "@context": "http://schema.org/",
  "@id": "#notebook",
  "@type": "Product",
  "additionalType": "urn:pcs:eclass:10.0.1:c:AEI956006",
  "name": "ACME Notebook",
  "additionalProperty": {
   "@type": "PropertyValue",
   "name": "battery capacity",
   "value": "6600",
   "unitCode": "E09",  # UN/CEFACT for mAh
   "propertyID": "urn:pcs:eclass:10.0.1:p:02-AAR570"
  }
}
```

Fig. 3. JSON-LD example of the property-value mechanism

The example above describes a Notebook but extends it with a standard product feature "battery capacity". Via the property propertyID, we can link to the respective property in the eCl@ss standard. eCl@ss 10.0.1 is currently not published on the Web, but should it once become available, a corresponding mapping from the URN to the URI would be trivial. The "battery capacity" feature describes a quantitative value and thus uses a unit of measurement code from the UN/CEFACT Common Code table [13]. If the data publisher cannot easily provide such a standard unit code, the more liberal unitText property could be used instead of unitCode.

Our example here describes a point value, but range intervals with minValue and maxValue properties are also possible. A valueReference property can further be used to model ratios (e.g. "6 l/100 km", where 100 km is the value reference). Boolean and qualitative values do not need unitText or unitCode. In the first case, the value is either "True" or "False". In the latter case, the value property should contain an additional PropertyValue instance that describes the predefined value and refers with propertyID to the value identifier in the classification standard, e.g. (Fig. 4).

Alternatively, the value property could directly point to the URN of the eCl@ss value.

```
{
 "@context": "http://schema.org/", ...
 "additionalProperty": {
  "@type": "PropertyValue",
  "name": "Energy efficiency class (2010/30/EC)",
  "value": {
   "@type": "PropertyValue",
   "value": "A++",
   "propertyID": "urn:pcs:eclass:10.0.1:v:07-AAA821"
  },
  "propertyID": "urn:pcs:eclass:10.0.1:p:02-AAR804"
 }
}
```

Fig. 4. JSON-LD example of qualitative values defined in eCl@ss

4 Evaluation

The evaluation of our schema.org extension proposal consists of two steps:

(1) We show that, as long as the same version of product ontologies in OWL exists (e.g. from PCS2OWL [6] or eClassOWL [4]), a consumer is able to regenerate the same triples from our schema.org markup. To achieve this, we define a SPARQL CONSTRUCT rule (cf. [11]) that maps from our markup to PCS2OWL markup. Assume the following JSON-LD data example that uses the additionalProperty property with a URN that represents a product feature within eCl@ss 10.0.1 (Fig. 5).

```
{
 "@context": "http://schema.org/",
 "@id": "#notebook", ...
 "additionalProperty": {
  "@type": "PropertyValue",
  "name": "battery capacity",
  "value": "6600",
  "unitCode": "E09",
  "propertyID": "urn:pcs:eclass:10.0.1:p:02-AAR570"
 }
}
```

Fig. 5. "battery capacity" feature modeled with the property-value mechanism in schema.org, in JSON-LD syntax

From the above markup, we want to get the following data that relies on product ontologies (note the specific property linking to a quantitative value) (Fig. 6):

```
{
  "@context": "http://schema.org/",
  "@id": "#notebook", ...
  "http://eclass.eu/10.0.1/P_02-AAR570": {
    "@type": "QuantitativeValue",
    "name": "battery capacity",
    "value": "6600",
    "unitCode": "E09"
  }
}
```

Fig. 6. "battery capacity" feature modeled with property from the "virtual" eCl@ss product ontology, in JSON-LD syntax

The mapping is achieved by executing the SPARQL CONSTRUCT query below (Fig. 7):

```
CONSTRUCT {
  ?product ?propuri [ a schema:QuantitativeValue ;
  ?p ?v ] .
} WHERE {
  ?product schema:additionalProperty ?aprop .
  ?aprop schema:propertyID ?pid .
  ?aprop ?p ?v .
  VALUES ?p {schema:name schema:unitCode schema:value
schema:minValue schema:maxValue}
  BIND(IRI(CONCAT("http://eclass.eu/", SUBSTR(?pid, 16,
6), "/", UCASE(SUBSTR(?pid, 23, 1)), "_", SUBSTR(?pid,
25, 9))) AS ?propuri)
}
```

Fig. 7. Mapping from property-value modeling approach to product ontology

(2) We show that the same queries we used to demonstrate eClassOWL can also be directly executed over the schema.org markup. In the following, we show the first two SPARQL queries from the eClassOWL documentation [14][9], that take advantage of product types, properties, and values from eCl@ss 5.1.4 (Figs. 8 and 9).

---

[9] http://www.heppnetz.de/projects/eclassowl/#usage-sparql-queries

```
SELECT ?pencil, ?length WHERE {
 ?pencil a schema:Product .
 ?pencil schema:additionalType
<urn:pcs:eclass:5.1.4:c:AKF30003> .
 ?pencil schema:additionalProperty [
  a schema:PropertyValue ;
  schema:maxValue ?length ;
  schema:unitCode "MMT" ;
  schema:propertyID <urn:pcs:eclass:5.1.4:v:BAF559001> ].
 FILTER(?length >= 100)
}
```

Fig. 8. Example 1: find all pencils that are at least 100 mm long

```
SELECT ?model WHERE {
 ?model a schema:ProductModel .
 ?model schema:additionalType
<urn:pcs:eclass:5.1.4:c:AKF303003> .
 ?model schema:additionalProperty [
  a schema:PropertyValue ;
  schema:propertyID <urn:pcs:eclass:5.1.4:v:BAG073001> ].
}
```

Fig. 9. Example 2: find all product models of pencils that have a pointed tip

5 Conclusion

In this paper, we have presented a generic and light-weight mechanism to describe products and services using product classification standards (PCS) in schema.org. With only a minimal extension of schema.org, we can attach additional type information, standardized properties, and enumerated values to products, and complement them by boolean values, point values, or range intervals.

In comparison to previous works, our main idea is to defer the creating of an OWL model of the PCS from the time before marking up and publishing data to the consumer, taking the burden from the many operators of Web content to the few data consumers.

In essence, we could demonstrate that our approach is functionally equivalent to conversion approaches like PCS2OWL and eClassOWL, while being much simpler for the publishers of data, who just need to insert product categorization system identifiers from back-end databases into rather light-weight schema.org markup in JSON-LD or Microdata. We have already submitted our proposal to schema.org and it has been included in the official release, see e.g. http://schema.org/additionalProperty.

References

1. McGuinness, D.L.: UNSPSC Ontology in DAML+OIL. http://www.ksl.stanford.edu/projects/DAML/UNSPSC.daml
2. Klein, M.: DAML+OIL and RDF Schema Representation of UNSPSC. http://www.cs.vu.nl/~mcaklein/unspsc/
3. Fensel, D., Ding, Y., Omelayenko, B., Schulten, E., Botquin, G., Brown, M., Flett, A.: Product data integration in B2B e-commerce. IEEE Intell. Syst. **16**, 54–59 (2001)
4. Hepp, M.: eClassOWL: a fully-fledged products and services ontology in OWL. In: Poster and Demo Proceedings of the 4th International Semantic Web Conference (ISWC 2005), Galway, Ireland (2005)
5. Hepp, M.: Products and services ontologies: a methodology for deriving OWL ontologies from industrial categorization standards. Int. J. Semant. Web Inf. Syst. **2**, 72–99 (2006)
6. Stolz, A., Rodriguez-Castro, B., Radinger, A., Hepp, M.: PCS2OWL: a generic approach for deriving web ontologies from product classification systems. In: Presutti, V., d'Amato, C., Gandon, F., d'Aquin, M., Staab, S., Tordai, A. (eds.) ESWC 2014. LNCS, vol. 8465, pp. 644–658. Springer, Cham (2014). https://doi.org/10.1007/978-3-319-07443-6_43
7. Hepp, M., de Bruijn, J.: GenTax: a generic methodology for deriving OWL and RDF-S ontologies from hierarchical classifications, thesauri, and inconsistent taxonomies. In: Franconi, E., Kifer, M., May, W. (eds.) ESWC 2007. LNCS, vol. 4519, pp. 129–144. Springer, Heidelberg (2007). https://doi.org/10.1007/978-3-540-72667-8_11
8. Hepp, M.: Possible ontologies: how reality constrains the development of relevant ontologies. IEEE Internet Comput. **11**, 90–96 (2007)
9. eCl@ss e.v.: Category:Products – wiki.eclass.eu. http://wiki.eclass.eu/wiki/Category:Products
10. Daigle, L., van Gulik, D., Iannella, R., Faltstrom, P.: URN Namespace Definition Mechanism. https://tools.ietf.org/rfc/rfc2611
11. Harris, S., Seaborne, A.: SPARQL 1.1 Query Language. http://www.w3.org/TR/2013/REC-sparql11-query-20130321/
12. McCathie Nevile, C., Brickley, D.: HTML Microdata. https://www.w3.org/TR/2017/WD-microdata-20170626/
13. United Nations Economic Commission for Europe (UNECE): Recommendation No. 20: Codes for Units of Measure Used in International Trades (2006)
14. Hepp, M., Radinger, A.: eClassOWL - The Web Ontology for Products and Services. http://www.heppnetz.de/projects/eclassowl/20100418/

Ontology-Based Personalized Resource Efficiency Management for Residential Users of Smart Homes

Short Paper

Mihaela Teoca and Ioana Ciuciu[(✉)]

University Babes-Bolyai, Cluj-Napoca, Romania
Ioana.Ciuciu@cs.ubbcluj.ro

Abstract. The paper proposes an ongoing application and its corresponding use cases for managing user preferences and resource consumption (electric energy, gas, water) in a smart home. The application brings innovation both at front end and back end levels, via intuitive computer-human interaction and ontology-based user modeling, aiming to (1) provide an easy to use graphical user interface in order to assist residential users in managing their resources in a smart home setting; (2) collect resource consumption data and perform analysis on these data for prediction of future consumption rates and costs; (3) make recommendations for the resource management in a smart home; and (4) provide statistics regarding resource consumption management. The concept will be validated with families of residential users from the city of Cluj-Napoca.

Keywords: Ontology · User profiling · Graphical user interfaces
Recommender systems · Decision support · Smart home · Internet of things

1 Context and Motivation

The paper introduces an ongoing application and the corresponding use case(s) for managing household appliances in a smart home, based on user profiling and recommendations for resource consumption saving. The current work considers electric energy, water and gas for resource consumption management. The paper presents ongoing work done in the context of a software engineering master thesis.

Several approaches exist which aim at resolving the resource management, usually in a smart home setting. Some of them focus on modeling the user interfaces for friendly and efficient setup of rules [1]. Others place the focus on modeling the user behavior [2] or on the semantics underlying such frameworks [3, 4]. In [5] it is discussed how to provide semantic decision support for energy efficiency in smart metered homes. The idea of supporting energy efficiency via social networks and the importance of ontologies in such a setting is introduced in [6].

Other approaches focus on multi-agents, web services, sometimes combined with semantics in order to improve energy saving in a smart home setting. A rule-based approach for energy saving in an ambient intelligence environment based on a semantic

C. Debruyne et al. (Eds.): OTM 2017 Workshops, LNCS 10697, pp. 114–119, 2018.
https://doi.org/10.1007/978-3-319-73805-5_12

web service middleware is proposed in [7]. Klein et al. [8] proposes an approach for occupant behavior coordination based on a multi-agent system.

The present paper contributes with respect to the above-mentioned related work (which is not exhaustive) with the ontology-based user profiling and the personalized recommendations that constitute a basis for decision making in the context of smart home resource consumption management. While most of the approaches in the literature focus on energy saving, this work proposes to take into account simultaneously the management of multiple resources (electric energy, gas and water). Moreover, this approach looks at how to learn from communities of residential users, both from the system and the end user perspective. The novelty of the proposed solution mainly resides in the semantics underlying the user interactions with the system and with other users, resulting in better understanding of the user preferences and behavior and consequently in better decision-making.

2 Use Case Scenarios

The case studies in this paper are related to the *resource consumption* management in (smart) residential buildings. Besides the consumption monitoring via smart meters, the application interacts with various *sensors* (e.g., smoke sensor, motion sensor, etc.) in order to be able to provide accurate management and predictions. The residencies are also equipped with Wi-Fi cameras for real-time remote monitoring. The identified *users* of the application are residential users in the city of Cluj-Napoca. Users are clustered according to various criteria for better system learning and prediction: geographically clustered, clustered by profile similarities, by interests (e.g., energy saving during sunny weather), etc. The users are able to exchange experiences related to their smart home management via social media. The application is designed as a web application, accessible on PCs and mobile devices. User interfaces are simple and allow users to (i) have a global view of their home in a dashboard; (ii) monitor and setup devices (i.e., sensors) and household appliances; (iii) create scenarios for each room of the house (e.g., flood, entry monitoring); (iv) receive statistics and recommendations according to various criteria (e.g., outside temperature, user profile, etc.). In the following, we present two possible use case scenarios:

Use case scenario 1: Mario and Alexandra, a freshly married couple, have just moved into their new apartment. It's August and the weather is dry and hot. As their home is equipped with a series of sensors and smart meters, they need to log into their Smart Home application in order to setup desired functionalities for their household appliances. Mario is trying out the smart device in their home in order to make some basic configurations. He starts the application and logs in with his credentials. Then he follows a few basic steps for the profile setup. He provides the age, the desired comfort temperature for the entire house, the desired price thresholds for resource consumption, etc. Then he activates the dashboard and starts building preferences for several modes: home, day, night, away, and on vacation, as Alexandra and he will soon travel for their honeymoon. In the meanwhile, Alexandra has logged into the application from her smart phone and starts configuring the security devices, to have the flood and smoke sensors activated. The building is equipped with solar panels, with the possibility to switch from classical energy provider to the energy produced by their PVs. Also, some of their house appliances can switch from gas to electricity, which is very convenient for the summer period. The couple is not sure how this works and so Mario enters the social media portal to get advice from their neighbors. Alexandra finds it useful to interrogate the application for some statistics on their building's resource consumption from previous years and also to ask the system for recommendations of savings for the following period, taking into account their honeymoon travel and the local weather predictions.

Use case scenario 2: Ana is preparing to go to ski for the winter break. She configures the settings for the resource management of her apartment while she is away. She sets up the security settings, and enables the flood, fire and motion alerts. Then sets the desired temperature for the whole apartment and separately the temperature for the living room where she keeps the plants. The system sends an alert to Ana's mailbox to ask for permission to switch from classical energy to energy generated by the solar panels of the building. Ana accepts the recommendation and now the configuration will switch automatically to PVs whenever there is enough sun. The day Ana returns home, she accesses the application in order to setup the comfort in the house for her return. She would like to avoid setting the temperature too high for so many hours in order to save resources. She asks the application to suggest the actions to take in order to have the desired comfort the moment she enters the house.

3   Semantic Layer

The semantic layer enables interoperability between the different layers of the architecture. It is based on our SmartHome ontology and an integrated knowledge base that form the basis for the recommender system. Ontologies are used in this study in order to enable semantic interoperability and inference as a basis for the recommendations and to enable knowledge sharing. The similarity metrics used for information retrieval in view of recommendations are ontology-based, i.e., the similarity is computed using an ontology graph, as illustrated in [9]. The ontology in this paper is expressed using owl^1 in order to ensure future ontology reuse. We are planning to identify and reuse existing relevant ontologies such as EBIO[2] or FOAF[3].

3.1   Ontology

The ontology used by the Smart Home application consists of five main categories: *home*, *resource*, *user*, *settings* and *action*. The core categories will be extended in the future, in order to cope with the complexity of the application. The *home* category

---

[1] https://www.w3.org/OWL/.

[2] ENTROPY Behavioural Intervention Ontology, http://entropy-project.eu.

[3] Friend-of-a-Friend, http://xmlns.com/foaf/spec/.

relates with categories room, device and appliance, as illustrated in Fig. 1. Every home disposes of several rooms. Every room is equipped with devices (i.e., sensors, cameras, smart plugs) and has household appliances installed (i.e., air conditioning, refrigerator, washing machine). There are three types of *resources* taken into account, i.e., electricity, water and gas. Resources are being measured by various metrics and are characterized by their price. The *user* is described by his personal information, his preferences and profile. The *user profile* describes the user preferred settings and user behavior as a resident and consumer. The user can have several modes: at home, away, night and vacation. The *settings* are done by the user and apply on the home and the resources. Examples of settings imply activating/deactivating the home devices and appliances based on specific conditions (e.g., while vacation mode is activated, activate motion sensor and alarm). *Action* can be performed on the home subcategories, and on the resources. Examples include activating/deactivating sensors and cameras, measuring temperature and humidity, turning home appliances on/off, switching between resources, measuring resource consumption, etc. Several actions compose a *scenario*. Examples of scenarios include monitoring consumption by appliance/group of appliances, flood, smoke, motion at the main entrance, etc. and the associated actions.

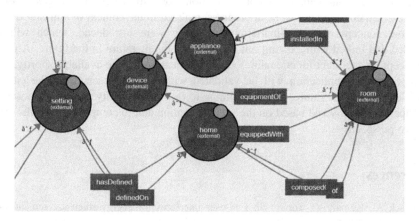

Fig. 1. Concept 'home' in the 'SmartHome' ontology, visualized with WebVOWL (http://vowl. visualdataweb.org/webvowl.html)

3.2   Recommendations

Of main importance are the *user profile* and the *scenario* concepts, as they are used as input to the web services in charge of recommending actions to take based on similar user profile. The web service receives in input a (partial of complete) user profile and returns various actions to take based on similarity metrics computed on user profiles stored in the knowledge base. Reversely, the web service takes in input a scenario or part of it (just actions) and returns contact details of users with similar profiles for the social media interactions, as discussed in Use case 1.

In Use case 2 described above, Ana is a user with a profile that falls under the 'economy' category. That means that resources are being saved regularly in Ana's house and the consumption prices are kept low all over the year. Therefore, when Ana asks for a recommendation in order to have the desired comfort when she returns from vacation while saving resources, the system works as follows: the web service is invoked with Ana's profile as input. The WS searches the knowledge base for profiles similar to Ana's, which fall under the 'economy' category. For the identified profiles, the WS performs a similarity check regarding the modes (i.e., for this specific case, mode is 'vacation'). Then it returns a list of actions (scenarios) to take for the most similar profiles. The web service is using ontology-based algorithms for data matching and similarity, as described in [9].

4   Conclusion

The paper proposes ongoing use cases and application for efficient resource consumption management in a Smart Home setting. The contribution of this work resides mainly in the semantic-enabled recommendations for resource consumption scenarios. The presented concepts are work in progress, realized in the context of a master thesis. The core concepts of our SmartHome ontology were introduced, which will be extended and linked with existing ontologies from the literature in the future. A proof of concept for the main functionalities of the application will be available shortly. The concept and the application will be validated with real end users from the city of Cluj-Napoca. For the future, we are planning to test the similarity metrics proposed in the paper technically and based on the user perception and to compare the results from the two perspectives.

References

1. Fensel, A., Kumar, V., Tomic, S.: End-user interfaces for energy-efficiency semantically enabled smart homes. Energy Effi. J. 7(4), 655–675 (2014)
2. Martinez-Gil, J.: Realistic user behavior modeling for energy saving in residential buildings. In: DEXA Workshops, pp. 121–125 (2014)
3. Tomic, S., Fensel, A., Schwanzer, M., Veljovic, M.K., Stefanovic, M.: Semantics for energy efficiency in smart home environments. In: Applied Semantic Web Technologies, chap. 16, pp. 429–454 (2012)
4. Fensel, A., Tomic, S., Kumar, V., Stefanovic, M., Aleshin, S., Novikov, D.: SESAME-S: Semantic Smart Home System for Energy Efficiency, Energieinformatik (2012)
5. Tang, Y., Ciuciu, I.: Semantic decision support models for energy efficiency in smart metered homes. In: Proceedings of 11th IEEE International Conference on Ubiquitous Computing and Communications, pp. 1777–1784, UK (2012)
6. Ciuciu, I., Meersman, R., Dillon, T.: Social network of smart-metered homes and SMEs for grid-based renewable energy exchange. In: Proceedings of IEEE International Conference on DEST-CEE, Italy (2012)
7. Stavropoulos, T.G., et al.: Rule-based approaches for energy savings in an ambient intelligence environment. Pervasive Mob. Comput. 19, 1–23 (2015)

8. Klein, L., et al.: Coordinating occupant behavior for building energy and comfort management using multi-agent systems. Autom. Constr. **22**, 525–536 (2012)
9. Tang, Y., Meersman, R., Ciuciu, I.G., Leenarts, E., Pudney, K.: Towards evaluating ontology based data matching strategies. In: Proceedings of 4th IEEE Research Challenges in Information Science (RCIS 2010), pp. 137–146, France (2010)

Towards Linking DBpedia's Bibliographic References to Bibliographic Repositories

David Nazarian and Nick Bassiliades(✉)

Department of Informatics, Aristotle University, Thessaloniki, Greece
{dnazarian,nbassili}@csd.auth.gr

Abstract. The widespread usage of semantic resources such as SPARQL endpoints and RDF data dumps by an ever growing number of users requires steps to be made in order to ensure the correctness of the provided data. DBpedia, a major node of the LOD cloud is a contributor of both types with its content deriving from Wikipedia. This paper presents our effort towards creating alternative links for the DBpedia's bibliographic references motivated by the "DBpedia citations & references challenge". We present the procedure of the link creation by utilizing a Java library that we have developed, called BibLinkCreator, which extracts data from the DBpedia's references RDF data dump provided during the competition, and other RDF data dumps (available for download or collected via APIs) relevant to bibliographic records, based on unique identifiers such as ISBN, and links citation URIs after matching identifiers and ensuring the similarity of other properties.

Keywords: Linking bibliographic references · Link discovery
Linked open data · Semantic web

1 Introduction

The web is evolving gradually into a machine-understandable platform through the introduction of semantics into it. From a Web of Documents, it is transforming into a Web of Data [1, 2] with a number of potential benefits for the users. Rich content is being made available by a variety of sources through RDF data dumps (datasets) and Simple Protocol and RDF Query Language (SPARQL) endpoints. The linking of such content creates a global data space [1, 3], a semantic cloud.

A huge amount of interconnected datasets are already available for free usage forming a cloud known as the Linked Open Data (LOD). Each of its nodes is a contribution of RDF content by individuals or organizations, linked to one or more datasets through RDF links. DBpedia, which extracts knowledge from Wikipedia, is one of its main nodes connected to a multitude of other through incoming and outgoing RDF links [4]. Many of these RDF datasets are made available by libraries from around the world providing metadata about digitized content such as books, serial publications (e.g. journals), maps, printed music and other library related material [2]. Such bibliographic datasets are being produced by mapping from existing library metadata standards such as the Machine-Readable Cataloging (MARC) and the Encoded Archival Description (EAD) [2].

© Springer International Publishing AG 2018
C. Debruyne et al. (Eds.): OTM 2017 Workshops, LNCS 10697, pp. 120–129, 2018.
https://doi.org/10.1007/978-3-319-73805-5_13

Since the content of the LOD cloud is changing constantly, some of its links may become obsolete, pointing either to outdated resources or to nonexistent ones. In order to ensure the correctness of the provided data, maintenance of the links is an important issue [1]. Providing alternative outgoing links for a source dataset is one way to increase its connectedness and ensure that other paths will exist for its pointed resources. Of course, the role of metadata about the temporal, provenance and trust dimensions of LOD should not be ignored.

This paper will present our effort towards creating alternative links for the DBpedia's references. For this purpose, we have created a Java Library that is capable of extracting and preprocessing data from pairs of RDF repositories, and linking them based on a combination of key-based and similarity-based approaches [3]. For the data extraction, we have used a number of unique identifiers, such as ISBN, ISSN, DOI, LCCN etc., as keys. A link is then created after ensuring the similarity of content such as identifier, title and publication year.

By using a number of link destination repositories, downloaded or created after collecting data through APIs, we managed to create 1,084,445 alternative links for the DBpedia's bibliographic references, with 761,235 corresponding to distinct URIs.

The paper is organized as follows: Sect. 2 discusses about related work done by the Semantic Web community, Sect. 3 presents details about the source and destination RDF data dumps downloaded or collected via APIs, Sect. 4 describes the Bib-LinkCreator library that we developed in order to create the links, Sect. 5 presents the link creation results, and Sect. 6 presents our conclusions and future steps.

2   Related Work

Although our main intention was the creation of links for the DBpedia's bibliographic references, it also led us to the development of a domain-specific bibliographic link creator library called BibLinkCreator which relies mainly on bibliographical identifiers. The use of such identifiers to link data is a common practice. An example of an application which exploits them is the RDF Book Mashup, which uses APIs from sources such as Amazon, Google and Yahoo in order to integrate information into Semantic Web. For this purpose, it uses the ISBN or the author name encoded into a URI sent during a lookup call to query data sources [5].

There are many applications in which domain-specific data are collected and merged or linked in order to provide an easier way of access to information. URank is an application that collects data from various web sites containing information about university rankings, uniquely identifies the University entities by linking them to DBpedia LOD set and constructs a merged University ranking dataset [6]. The author in [7] presents an approach to create an active Linked Life Sciences Data Compendium which dynamically assembles queries retrieving data from multiple SPARQL endpoints, in order to easily navigate through different datasets.

Many link discovery frameworks have been developed and are available to facilitate the linking of datasets [8]. KnoFuss, LIMES and Silk are some of the well-known ones which include diverse capabilities. They are universal, not specific to a domain and incorporate different algorithms to reduce the search space for a given task.

3   Bibliographic Resources Used

Throughout the paper, the terms references and citations will be used interchangeably referring to the same concept. For the task of linking DBpedia's bibliographic references we used as a link source, the enwiki-20160305-citation-data[1] RDF data dump file provided during the "DBpedia citations & references challenge"[2] containing extracted metadata related to citation URIs from the English version articles of Wikipedia. In the majority of cases these URIs are actual web addresses (URLs) pointing to the cited resources. RDF data dumps and APIs providing the link destinations were chosen after analyzing the structure of the link source, and determining the portion of the citations for which an alternative link can be found. A total of five RDF data dumps and five APIs providing bibliographic record information about books, journals, periodicals, magazines etc. were chosen.

The greater portion of the citation URIs contained in the link source either refers to resources for which an alternative link does not exist or is difficult to be found. By alternative, we mean a content describing the same thing found elsewhere (in a different URI) not a related content. For example, there are many cases when a citation is being made to a website of an individual presenting his or her work which has not been published elsewhere and consequently no alternative link can exist. Many citations are being made to content such as YouTube videos not published elsewhere, or even to newspaper articles for which an alternative cannot be found easily. These reasons made us to concentrate on the portion of the link source which contains citations to bibliographic records available from many sources.

3.1   Link Source RDF Data Dump

As mentioned earlier the enwiki-20160305-citation-data file was used as a link source for the citations. It contains 97,468,830 triples which are reduced to 76,223,926 because of duplicates after inserting the file into a triplestore. The subjects of all the triples represent citation URIs with the majority of them (70.636.663 triples) representing actual URLs pointing to the cited resources, and the rest pointing to non-dereferenceable links of citation.dbpedia.org. There are 12,391,363 distinct citation subject URIs of different categories.

In order to distinguish which predicates are important and can be used during link creation, we sorted them by their counts and selected for examination the ones that had multiplicity greater than 5,000, since there are 3,620 predicates in total. From the 148 that resulted, only 16 predicates relevant to bibliography were selected for further examination as shown in Table 1. There are cases when a subject contains more than one of these predicates simultaneously.

A search was conducted for each predicate and based on availability in online libraries and other criteria, only 11 of them were eventually selected. The predicates that were rejected are the following: newspaper, pmc, bibcode, jstor and encyclopedia.

---

[1] http://downloads.dbpedia.org/temporary/citations/enwiki-20160305-citation-data.ttl.bz2.

[2] http://wiki.dbpedia.org/blog/dbpedia-citations-references-challenge.

Table 1. Bibliography relevant properties and their counts.

	Property name	Count		Property name	Count
1	journal	998,460	9	oclc	48,463
2	newspaper	664,742	10	issn	46,265
3	isbn	646,153	11	jstor	30,968
4	doi	584,056	12	magazine	27,833
5	pmid	347,067	13	encyclopedia	24,244
6	series	85,953	14	periodical	13,992
7	pmc	76,546	15	arxiv	13,624
8	bibcode	56,518	16	lccn	5,689

From the selected predicates, seven of them (isbn, issn, doi, pmid, oclc, arxiv and lccn) represent unique identifiers and the rest (journal, series, magazine and periodical) refer to titles of serial publications. The description of each identifier is given below:

- International Standard Book Number (ISBN): A code that uniquely identifies each edition of a book. Two forms exist, the ISBN10 and the ISBN13. A conversion algorithm exists in order to convert an ISBN10 to an ISBN13.
- International Standard Serial Number (ISSN): An eight-digit code that uniquely identifies a serial publication such as a journal, a magazine etc. To each successive edition of the serial publication, the same ISSN is assigned.
- Digital Object Identifier (DOI): A unique identifier that is assigned to a variety of things such as books, websites, articles etc. It is a string consisted of two parts, a prefix and a suffix separated by a forward slash.
- PubMed identifier (PMID): A sequentially assigned integer number to content that can be queried and retrieved via the PubMed search engine.
- Online Computer Library Center (OCLC) control number: A sequentially assigned integer number to records of WorldCat.
- ArXiv identifier: A unique identifier assigned to content submitted to arXiv.org.
- Library of Congress Control Number (LCCN): A unique identifier assigned to records of the United States Library of Congress.

3.2   Link Destination RDF Data Dumps/APIs

Five link destination RDF Data Dump files were selected after the examination of the content provided by a number of libraries and bibliography relevant sources. We discovered many of these files through the datahub[3] website which hosts information about a multitude of datasets, and through searching for RDF content directly from different publishers and libraries.

In order for a file to be selected, a part of its content had to be described through one or many unique identifiers such as those described in Sect. 3.1, and had to have dereferenceable subject URIs. There are many libraries providing a rich RDF content

---

[3] https://datahub.io.

but lacking an identifier such as an ISBN. For example, TEL[4] (The European Library) which allows online access to resources of many European national libraries provides its RDF content based on an ontology that lacks a property related to ISBN, even though it contains information about books. There are also cases of libraries whose content is provided without dereferenceable URIs and consequently a link cannot be created by using them. Eventually we selected data dumps provided by DBLP, Springer, **B**iblioteca **N**acional de **E**spaña (BNE), **B**ritish **N**ational **B**ibliography (BNB) and **D**eutsche **N**ationalbibliografie (DNB).

There are many bibliography-related websites that provide their material through APIs in different serializations and formats, allowing individual or groups of items to be queried in most of the cases through unique identifiers, keywords or by other search criteria. Each website has its own policy in regard to the terms that apply to its API usage. Consequently, there can be limitations on the number of daily requests made, the number of items that can be queried in a single request, the interval between consecutive requests and other parameters. Although usually the provided content is not in a semantic form, it can be mapped to vocabularies in order to incorporate them into semantic applications.

Five APIs were selected based on a number of criteria such as, the types of the unique identifiers that could be queried, their limitations, their content, their responsiveness etc. We discovered many of them through a list of APIs[5] provided by MIT Libraries and through searching directly from publishers. Four of these are as described previously, and one of them provides data about individual items directly in different semantic forms. The selected link destination API providers are: arXiv, HathiTrust, Open Library, PubMed and WorldCat.

4 Bibliographic Link Creator Library

For the purpose of citation linking, a Java library called BibLinkCreator[6] (Bibliographic Link Creator) was developed. It is a domain-specific library which can be used to link URIs from any pair of bibliographic RDF datasets, if they contain metadata about unique identifiers such as those described in Sect. 3.1, titles and publication years (optional in some cases). In order to communicate with these datasets which must be stored in a triplestore,[7] it utilizes the Sesame API. Its main functionality is provided through a data extractor and a data linker class which are described below.

The abstract link creation procedure comprised of data extraction from two repositories (sources) followed by the data linking is illustrated in Fig. 1. The source X represents the repository providing the subject URIs of the links, while the source Y represents the repository providing the object URIs of the links. The parameters provided to the Data Extractor represent other inputs, such as SPARQL queries,

---

[4] http://www.theeuropeanlibrary.org.

[5] http://libguides.mit.edu/apis.

[6] https://github.com/DavidNazarian/BibLinkCreator.

[7] We have used the Ontotext GraphDB 7 Free edition http://ontotext.com/products/graphdb.

user-defined string replacement data etc. The identifier and data collection steps include their preprocessing and validation. The identifier set C represents the distinct identifiers that are present in both repositories.

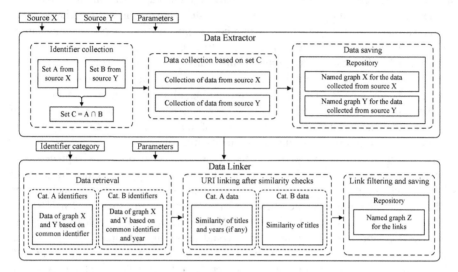

Fig. 1. Abstract link creation procedure.

The data saved by the Data Extractor is used by the Data Linker for the link creation. The identifier category determines the query category that will be used in order to retrieve data from the two sources and the similarity checks that will be employed. The parameters provided to the Data Linker include inputs such as source repository names (aliases), the string similarity thresholds, the year maximum absolute difference threshold etc.

4.1   Data Extractor

Since data from different sources can differ even though they describe the same entities, a mechanism is needed in order to make them uniform. The data extractor's main purpose is to extract, preprocess, validate and save specific data from the provided semantic repositories, which will be later used by the data linker for the link creation. There are three categories of data that are being extracted, unique identifiers, titles and publication years.

Unique identifiers depending on their structure may be converted in other forms and may be validated if a validation algorithm exists for them. For example, preprocessing and validation steps for an extracted ISBN are the following:

1. Hyphens and other non-numeric characters are removed, except the letter x.
2. Then, it is checked for validity based on the ISBN algorithm and is kept or rejected accordingly.
3. If it represents an ISBN10 then it is converted to an ISBN13 because there are cases when the same ISBN is represented with different forms in different sources.

Extracted titles are strings representing the titles of books, specific editions of serial publications etc., which may contain letters (upper- and lower-case), numbers, and punctuation marks such as brackets, quotation marks, dashes and other. Since the same title can be present in different sources with different capitalization rules and with alternative punctuation marks, the preprocessing step converts all of their characters to lowercase and removes from them a number of punctuation marks (leaving single spaces between words). A 0-length resulting string is considered invalid.

Extracted publication years represent the years when books, specific editions of serial publications and other works were published. Usually they are provided either as a string, a date or a gYear. During the preprocessing, all the non-numeric characters are removed from a string representation of the year, whereas from a date representation of year, only the year is kept, resulting in a string of four digits in both cases. A resulting string of length different than four is considered invalid.

The default preprocessing steps for each of these data categories can be preceded by user-defined string replacements. Sometimes this is necessary for removing parts of strings which if not removed can lead to corrupted results or as a step to increase the quality of the data. For example, there are cases when a prefix such as "ISBN10:" or "ISBN13:" exists in front of ISBN strings. If not removed, the default preprocessing (described previously by the three steps) would leave an undesired "10" or "13" in them leading to invalid ISBNs. To prevent it, a string replacement list containing both of these prefixes would ensure that they are replaced, for instance by an empty string.

In order to extract the three kinds of data described previously (identifiers, titles and publication years), a SPARQL query for each of the data sources is employed. Each query must expose a number of variables with specific names or aliases. There are two query categories depending on the identifier involved during the data extraction. The first (category-A) includes those that identify a specific bibliographical item, such as a book, and the second (category-B) includes those that identify a range of biblio-graphical items, such as a journal.

The identifiers extracted from the link source repository (set A in Fig. 1) are used to filter the data that will be extracted from the link destination repository (set B in Fig. 1), thus only absolutely relevant data are extracted (set C in Fig. 1).

4.2 Data Linker

The purpose of the data linker is to link URIs from two sources (identified as X and Y in Fig. 1) based on the similarity of identifiers, titles and years, by using a provided URI representing the type of the link, such as owl:sameAs [9], rdfs:seeAlso [10] etc. The data of the two sources are retrieved from the repository where the extracted data were saved. Depending on the identifier used to retrieve the data, there are two pre-defined SPARQL query categories directly corresponding to the ones described in the previous section.

The first category (category-A) data are retrieved from the two sources by using a common unique identifier variable name. This results into retrieving only the data accompanied with matched identifiers from both sources. The second category (category-B) data are retrieved from the two sources by using a common identifier and a common year variable name for both sources. This ensures that only editions of serial publications published during the same year are retrieved from both sources, since there are cases when the same title is being reused for editions of different years (e.g. recurrent conferences).

The usage of identifiers alone to link the data proved to be insufficient, because there are cases when by human error they are assigned to irrelevant URIs. These kinds of errors are considerably higher in datasets produced by community effort. Identifiers combined with titles and years ensure that the metadata of the two sources are relevant to each other and increase confidence on the correctness of the result.

The string similarity measures that have been incorporated into the library, to compare the titles are the Jaccard, Dice, Overlap and Cosine coefficient [11]. All of them take as an input two strings, and return a real number ranging from 0 (no similarity) to 1 (absolute similarity). They can be parameterized in regard to the string segmentation type which will be used to create the comparison sets for each input.

To compare the titles retrieved by the category-B queries, a stricter threshold should be used in contrary to those of the category-A. This is because, even different editions of serial publications published during the same year and identified by the same ISSN can have very similar titles. For example, "The History of Poland" and the "The History of Portugal" are different editions of the "The Greenwood Histories of the Modern Nations" (ISSN 1096-2905) both published in the year 2000, and have very similar titles. A low threshold would wrongly deem these different titles similar, whereas a high threshold would correctly differentiate them.

After data from the two sources have been found to refer to the same entity, the last step before the link creation is to check whether the subject and object URIs of the created links are different. For URIs referring to doi.org, there is an optional capability of resolving their redirected addresses in order to ensure that even after the redirection the URIs remain different. This is done by retrieving metadata[8] from doi.org in JSON format which contain the redirection information.

5   Results

By utilizing the BibLinkCreator library, we managed to create 1,084,445 alternative links for the DBpedia's bibliographic references with 761,235 corresponding to distinct subjects. This covers $761,235/12,391,363 = 6.14\%$ of the distinct subjects found in the entire file and $761,235/1,719,223 = 44.3\%$ of the distinct subjects that contain one of the 11 selected predicates described in Sect. 3.1. Notice that although the coverage seems to be small, the majority of the uncovered links are not about bibliographic references but other stuff, such as YouTube videos, newspaper articles, etc., as mentioned in Sect. 3. In order to have more accurate results, we excluded the subjects containing a "chapter" predicate, because usually its presence indicates that a subject URI is referring to a specific chapters of bibliographical item, and thus cover $761,235/1,646,484 = 46.23\%$.

---

[8] http://www.doi.org/factsheets/DOIProxy.html.

For the link category-A, we used the Overlap coefficient as a string similarity measure, parameterized with a threshold $\geq 80\%$ for the title comparisons, when year data have been retrieved, and $\geq 90\%$ otherwise. The years have been compared with 1-year maximum absolute difference threshold. For the link category-B, the Dice coefficient, which is equivalent to the F1 score, has been used with a threshold $\geq 97\%$ for the title comparisons. Both similarity coefficients have been parameterized with character level shingles of $k = 2$. We chose those parameter values by experimenting with different string similarity measures, thresholds, shingle types and shingle sizes, but mostly taking into account the nature of the data.

The accuracy of the results cannot be evaluated using automated methods since URL content comparisons are involved. A sampling of the results showed that inaccuracies are negligible relative to the number of the links found and are largely due to inaccurate metadata of the DBpedia's citations. Proportionally, the majority of inaccuracies occur in the category-B links, because of cases when a URI describing a serial publication is provided instead of a URI describing a specific edition of that serial publication, even though the provided metadata describe the specific edition.

As a predicate for the created links we have used rdfs:seeAlso instead of owl:sameAs because (a) it is more "safe" considering the uncertainties that can exist in the results, (b) because there are links pointing to metadata URIs and (c) because the resources involved in the link creation from the two sources do not share all the same properties as needed for owl:sameAs [9, 12]. The created links are available to be queried through different named graphs from a SPARQL endpoint.[9]

6   Conclusions and Future Work

We have presented our effort towards the link creation procedure for the bibliographic references of DBpedia which is one of the main nodes of the LOD cloud by utilizing a bibliographic link creator library called BibLinkCreator that we developed for this purpose. A combination of key-based and similarity-based approaches were used, because of errors present in the data or the sources.

Future work can include the use of more link destination data sources (RDF data dumps and APIs) in order to create new links, using already existing links in the metadata of the destination data sources to increase the number of alternative links, the incorporation of the ability to use SPARQL endpoints and other communication APIs such as Jena to retrieve data, and the incorporation of Machine Learning techniques in order to reduce the user effort into specifying the parameters needed for the two link categories discussed in the Sect. 4.2. Finally, a proper evaluation for accuracy and completeness should be performed by crowdsourcing methods, as well as a comparison with general-purpose tools, such as Silk, LIMES, etc., in order to be used as a baseline of comparison for the performance of our tool.

---

[9] http://lod.csd.auth.gr:7200/sparql.

References

1. Bizer, C., Heath, T., Berners-Lee, T.: Linked data - the story so far. IJSWIS **5**(3), 1–22 (2009)
2. Godby, C.J., Wang, S., Mixter, J.K.: Library Linked Data in the Cloud: OCLC's Experiments with New Models of Resource Description. Morgan & Claypool, San Rafael (2015)
3. Heath, T., Bizer, C.: Linked Data: Evolving the Web into a Global Data Space. Morgan & Claypool, San Rafael (2011)
4. Lehmann, J., Isele, R., Jakob, M., Jentzsch, A., Kontokostas, D., Mendes, P.N., Hellmann, S., Morsey, M., van Kleef, P., Auer, S., Bizer, C.: DBpedia – a large-scale, multilingual knowledge base extracted from wikipedia. Semant. Web **6**(2), 167–195 (2015)
5. Bizer, C., Cyganiak, R., Gauß, T.: The RDF book mashup: from web APIs to a web of data. In: Auer, S., Bizer, C., Heath, T., Aastrand Grimnes, G. (eds.) SFSW 2007, vol. 248, CEUR Workshop Proceedings, Aachen (2007)
6. Bassiliades, N.: Collecting university rankings for comparison using web extraction and entity linking techniques. In: Ermolayev, V., Mayr, H.C., Nikitchenko, M., Spivakovsky, A., Zholtkevych, G. (eds.) ICTERI 2014, vol. 469. Springer, Heidelberg (2014). https://doi.org/10.1007/978-3-319-13206-8_2
7. Hasnain, A.: Improving discovery in life sciences linked open data cloud. In: Ciravegna, F., Vidal, M.E. (eds.) ISWC 2015, vol. 1491, CEUR Workshop Proceedings, Aachen (2015)
8. Nentwig, M., Hartung, M., Ngonga Ngomo, A.C., Rahm, E.: A survey of current link discovery frameworks. Semant. Web **8**(3), 419–436 (2017)
9. Halpin, H., Hayes, P.J.: When owl: same as isn't the same: an analysis of identity links on the semantic web. In: Bizer, C., Berners-Lee, T., Hausenblas, M. (eds.) LDOW 2010, vol. 628, CEUR Workshop Proceedings, Aachen (2010)
10. Matinfar, F., Nematbakhsh, M.: Specializing RDFS: see also in semantic web. In: IJWesT 2012, vol. 3, no. 1, AIRCC, Chennai (2012)
11. Manning, C.D., Schütze, H.: Foundations of Statistical Natural Language Processing. MIT Press, Cambridge (1999)
12. Jaffri, A., Glaser, H., Millard, I.C.: Managing URI synonymity to enable consistent reference on the semantic web. In: Bouquet, P., Halpin, H., Stoermer, H., Tummarello, G. (eds.) IRSW 2008, vol. 422, CEUR Workshop Proceedings, Aachen (2008)

International Workshop on Fact Based Modeling (FBM) 2017

FBM 2017 PC Chair's Message

The FBM 2017 workshop gives insight into the professional application of Fact Based Modeling in government and business practice. Our main theme for this workshop is versatility in conceptual modeling. For FBM 2017, 10 high quality papers were selected for presentation including 2 invited papers on ontology and agile enterprise design. We congratulate the authors of these contributions. FBM 2017 will be centered around the presentation of practice reports and theoretical papers on Fact Based Modeling. The focus of this year's workshop will once again be on versatility of the fact-based approach for conceptualizing knowledge in a broad range of domains, i.e. financial and insurances services, engineering, governmental agencies, by offering modeling protocols that are tailored to such a domain.

For regulation based services there are currently research groups that have as objective to design and test out a protocol how to produce the complete and IT-independent specifications for regulation based services. One paper at this workshop is dedicated to an IT- independent reference model for these types of services. Another paper will present the role of states and transitions in IT-supported, interactive, regulation based services.

Within the context of requirements modeling a paper on grounded enterprise modeling will be presented and another paper will discuss the issues related to the requirements for regulatory services.

The first day of the workshop will be concluded by an invited presentation on ontology dependency relationships that deliver an empirically-founded semantic normal form by Prof. Ronald Stamper.

The first presentation session of the 2nd day of the workshop will be on the application of Fact Based Modeling on law and legal code.

In the second paper session of the second day, a paper on FBM as a mandatory subject in a knowledge engineering master program will be presented. Furthermore, a paper that gives a FBM model of the ISO cloud computing architecture will be presented.

The paper sessions will be completed by the 2nd invited paper on Agile Enterprise Design by Klaas Meijer.

The 2nd day of the workshop will be concluded by an open discussion on the future of FBM chaired by Maurice Nijssen.

October 2017

Robert Meersman
Peter Bollen
Hans Mulder
Maurice Nijssen

Fact Based Modeling as Mandatory Subject in the First Year of a Knowledge Engineering Program

Peter Bollen[(✉)]

Maastricht University, Maastricht, The Netherlands
p.bollen@maastrichtuniversity.nl

Abstract. In this paper we discuss the introduction of a course on fact-based modeling in the first year of the bachelor program Knowledge Engineering at Maastricht University. We will discuss the course built-up and the course assessment.

1 Introduction

Since 1993 Maastricht University has a bachelor program on Knowledge Engineering. In the first year of this program students will be introduced to subjects like *computer science, discrete mathematics, knowledge representation and cognitive psychology, linear algebra, calculus, data structures and algorithms, logic, numerical mathematics* and *software engineering*. In the academic year 2016/2017 students have been introduced to the concepts of fact-based modeling in the newly designed course *ICT and Knowledge Management*.

2 Knowledge Management Approaches

Knowledge Management studies how organizations can manage, retain and exploit their knowledge resources. Having insight in its knowledge is important for an organization because the world changes rapidly and therefore organizations have to be able to respond to that change in an ever increasing pace. The amount of knowledge grows but this doesn't mean that this growing amount of knowledge is accessible at all times. Knowledge in many cases is bound to individual persons, making organizations more and more dependent on these individuals. For an ever growing number of organizations, the intellectual capital of an organization determines the value of that organization.

Knowledge is a fundamental prerequisite in the ability of a person to execute a task. This ability consists of explicit knowledge or information, implicit knowledge or experiences, skills and attitudes.

Knowledge can be analyzed from different perspectives, depending on which element in the definition the emphasis is placed. In knowledge management, basically three dominant approaches exist:

C. Debruyne et al. (Eds.): OTM 2017 Workshops, LNCS 10697, pp. 133–140, 2018.
https://doi.org/10.1007/978-3-319-73805-5_14

– The *ICT approach (or technocratic school* [1]*)*, with focus on making knowledge explicit and structuring the knowledge in such a way that the knowledge can be objectively shared.
– The *Economic school,* with focus to see knowledge as an asset [1].
– The *Behavioral school* [1], with focus on providing means to stimulate the pooling and exchange of knowledge.

Independently of the approach, *the aim of knowledge management is expliciting the relevant knowledge to the highest possible extent.* In the knowledge engineering course *ICT and Knowledge Management* we have focused on the first approach (the ICT approach) in which we also clearly make a link to other courses in the first year of the bachelor of Knowledge Engineering. Knowledge Management is an integral approach for the identification, the structuring, the sharing and evaluation of knowledge in the organization.

The educational goal of a course on ICT and Knowledge Management is to provide the knowledge engineering students the basic tools for capturing *fact types, integrity rules, concept definitions, derivation rules* and *business processes.*

3   The Modeling of Knowledge in the Course ICT and Knowledge Management

In this course the identification and structuring of knowledge is considered as a modeling process that will result in models that represent the structure of the knowledge. The knowledge model that has been used in this course consists of 4 dimensions: *Data, Semantics, Rules* and *Processes.*

Table 1. Content of sessions/tutorials

Session	Content
Session 1: Knowledge management 1	Introduction to 4 dimensions Knowledge Management: Importance of modeling
Session 2: Tutorial	Data, semantics and integrity rules 1
Session 3: Knowledge management 2	More Integrity rules
Session 4: Tutorial	Data, semantics and integrity rules 2
Session 5: Knowledge management 3	Derivation rules and DMN[a]
Session 6: Tutorial	Integrity rules and derivation rules
Session 7: Mid-term test	
Session 8: Tutorial	Integrity rules and DMN
Session 9: Knowledge management 4	BPMN[b]
Session 10: Tutorial	BPMN and Data
Session 11: Tutorial	BPMN and data and derivation rules
Session 12: Tutorial	Application to laws and regulations

[a]DMN stands for Decision Model and Notation. DMN is an OMG standard for modeling structured decisions in organizations an make them interchangeable [2].
[b]BPMN stands for Business Process Model and Notation. BPMN is an Omg standard that will facilitate the description and understanding of business processes within and between organizations [3].

In the course *ICT and Knowledge Management* a variety of educational formats is used. It is a combination of lectures in which the theory is presented and illustrated by exercises and cases, and tutorials in which students are expected to have prepared exercises and small case studies. During the tutorial sessions, feedback on the exercises and case studies is provided. During the tutorial hands-on explanations with respect to the case studies is provided. In the *lectures* and *problem based tutorials* the focus is on the given dimensions one by one first and gradually those perspectives will be integrated in application exercises and cases. In Table 1 an outline of the content for the lectures/sessions is given [4].

4 The Content of the Lectures and Tutorial Sessions

4.1 Session 1 (Lecture): Introduction to 4 Dimensions Knowledge Management: Importance of Modeling

In the course we demonstrated that a knowledge specification consists of 4 dimensions, namely: *data*, *semantics*, *processes* and *rules*, that form an integrated whole. The integration of these dimensions within the context of Knowledge Management can be depicted clearly by means of the *knowledge triangle* (see Fig. 1).

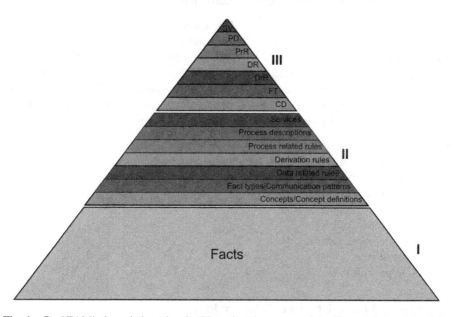

Fig. 1. CogNIAM's knowledge triangle (Note that the names of the 'layers' in level 3 of the knowledge triangle are abbreviated. Their full description can be found on the corresponding color 'slice' of level 2)

During the first session we have focused on the data dimensions by introducing a framework and protocol for developing these model dimensions. The lecture ended with a perspective on the integration: how are the 4 dimensions related to each other, and provide some insight on the dependencies between them.

The following steps of the CogNIAM modelling protocol were introduced and explained during the first lecture:

Step 1: Verbalise
Step 2: Denote variable and constant parts
Step 3: Qualification of variables
Step 4: Identification of concepts
Step 5: Generalization towards fact type forms and fact types
Step 6: Adding Uniqueness rules

4.2 Session 2 (Tutorial): Data, Semantics and Data Related Rules 1

In this session the students were expected to have prepared a number of (modeling) exercises and they were asked to hand-in the workouts of these tasks at the beginning of the tutorial. The students were asked to derive level I and the first three layers of level II of the knowledge triangle by applying the CogNIAM modelling protocol on some 'scaled-down' real-life (business) examples. In terms of integrity rules only *uniqueness* rules needed to be derived.

4.3 Session 3 (Lecture): More Data-Related Rules

One of the important elements of the data dimension are the data-related integrity rules that ensure that the data specified are useful and correct. In this session, we have discussed and applied the protocol for deriving additional data-related rules. The semantic dimension of the knowledge model specifies the meaning of concepts, how concept definitions can be formed, and we have introduced a maturity model for determining the quality of such a concept definition structure. In this lecture we have extended the CogNIAM protocol with further modeling steps 7 and 8:

Step 7: Add other integrity rules:
  • Set comparison rules: subset, equality, exclusion
  • Mandatory (non-empty) rule
  • Value rule
  • Occurrence frequency rule
  • Non-overlap rule
  • Value comparison rule
  • General rule
Step 8: Define concepts

4.4 Session 4 (Tutorial): More Integrity Rules

In this session the students were asked to have prepared an additional number of tasks. These tasks were worked on during the tutorial, by asking students to come forward and present their solutions. That served as a starting point for the instructional process in which in a tutorial class-room setting (maximally 15 students) the educational process will lead to an agreed solution.

4.5 Session 5 (Lecture): Derivation Rules and DMN

The third dimension of the complete knowledge model is the rules dimension, in particular the *derivation rules*. *Derivation rules* define the way how new facts are determined from existing facts. One of the major types of derivation rules that is of importance for an organization's agility are the decision rules. In this lecture we have focused on *DMN (decision modeling notation)* the standard for modeling decision rules. The session ended with a perspective on the integration: how are the 4 dimensions related to each other, and the dependencies between them. Furthermore, we have introduced step 9 of the CogNIAM modeling protocol: Derive derivation rules.

4.6 Session 6 (Tutorial): Integrity Rules and Derivation Rules

In this session the students were once again asked to have prepared a number of tasks. These tasks were worked on during the tutorial, by asking students to come forward and present their solutions. This once again served as a starting point for the instructional process in which in a tutorial class-room setting (maximally 15 students) the process will lead to an agreed solution. In this session the types of cases were of an integrated nature in which all steps of the modeling protocol needed to be applied on these integrated knowledge domain exercises and case studies.

4.7 Session 7: Mid-Term Test

This was a 2 h open book test on the subjects from sessions 1, 2, 3, 4, 5 and 6 and accounts for 40% in the final grading of the course.

4.8 Session 8 (Tutorial): Integrity Rules and DMN

In this session the students were once again asked to have prepared a number of tasks. These tasks were once again used in the tutorial, by asking students to come forward and present their solutions. This as a starting point for the instructional process. In this session the types of cases were of an integrated nature in which all steps of the modeling protocol needed to be applied. During the teaching of the course it turned out that the initial exercises for session 4 and 6 were of such a level, that it was decided to use the respective sessions as guiding sessions in which (significant) parts of the work-outs were presented and internalized, and hence the final complete work-out was postponed till the following tutorial session.

4.9 Session 9 (Lecture): BPMN

This lecture was focused on the fourth dimension of the knowledge management framework: (business) processes. Until this session the CogNIAM modeling protocol had been applied to model the *data, semantics* and *integrity rules* of a subject domain. It was also shown that in certain application domains derived fact types play an important role and hence, we have introduced the DMN standard that allowed us to easily model relatively complex derivation rules. The focus of this lecture was on the *business process* dimension and the accompanying process description and process related rules in level II of the *knowledge triangle*. We have introduced the business process modeling constructs and notation as laid down in the BPMN standard. A business process defines the order in which activities are performed, by whom they are performed, which decisions are made and what events influence this order. In CogNIAM, the prescriptions of the activities and decisions are expressed using exchange rules and derivation rules. In this session we have introduced a best practice, covering a subset of the BPMN symbols and introducing a structured way of working for modeling business processes with BPMN.

4.10   Session 10 (Tutorial): BPMN and Data

In this tutorial the integrated CogNIAM protocol for process and data modelling has been applied (steps 1 through 9 in Sect. 4 and the BPMN protocol). The modeling results will consist of a CogNIAM data model and the accompanying (excerpts of) a BPMN model. In this session the students were expected to have prepared a number of integrated tasks and they have finalized s set of tasks that were introduced in the tutorial of session 8 and were only partly discussed in session 8.

4.11   Sessions 11 and 12: Application to Laws and Regulations

In this final tutorial the knowledge triangle was applied (steps 1 through 9 in Sect. 4 and the BPMN protocol) in the context of regulations. As an example the regulation 261.2004 of the European commission on compensation and assistance to passengers in the event of denied boarding, flight cancellations or long delays of flights has been used to apply the modeling protocol on all 4 dimensions: *Data, Semantics, Rules* and *Processes*.

5   Assessment and Attendance for the Course ICT and Knowledge Management

In order to pass this block the following requirements should have been met: fulfilling presence requirement, a grade for the final exam on ICT and Knowledge Management in the exam period that is at least a 5.0 and sufficient participation in the 7 tutorials of the course.

The final grade for the block is composed as follows: Mid-term test in week 3 (relative weight 40%), participation in the tutorials (relative weight 20%) and the result of the final exam (relative weight 40%).

5.1   Example of Assessment

In this section an example is given of an exam question in which students have to assess a description of a use case and evaluate which fact type and integrity rule is applicable.

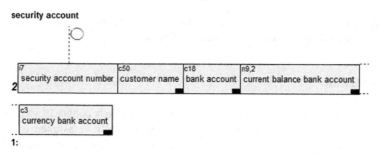

security account

1:

2: Security account <security account number> belongs to customer <customer name>
3: Security account <security account number> is attached to bank account <bank account>.
4: The current balance of the bank account security account <security account number> is attached to is <current balance bank account> <currency bank account>.

Question 1.1

An integrity constraint applies to the security type as shown in the fact type diagram 'security' (marked with a '1.'). Which integrity rules applies? Choose the symbol associated with this rule from the options below.

a) ⓘ   b) ⊕   c) ⓒ

d) ⓘ   e) ⊜   f) no integrity rule applies

In the mid-term exam the focus was on the *data*, *semantics* and *integrity rules*. In the final exam this was extended with the *derivation rules* and *processes*.

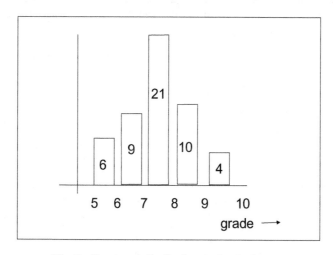

Fig. 2. Frequency distribution grades final exam

5.2   Grade Distribution for Final Exam

In Fig. 2 we have shown the frequency distribution of the grades for the final exam. A perfect normal distribution with a mean of around 7.5.

6   Conclusion

The course on ICT and knowledge management for this year's cohort 1st year students for the bachelor in Knowledge Engineering has been totally redesigned in order to cover all relevant aspects of data, semantics, rules and processes. A few lessons that we have learned from the course evaluations is that the mid-term and final test should be more in line with the type of exercises and case study that is used during instruction. This year we had for most subjects, questions in a multiple-choice format. These questions were created in a way that it took students a long time to read each of the 8 answering options and compare the options as a kind of 'find-the-difference' exercise. Furthermore, the educational material will be changed in order to make it more challenging for this type of student, by creating smaller exercises in terms of volume but at the same time make them more interesting by adding additional complexity in the use cases and henceforth looking for more challenging domains in which Knowledge Management can be applied.

References

1. Earl, M.: Knowledge management strategies: toward a taxonomy. J. Manag. Inf. Syst. **18**(1), 215–233 (2001)
2. OMG, Documents associated with DMN (2016). http://www.omg.org/spec/DMN/1.1/PDF
3. OMG, Documents associated with BPMN (2011). http://www.omg.org/spec/BPMN/2.0/
4. Maastricht University. Course manual: 1.4 ICT and Knowledge Management (2017)

Towards Grounded Enterprise Modelling

Henderik A. Proper[1,4,5]([✉]), Marija Bjeković[1], Bas van Gils[2],
and Stijn J. B. A. Hoppenbrouwers[3,4]

[1] Luxembourg Institute of Science and Technology (LIST),
Belval, Esch-sur-Alzette, Luxembourg
`e.proper@acm.org, marija.bjekovic@list.lu`
[2] Strategy Alliance, Lelystad, The Netherlands
`bas.vangils@strategy-alliance.com`
[3] HAN University of Applied Sciences, Arnhem, The Netherlands
`stijn.hoppenbrouwers@han.nl`
[4] Radboud University Nijmegen, Nijmegen, The Netherlands
[5] University of Luxembourg, Luxembourg City, Luxembourg

Abstract. This paper is concerned with the concept of grounding enterprise models in terms of an underlying fact-based model, as a way to add more meaning to these enterprise models. We motivate the need for doing so in terms of a fundamental understanding of conceptual modelling, and enterprise modelling in particular. We also clarify why, next to e.g. adding more meaning by using formal semantics, or mapping the model to a foundational ontology, it remains important to ground enterprise models on fact-based models that capture the natural way in which people converse about/in their domain. The presented concepts are illustrated by means of a running example, while also reflecting on, and summarising, the results of earlier experiments in grounding different enterprise models.

1 Introduction

Conceptual models, in their many different purpose and/or domain specific variations, play an increasingly important role in society. From conceptual database designs, via ontologies, domain models, process models, and actor models, to enterprise models in general, models are increasingly first class citizens in the organisations using them. Such models are not created as mere "one off" artefacts. They rather have a life of their own, covering a broad range of uses (from analysis and understanding, via simulation and design, to execution and monitoring), while involving an even broader variety of stakeholders/audiences.

This work has been partially sponsored by the *Fonds National de la Recherche Luxembourg* (www.fnr.lu), via the ValCoLa and CoBALab projects.

C. Debruyne et al. (Eds.): OTM 2017 Workshops, LNCS 10697, pp. 141–151, 2018.
https://doi.org/10.1007/978-3-319-73805-5_15

In this paper, we take the perspective that conceptual models should (unless they only serve a temporary "throw away" purpose) include a definition of their meaning[1] in a way that is understandable to the model's audience. We therefore posit that a conceptual model should be grounded on an (underlying) fact-based model involving verbalisations using the terminology as it is actually *used* (naturally) by the people involved in/with the modelled domain. We see this as a key enabler for the transferability of models across time and among people, in particular in situations where the model needs to act as a *boundary object* [2].

At the same time, we can see how purpose/domain specific modelling language (e.g. process models, goal models, actor models, value models, architectural models, etc.) create models using "boxes and lines" based constructs/abbreviations that only provide a limited linkage to the (natural) language as used by the model's audience. In general, the only link in this regard are the names used to label the "boxes". Relationships are replaced by generic graphical representations in terms of arrows and lines capturing relations such as "assigned to", "part of", "realises", "aggregates", "triggers", while leaving no room for situation specific nuance. Examples of such enterprise modelling languages/frameworks include a.o. ArchiMate [17], ARIS [29] and BPMN [23].

While the abstract, and more compact, notations of purpose/domain specific modelling languages enable a more compact representation of models, they offer no means to provide a "drill down" to an underlying grounding in terms of well verbalised fact types that capture, and honour, the original natural (language) nuances. The basic idea, as presented in this paper, is therefore to ground enterprise models on a fact-based model of the domain being modelled and, in line with the tradition of fact-based modelling, do so based on sample facts drawn from the domain being modelled. A fact model, grounding an enterprise model, might actually have a broader scope than the enterprise model, so as to capture even more of the relevant context.

The remainder of this paper is structured as follows. In Sect. 2, we discuss our fundamental view conceptual modelling, and enterprise modelling in particular. Section 3 then continues with a discussion on the need for a better grounding of enterprise models. In Sect. 4, we then illustrate this grounding in terms of a concrete example. In that section, we will also briefly revisit some of the earlier experiments in grounding enterprise models. Section 5 then concludes the paper.

2   A Fundamental View on Conceptual Modelling

This section is concerned with our fundamental view on conceptual modelling. We consider a model to be: *"an artefact acknowledged by an observer as representing some domain for a particular purpose"* [5]. This definition of model is strongly based on the work reported in e.g. [10, 28, 30, 31], as well as our own earlier work [15, 16].

---

[1] In principle, we would prefer to use the word "semantics" here. However, since the word "semantics", in our computer science oriented community, tends to be equated to only mean "formal semantics", we will use the word *meaning*.

The *observer* in our definition refers to the group of people consisting of model creators and model audience. On one extreme, it can refer to the entire society, on the other extreme, it can refer to an the individual.

Similar to [10], we define *domain* as any "part" or "aspect" of the world *considered relevant by the observer*. The term *world* here refers to "reality", as well as to possible worlds [35]. In the context of conceptual database design, this notion of *domain* is also referred to as the *universe of discourse* [18].

The *purpose* of a model is often considered as the main discriminant of the added value of a model [28,30,31]. We understand *purpose* as aggregating two interrelated dimensions: (1) the *domain* that the model (should) pertains to, and (2) the intended *usage* of the model by its intended *audience*.

In terms of the above, we define a conceptual model as being *a model where its purpose involves a need to capture knowledge about the represented domain*. In other words, a model answering a need to understand and/or articulate the workings and/or structure of some domain. Such a model needs to reflect human cognition in that it concerns concepts, their relationships, and relevant properties. This is what makes it a *concept*ual model. In line with this, we consider an *enterprise model* to be a *conceptual model that represents some part and/or aspect of an organisation/enterprise* [20].

A specific class of conceptual models are *conceptual (database) schemas*, which are conceptual models of the (implementation free) structure of a *universe of discourse* as it is to be captured in a database [18]. Or, as [18] puts it: "*The description of the possible states of affairs of the universe of discourse including the classifications, rules, laws, etc., of the universe of discourse*".

This brings us to the role of modelling languages. As defined in [3], we regard a modelling language as having a *linguistic function* and a *representational function*.

The *linguistic function* refers to the ability of a modelling language to frame the discourse about a domain and shaping the observer's conception of a domain. In this regard, a modelling language should provide a *linguistic structure*, involving a specific classification of concepts to be used in the discourse about the world (the embodied *world view*, or *Weltanschauung*). This linguistic structure will differ between e.g. a modelling language for value modelling and one for process modelling.

For modelling languages, the so-called meta-model will largely define the linguistic structure. Additional (linguistic) structure may be added by combining this with e.g. formal semantics, providing a normative view on what models are semantically sound/correct, and which are not [13]. Another way to increase the linguistic structure, is by the (enforcement of the) use of e.g. a foundational ontology [11].

The *representational function* refers to the ability of the language to express the conceived domain in a purposeful model. This generally involves a *representation system* involving an abstract and a concrete syntax of the modelling language.

It is important to acknowledge that the *linguistic structure*, being its essential world view (*Weltanschauung*), may not only limit the freedom of what can be expressed in a model. It may even limit, or at least influence, the way in which modellers observe the domain. This may lead to situations where a modelling language may "feel unnatural", in the sense that the linguistic structure puts to many restrictions on a modeller's "freedom of expression". This may, especially, become problematic when a model is used as a boundary object across communities [2].

At an anecdotical level, the influence of a specific (restricted) world view corresponds to the *hammer* and *nail* paradigm. At a more fundamental level, it corresponds to the notion of linguistic relativity [32][2], which states that the structure of a language determines, or greatly influences, the modes of thought and behaviour characteristic of the culture/context in which it is spoken. As we will see in the next section, this point is also key in our observations that a non-normative means is needed to be able to add more (natural language based) meaning to enterprise models.

3   The Need to Ground Enterprise Models

Enterprise models, being conceptual models, involve *concepts* and their *relations*, as well as possibly a *typing* of these in terms of modelling constructs. Consider, as an example, the ArchiMate [17] model as shown in Fig. 1. It contains, a.o., the concepts Patient, Doctor, Form, Examine and Diagnose. The icons in the boxes indicate whether a concept is a *role* (e.g. Patient), *activity* (e.g. Examine) or a passive *object* (e.g. Form). The line with the double dots is a so-called *assignment* relation. For example, Doctor and Patient are assigned to the Examine activity. The arrows correspond to triggering rules, so e.g. the Examine activity is triggered by the Register activity.

The example in Fig. 1 also illustrates the point that such models only provide a limited linkage to the (natural) language as used by the model's audience. Consider the assignment of Doctor and Patient to the Examine activity. One can only infer that a Doctor examines a Patient, when using contextual knowledge about what Doctors and Patients are, and what usually happens in an Examination. This is, of course, a rather simple example. However, in real-world cases, it is likely to become more difficult to "re-construct" the more precise meaning, in particular when a broader audience with a higher variety of backgrounds are involved (e.g. when a model acts as a *boundary object* [2]), or when a longer period of time has passed since the model was created.

Different ways of adding more meaning, and precision, to models can be used. We already mentioned formal semantics and the use of foundational ontologies. At a more fundamental level, these lead to refinements of the *linguistic structure* of the modelling language used, and as such provide *normative* restrictions on the freedom to express models. These normative restrictions, which might be said to *freeze* the (modelling) language [14], are likely to hamper, and stress, the actual

---

[2] More colloquially also known as the Sapir-Whorf hypothesis.

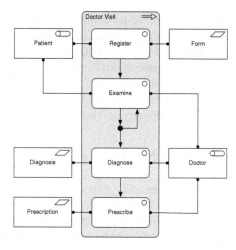

Fig. 1. Example ArchiMate model of a Doctor Visit

modelling process. At the same time, these normative restrictions certainly have a clear benefit, depending on the *purpose* of the model [4,5]. When an enterprise model is to act as a sector/industry wide reference model, it is certainly good to use a shared foundational ontology. Also, when a model is to be used as a base for formal analysis, code generation, or even execution, then a formal semantics is indeed called for.

In this paper, however, we focus on another approach to capture more meaning in an enterprise model, targeting situations where it is necessary to capture more *organisation specific* meaning, and enable those who are involved in modelling processes, to stay close to the language/terms they are used to. In such situations, we suggest a more *descriptive* approach, rather than a *normative* approach, when adding more meaning. This, we think, resonates well with the objectives of fact-based modelling [12,22], where the conceptual structures of a domain are expressed using fact(s) (types) in an explicit format, capturing the deeper conceptual meanings in a language that is understandable to the various stakeholders involved.

Grounding an enterprise model on a fact-based model has the potential added advantage that enterprise modelling can also benefit from the use of sample facts to validate the models (by e.g. a population check), in the sense that they can be more easily validated by domain experts. Here, we also see a strong analogy to grounded theory [21], which requires theories to be grounded in actual observed data; i.e. the sample facts that fact-based approaches start out from. This is also why we use the word *grounding*. An additional advantage is that the modelling procedure as suggested by most fact-based modelling approaches, ensures one starts out from *elementary* facts. Applying this in the context of enterprise modelling, could also lead to better models in terms of normalised relations in the model.

Each of the strategies to add more meanings to a model is bound to add a *specification burden* to the modelling process. The approach as suggested in the next section, does so by requiring more elaborate verbalisations, and even the identification of elementary sample facts. Adding more formal semantics to models, or using foundational ontologies, adds more burden on the modelling process by putting normative restrictions on the linguistic function. Whether these extra "burdens" are worth the effort, depends on the purpose(s) of the model.

4   Grounded Enterprise Modelling

The aim of this section, is to exemplify the grounding of enterprise models. Inspired by (1) earlier experiences with the need to better manage domain concepts during software and/or information system development [25], (2) work on explicitly identifying the need to introduce modelling concepts into a modelling language [16], as well as (3) the way in which the ArchiMate language was designed in terms of a series of layers with increasingly more specific modelling concepts [19], we developed the idea to use generic conceptual models to ground other, more specific, models on top of a semantically rich understanding of the domain in terms of a fact-based model [24]. In developing this approach, we also conducted some initial experiments in grounding enterprise models, involving (1) activity models [8,9,26], (2) system dynamics models [33,34], and (3) architecture principles [6].

A concrete example of how the ArchiMate model from Fig. 1 can be grounded on an ORM fact-based model has been depicted in Figs. 2, 3 and 4 respectively. In Fig. 2, we see an ORM model[3] dealing with patients visiting a doctor. Patients fill out forms in order to register, they can be examined by a doctor, doctors produce diagnoses, as well as prescribe possibly prescriptions.

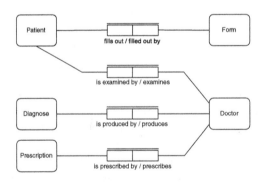

Fig. 2. Doctor Visit example; ORM grounding

---

[3] To keep the diagram clean, we have omitted all of the so-called reference schemes, which identify how e.g. a Doctor or a Patient is referred to in this domain.

When applying the ORM CSDP [12], one is also "invited" to carefully reflect on the question if Doctor and Patient should be treated as specialisation of a same super-type, such as Person. Especially, since a Doctor may also become a Patient. In the example, we assume that such a choice was not made. However, *making* such a conscious choice should be part of the grounding process.

What is missing in Fig. 2 is the temporal order in which these facts occur, as well as the fact that these activities take place in the context of a Doctor Visit. This leads to the situation as shown in Fig. 3, where we have also adorned the roles with icons corresponding to the modelling concepts of the ArchiMate language [17].

In adding a temporal semantics to ORM [7, 27] we assume that the regular ORM constraints (cardinality, etc.) need to apply at each individual moment in time. So, a mandatory role constraint, such as the one marked with (a), should apply at each individual moment in time. In other words, if a Register occurrence takes place during some period in time, then (also during that period in time), it must be taking place in the context of some Doctor Visit.

Normally, ORM uniqueness constraints are represented with a single bar over the involved roles. Now, consider the uniqueness constraint marked with (b). If this one would have been marked with only a single bar, it would have signified that at each moment in time, a Register occurrence can only be for one Doctor Visit. This would still make it possible for one Register occurrence during some time period T to be assigned to two different Doctor Visits, but at non coinciding intervals in time T_1 and T_2, with $T_1, T_2 \subset T$. The double bar, therefore, signifies that the Register occurrence can be part of a Doctor Visit once, ever. The patient can of course register for *an other* Doctor Visit by filling out *an other* form.

The required temporal order of events is depicted with an open arrow connecting the involved roles. See, for example, the one marked with (c). This states that for Doctor Visit, we cannot see a Register occurrence after we have started to see (an) Examine occurrence(s). We also see (indicated by the open arrow further below) that (the way it is modelled in the *example*) after a Diagnose occurrence has taken place, for a given Doctor Visit, we can no longer see further Examine occurrences in the context of *this* Doctor Visit. Note also, that a Doctor Visit is only allowed to have one Diagnose occurrence, but multiple Examine occurrences, as signified by the double bars.

The constraint pattern marked (d) is also of interest. It insures that the Patient filling out the Form is also the Patient who is to be examined (in the context of one Doctor Visit). Similarly the Doctor doing the diagnosing is also required to be the Doctor writing the prescription.

The process flow as depicted in Fig. 3 does not involve split/join junctions. Such structures could, however, also be modelled using similar temporal constraints. However, advanced workflow/temporal-ordering patterns, are probably best left to a dedicated modelling language [1]. In grounding enterprise models, we think it is wisest to focus on grounding the main conceptual structure of the domain.

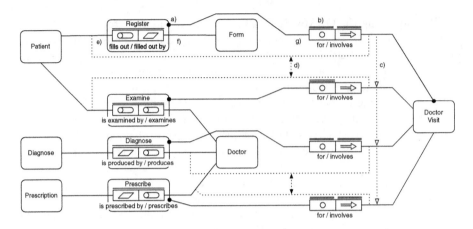

Fig. 3. Doctor Visit example with temporal ordering and ArchiMate mapping

Figure 3 also shows the a classification, by means of icons, of roles in terms of the modelling concepts from the ArchiMate language [17]. Consider, for instance, the role marked with (e). When a Patient fills out a form, then they are, in terms of ArchiMate enacting a *business role*. The form, see (f), then plays the passive role of a *business object*. The Register occurrence, see (g), plays the role of a *business activity* in the context of a composed *business process* Doctor Visit.

In the case of larger examples, even when limited to educational settings, diagrams in the style of Fig. 3 can easily become rather large. Therefore, we would suggest to use a graphical abbreviation in the ORM diagrams, in terms of a State Sequence (complex) object type, as used on the left hand side of Fig. 4.

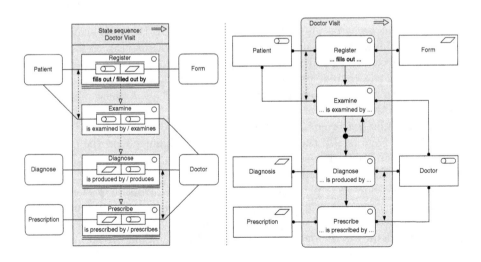

Fig. 4. Doctor Visit example, notational variations

The version represented on the right hand side, would actually result in a more ArchiMate-alike notation. Note the added fact verbalisations, as well as the addition of the more specific constraints on role participations of Doctors and Patients.

5   Conclusion

In this paper, we presented the idea of grounding enterprise models in terms of fact-based models, in order to add more domain specific meaning to enterprise models. We discussed the need for doing so in terms of a fundamental understanding of conceptual modelling. We also argued why grounding enterprise models on fact-based models provides a complementary (descriptive) approach next to (more normative) alternatives. A grounding on fact-based models, allow us to leverage the traditional fact-based modelling advantages of capturing the deeper conceptual meanings in a language that is understandable to the various stakeholders involved. The presented concepts were illustrated by means of a running example, while also reflecting on, and summarising, the results of earlier experiments in grounding different enterprise models.

As a next step, we aim to further elaborate the grounding of ArchiMate models, as well as other enterprise modelling languages, while also formalising the used mapping mechanisms. In addition, to the theoretical underpinning as discussed in Sect. 2, and the early experiments as reported in [6,8,9,26,33,34], we also plan to conduct more usage oriented experiments. Does adding a grounding to enterprise models lead to: *Models of higher quality? Models that can be more easily communicated among different actors? Models that can more easily understood at a later point in time?*

References

1. van der Aalst, W.M.P., ter Hofstede, A.H.M., Kiepuszewski, B., Barros, A.P.: Workflow patterns. Distrib. Parallel Databases **14**(1), 5–51 (2003)
2. Abraham, R., Niemietz, H., de Kinderen, S., Aier, S.: Can boundary objects mitigate communication defects in enterprise transformation? Findings from expert interviews. In: Jung, R., Reichert, M. (eds.) Proceedings of the 5th International Workshop on Enterprise Modelling and Information Systems Architectures (EMISA 2013). LNI, vol. 222, pp. 27–40. Gesellschaft für Informatik, Bonn (2013)
3. Bjeković, M., Proper, H.A., Sottet, J.-S.: Embracing pragmatics. In: Yu, E., Dobbie, G., Jarke, M., Purao, S. (eds.) ER 2014. LNCS, vol. 8824, pp. 431–444. Springer, Cham (2014). https://doi.org/10.1007/978-3-319-12206-9_37
4. Bjeković, M., Proper, H.A., Sottet, J.-S.: Enterprise modelling languages – just enough standardisation? In: Shishkov, B. (ed.) BMSD 2013. LNBIP, vol. 173, pp. 1–23. Springer, Cham (2014). https://doi.org/10.1007/978-3-319-06671-4_1
5. Bjeković, M., Sottet, J.S., Favre, J.M., Proper, H.A.: A framework for natural enterprise modelling. In: Proceedings of the 15th IEEE Conference on Business Informatics (CBI 2013), pp. 79–84. IEEE Computer Society Press, Los Alamitos (2013)

6. van Bommel, P., Buitenhuis, P.G., Hoppenbrouwers, S.J.B.A., Proper, H.A.: Architecture principles – a regulative perspective on enterprise architecture. In: Reichert, M., Strecker, S., Turowski, K. (eds.) Proceedings of the 2nd International Workshop on Enterprise Modelling and Information Systems Architectures (EMISA 2007). LNI, no. 119, pp. 47–60. Gesellschaft für Informatik, Bonn (2007)
7. van Bommel, P., Frederiks, P.J.M., van der Weide, T.P.: Object-oriented modeling based on logbooks. Comput. J. **39**(9), 793–799 (1996)
8. van Bommel, P., Hoppenbrouwers, S.J.B.A., Proper, H.A., van der Weide, T.P.: On the use of object-role modeling for modeling active domains. In: Research Issues in System Analysis and Design, Databases and Software Development, pp. 123–145. IGI Publishing, Hershey (2007)
9. van Bommel, P., Hoppenbrouwers, S.J.B.A., Proper, H.A., van der Weide, T.P.: On the use of object-role modelling to model active domains. In: Halpin, T.A., Krogstie, J., Proper, H.A. (eds.) Proceedings of the 13th Workshop on Exploring Modeling Methods for Systems Analysis and Design (EMMSAD 2008), Held in Conjunction with the 20th Conference on Advanced Information Systems Engineering (CAiSE 2008), Montpellier, France, vol. 337, pp. 473–484. CEUR-WS.org, June 2008
10. Falkenberg, E.D., Verrijn-Stuart, A.A., Voss, K., Hesse, W., Lindgreen, P., Nilsson, B.E., Oei, J.L.H., Rolland, C., Stamper, R.K. (eds.): A Framework of Information Systems Concepts. IFIP WG 8.1 Task Group FRISCO, IFIP, Laxenburg, Austria (1998)
11. Guizzardi, G.: On ontology, ontologies, conceptualizations, modeling languages, and (meta)models. In: Vasilecas, O., Eder, J., Caplinskas, A. (eds.) Databases and Information Systems IV - Selected Papers from the Seventh International Baltic Conference, DB&IS 2006, 3–6 July 2006, Vilnius, Lithuania. Frontiers in Artificial Intelligence and Applications, vol. 155, pp. 18–39. IOS Press (2006)
12. Halpin, T.A., Morgan, T.: Information Modeling and Relational Databases. Data Management Systems, 2nd edn. Morgan Kaufman, San Francisco (2008)
13. ter Hofstede, A.H.M., Proper, H.A.: How to formalize it? Formalization principles for information systems development methods. Inf. Softw. Technol. **40**(10), 519–540 (1998)
14. Hoppenbrouwers, S.J.B.A.: Freezing language; conceptualisation processes in ICT supported organisations. Ph.D. thesis, University of Nijmegen, Nijmegen, The Netherlands (2003)
15. Hoppenbrouwers, S.J.B.A., Proper, H.A., van der Weide, T.P.: A fundamental view on the process of conceptual modeling. In: Delcambre, L., Kop, C., Mayr, H.C., Mylopoulos, J., Pastor, O. (eds.) ER 2005. LNCS, vol. 3716, pp. 128–143. Springer, Heidelberg (2005). https://doi.org/10.1007/11568322_9
16. Hoppenbrouwers, S.J.B.A., Proper, H.A., van der Weide, T.P.: Understanding the requirements on modelling techniques. In: Pastor, O., Falcão e Cunha, J. (eds.) CAiSE 2005. LNCS, vol. 3520, pp. 262–276. Springer, Heidelberg (2005). https://doi.org/10.1007/11431855_19
17. Iacob, M.E., Jonkers, H., Lankhorst, M.M., Proper, H.A., Quartel, D.A.C.: ArchiMate 2.0 Specification. The Open Group (2012)
18. ISO/IEC JTC 1/SC 32 Technical Committee on Data management and interchange: Information processing systems – Concepts and Terminology for the Conceptual Schema and the Information Base. Technical report. ISO/TR 9007:1987, ISO (1987)
19. Lankhorst, M.M., Proper, H.A., Jonkers, H.: The anatomy of the ArchiMate language. Int. J. Inf. Syst. Model. Design (IJISMD) **1**(1), 1–32 (2010)

20. Magalhães, R., Proper, H.A.: Model-enabled design and engineering of organisations. Organ. Design Enterp. Eng. **1**(1), 1–12 (2017)
21. Martin, P.Y., Turner, B.A.: Grounded theory and organizational research. J. Appl. Behav. Sci. **22**(2), 141–157 (1986)
22. Semantics of Business Vocabulary and Rules (SBVR). Technical report. dtc/06-03-02, Object Management Group, Needham, Massachusetts, March 2006
23. OMG: Business Process Modeling Notation, V2.0. Technical report. OMG Document Number: formal/2011-01-03, Object Management Group, January 2011
24. Proper, H.A.: Grounded Enterprise Modelling. DaVinci Series, Nijmegen Institute for Information and Computing Sciences, Radboud University, Nijmegen, The Netherlands (2008)
25. Proper, H.A., Bleeker, A.I., Hoppenbrouwers, S.J.B.A.: Object-role modelling as a domain modelling approach. In: Grundspenkis, J., Kirikova, M. (eds.) Proceedings of the Workshop on Evaluating Modeling Methods for Systems Analysis and Design (EMMSAD 2004), Held in Conjunctiun with the 16th Conference on Advanced Information Systems 2004 (CAiSE 2004), Riga, Latvia, vol. 3, pp. 317–328, June 2004
26. Proper, H.A., Hoppenbrouwers, S.J.B.A., van der Weide, T.P.: A fact-oriented approach to activity modeling. In: Meersman, R., Tari, Z., Herrero, P. (eds.) OTM 2005. LNCS, vol. 3762, pp. 666–675. Springer, Heidelberg (2005). https://doi.org/10.1007/11575863_86
27. Proper, H.A., van der Weide, T.P.: EVORM – a conceptual modelling technique for evolving application domains. Data Knowl. Eng. **12**, 313–359 (1994)
28. Rothenberg, J.: The nature of modeling. In: Artificial Intelligence, Simulation & Modeling, pp. 75–92. Wiley, New York (1989)
29. Scheer, A.W., Schneider, K.: ARIS - architecture of integrated information systems. In: Bernus, P., Mertins, K., Schmidt, G. (eds.) Handbook on Architectures of Information Systems, pp. 605–623. Springer, Heidelberg (1998). https://doi.org/10.1007/3-540-26661-5_25
30. Stachowiak, H.: Allgemeine Modelltheorie. Springer, Vienna (1973)
31. Thalheim, B.: The theory of conceptual models, the theory of conceptual modelling and foundations of conceptual modelling. In: Embley, D., Thalheim, B. (eds.) Handbook of Conceptual Modeling, pp. 543–577. Springer, Heidelberg (2011). https://doi.org/10.1007/978-3-642-15865-0_17
32. Tohidian, I.: Examining linguistic relativity hypothesis as one of the main views on the relationship between language and thought. J. Psycholinguist. Res. **38**(1), 65–74 (2009)
33. Tulinayo, P.F., Hoppenbrouwers, S.J.B.A.S., Proper, H.A.: Integrating system dynamics with object-role modeling. In: Stirna, J., Persson, A. (eds.) PoEM 2008. LNBIP, vol. 15, pp. 77–85. Springer, Heidelberg (2008). https://doi.org/10.1007/978-3-540-89218-2_6
34. Tulinayo, F.P., van Bommel, P., Proper, H.A.: Enhancing the system dynamics modeling proces with a domain modeling method. Int. J. Coop. Inf. Syst. **22**(02), 1350011 (2013)
35. Wyssusek, B.: On ontological foundations of conceptual modelling. Scand. J. Inf. Syst. **18**(1), 63–80 (2006)

An FBM Model of ISO Cloud Computing Architecture

Baba Piprani[✉]

MetaGlobal Systems, Ottawa, Canada
babap@attglobal.net

Abstract. With the ever-changing dynamic Information and Communications Technology environment and the new shared deployment options for computing, a paradigm shift has occurred, which enables ubiquitous and convenient computing on a pay-as-you-go basis. Access on demand has become available to networks of scalable, elastic, self-serviceable, configurable physical and virtual resources. This paper updates the previous paper that addressed early ISO Committee Draft (CD) work on Cloud Computing by ISO ISO/IEC JTC1 SC38 (in collaboration with ITU-T SG13/WP6 for Cloud Computing), and models the full and expanded ISO Cloud Computing Reference Architecture and Service Level Agreement (SLA) using Fact Based Modeling (FBM) methodology. FBM has allowed us to distill the concepts, relationships and business rules - thereby capsulizing the Cloud Computing standards to enable understanding, and also exposing the strengths and weakness of the models, and thus allowing for identification of any gaps towards furthering the ISO standard.

Keywords: Cloud Computing · Cloud computing reference architecture
CCRA · SLA · Service level agreement · ISO · Fact Based Modeling
FBM · SLO · SQO · Cloud service
Cloud computing interoperability and portability · ODP

1 Introduction and Background

Information and Communications Technology (ICT) is being transformed to a model based on services that are commoditized and delivered in a standardized manner. In a cloud service-based model, users access cloud services based on their requirements without regard to where the cloud services are hosted or how they are delivered.

Several computing paradigms have promised to deliver this computing vision, of which the latest is Cloud Computing. The term "Cloud" denotes a computing infrastructure from which businesses and users are able to access applications from anywhere in the world, on-demand. Thus, the ICT world is rapidly evolving to develop software for millions to consume as a cloud service, rather than to run on individual computers. Cloud computing represents a paradigm shift that has redefined the relationship between buyers and sellers of IT-related products and services [1]. The ISO (International Organization for Standardization) SC38 Study Group on Cloud Computing in their 2011 report [1] identified at least 23 Cloud Computing industry initiatives that had published material, were developing standards or were doing at least some work in this area.

C. Debruyne et al. (Eds.): OTM 2017 Workshops, LNCS 10697, pp. 152–162, 2018.
https://doi.org/10.1007/978-3-319-73805-5_16

With multiple and often confusing Cloud Computing approaches being offered to the IT community, ISO initiated standardization work on a Cloud Computing vocabulary and a Cloud Computing reference architecture in 2010. On a parallel front, ITU-T was also in the process of developing Recommendations for Cloud Computing terminology and reference architecture. The two groups successfully launched collaborative work on the development of a common set of standards/recommendations for Cloud Computing vocabulary and reference architecture.

The ISO Joint Technical Committee (JTC1) formed a Sub-Committee, called SC38 named Distributed Application Platform and Services, to harmonize the ISO work on standardization for: Web Services, Service Oriented Architecture and Cloud Computing. This initiative was largely driven by the IT marketplace having to face multiple incompatible choices of product sets, which essentially creates barriers to interoperability efforts.

This paper updates the previous work [10] of the basic Cloud Computing terminology and Reference Architecture that was based on the Committee Draft (CD) document. This update reflects removal of some overlapping items between the Vocabulary and Reference Architecture documents, along with minor clarifications of relationships. This paper illustrates how Fact Based Modeling (FBM) provides a useful means to capture and understand the Cloud Computing standards, hopefully leading to a more cohesive and consistent direction for the next generation of ICT.

NOTE: The standards for Cloud Computing are under continuing development and are subject to change. The contents of this paper are intended to be illustrative and should not be considered as an authoritative description of the emerging ISO standards.

In this paper, we have used the FBM notation and methodology as a description technique to define semantic models abstracted from the current Cloud Computing and SOA documents being progressed for standardization. FBM is a methodology for modeling the semantics of a subject area.

FBM is based on logic and controlled natural language, whereby the resulting fact based model captures the semantics of the domain of interest by means of fact types, together with the associated concept definitions and the integrity rules [9].

The roots of FBM go back to the 1970s. NIAM, a FBM notation style, was one of the candidate methodologies used for developing conceptual schemas as defined in ISO Technical Report TR9007:1987 Concepts and Terminology for the Conceptual Schema and the Information Base. Subsequently, several developments have taken place in parallel, resulting in several Fact Based Modeling "dialects", like NIAM, ORM2, CogNIAM, DOGMA and FCO-IM. The notation used in this paper is ORM2 notation.

A simplistic description of usage and reading the ORM2 notation follows. The subject area Universe of Discourse is seen as consisting of semantic objects (representing objects in the real world model) that can be described using natural language sentences—consisting of an object, predicate and possibly one or more objects, each connected with a predicate-object pair. A real world object is represented by an object type denoted by a circle, also known as an entity type. Object types may have subtypes denoted by arrows from the subtype to supertype (e.g. object type Role has subtype Sub-role). Object types are involved in 'fact type' sentence descriptions that can be binary, or n-ary (ternary, quaternary etc.), as depicted by rectangle boxes, each box representing a 'role' that the object type plays in that sentence. Integrity rules are then associated with the fact types, like mandatory (shown as a dark dot on the object type connector). A horizontal bar on top of a role of a fact type denotes a uniqueness restriction on the occurrence of the set of role populations. The ORM2 notation contains several other rules that can be graphically depicted but are out of scope for our discussions. An example of a fact type reading from Fig. 1 is: A Party (in the cloud computing paradigm schema) *must* be assigned to one or more CCRole(s). A CCRole *may* be assigned to one or more Parties.

2 Cloud Computing Concepts

Figure 1 depicts the main Cloud Computing concepts using FBM, along with examples, as defined in the ISO Overview and vocabulary document [2]. The concepts are defined in terms of the cloud services that are available to cloud service customers and the cloud deployment models that describe how the computing infrastructure that delivers these cloud services can be provided and shared by users.

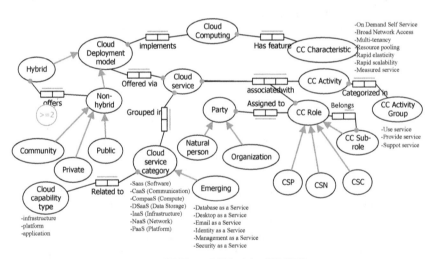

FBM Schema of CC Vocabulary (ISO 17788)

Fig. 1. Basic Cloud Computing concepts from ISO 17788

It is interesting to note that the Cloud Computing vocabulary and concepts were developed prior to an agreed upon architecture. The architecture itself takes its basis from the approach used in the ISO Open Distributed Reference Model (ODP) [4] by utilizing the user view and functional view.

The cloud paradigm is composed of key characteristics, roles and activities, cloud service capabilities and cloud service categories, deployment models, and cross cutting aspects as shown. The concept relationships generally appear in the cloud computing reference architecture.

Table 1 is the relevant definitions pertaining to the cloud computing models shown.

Table 1. Definitions of concepts used in Cloud Computing ISO 17788, ISO 17789

Concept	Definition	Examples
Party	Entities that play one or more roles (and sub-roles)	Natural person, or an organization
Role	Sets of activities	Cloud service customer Cloud service provider Cloud service partner
Subrole	A subset of the activities associated with a role	Sub-roles for a partner role are: service integrator, auditor, and cloud broker
Activity	A logical functional element of a cloud service	Using cloud services, providing cloud services, and supporting cloud services
Component	An implementation of an activity	
Cross-cutting aspect	Behaviors or capabilities that need to be implemented & coordinated across roles	Interoperability, portability, reversibility, security, privacy, governance, etc.
Cloud Computing	Paradigm for enabling network access to a scalable and elastic pool of shareable physical or virtual resources with on-demand self-service provisioning and administration	
Cloud characteristic	Basic user-oriented features of a Cloud Computing environment	On-demand self-service, Broad network access, Multi-tenancy, Resource pooling, Rapid elasticity & scalability, Measured service
Cloud service	One or more capabilities offered via cloud computing invoked using a declared interface	Natural person, or an organization

(continued)

Table 1. (*continued*)

Concept	Definition	Examples
Cloud service category	Group of cloud services that possess some qualities in common with each other	Infrastructure as a service, Platform as a service, Software as a service, Network as a service, Data Storage as a service, Compute as a service, Communication as a service
Capability	A quality of being able to perform a given activity	
Cloud capability type	Classification of the functionality, based on the type of resources used. Cloud capability types follow the principle of separation of concerns, i.e. they have minimal functionality overlap between each other.	Infrastructure capabilities, Platform capabilities, Application capabilities
Cloud deployment model	The way in which cloud computing can be organized based on control of physical or virtual resources and how those resources are shared	Community cloud, Public cloud, or Private cloud
Hybrid cloud	A cloud deployment model that includes at least two different deployment models	Interoperability, portability, reversibility, security, privacy, governance, etc.

3   Cloud Computing Reference Architecture

A Fact Based Model for the Cloud Computing Reference Architecture (CCRA) is shown in Fig. 2. As noted earlier, the CCRA takes as its basis the ODP reference model but focuses only on the user and functional views. The CCRA does not address the implementation and deployment views. The user view is the ecosystem (or system context) including the parties, the roles, the sub-roles and the activities. The functional view is the distribution of functions necessary for the support of cloud activities.

The Fact Based Models in this paper represent the distillation and transforms as interpreted from the vocabulary text [2] and the CCRA text [3]. The purpose of these diagrams is being able to understand and analyze them using a formal modelling methodology to represent the involved facts and relationships as opposed to text paragraphs.

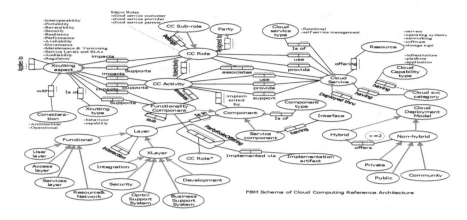

Fig. 2. Cloud computing reference architecture model from ISO 17789

4 Cloud Computing Service Level Agreement (Cloud SLA)

A service level agreement is part of a cloud service agreement that includes cloud service level objectives and cloud service qualitative objectives for the covered services. The cloud SLA accounts for the key characteristics of cloud computing that include: Self-service, resource pooling, multi-tenancy, rapid elasticity and scaling, tradeoff between cost and control, and more importantly, the ability to 'measure' cloud services.

Figure 3 relates cloud services with service level agreements, SLOs and SQOs.

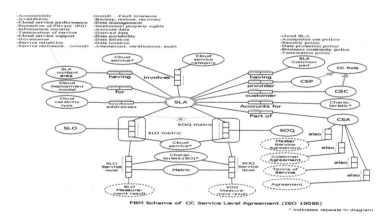

Fig. 3. FBM schema depicting ISO 19086-1 CC SLA

The use of FBM enables the capture of SLA standard semantics [5–7] in a succinct capsulated form in the FBM schema shown in Fig. 3 (Table 2).

Table 2. Definitions of concepts used in CC SLA ISO 19086

Concept	Definition	Examples
CSA	Cloud service agreement	Contract vehicle for organizations, enterprises and individuals, software and hardware
CSC	Cloud service customer	
CSP	Cloud service provider	
Cloud service	One or more capabilities offered via cloud computing invoked using a defined interface	
Metric	Standard of measurement that defines the conditions and the rules for performing the measurement and for understanding the results of a measurement	
SLO	Cloud service level objective - commitment a cloud service provider makes for a specific, quantitative characteristic of a cloud service, where the value follows the interval or ratio scale	
SQO	Cloud service qualitative objective: commitment a cloud service provider makes for a specific, qualitative characteristic of a cloud service, where the value follows the nominal or ordinal scale	

5   Cloud Computing Interoperability and Portability

The cloud computing interoperability standard [8] is aimed at all parties involved in cloud computing—cloud service customers (CSCs), cloud service providers (CSPs), and cloud service partners (CSNs) acting as cloud service developers. ISO DIS 19941 provides a common understanding of interoperability and portability as it applies to cloud computing. This common understanding helps to achieve interoperability and portability in cloud computing by establishing common terminology and concepts that are involved.

Figure 4, describes cloud computing portability and depicts the terminology used. Figures 5, 6, 7 and Table 3 describe cloud computing interoperability the terminology used.

It is important to note that using FBM and strongly typed subtypes, it was possible to abstract and condense much of the formal descriptions in the standard [8].

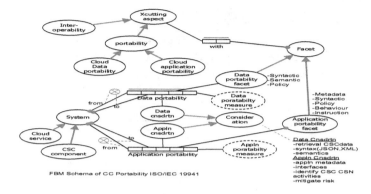

Fig. 4. FBM schema of CC portability ISO 19941

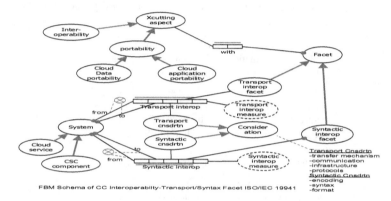

Fig. 5. FBM schema of CC interoperability – transport/syntax facet ISO 19941

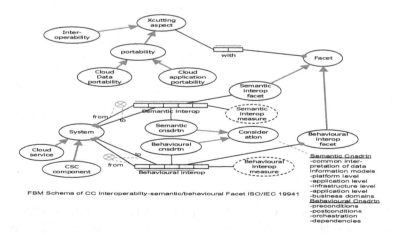

Fig. 6. FBM schema of CC interoperability – semantic/behavioural facet ISO 19941

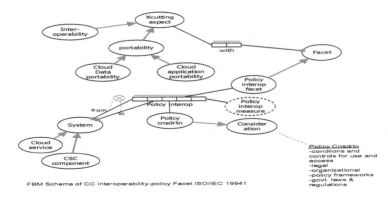

FBM Schema of CC Interoperability-policy Facet ISO/IEC 19941

Fig. 7. FBM schema of CC interoperability – policy facet ISO 19941

Table 3. Definitions of concepts used in CC interoperability and portability ISO 19941

Concept	Definition	Examples
Interoperability	Ability of two or more systems or applications to exchange information and to mutually use the information that has been exchanged	
Cloud interoperability	Ability of a CSC's system to interact with a cloud service, or the ability for one cloud service to interact with other cloud services, by exchanging information according to a prescribed method to obtain predictable results	
Data portability	Ability to easily transfer data from one system to another without being required to re-enter data	
Cloud data portability	Data portability from one cloud service to another cloud service, or between a CSC's system and a cloud service	
Application portability	Ability to migrate an application from one cloud service to another cloud service or between a CSC's system and a cloud service	
Cloud application portability	Ability to migrate an application from one cloud service to another cloud service, or between a CSC's system and a cloud service	
Functional component	A functional building block needed to engage in an activity backed by an implementation	Cloud service client component

6   Cloud Computing Suite of Standards

By transforming each of the Cloud Computing concepts, terminology and architectures using Fact Based Modeling, we are able to distill the salient object types, relationships and some of the business rules to enable a comparative analysis of the involved architectures—the Cloud computing reference architecture (CCRA), the cloud computing service level agreement suite of multi part standards (some are still in development), cloud computing interoperability and portability architecture, and cloud computing cloud service and devices: data flow, data categories and data use.

By using FBM any deviations from the established vocabulary immediately become apparent. Cloud computing reference architecture uses ODP views whereas the follow on standards do not. These are only some of the examples of divergence between the cloud computing and companion architectures.

It is clear that there needs to be an accord between the Cloud Computing standards group and other CC related standards groups like Security and Privacy, Metadata, Open-edi, Internet of Things (IoT RA), Blockchain and distributed ledger technologies, with other standards developing organizations (SDO), and industry consortia.

7 Conclusions

In this paper we have demonstrated the use of Fact Based Modeling to facilitate an analysis of the ISO vocabulary and reference architecture standards for Cloud Computing, cloud computing service level agreement framework, cloud service level agreement metrics, cloud computing interoperability and portability. As a result, we have identified a number of areas where the concepts in the vocabulary and architecture documents are generally aligned and provide a mechanism to explore any misalignments. We have also identified a number of areas where Cloud Computing and associated standards are using similar concepts, typically in ways that may be readily compared.

Fact Based Modeling appears to provide significant assistance both in the development of consistent architectures based on sound concepts and also in the analysis and comparison of different architectures.

Further effort to analyze the models in more detail would provide valuable insight into the complex relationships within Cloud Computing suite of standards.

References

1. ISO/IEC JTC1 SC38 N430 JTC1 SC38 Study Group on Cloud Computing Report – Final Version, 30 September 2011
2. ISO/IEC 17788 Information technology — Distributed application platforms and services — Cloud computing — Overview and vocabulary, 23 April 2013
3. ISO/IEC 17789 Information technology — Distributed application platforms and services — Cloud computing — Reference Architecture, 23 April 2013
4. ISO/IEC 10746-1:1998, Information technology – Open distributed processing – Reference Model: Overview
5. ISO/IEC DIS 19086-1, Cloud Computing – Service Level Agreement (SLA) framework – Part 1: Overview and concepts
6. ISO/IEC DIS 19086-2, Cloud Computing – Service Level Agreement (SLA) framework – Part 2: Metric Model

7. ISO/IEC DIS 19086-3, Cloud Computing – Service Level Agreement (SLA) framework – Part 3: Core conformance Requirements
8. ISO/IEC DIS 19941, Cloud Computing – Interoperability and portability
9. Nijssen, G.M., Halpin, T.A.: Conceptual Schema and Relational Database Design. Prentice Hall, Victoria (1989)
10. Piprani, B., Sheppard, D., Barbir, A.: Comparative analysis of SOA and cloud computing architectures using fact based modeling. In: Demey, Y.T., Panetto, H. (eds.) OTM 2013. LNCS, vol. 8186, pp. 524–533. Springer, Heidelberg (2013). https://doi.org/10.1007/978-3-642-41033-8_66

Analyzing the New 2019 Dutch Environment and Planning Act

John Bulles[1]([☒]), Bas Cartigny[1], and Peter Bollen[2]

[1] PNA Group, Heerlen, The Netherlands
{john.bulles,bas.cartigny}@pna-group.com
[2] Maastricht University, Maastricht, The Netherlands
p.bollen@maastrichtuniversity.nl

Abstract. In The Netherlands, all legislation regarding infrastructure and environment is described in more than 250 legal documents. In 2019 the new "Omgevingswet" (translated as "Environment and planning act" [1, 4]) was supposed to come into force. This law modernizes, harmonizes and simplifies the mentioned regulation and integrates this myriad of legislations, decrees and regulations into one legal framework.

To be able to apply the environment and planning act, legal analysis of this legislation is required. The Dutch Rijkswaterstaat ministerial department [2, 3] has developed an approach to analyze (interpret), structure and store the rules contained in the legislation. In their approach, all rules are associated with activities, which form a functional structure. This functional structure is the baseline from which relevant parts of the legislation is grouped. This paper describes how this approach works, how it is supported by Fact Based Modeling and the software environment used (Cognitation) to perform the document analysis.

Keywords: Laws · Regulations · Cognitation · Omgevingswet
Analysis of legal documents · Fact based modeling (FBM)

1 Introduction

Currently any person or organisation in the Netherlands that wants to interact with the environment, is forced to adhere to many laws and regulations. The legislation concerning infrastructure and environment is described in more than 26 laws, 120 governmental decrees and 120 ministerial regulations. The legislation was never meant to become this extensive, but it grew over time.

In 2015, the Dutch government accepted the law proposal for the new "Omgevings-wet" (translated as "Environment and planning act" [1, 4]). Together with 4 governmental decrees and 10 ministerial regulations, this new legislation will replace (parts of) the current legislation with the intent to modernize, harmonize and simplify the rules on land use, environmental protection, environmental conservation, construction of buildings, protection of cultural heritage, water management, urban and rural redevelopment, development of major public and private works and mining and earth removal.

© Springer International Publishing AG 2018
C. Debruyne et al. (Eds.): OTM 2017 Workshops, LNCS 10697, pp. 163–172, 2018.
https://doi.org/10.1007/978-3-319-73805-5_17

The new legislation still adds up to multiple thousands of pages. Therefore the Dutch Rijkswaterstaat (abbreviated into RWS) ministerial department (the Ministry of Infrastructure and the Environment) developed an approach to analyse, structure and store the legislation in order to prepare them for the specification of the underling rules that, eventually, must be implemented in a so-called digital counter. Individuals and organizations will be able to use this digital counter to obtain further information about necessary building permits, notification obligations, etc. needed for particular projects that have an effect on the environment.

Because of the impact this new legislation has on municipalities, provinces and other local governments, the date that this legislation will come into force has already been delayed. It was supposed to come into force in 2019. The described approach makes it possible for RWS to be able to enforce their part of the legislation on time.

Such an approach requires sufficient support in tooling as the amount of legislation makes it impossible for individuals to oversee everything. Therefore RWS put out a tender on support for their approach. PNA has developed a legal analysis software tooling, named Cognitation, which PNA offered for this tender. Cognitation is developed in collaboration with the Dutch Tax Office, after winning the tender for an Annotation environment of "Wendbare Wetsuitvoering" in 2014 [6, 7]. After winning the tender of RWS in February 2017 [5], PNA, in collaboration with RWS, added the necessary changes to Cognitation to be able to fully support the analysis process of RWS.

2 Outline of the Approach

The first step of the approach is building up (part of) a functional structure of activities. Therefore the text is analyzed and all activities and subjects in the documents are identified and annotated. This functional structure describes hierarchical relations between activities and subjects, but also the non-hierarchical relations between two activities, an activity and a subject or two subjects. A subject is a special kind of activity in the hierarchical structure that has no more sub-activities. One of the important demands of RWS for support tooling was to be able to trace the existence of an activity or subject back to a particular piece of text in one (or more) of the legal documents.

After defining the functional structure, a document is analyzed in more depth by defining which sections of a document are linked to a certain activity or subject. When finished, these sections are classified into different categories. The categories indicate, e.g. whether the text describes the scope of the application of the activity/subject, a filling requirement for a permit, or whether a permit is necessary for a certain activity, etc.

Finally the actual set of words which describe a rule for such a category of an activity/subject are annotated in the text. These annotations also belong to a certain category like what, where, who, how much, etc.

Operation areas are determined for the activities and subject as well for some of the rules that are annotated. An operation area describes the actual are of the Netherlands a rule applies to.

All annotations concerning (a set of) activities and/or subjects spanning one or more documents will be subject to a set of validations, which will validate the consistency of the annotations. After this check, the documents together with the annotations are sent to the specification tooling in which the rules are formalized. After the formalization the rules are implemented in a rule based environment.

Because of the detailed analysis at the start of this process, all parts of the resulting model are traceable to a specific part in the legal documents. Through support of Cognitation, RWS has the possibility to trace all implemented rules back to their source. This leads to full traceability of all implemented rules.

Legislation often changes, in case of changes Cognitation supports in identifying and processing the new, changed or deleted parts in the new legislation. This helps to stay compliant at all times.

3 Step 1 - Defining a Functional Structure

An activity describes what type of work an individual or organization can perform on the environment. In the legal documents of the Environment and planning act, a lot of these activities are mentioned. The legal texts are defined in a way that they describe a hierarchical structure of these activities.

For example, two parts from the translation of the Omgevingswet [1]:

"

Article 1.2 (physical environment)

1. This Act is concerned with:

   a. the physical environment, and
   b. activities that affect or may affect the physical environment."

...   ·

Article 4.21 (government regulations relating to buildings)

1. The rules referred to in Article 4.3 relating to construction activities, demolition activities and the use and maintenance of buildings are laid down for the purpose of:

   a. ensuring safety,
   b. safeguarding health,
   c. sustainability.

"

Article 1.2, 1. b. is the description of the root activity which is defined as "activities that affect or may affect the physical environment". In article 4.21, 1. the activity "the use and maintenance of buildings" is mentioned. This activity is hierarchically placed beneath the root activity in article 1.2, 1. b.

This functional structure of activities is not limited to one document. In another document, the "Besluit bouwwerken leefomgeving" (freely translated as Decree buildings living environment), the activities "the use of buildings" and "the maintenance of buildings" are described. These activities are again hierarchically beneath the activity of article 4.21, 1. When activities do not have any more sub-activities, they will be set as a subject.

This kind of relation between activities and subjects is called a "is subactivity of"-relation in the RWS approach. Cognitation is built in a way that it is highly configurable. Therefore this relation can easily be supported by adding an annotation type "Activity", which is used to link concepts of the type activity to parts in the actual documents as shown below (Fig. 1).

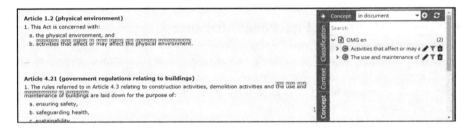

Fig. 1. Identifying activities

The created concepts can then be linked using the "is subactivity of" hierarchical relation by creating a binary concept relation. The type of relation is also configured by an administrator, who is able to add multiple types of relations. In the example of above, three relations are defined:

1. "the use and maintenance of buildings" is subactivity of "activities that affect or may affect the physical environment"
2. "the use of buildings" is subactivity of "the use and maintenance of buildings"
3. "the maintenance of buildings" is subactivity of "the use and maintenance of buildings"

Because the complete set of activities will add up to more than 100 different activities, Cognitation offers the user the possibility to filter a part of the functional structure and to display the hierarchical relations in a tree view.

When performing a certain activity other activities are often involved. For example, when building a new garage, you possibly also need a drive-in from the public road. These kind of relations between activities and/or subjects are necessary to support people and organizations when requesting information about particular activities. For this purpose another concept relation type is introduced: "is legally related to". This relation offers the possibility to define that, when requesting information about a particular activity, other activities are listed as worthwhile looking at as well.

4   Step 2 - Adding Rule Maintenance Objects

Laws, governmental decrees and ministerial regulations are divided into different types of document structure elements, like parts, chapters, sections and articles. An article again can be divided into clauses which can contain lists. These different text parts of a legal document are used to navigate in a legal document (index), but also are the basis for the next part of the analysis.

In the RWS approach these document structure elements of a legislation are linked to the defined activities and subjects. Such a link states that this part of the document concerns this activity or subject. The hierarchical structure of the activities is used to link the document structure elements as high as possible in this structure. All rules that are defined for an activity will by default also apply to the sub-activities of this activity. Therefore linking as high as possible in the hierarchical structure is preferable.

The next step is to classify the document structure elements as irrelevant for the rule analysis process or as a particular rule maintenance object. If a document structure element is irrelevant for the rule analysis process, this part of the document is no longer issue of further analysis. A rule maintenance object describes a certain field of interest for a specific activity or subject. These fields of interest are categorized as follows:

- Scope of the application,
- Permissions,
- Filing requirements,
- Measures,
- Notification requirements,
- Permit requirements,
- Etc.

A categorized document structure element in Cognitation is called a context. As Cognitation is not a RWS application all these categories, similarly to the concepts and relations, are also configurable. Contexts offer the possibility to add traceability to parts of documents up to single paragraphs. Furthermore, it is possible to filter the actual text of a legal document on basis of these contexts. If a document has multiple hundreds of pages, it is convenient to have the possibility to filter the view, so that only the text which is relevant for the activities is shown. Also Cognitation offers the users navigation possibilities between text, contexts and document structure elements, which helps further analysis.

After performing this step in the RWS approach, it is clear what parts of what documents are needed for a particular activity or set of activities. A filter option in

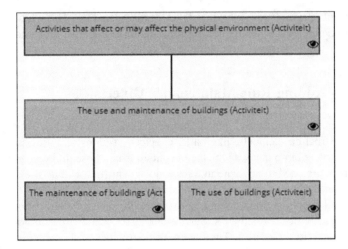

Fig. 2. Functional structure view

Cognitation helps a user to focus on these linked contexts. Also, as shown in the overview of Fig. 2, the user has the possibility to see the linked contexts.

5   Step 3 - Adding the Actual Rules

Now it is clear what parts of the documents are relevant for a particular activity, more thorough analysis can be performed on these sections. Within such a section, one or more legal bases for rules which need to be formalized can be found. A legal base is often a set of words and belongs to a certain category. Again these categories are configurable, but in the RWS approach the following legal base categories are used:

- What
- Where
- How
- How much
- For what
- Who
- When
- Filing requirement

These legal bases are indicated in the text as text annotations of the particular category. The text annotations are all part of the earlier defined contexts, therefore it is also possible to filter out the relevant text annotations for certain activities.

In Cognitation these text annotations can span words from different parts of a document structure element and don't need to be contiguous. Also the same word can be part of multiple text annotations. For lists, the text before the list is often part of text annotation for multiple items of that list.

Additionally, interpretations as to why a certain part of the text is categorized as a particular legal base can be added as well. This helps to understand why a legal analyst made a certain decision.

An example of a categorized text is shown below. As the shown example concerns Dutch legislation the text is also in Dutch (Fig. 3).

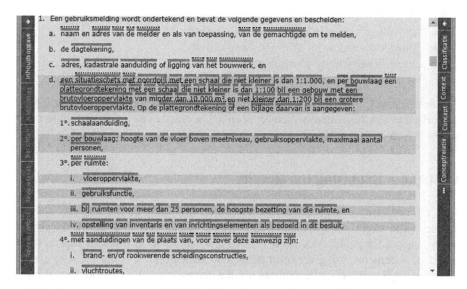

Fig. 3. Annotated legal bases

6 Step 4 – Determining Operating Areas

Parts of the legislation of the Environmental and planning act are limited to certain operating areas. Some rules apply to all of the Netherlands, others only to parts of the Netherlands, like the coastal area or surface water areas. For local governments, an operating area could even be limited to a certain district of a city. Such an operating area exists of one or more polygons. These polygons are described as a set of coordinates.

In the RWS approach, these polygons that describe an operating area are identified with a unique number. This number is used to link an activity or legal base of the category "Where" to an operating area. When formalizing the rules, these are also linked to this operating area number. With this information (rules and operating areas) bundled, a user of the digital counter can easily see which ever set of rules apply to his location in combination with a specific activity.

7 Step 5 – Validating the Annotations

After analyzing a certain part of the functional structure, one wants to be sure that the different annotations (activities, categorized context, legal bases and relations) are consistent. This can be checked using self-defined validations. For example, to have a good functional structure, there are some demands for the activities, subjects and the "is subactivity of"-relations, namely:

- Each activity is subactivity of at most one activity.
- Each subject is subactivity of exactly one activity.
- No activity is subactivity of a subject.
- Is subactivity of-relation has no circularity.

Another check that needs to be performed verifies whether each context that is categorized as a rule maintenance object is linked to exactly one activity or subject and that each such a context has at least one legal base.

8 Step 6 – Exporting the Results

After all violations of validations are resolved, the result of the analysis can be exported. The export of Cognitation exports the documents to a newly developed Dutch standard for public documents [9]. All annotations are exported separated from the actual documents, using the open annotation standard [10].

In the RWS approach, rule analysts use the output to be able to write formal rules which can be used in the digital counter. At all times, all information of the performed analysis is available. This provides traceability of the legal base for all rules used in the digital counter. This is possible because Cognitation has a unique URL for each annotation of the analysis. Entering such an URL into a common browser will lead to the particular part of the document of this annotation.

9 Step 7 – Performing Legal Maintenance

Of course, these legal documents are subject to change. Either to improve them, but also because of changes in other regulations, or just because politicians agree to change some rules.

Instead of repeating the analysis again on the changed document, the document will be uploaded as a new version of an existing document. Cognitation helps the user in viewing the changes of such documents (up to word-level). The user can then migrate all annotations to the newer version, only having to change annotations which contain text changes or adding new annotations for new texts. Also it is possible that a new activity is added, which also influences the functional structure. After applying the necessary changes, the analysis is compliant to the changed regulations.

Cognitation also keeps track of all made changes, which helps in overviewing all changes over time. Also the possibility of defining when which annotation is valid exists, which can help to determine what rules apply at what time.

10   Future Development

RWS is only responsible for a part of the analysis and implementation of the new regulations. Other local governments, like hydrographic confederations, counties and municipalities in the Netherlands also need to apply similar analysis to their part of the process. In the upcoming years this will lead to a lot of changes for these local governments in their process of writing environmental visions, plans, zoning plans, etc.

Because of the complexity of the regulations and current state hereof at these local governments, the intended deadline for compliance to the new law is postponed [8].

11   Summary

The RWS approach for analyzing the legislation of the new Environmental and planning act contains the following steps:

1. *Defining the functional structure*
   A hierarchical structure is defined using the "is subactivity of"-relation between activities and/or subjects. Also the non-hierarchical "is legally related to"-relations are added.
2. *Adding rule maintenance objects*
   For a specific activity or subject it is determined which sections of the legislation describes this activity or subject in more detail. These sections are linked to the activity or subject and then classified into a specific category.
3. *Adding the actual rules*
   Within the rule maintenance objects, legal bases for rules are annotated and classified. Interpretations of the analysts, as to why these annotations are added, are also included.
4. *Determining Operating areas*
   The operating area of an activity or subject is determined and stored. The operating area for specific legal bases of the category "Where" are determined as well.
5. *Validating the annotations*
   All annotations (step 1 to 4) are validated against predefined validation rules. Violations of the validations are repaired.
6. *Exporting the results*
   The results of the previous steps are exported into standardized files (Standaard officiële publicaties (STOP) [9] and Open Annotation standard [10]). These files are used in the tooling for formalizing the rules.
7. *Performing legal maintenance*
   Changes in the legislation are identified and processed.

The support of Cognitation is needed for this process to be able to easily annotate the documents and link all parts of the analysis together. Supporting the user in doing this quickly, but correctly is the main issue for Cognitation. When handling changes in the legislation, Cognitation determines the changes in the documents automatically and where possible migrates the annotations into the new document version.

References

1. Ministerie van Infrastructuur en Milieu, Engelse vertaling Omgevingswet, 24 January 2017. https://www.omgevingswetportaal.nl/documenten/publicaties/2017/01/24/engelse-vertaling-omgevingswet-en-mvt
2. Website Rijkswaterstaat. https://www.rijkswaterstaat.nl/english/index.aspx
3. Rijkswaterstaat, Heading towards 2020. https://staticresources.rijkswaterstaat.nl/binaries/Horizon%20Rijkswaterstaat%202020_tcm21-95317.pdf
4. Informatiepunt omgevingswet, Aan de slag met de omgevingswet. https://aandeslagmetdeomgevingswet.nl/
5. PNA, Rijkswaterstaat kiest Cognitatie. http://www.pna-group.com/rijkswaterstaat-kiest-cognitatie/
6. Dulfer, D., Nijssen, S., Lokin, M.: Developing and maintaining durable specifications for law or regulation based services. In: Ciuciu, I., et al. (eds.) OTM 2015. LNCS, vol. 9416, pp. 169–177. Springer, Cham (2015). https://doi.org/10.1007/978-3-319-26138-6_20
7. Lokin, M., Dulfer, D., Straatsma, P.: Wetsanalyse voor wendbare wetsuitvoering; Voor het bouwen van bruggen tussen wet- en regelgeving en beleid en de informatievoorziening van de overheid, versie 2013-05-13-0755, 057 (2013)
8. Binnenlands bestuur, Begrip voor uitstel invoering Omgevingswet. http://m.binnenlandsbestuur.nl/nieuws/begrip-voor-uitstel-invoering-omgevingswet.184431.lynkx
9. Geonovum, Standaarden omgevingsdocumenten. https://www.geonovum.nl/onderwerpen/omgevingswet/nieuws/standaarden-omgevingsdocumenten
10. W3c, web annotation data model. http://www.w3.org/TR/annotation-model/

An IT-Independent Reference Model for IT-Supported, Interactive, Regulation Based Services

Sjir Nijssen[1]([⊠]), Diederik Dulfer[2], Peter Bollen[3], and Jos Rozendaal[4]

[1] Heerlen, The Netherlands
sjir.nijssen@pna-group.com
[2] Dutch Tax and Customs Administration Apeldoorn,
Apeldoorn, The Netherlands
dph.dulfer@belastingdienst.nl
[3] University of Maastricht, Maastricht, The Netherlands
p.bollen@maastrichtuniversity.nl
[4] Braincap BV, Beverwijk, The Netherlands
jos.rozendaal@gmail.com

Abstract. In 2012 some Dutch government services organizations, academia and innovative companies decided to establish a co-creation, named Blue Chamber, with the aim to develop a national protocol to "translate regulations" into a durable, IT-independent model or specifications for interactive regulation based services. Regulation here means the union of laws and decrees, both government and ministerial. Such a protocol acts like a process and each process requires a conceptual data structure or IT-independent reference model. After 5 years of research, development and validation, version 1 of the Reference model is ready for publication. The Dutch Government has decided to provide IT-based services and enforcement actions based on as many laws and decrees as appropriate. The core of this Reference model will be described in this paper. The CogNIAM variant of Fact Based Modeling has been used to develop the Reference model, using field-testing with the associated prototypes.

Keywords: IT-independent durable model for regulation based services
Legal services · Legal relations · Legal facts · Fact Based Modeling (FBM)
Legal domain reference protocol

1 Introduction

The Netherlands, like many other countries, has a number of governmental bodies responsible for the execution and enforcement of the applicable regulation. Regulation in this paper means the union of laws, government decrees, ministerial decrees and several other policies, including decisions by the courts. The intent of the regulation needs to be faithfully applied in all practical scenarios or cases. The legislation

S. Nijssen—Retired from PNA Group, Heerlen, The Netherlands

C. Debruyne et al. (Eds.): OTM 2017 Workshops, LNCS 10697, pp. 173–182, 2018.
https://doi.org/10.1007/978-3-319-73805-5_18

describes roughly speaking which rights and duties are applicable for a specific citizen or enterprise and under which circumstances; it furthermore describes the consequences of legal facts. For a faithful application of the regulation in all practical scenarios it is needed to model explicitly all the semantics *intended* in the practical scenarios or cases.

In Sect. 2 we describe very briefly the AS-IS situation as of 2013. In Sect. 3 we describe the TO-BE situation as of 2017. In Sect. 4 the Conceptual Architecture for regulation based services, as developed in the period 2013–2015, will be briefly described. In Sect. 5 we present the principles on which the Reference Model for IT-supported, interactive, regulation based services is based. In Sect. 6 we present the core of the IT-independent reference model, a domain model for IT-independent, interactive, regulation based services. In Sect. 7 we present a summary and suggestions for the road ahead.

2   The AS-IS Situation as of 2013 for Regulation Based Services

In the initial period of Q1 2012 through Q3 2013 the focus of the Blue Chamber was to describe the then current situation.

We quote a part of the first report [6] of the Blue Chamber below.

"In recent decades, public administration has changed under the influence of digitization. These changes affect the processes of implementing public services. Both the large-scale processes for handling cases of large groups of citizens, and processes for the treatment of individual cases in complex situations are affected. Examples can be found in the area of benefit provision, granting of subsidies, licensing and taxation. Central government, provincial governments and municipalities strive, as much as possible, to process applications for licenses, benefits and the provision of other public services electronically."

Intermediate results of the Blue Chamber have been reported in [1, 4, 5, 7–9, 19], [20] and [21]. The approach adopted by the Blue Chamber has several concepts adopted from [2, 3, 10, 11, 15].

3   The Goals for the TO-BE Situation as Seen in 2017

In the first report of the Blue Chamber, the TO-BE situation, was described as follows: "In legislation rights and obligations are defined: among citizens, citizens towards the government and vice versa. Legislation contains concepts, rules and conditions that directly affect the actions of citizens, businesses and government organizations. These concepts, rules and conditions form the basis for the services and processes of public implementing bodies. For the following reasons, it is important to be able to distill concepts, rules and conditions from the legislation in an unambiguous and repeatable manner:

A. It promotes legal certainty for citizens and prevents unnecessary disputes and proceedings in court.
B. It enhances the transparency of government. The government can show that what they are doing is in accordance with the democratically established legislation.

This includes providing insight into the rules that give the authorities a margin of discretion to do justice in special cases.

C. It simplifies implementation of legislation in services and processes. Thus, orders from politics and public demands can be accommodated more rapidly.

D. It improves an implementing body's capacity to, as part of ex ante feasibility tests, to provide feedback on proposed changes in legislation. This contributes positively to the effectiveness and efficiency of the implementation.

E. It provides insight into the coherence of the complex of legislation. Consequently, generic and specific elements in processes and services can more easily be distinguished. This offers possibilities for reuse, not only within an organization, but also between organizations.

In short, the added value of a repeatable approach to the organization of the implementation of legislation comes from the ability to transform legislation into legitimate and meaningful services for citizens and businesses and to perform this in a truthful, efficient, multidisciplinary and timely fashion [6].

This is still the TO-BE situation as of 2017.

4 The Durable Architecture for the TO-BE Situation

Since late 2013 it became clear in the co-creation group that there was a need for an overall durable architecture covering the main groups and results involved. The status of it as of mid-2016 has been reported in [19].

After many lengthy discussions in 2016 it became clear that one has to distinguish two different phases in this process, the preparation phase and the phase in which the citizens and companies consume the regulation based. The preparation phase is hardly known to the average citizen. Why should the citizen care about this? The preparation phase is on the other hand essential for the quality of the IT-supported, interactive, regulation based services (Table 1).

The actor group in preparation phase 1 consists of members of Parliament, and members of government and civil servants legally trained to produce regulations. Often the coalition agreement is one of the most important starting documents in the process of defining new (versions of) regulations.

For the regulation based services there is another set of actors very important, namely the judges in the courts. In time they come after the regulation based service has been consumed, but they have a similar effect on the services thereafter as the original regulation as their decisions have a clear effect on similar cases of services.

Regulations are produced to provide services for the citizens and enterprises, or require them to perform certain duties. These services are in The Netherlands primarily IT-based. The IT based services outnumber the lawyer assisted services by far, although there is hardly any mention of IT-supported services in the academic education of legal experts in The Netherlands.

The traditional textual representation of the regulation is not adequate to be used as drawings for the IT regulation based service engineers.

Table 1. Different phases in implementation of IT supported, interactive, regulation based services

	Preparation phase			Service consumption
	1	2	3	
	Formulate and decide on a new (version of) regulation	Translate regulation into the IT-independent specifications for IT-supported, interactive, regulation based services	Translate IT-independent specifications into a specific IT-solution	
Major actors	Members of Parliament and regulation specification experts	Multidisciplinary team consisting service experts, regulation experts and durable specification experts	Software engineers	Citizens and companies
Major challenge	To be completed	From logically informal to logically formal	From IT-independent, logically formal to IT-dependent, logically formal	
Legally formal	Yes	Yes	Yes	Yes
Logically formal	No	Yes	Yes	Yes
IT-independent	Yes	Yes	No	No

What is needed for IT-supported, interactive, regulation based services is a complete specification that takes the regulation as input and produces a testable IT-independent specification of the interaction between the government service providers and the citizens or enterprises. This is a multidisciplinary effort and in principle independent of IT such that new IT technologies can be based on the durable specifications or model. The actor group 2 in preparation phase 2 consists of legal experts, service experts, specification experts and service architects.

An essential task of the actors in preparation phase 2 is to provide the two-way references between the durable model of the services and the regulations as it is required in The Netherlands that all regulation based services need to be based on approved regulations. This is also needed for impact analysis and certification. Often this is also referred to as annotation services. However the concept annotation service in the traditional legal field consists of a free format text; we mean here with annotation the classification of pieces of texts in the regulations to one of the elements of the classification scheme or Reference model. The specifications of the durable model can be represented with traditional Word, PDF or Excel documents, or by the so-called a *fully classified model*, a representation that can be consulted with a logical language. An organization has a choice. No matter what the choice is, there is a need to know which requirement is based on which pieces of texts in the regulations.

Actor group 3 consists of the engineers of the IT-supported services. The engineers take as input the logically formal and legally formal IT-independent specifications of the interaction and the function of the services (the durable model) just like a builder of a large office block receives as input the drawings of the architect, and build the services. The goal is to maximize the functionality that provides the automatic mapping from the durable specifications into an executable IT-supported service.

Actor group 4 consists of the citizens or enterprises that receive the services of the government service provider or the duty dispatching service.

5 The Principles That Have to be Satisfied by a Reference Model for IT-Supported, Interactive, Regulation Based Services

In the section we present the principles upon which the Reference model is based.

5.1 Legality Principle

One of the requirements for which the law makers are not willing to compromise, is that the services provided should be fully based on the regulation and faithfully represents the intent of the regulation in all relevant practical cases. Hence that means that the durable model must represent the full semantics as intended in the regulation (knowledge level II [16]) to apply to all the foreseen cases or scenarios (knowledge level I). This means that the language to describe the durable model (knowledge level II) must be capable of describing explicitly what the semantics as specified in the regulation mean in the associated practical cases (knowledge level I). Here we see a strong link between the level I of the knowledge triangle (the level of the facts) and the domain specific regulation, knowledge level II. Further description of the elements at knowledge level II can be found in [16].

5.2 The Knowledge Microscope Principle

The approach taken here is that of observation, detect patterns and draw generalized conclusions. This principle is re-used from a well-accepted principle in natural sciences: "Use a microscope, describe what you see and generalize towards a consistent theory".

In this approach we make use of the so called knowledge microscope. Hence put a sufficient set of regulation texts under the knowledge microscope and a representative set of associated services and conclude which knowledge elements are needed to fully describe the semantics for all relevant practical cases. This process is not new and listens to the term ex-ante in legal textbooks.

The knowledge microscope is operated by a durable knowledge modeler (2nd, 3rd and 4th author) who submits questions on concrete scenarios to a legal expert (1st author). Specifying a durable model is a multi-disciplinary task, not a durable modeler as a hermit.

6   The Core of the Reference Model

Several regulations have been analyzed in the last 5 years to find out which constructs are observable that play a role in the regulation based services.

It is the intent of the group to publish the complete Reference model after it has been discussed in a number of external groups in the coming months.

The main aspects of the Reference model are the following:

I. Make a clear distinction between law (objective perspective) and rights and duties of an individual legal subject (subjective perspective).
II. Define explicitly the context that applies to the regulation based services. A context may consist of any number of texts, not necessarily consecutive, from one or more different regulations.
III. Define the legal subjects, within the context and distinguish the objective and subjective perspective.
IV. Add to this the state aspects, the legal relationships, forming the legal situation of a legal subject, and the conditions that apply to the legal relationships.
V. Add to this the transition aspects (Legal facts) between a legal situation and the legal consequences that lead to a different legal situation.

6.1   The First Shell: The Legal Subjects Within the Context and Subjective Perspective

If there are no legal subjects, there is no law or regulation. Legal subjects are natural persons or legal constructs like foundation, union or company. Be aware that each jurisdiction (country, and sometimes a part of a country) has its own set of legal constructs (Fig. 1).

Fig. 1. The legal context

6.2   The Second Shell: Legal Subjects and Legal States

A legal relationship type is a relationship type between two legal subject types, one of which holds the right side, while the other legal subject holds the duty side, with respect to a certain item (e.g. the power to modify the existing number of working hours in a labor agreement). This is part of the law, hence the objective perspective (Fig. 2).

Law

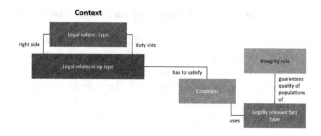

Fig. 2. Legal subjects and legal states

Different cases and scenario's happen in the world of the subjective perspective, and therefore each individual legal relationship has a start date and sometimes a known end date.

In the law a legal relationship has an associated set of conditions that must be met to make the legal relationship valid.

Associated with every condition in the case are one or more fact instances of fact types that have to be properly specified. These fact types could be named legally relevant fact types. Please note that each legal fact is a legally relevant fact, but only some legally relevant facts are legal facts.

There are a number of quality control rules (integrity rules) that apply to the legally relevant facts. It is unfortunate that lawmakers seldom specify the complete set of integrity rules. These are required for the specification for IT-supported, interactive, regulation based services. Of course having them all explicitly available takes some jobs away. At the time of writing of this paper a discussion has emerged whether POTUS (President Of The United States) can pardon himself. This is a typical example of a missing integrity rule. We have observed in the last three years that many integrity rules are missing in Dutch regulations. If the US constitution had been specified with this Reference model as guideline, then it would certainly have included the integrity rule that POTUS can pardon himself.

The code in the Constitution says:

`Section 2. \1\The President [...] shall have Power to grant Reprieves and Pardons for Offences against the United States, except in Cases of Impeachment.`

Here clearly the integrity rule is forgotten to specify explicitly: `No President has the power to pardon himself.`

In the years since 2013 the research of various Dutch regulations has resulted in the observation that there are at least 7 kinds of legal relationships, three kinds of claim-duty and two kinds of power-liability, one liberty-noright and immunity-nopower, that can be grouped into the four kinds of legal relationships similar to the Hohfeld classification of ref. 10.

So far we have only discussed the legal subjects and the legal states. As we live in a dynamic world, we need transitions from one legal state to another, as we will see in the third shell. Legal transitions are usually called legal facts in traditional law books.

6.3   The Third Shell: Legal Subjects, Legal States and Legal Transitions

The term for a legal transition in the traditional law textbooks is legal fact. A legal fact may result in the creation of zero, one or more legal relationships, in the modification of an attribute of zero, one or more existing legal relationships and/or the ending of zero, one or more legal relationships, with the rule that there is at least one of these three, guaranteeing that the legal situation before and after the legal fact are different.

There are two subtypes of legal facts, one with an active legal subject, which can be further subtyped into a legal act (of a legal subject) and an act with legal consequences of a legal subject; in the other subtype no legal subject is an actor and this can be further subtyped into events with legal consequences and time laps with legal consequences (Fig. 3).

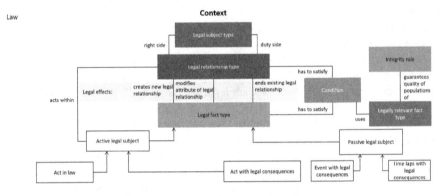

Fig. 3. Legal subjects, legal states and legal transitions

The reference model has been prototyped using a language workbench in which the reference model has been implemented as a set of Domain Specific Languages. Based on these language specifications the interactive regulation based service have been written of a specific law. The language workbench was configured in such a way that based on the specifications a simulation (ex-ante) could be executed of the interactive regulation based service. During the simulation the legal position of each of the legal subjects is shown. Based on the legal position a list of possible acts is derived. Based on this list an act can be executed. Executing the act resulted in legal consequences which changed the legal positions of the legal subjects.

7   Conclusions and Future Work

The Blue Chamber has adopted the knowledge microscope principle. A working group of the Blue Chamber will present the Reference model later this year in open sessions in The Netherlands. The Reference model is the result of observation and generalization. There is at the time of writing no single ISO, OMG or W3C standard modeling language that has the representational power required by the Reference model. Hence one needs a smart combination of various standards and of course some interfaces between the various standards. It is currently under consideration that the Blue Chamber will publish a proposal for such a standard language.

Acknowledgements. The authors gratefully acknowledge the many discussions in the Blue Chamber and in particular Mrs. Mariette Lokin since June 2012. The Blue Chamber a multi-disciplinary group with the principle that each member brings more sandwiches to the lunch than he intends to eat and users are the ultimate decision makers whether or not a modeling approach is accepted. The authors express their thanks to the colleagues of the Blue Chamber for their inspiring sessions. The Blue Chamber will continue in the future to improve the development and maintenance of regulation based specifications for services.

References

1. Brattinga, M., Nijssen, S.: A sustainable architecture for durable modeling of laws and regulations and main concepts of the durable model. In: Ciuciu, I., et al. (eds.) OTM 2015. LNCS, vol. 9416, pp. 254–265. Springer, Cham (2015). https://doi.org/10.1007/978-3-319-26138-6_29
2. Corbin, A.: Legal Analysis and Terminology. Yale Law School (1919)
3. Corbin, A.: Jural Relations and Their Classification. Yale Law School (1921)
4. Dulfer, D., Nijssen, S., Lokin, M.: Developing and maintaining durable specifications for law or regulation based services. In: Ciuciu, I., et al. (eds.) OTM 2015. LNCS, vol. 9416, pp. 169–177. Springer, Cham (2015). https://doi.org/10.1007/978-3-319-26138-6_20
5. van Engers, T.M., Nijssen, S.: Bridging social reality with rules. Paper presented at IRIS 2014, Das Internationale Rechtsinformatik Symposion, Salzburg, Austria, 21 February 2014
6. Van Engers, T., Nijssen, S.: Connecting people: semantic-conceptual modeling for laws and regulations. In: Janssen, M., Scholl, H.J., Wimmer, Maria A., Bannister, F. (eds.) EGOV 2014. LNCS, vol. 8653, pp. 133–146. Springer, Heidelberg (2014). https://doi.org/10.1007/978-3-662-44426-9_11
7. van Engers, T., Nijssen, S.: From legislation towards the provision of services – an approach to agile implementation of legislation. In: Kő, A., Francesconi, E. (eds.) EGOVIS 2014. LNCS, vol. 8650, pp. 163–172. Springer, Cham (2014). https://doi.org/10.1007/978-3-319-10178-1_13
8. van Engers, T.M., van Doesburg, R.: First steps towards a formal analysis of law. In: Malzahn, D., Conceição, G. (eds.) eKNOW 2015, pp. 36–42. IARIA (2015)
9. van Engers, T.M., van Doesburg, R.: At your service, on the definition of services from sources of law. In: Proceedings of the 15th International Conference on Artificial Intelligence and Law (ICAIL 2015), pp. 221–225. ACM, New York (2015)
10. Hohfeld, W.N.: Fundamental Legal Conceptions as Applied in Judicial Reasoning (2010). Cook, W.W. (ed.) ISBN-13: 978-1-58477-162-3
11. ISO TR9007, Concepts and terminology for the Conceptual Schema and the Information Base, ISO Technical report (1987)
12. Saton, J., Kleemans, F.: Developing the uniform economic transaction protocol: a fact based modeling approach for creating the economic internet protocol. In: Ciuciu, I., et al. (eds.) OTM 2015. LNCS, vol. 9416, pp. 276–285. Springer, Cham (2015). https://doi.org/10.1007/978-3-319-26138-6_31

13. Lemmens, I., Pleijsant, J.M., Arntz, R.: Using fact-based modelling to develop a common language - a use case. In: Ciuciu, I., et al. (eds.) OTM 2015. LNCS, vol. 9416, pp. 197–205. Springer, Cham (2015). https://doi.org/10.1007/978-3-319-26138-6_23

14. Lemmens, I., Koster, J.-P., Valera, S.: Achieving interoperability at semantic level. In: Ciuciu, I., et al. (eds.) OTM 2015. LNCS, vol. 9416, pp. 206–215. Springer, Cham (2015). https://doi.org/10.1007/978-3-319-26138-6_24

15. Nijssen, G.M.: A Framework for Discussion in ISO/TC97/SC5/WG3, 78.09/01 (1978)

16. Nijssen, S., Valera, S.: An architecture ecosystem for the whole systems perspective, including system dynamics, based on logic & set theory and controlled natural languages. Working paper for the OMG Architecture Ecosystem SIG (2012)

17. Rozendaal, J., Nijssen, S.: A durable architecture as a foundation for regulation based services. In: Ciuciu, I., Debruyne, C., Panetto, H., Weichhart, G., Bollen, P., Fensel, A., Vidal, M.-E. (eds.) OTM 2016. LNCS, vol. 10034, pp. 164–173. Springer, Cham (2017). https://doi.org/10.1007/978-3-319-55961-2_16

18. Rozendaal, J., Nijssen, S.: A proposal for a regulations based services language. In: Ciuciu, I., Debruyne, C., Panetto, H., Weichhart, G., Bollen, P., Fensel, A., Vidal, M.-E. (eds.) OTM 2016. LNCS, vol. 10034, pp. 174–182. Springer, Cham (2017). https://doi.org/10.1007/978-3-319-55961-2_17

19. Straatsma, P., Dulfer, D.: Wendbare Wetsuitvoering. In: DREAM 2014 (2014)

The Role of States and Transitions in IT-Supported, Interactive, Regulation Based Services

Sjir Nijssen[1(✉)], Diederik Dulfer[2], Peter Bollen[3], and Jos Rozendaal[4]

[1] Heerlen, The Netherlands
sjir.nijssen@pna-group.com
[2] Dutch Tax and Customs Administration, Apeldoorn, The Netherlands
dph.dulfer@belastingdienst.nl
[3] University of Maastricht, Maastricht, The Netherlands
p.bollen@maastrichtuniversity.nl
[4] Braincap BV, Beverwijk, The Netherlands
jos.rozendaal@gmail.com

Abstract. The theory and engineering of states and transitions has been developed since WWII, with considerable success. Since 2012 some Dutch government services organizations, academia and innovative companies decided to establish a co-creation, named Blue Chamber, with the aim to develop a national protocol to "translate the regulations" into a durable, IT-independent model or specifications for IT-supported, interactive, regulation based services. Regulation here means the union of laws, associated decrees and policies, both government and ministerial. Such a protocol acts like a process and each process requires a conceptual data structure or IT-independent reference model. During the analysis of the deep structure of regulations and the associated services it became clear that the theory and application of states and transitions could be applied as innovative tool in the process of specifying the durable specifications. In this paper we describe this approach using a small but significant law and associated services.

Keywords: States and transitions as a modeling tool in IT-supported · Interactive
Regulation based services · Diagrammatic representation of scenario's
using extended state and transition diagrams · Fact based modeling (FBM)

1 Introduction

IT-supported, interactive, regulation based services are on the rise in The Netherlands, like in many other countries in recent decades. The community that defines these regulations is not always fully aware that the regulations need to take into account the new opportunities of IT-supported, interactive, regulation based services as that trade is so far hardly using any intelligent software applications.

S. Nijssen—Retired from PNA Group, Heerlen, The Netherlands.

C. Debruyne et al. (Eds.): OTM 2017 Workshops, LNCS 10697, pp. 183–192, 2018.
https://doi.org/10.1007/978-3-319-73805-5_19

One of the results of the co-creation was the discovery that there is a solid base to unify the various approaches to laws and IT-supported, interactive, regulation based services. We mention with pleasure the paper of reference [2]. Regulation in this paper means the union of laws, government decrees, ministerial decrees and several other policies, and also including decisions by the courts.

The legality principle specifies that the intent of the regulation needs to be faithfully applied in all practical scenarios or cases or service.

The legislation describes roughly speaking which rights and duties are applicable for a specific citizen or enterprise and under which circumstances; it furthermore describes the consequences of legal facts. For a faithful application of the regulation in all practical scenarios it is needed to model explicitly all the semantics *intended* in the practical scenarios. In another paper we have described the core of the Reference model for IT-supported, interactive regulation based services [7].

In Sect. 2 we summarize the core of the Reference model. In Sect. 3 we turn our focus to testing the service before issuing the legislation. In the Dutch legal system testing in advance (called ex-ante) of issuing the legislation is part of the way how to specify a regulation, but it is seldom completed and unfortunately not part of the official Government publications. [9] For testing the services in advance it is recommended by the Blue Chamber to go through the experience that the citizen or company will have to go through. In doing so in the working group it was discovered that the knowledge about states and transitions can be adequately re-used in this field to model the actual experience. We describe in Sect. 4 that there is a need to distinguish three different types of states, legal, intermediate legal and interactive, the last two with no legal change with the respect to the most recent legal state. In Sect. 5 we quote part of a small but representative law for which we will describe in the next section how the graphical tool of states and transitions can be applied. In Sect. 6 we model the experience that an employee and the employer go through when the employee makes use of his power to request an adjustment to the number of his agreed working hours of the contract signed or the small employer fulfils his duty to specify a regulation for his situation. The Government has given in this act a qualified power to employees to adjust their obligated number of working hours to help in the new situation that there is a need for more adjustment of working hours. The old system 8 till 5, Monday through Friday, is not any longer adequate in this situation. A small employer has the duty to specify a regulation fit for his small company. This modeling is done with extended state transition diagrams. It clearly demonstrates the higher productivity of structured legal information over the traditional textual representation. In Sect. 7 we present a summary and suggestions for the road ahead.

2   The Core of the Reference Model for Regulation Based Services

During the last 4 years the co-creation effort also included what is called Comparative Law [6]. However where Comparative Law in the Law Faculties focus on the different surface structure languages, we came to the conclusion that we had to focus on the deep structure meaning of an expression for its intent in the regulation based service. For several regulations a deep structure analysis has been performed to find out which constructs are observable that play an essential role in the IT-supported, interactive, regulation based services.

The main aspects of the Reference model are the following:

I.   Define explicitly the context for the regulation based services. A context may consist of any number of texts, not necessarily consecutive, from one or more different regulations. For regulation based services it may be necessary to specify e.g. the company as its Collective Labor Agreement may have an impact.
II. Define the legal subjects, within the context and distinguish the objective and subjective perspective. If there are no legal subjects, there will be no regulation based services. A legal subject is a bearer of right and duties, that can perform legal acts and acts with legal consequences.
III. Context and legal subjects the state aspects. The core of the state aspects are the legal relationships, forming the legal situation of a legal subject. A legal relationship is a relationship in which one legal subject has the right side and another legal subject has the duty side, with respect to a certain subject, e.g. the right to adjust the agreed working hours. So far there have been detected 7 different kinds of legal relationships in the European Dutch jurisdiction.
IV. The conditions that apply to the legal relationships.
V.   The transition aspects (Legal facts) between a legal situation and the legal consequences that lead to a different legal situation.
VI. Add the conditions that apply to the transitions.
VII. Make a clear distinction between law (objective perspective) and rights and duties of an individual legal subject (subjective perspective).
VIII. The fact types for all legally relevant facts.
IX. The integrity rules for the fact populations.
X.   The required concept definitions.
XI. Add the legal provisions for delegator and the delegee.

For more on the Reference model for IT-supported, interactive, regulation based services see ref. [3].

3   Testing the Services Before Issuing the Legislation: Ex-Ante

Testing is an essential process in any non-trivial endeavor. As many people know that have experience with large scale systems, testing is key in the success and the earlier the better.

It is interesting to note that testing has been prescribed in the Netherlands for the specification of regulations since a long time. It is referred to by the term ex-ante. However it is seldom or never performed completely. And very unfortunately, the test records are not part of the official publications.

It became clear in the co-creative effort that systematic, multidisciplinary testing is part of the most productive approach to get to high quality regulations, and associated high quality IT-supported, interactive, regulation based services. In a multidisciplinary group the services are "lived through" on the basis of the draft legislation. This gives valuable insights to improve the regulations.

In the last two years it became clear that we could re-use of valuable theory and engineering practices developed in other scientific disciplines, and that was the theory of states and transitions that has been developed since WWII. Most people in the world that use a smart phone have extensive experience with operating a state and transition service.

In looking at the conventional legal services, states and transitions are a welcome re-use and greatly helps in the understanding and application of regulations. However, when taking into account that we want to work with IT-supported and interactive services, this requires a few extensions to the classical state and transitions diagrams as will be described in the next section.

4   Why Three Different Kinds of States?

During the development of the Reference model using extensive test cases of IT-supported, interactive, regulation based services it became clear that there is a need to distinguish three different kinds of state.

A legal state contains all the legal relationships of a certain number of legal subjects within a certain context.

A legal intermediate state has the same legal state as the last visited but contains already parts of a transaction that needs other parts for completion and the completion is a new legal state.

An interactive state contains no modification with the last visited legal or legal intermediate state; it is part of an interactive service to assist a legal subject in getting errors out of the way.

5   Working Hours Adjustment Act (WHAA): A Small but Representative Act

Below we present a small but representative regulation for the discussion of the states and transitions.

(Entry into force of this version: July 1st, 2000)

Act of February 19, 2000, concerning rules on the right to adjust the working hours (Working Hours Adjustment Act)

General Clause

Article 1

In this act and the decrees based thereon, the following definitions apply:

a. employer: one who – based on a contract of employment subject to civil law or public appointment – lets another perform labor;
b. employee: the 'another', as mentioned under a.

Right of adjustment of number of working hours
Article 2

1. The employee can request the employer for adjustment of the working hours arising from his contract of employment or public appointment, if the employee has been in the employment of said employer for the duration of at least one year prior to the intended date of commencement of the adjustment. For the calculation of the one year term, consecutive periods in which work is performed shall be aggregated if the interval between periods amounts to no more than three months. The preceding sentence shall apply mutatis mutandis to periods in which work is performed for different employers, when said employers can reasonably be deemed to be each other's successor with respect to the work performed.
2. For military officials the right to adjust working hours is governed by Order in Council on the recommendation of Our Minister of Defence and Our Minister of Social Affairs and Employment using unpaid leave for part-time work.
3. The request for adjustment of working hours will have to be submitted in writing to the employer at least four months prior to the intended commencement date of the adjustment, stating the commencement date, the magnitude of the adjustment of working hours per week or, if hours of work has been established for a different period the adjustment for said period, and the desired distribution of hours over the week or other period agreed upon. The employee can resubmit a request for adjustment of working hours at most once every two years, after the employer has granted or rejected a previous request.
4. The employer shall consult with the employee concerning the employee's request.
5. The employer shall grant the employee's request for adjustment of working hours in so far as it concerns the date of commencement and the magnitude of the adjustment, unless substantial business or service interests dictate otherwise.
6. The employer shall determine the distribution of hours in accordance with the wishes of the employee. The employer can change the distribution of the hours if the interests of the employee must yield for reasons of reasonableness and fairness.
7. The employer shall notify the employee in writing with respect to the decision on the request for adjustment of working hours. If the employer does not grant the request or determines a distribution of the working hours in deviation from the wishes of the employee, this shall be notified in writing providing a statement of the reasons.
8. [...]
9. If the employer has not provided a decision on the request one month before the intended commencement date of the adjustment, the working hours will be adjusted according to the request of the employee.
10. [...]
11. This article does not apply to an employer with fewer than 10 employees. This employer must make arrangements regarding the right of employees to adjust their working hours.

6   Modeling the Experience of the Service

In this section we will describe the experience initiated by the employee exercising his power to request adjusting his working hours, in terms of different states of different types, the transitions and its justification in the regulation.

To be representative it is strongly recommended to start with the first legal state before the start of the act. Why? It happens that legal subjects asked at any time what their rights and obligations are in the context of the WHAA. It is actually part of a legal case as published in jurisprudence about the WHAA. In the time before the start of the validity of the act, no employee nor employer has a right or obligation in the *context* of the WHAA. This is represented as Legal State 0, LS0 in Fig. 1. A legal state is represented as a rectangle with solid thick lines, with a short identifying code and a brief description of the legal relationship.

The legal state before the start of the WHAA 2000

Fig. 1.   Start state

The next interesting legal state is the result of the time becoming the first of July, 2000. This transition is represented as a solid arrow in the diagram of Fig. 2, with a clock to denote that this transition is performed by the time becoming 2000-07-01 ISO Date Convention. It is the time has as legal result the associated legal relationship as is represented in Fig. 2. Here we see that the employee has the power to request an adjustment of the agreed working hours from his employer. The transition from legal state LS0 to LS1 is the time 2000-07-01, the start date of the WHAA.

The WHAA 2000 becomes valid

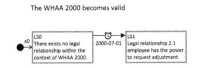

Fig. 2.   WHAA 2000 becomes valid

In Legal state LS1 there exist a legal relationship between the legal subject employee as the right holder (power) and the legal subject the employer as the duty holder (liability), with respect to an adjustment of the working hours. The employee can in legal state LS1 decide to make use of his power to request an adjustment in working hours. This act by the employee is *intended* as a legal act. However, there are conditions to the legal act and they need to be agreed by the employer, for the legal act to have the legal consequences. That is the reason that in Fig. 3 the arrow between legal state LS1 and legal intermediate state LIS1 is a an arrow with dots and small line, while the act is in a similar circle to denote that it is part of the acts that are required from the legal subjects. Hence this *intended* legal act by the employee results in a Legal Intermediate State.

Why? There can be errors in the request (e.g. number of working hours is inconsistent with the desired distribution; or the commencement date has been forgotten, or is in the past and so on). Hence legal intermediate state is the same legal state as LS1, but has an intermediate effect as the employer can now communicate the errors to the requesting employee. An intermediate legal state is represented by a rectangle with thick interrupted lines.

Fig. 3. Request employee

The current version of the Dutch Civil Code was specified in the period roughly 1960–1990 and in that period it was not known that we would have IT-supported, inter-active, regulation based services. Hence the Dutch Civil Code does currently not describe sufficiently precise, how to specify an IT-supported, interactive, regulation based service. Hence the Dutch Civil Code needs to be extended to cater for IT-supported, interactive, regulation based services. In the meantime however the serv-ices are already needed and in operation. The abbreviation eE stands for employee, the abbreviation eR for employer.

The employer identifies the errors in the request of the employee and notifies the employee via arrow a, and this generates a new interactive state (still the same legal state), see Fig. 4. An interactive state is represented by a rectangle with thin lines.

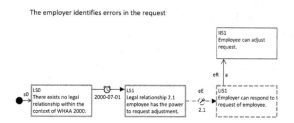

Fig. 4. Errors in the request

In the interactive intermediate state IIS1 the employee can correct the errors and re-submit the request to the employer via arrow b. This is represented in Fig. 5.

The employee responds to the errors

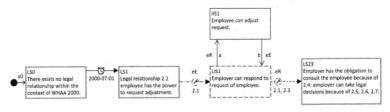

Fig. 5. Responding to the errors

The employer declares that all conditions are satisfied

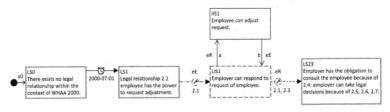

Fig. 6. All conditions satisfied

The employer now receives (hopefully) a modified request. It can still have one or more errors and then the actions of arrow a en b can be repeated. When there are no errors and all conditions are satisfied, the employer declares this and then the legal act by the employee (!) is finished and has the legal consequences as specified in 2.4, 2.5, 2.6 and 2.7 as presented in Fig. 6.

Please note there is a difference in arrow 2.1 and arrow 2.1, 2.3 to denote the different kinds of actions by the employee and the employer.

In Fig. 7 we present the graphical information about the possible paths. One can quickly see that the employer has three courses of action (mutually exclusive), in legal state LS23, use article 2.5 ls (last sentence), use article 2.5 fs (first sentence) or let the time decide (article 2.10). Applying article 2.5 first sentence leads to a legal intermediate

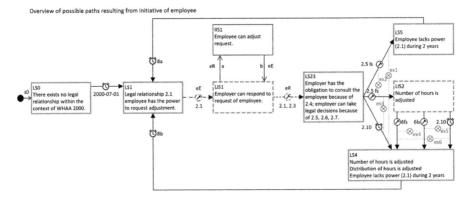

Fig. 7. Possible paths employee

state LIS2, in which the employer has again the choice using of three each other excluding options. And thereafter we see quickly that the situation comes back to Legal State 1 (LS1) via transition (legal fact) 8a or 8b as 2 years have passed.

In Fig. 8 we have represented the possible paths that can be followed from the initiative of the employer. The legal fact 1 (transition from legal state LS1 to LS2) means that the employer has grown to 10 or more employees, in which situation he has no duty to specify a specific provision for his enterprise. The opposite happens with legal fact 2, when the employment situation moves from 10 or more to less than 10. Please note that the code for a state is unique within an initiative.

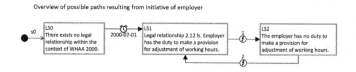

Overview of possible paths resulting from initiative of employer

Fig. 8. Possible paths employer

For the main legal subjects for the WHAA these are the two initiatives and the possible paths after the initiative.

It is our belief that this kind of graphical information to provides a more productive overview of the act than the traditional textual representation.

7   Conclusions and Future Work

The Blue Chamber been working on new ways to get to the complete and tested specification for IT-supported, interactive, regulation based services. During that effort it was detected that one could usefully make use of the state and transition theories developed in the sciences and engineering disciplines.

The working group is currently working on another concept to be added, the legal subject transaction.

Acknowledgements. The authors gratefully acknowledge the many discussions in the Blue Chamber and especially Mrs. Mariette Lokin, since June 2012. The Blue Chamber a multi-disciplinary group with the principle that each member brings more sandwiches to the lunch than he intends to eat and users are the ultimate decision makers whether or not a modeling approach is accepted. The authors express their thanks to the colleagues of the Blue Chamber for their inspiring sessions. The Blue Chamber will continue in the future to improve the development and maintenance of regulation based specifications for services.

References

1. Dulfer, D., Nijssen, S., Lokin, M.: Developing and maintaining durable specifications for law or regulation based services. In: Ciuciu, I., et al. (eds.) OTM 2015. LNCS, vol. 9416, pp. 169–177. Springer, Cham (2015). https://doi.org/10.1007/978-3-319-26138-6_20
2. Hohfeld, W.N.: Fundamental legal conceptions as applied in judicial reasoning. In: Cook, W.W. (ed.) (2010). ISBN-13: 978-1-58477-162-3
3. Lokin, M., Nijssen, S., Dulfer, D., Bollen, P., Rozendaal, J.: An IT-independent reference model for IT-supported, interactive, regulation based services. In: Debruyne, C., Panetto, H., Weichhart, G., Bollen, P., Ciuciu, I., Vidal, M.E., Meersman, R. (eds.) OTM 2017 Workshops. LNCS, vol. 10697, pp. 173–182. Springer, Cham (2018)
4. Rozendaal, J., Nijssen, S.: A durable architecture as a foundation for regulation based services. In: Ciuciu, I., Debruyne, C., Panetto, H., Weichhart, G., Bollen, P., Fensel, A., Vidal, M.-E. (eds.) OTM 2016. LNCS, vol. 10034, pp. 164–173. Springer, Cham (2017). https://doi.org/10.1007/978-3-319-55961-2_16
5. Rozendaal, J., Nijssen, S.: A proposal for a regulations based services language. In: Ciuciu, I., Debruyne, C., Panetto, H., Weichhart, G., Bollen, P., Fensel, A., Vidal, M.-E. (eds.) OTM 2016. LNCS, vol. 10034, pp. 174–182. Springer, Cham (2017). https://doi.org/10.1007/978-3-319-55961-2_17
6. Steenhof, G.: Teaching comparative law, comparative law teaching. Electron. J. Comp. Law **6.4** (2002). http://www.ejcl.org/64/art64-4.html

Meaning Based Structured Legal Code

Sjir Nijssen[1(✉)], Diederik Dulfer[2], Peter Bollen[3], and Jos Rozendaal[4]

[1] PNA Group, Heerlen, The Netherlands
sjir.nijssen@pna-group.com
[2] Dutch Tax and Customs Administration Apeldoorn,
Apeldoorn, The Netherlands
dph.dulfer@belastingdienst.nl
[3] University of Maastricht, Maastricht, The Netherlands
p.bollen@maastrichtuniversity.nl
[4] Braincap BV, Beverwijk, The Netherlands
jos.rozendaal@gmail.com

Abstract. The theory and engineering of states and transitions has been developed since WWII, with considerable success. Since 2012 some Dutch government services organizations, academia and innovative companies decided to establish a co-creation, named Blue Chamber, with the aim to develop a national protocol to "translate the regulations" into a durable, IT-independent model or specifications for IT-supported, interactive, regulation based services. Regulation here means the union of laws, associated decrees and policies, both government and ministerial.

Such a protocol acts like a process and each process requires a conceptual data structure or IT-independent reference model. During the analysis of the deep structure of regulations and the associated services it became clear that the theory and application of states and transitions could be applied as innovative tool in the process of specifying the durable specifications. In this paper we describe this approach using a small but significant law and associated services.

Keywords: States and transitions as a modeling tool in IT-supported
Interactive · Regulation based services
Diagrammatic representation of scenario's using extended state and transition
diagrams · Fact based modeling (FBM)

1 Introduction

IT-supported, interactive, regulation based services are on the rise in The Netherlands, like in many other countries in recent decades. The community that defines these regulations is not always fully aware that the regulations need to take into account the new opportunities of IT-supported, interactive, regulation based services as that trade is so far hardly using any intelligent software applications.

S. Nijssen—Retired from PNA Group.

© Springer International Publishing AG 2018
C. Debruyne et al. (Eds.): OTM 2017 Workshops, LNCS 10697, pp. 193–201, 2018.
https://doi.org/10.1007/978-3-319-73805-5_20

One of the results of the co-creation was the discovery that there is a solid base to unify the various approaches to laws and IT-supported, interactive, regulation based services [1, 2, 5] and [6]. Regulation in this paper means the union of laws, government decrees, ministerial decrees and several other policies, including decisions by the courts.

The legality principle specifies that the intent of the regulation needs to be faithfully applied in all practical scenarios or cases or service.

The legislation describes roughly speaking which rights and duties are applicable for a specific citizen or enterprise and under which circumstances; it furthermore describes the consequences of legal facts. For a faithful application of the regulation in all practical scenarios it is needed to model explicitly all the semantics *intended* in the practical scenarios. In another paper we have described the core of the Reference model for IT-supported, interactive regulation based services [7].

In Sect. 2 we briefly describe the aspect of spaghetti in earlier software. In Sect. 3 we summarize the core of the Reference model [4, 9, 10, 11]. In Sect. 4 we discuss a small but fairly representative Dutch act, WHAA (Working Hours Adjustment Act), representative with respect to states and transitions, with the first part expressed in meaning based, structured legal code. In Sect. 5 we take parts of the (traditional) legal code of the WHAA and demonstrate how the meaning can be expressed quite a bit better. In Sect. 6 we present a summary and suggestions for the road ahead.

2   Spaghetti in Software Code

In the early days of software code the notorious GO TO instruction was all over the place. It resulted in spaghetti code. It was the Dutch software scientist Edsger Dijkstra that published the famous article in 1968: The Go To statement considered harmful [3]. In software science this publication resulted in a lot of attention. Software languages were later adjusted to exclude the Go To statement. Hence a systematic improvement of the quality of the software code.

In 1975 an article was published in Datamation with the title. The ELSE must go, too. Although this would mean another major step away from complexification, the results so far have not received widespread adoption.

Most software code today is less of spaghetti than in was in the days of the GO TO; however the size of specification languages and software programs using the ELSE has resulted in almost unmanageable complexity. Hence there is a drive away from procedural specification and coding towards a larger percentage of declarative formulations.

Often the writing of acts is also called coding. How about the spaghetti aspect of legal coding? This will be illustrated later in this article.

3   Reference Model

During the last 4 years the co-creation effort of the Blue Chamber resulted in a clear distinction between state based constructs like legal relationships, with their conditions and transition based constructs, with their conditions [4, 8–10, 11].

The core of the state aspects are the legal relationships, forming the legal situation of a legal subject. A legal relationship is a relationship in which one legal subject has the right side and another legal subject has the corresponding duty side, with respect to a certain subject, e.g. the right to adjust the agreed number of working hours. So far there have been detected 7 different kinds of legal relationships in the European Dutch jurisdiction.

Every legal relationship has associated with it one or more conditions.

Needless to say that state aspects should be carefully distinguished from transition aspects. Hence take into account the transition aspects (Legal facts) between a legal situation and its successive legal situation as a result of the legal fact.

It is furthermore useful to have the concept of the legal consequences of a legal fact that lead to a different legal situation.

For more on the Reference model for IT-supported, interactive, regulation based services see ref. [7].

4   An Example of a Meaning Based Structured Legal Code

Below we present a small but representative regulation for the discussion of meaning based legal code and traditional legal code.

Article 2, item 1 and 2, are expressed in meaning based, structured legal code, the remainder is a copy of the current conventional legal code.

(Entry into force of this version: July 1st, 2000)

Act of February 19, 2000, concerning rules on the right to adjust the working hours (Working Hours Adjustment Act)

General Clause

Article 1

In this act and the decrees based thereon, the following definitions apply:

a. employer: one who – based on a contract of employment subject to civil law or public appointment – lets another perform labor;
b. employee: the 'another', as mentioned under a.

Right of adjustment of number of working hours
Article 2

1. The employee has the power to request the employer for adjustment of the working hours arising from his contract of employment or public appointment, if all of the following conditions are satisfied:
   a. the employer of the employee is not a military employer,
   b. the employer employs at least 10 employees,
   c. the employee has in the past two years not received a grant or rejection of a request for adjustment of working hours, and
   d. the employee is not within 4 months of the termination of the employment contract, or the employee has a contract without a termination date.

2. The request for adjustment of the working hours by the employee on the basis of the legal relationship described in 1 has legal consequences, if all of the following conditions are satisfied:

The request to the employer for the adjustment of the working hours by the employee is

a. submitted in writing,
b. at least four months prior to the intended commencement date of the adjustment,
c. stating the commencement date,
d. stating the magnitude of the adjustment of working hours,
e. stating the desired distribution of hours,
f. an employment started at least one year prior to the intended date of commencement of the adjustment, and
g. the intended commencement date is before the planned end date of the employment, or the employment has no planned end date.

Legal consequences
A valid legal act as described in 2.1 and 2.3 has the legal consequences described in 4, 5, 6 and 7, as far as applicable.
(from here on the traditional code)

4. The employer shall consult with the employee concerning the employee's request.
5. The employer shall grant the employee's request for adjustment of working hours in so far as it concerns the date of commencement and the magnitude of the adjustment, unless substantial business or service interests dictate otherwise.
6. The employer shall determine the distribution of hours in accordance with the wishes of the employee. The employer can change the distribution of the hours if the interests of the employee must yield for reasons of reasonableness and fairness.
7. The employer shall notify the employee in writing with respect to the decision on the request for adjustment of working hours. If the employer does not grant the request or determines a distribution of the working hours in deviation from the wishes of the employee, this shall be notified in writing providing a statement of the reasons.
8. [...]
9. If the employer has not provided a decision on the request one month before the intended commencement date of the adjustment, the working hours will be adjusted according to the request of the employee.
10. [...]
11. This article does not apply to an employer with fewer than 10 employees. This employer must make arrangements regarding the right of employees to adjust their working hours.

5 The Classification (Modeling) of the Traditional Legal Code

In this section we classify (model) the existing legal code.

(Entry into force of this version: July 1st, 2000)

Act of February 19, 2000, concerning rules on the right to adjust the working hours (Working Hours Adjustment Act)

General Clause

Article 1

In this act and the decrees based thereon, the following definitions apply:

a. employer: one who – based on a contract of employment subject to civil law or public appointment – lets another perform labor;
b. employee: the 'another', as mentioned under a.

Right of adjustment of number of working hours

Article 2

1. The employee can request the employer for adjustment of the working hours arising from his contract of employment or public appointment, if the employee has been in the employment of said employer for the duration of at least one year prior to the intended date of commencement of the adjustment. For the calculation of the one year term, consecutive periods in which work is performed shall be aggregated if the interval between periods amounts to no more than three months. The preceding sentence shall apply mutatis mutandis to periods in which work is performed for different employers, when said employers can reasonably be deemed to be each other's successor with respect to the work performed.
2. For military officials the right to adjust working hours is governed by Order in Council on the recommendation of Our Minister of Defence and Our Minister of Social Affairs and Employment using unpaid leave for part-time work.
3. The request for adjustment of working hours will have to be submitted in writing to the employer at least four months prior to the intended commencement date of the adjustment, stating the commencement date, the magnitude of the adjustment of working hours per week or, if hours of work has been established for a different period the adjustment for said period, and the desired distribution of hours over the week or other period agreed upon. The employee can resubmit a request for adjustment of working hours at most once every two years, after the employer has granted or rejected a previous request.
4. The employer shall consult with the employee concerning the employee's request.
5. The employer shall grant the employee's request for adjustment of working hours in so far as it concerns the date of commencement and the magnitude of the adjustment, unless substantial business or service interests dictate otherwise.
6. The employer shall determine the distribution of hours in accordance with the wishes of the employee. The employer can change the distribution of the hours if the interests of the employee must yield for reasons of reasonableness and fairness.

7. The employer shall notify the employee in writing with respect to the decision on the request for adjustment of working hours. If the employer does not grant the request or determines a distribution of the working hours in deviation from the wishes of the employee, this shall be notified in writing providing a statement of the reasons.

8. [...]

9. If the employer has not provided a decision on the request one month before the intended commencement date of the adjustment, the working hours will be adjusted according to the request of the employee.

10. [...]

11. This article does not apply to an employer with fewer than 10 employees. This employer must make arrangements regarding the right of employees to adjust their working hours.

The first question is: how to classify (model) the first 21 words of article 2.1, is it a state concept or a transition concept?

Right of adjustment of number of working hours

Article 2

1. The employee can request the employer for adjustment of the working hours arising from his contract of employment or public appointment

The title "Right of adjustment" denotes a legal *relationship*, hence a *state* concept. However the 21 words are expressed in a way that it comes very close to the legal act, or *transition* concept. This is one of the problems in the current legal coding convention that the distinction between state and transition is often not properly described.

Hence the 21 words are in blue (Fig. 1), corresponding with the color of legal relationship in the Reference model [7].

The employee can request the employer for adjustment of the working hours arising from his contract of employment or public appointment, if the employee has been in the employment of said employer for the duration of at least one year prior to the intended date of commencement of the adjustment.

Fig. 1.

However, at the same time we have to classify (model) the same 21 words as a legal fact (transition) as represented in Fig. 2.

The employee can request the employer for adjustment of the working hours arising from his contract of employment or public appointment, if the employee has been in the employment of said employer for the duration of at least one year prior to the intended date of commencement of the adjustment.

Fig. 2.

Hence the same 21 words have to be classified both as legal relationship (state) and legal act (transition). It would be much better if there would be in the legal coding an explicit description of the legal relationships (state) and the legal acts (transition). Why? State and transition are two entirely different concepts and each has its own conditions.

How to classify (model) the following 29 words in 2.1:

1. [...] if the employee has been in the employment of said employer for the duration of at least one year prior to the intended date of commencement of the adjustment.

The intended date of commencement has nothing to do with the legal relationship of power. It is a fact of the legal act to request an adjustment of working hours. Hence the text of 29 words is to be classified as a condition on the legal act (transition). That is the reason that we use the same color as legal act attached to the condition (Fig. 3).

The employee can request the employer for adjustment of the working hours arising from his contract of employment or public appointment if the employee has been in the employment of said employer for the duration of at least one year prior to the intended date of commencement of the adjustment.   I

Fig. 3.

This is the kind of confusion that can be avoided when using meaning based, structured, legal code.

How to classify (model): The request for adjustment of working hours (see Fig. 4).

The request for adjustment of working hours will have to be submitted in writing to the employer   II

Fig. 4.

2. The request for adjustment of working hours will have to be submitted in writing to the employer at least four months prior to the intended commencement date of the adjustment, stating the commencement date, the magnitude of the adjustment of working hours per week or, if hours of work has been established for a different period the adjustment for said period, and the desired distribution of hours over the week or other period agreed upon. The employee can resubmit a request for adjustment of working hours at most once every two years, after the employer has granted or rejected a previous request (Fig. 5).

The employee can resubmit a request for adjustment of working hours at most once every two years, after the employer has granted or rejected a previous request.   III

Fig. 5.

The request for adjustment of working hours is clearly a legal act, hence a transition. Hence the condition "submitted in writing" is a condition on the legal act, the transition.

However, the last sentence of 2.3:

The employee can resubmit a request for adjustment of working hours at most once every two years, after the employer has granted or rejected a previous request.

Is a condition on the legal relationship, while the text is part of 2.1, which starts with the legal act. This is the kind of confusion that can be avoided when using meaning based, structured, legal code.

Hence we have demonstrated that in the existing legal code there is hardly a clear classification of the core elements of legal code such as legal relationships, conditions on legal relationships, legal facts and conditions on legal acts and the legal consequences of legal acts.

If the proposal for meaning based, structured, legal code would be implemented it would likely result in substantial savings and increased quality in projects to produce IT-supported, interactive, regulation based services.

6   Conclusions and Future Work

While working in the co-creation the Blue Chamber we gradually came closer and closer to a meaning based, structured legal code. It then became clear how much productivity could be achieved if this would be systematically used in legal code. We have described above an example of an act in traditional legal code and in the proposed meaning based, structured legal code. It has been demonstrated that the traditional legal code causes quite a bit of avoidable confusion. We believe that the meaning based, structured legal code opens complete new opportunities in IT-supported, interactive, regulation based services.

Acknowledgements. The authors gratefully acknowledge the many discussions in the Blue Chamber and especially Mrs. Mariette Lokin, since June 2012. The Blue Chamber a multi-disciplinary group with the principle that each member brings more sandwiches to the lunch than he intends to eat and users are the ultimate decision makers whether or not a modeling approach is accepted. The authors express their thanks to the colleagues of the Blue Chamber for their inspiring sessions. The Blue Chamber will continue in the future to improve the development and maintenance of regulation based specifications for services.

References

1. Corbin, A.: Legal Analysis and Terminology. Yale Law School (1919)
2. Corbin, A.: Jural Relations and Their Classification. Yale Law School (1921)
3. Dijkstra, E.: Letters to the editor: go to statement considered harmful. Commun. ACM **11**, 147–148 (1948)
4. Dulfer, D., Nijssen, S., Lokin, M.: Developing and maintaining durable specifications for law or regulation based services. In: Ciuciu, I., et al. (eds.) OTM 2015. LNCS, vol. 9416, pp. 169–177. Springer, Cham (2015). https://doi.org/10.1007/978-3-319-26138-6_20

5. Hohfeld, W.N.: Fundamental Legal Conceptions as Applied in Judicial Reasoning (2010). ISBN-13 978-1-58477-162-3. edited by Walter Wheeler Cook
6. ISO TR9007, Concepts and terminology for the Conceptual Schema and the Information Base. ISO Technical report (1987)
7. Mariette, L., Sjir, N., Diederik, D., Peter, B., Jos, R.: An IT-independent reference model for IT-supported, interactive, regulation based services. In: Debruyne, C., et al. (ed.) Paper Submitted to FBM 2017 Workshop of the OnTheMove 2016 Conference, Rhodos, Greece, October 2017. LNCS, vol. 10697, pp. 173–182 (2018)
8. Nijssen, G.M.: A Framework for Discussion in ISO/TC97/SC5/WG3, 78.09/01 (1978)
9. Rozendaal, J., Nijssen, S.: A durable architecture as a foundation for regulation based services. In: Ciuciu, I., Debruyne, C., Panetto, H., Weichhart, G., Bollen, P., Fensel, A., Vidal, M.-E. (eds.) OTM 2016. LNCS, vol. 10034, pp. 164–173. Springer, Cham (2017). https://doi.org/10.1007/978-3-319-55961-2_16
10. Rozendaal, J., Nijssen, S.: A proposal for a regulations based services language. In: Ciuciu, I., Debruyne, C., Panetto, H., Weichhart, G., Bollen, P., Fensel, A., Vidal, M.-E. (eds.) OTM 2016. LNCS, vol. 10034, pp. 174–182. Springer, Cham (2017). https://doi.org/10.1007/978-3-319-55961-2_17
11. Straatsma, P., Diederik, D.: Wendbare Wetsuitvoering, DREAM (2014)

How to Fulfil Regulatory Requirements Consistently: A Semantic-Based Approach

Inge Lemmens[(✉)], Bas van de Laar, Johan Saton, and John Bulles

PNA, Heerlen, The Netherlands
{inge.lemmens,bas.van.de.laar,johan.saton,
john.bulles}@pna-group.com

Abstract. Organizations, and financial organizations in particular, have to fulfil an increasing amount of regulations imposed by external entities. Moreover, these regulations impose shorter lead times and require much more granularity of the data that needs to be reported than traditional reports. In addition, lineage requirements are imposed more strictly and at a faster pace. For organizations to fulfil all these requirements, having insight in the link between the reported data and the source provides (part of) the key to success. To achieve this insight, the creation of a common understanding forms the foundation.

Keywords: Fact-based model · Compliance · Regulation · Cognitation Cogniam

1 Introduction

Regulators, and bank regulators in particular, are requiring more frequent and more detailed information in addition to traditional reporting. Instead of aggregated information, regulators like the European Central Bank (ECB), request the underlying granular data sets such that they can perform the analysis themselves. Hereby, some of these regulations, among which the Basel capital adequacy principles and IFRS 9, require interoperability between the finance, risk and regulatory reporting functions within financial organizations.

Additionally, new requirements are coming at an increasing pace, with decreasing lead times for the financial institutions to realize the requirements.

While all of the above is already extremely challenging for financial institutions, the complexity does not stop there. Additional complexity is given by the fact that the regulators themselves are not aligned in terms and understanding. That is, between regulators (and even between departments within the same regulator), there is no guarantee that the used concepts are aligned in terms and understanding. One reason for this is that regulators may take different approaches to the same issue: they come up with similar requirements, designed with similar intents in mind, but are all slightly different. At the same time, different regulators can have different views on the same concept, resulting in similar terms with different interpretations.

© Springer International Publishing AG 2018
C. Debruyne et al. (Eds.): OTM 2017 Workshops, LNCS 10697, pp. 202–211, 2018.
https://doi.org/10.1007/978-3-319-73805-5_21

Many financial organizations have installed project programs to deal with the challenges mentioned above. Typically, they introduce a central data store to collect the granular data and connect this data store to the reporting chains. While this is a feasible solution, it only solves part of the issue. The major challenge is not only to connect all sources to the central data store, but to do so in a *meaningful* manner. In this paper, we introduce a semantic-based approach whereby a common understanding serves as the foundation to achieve the required lineage as well as to ensure correct answering of regulatory requirements.

2 Approaches to Regulatory Reporting

As stated in the introduction, organizations are facing new challenges because of an increase in regulatory demands. This requires organizations to rethink their strategy with respect to reporting in particular, and data management in general as reconciliation of date used for risk, finance and reporting is necessary to support the different regulatory reporting needs.

2.1 Traditional Approach to Reporting

Traditionally, reporting requirements were dealt with in a fragmented, isolated manner: for each regulatory reporting, a project was initiated, resulting in a customized reporting chain. That is: traditionally, each regulatory reporting was supported by exactly one reporting chain: the Basel chain being responsible for Basel reporting and Basel reporting only.

Looking into the details of such a project (i.e. in the traditional view), the activities performed are always the same: (1) analysis of the regulation, (2) mapping of the regulation to existing source systems and (3) defining the associated transformation rules to go from source system to final report. This leads to a myriad of relations, whereby consistency is hard to maintain as changes in the source systems have an impact on more than one reporting chain. At the same time, changes in regulations are hard to trace as one regulatory requirement is a transformation of data coming from several source systems as the regulatory requirements are not elementary in nature and the link between regulatory requirement and source system data element is not necessarily a one-on-one mapping.

This traditional approach to reporting is hard to maintain since consistency in reporting and consistency in supply of data to disparate business lines cannot be completely guaranteed and compliance thus comes at risk (Fig. 1).

2.2 A Common Approach to Reporting

One of the major shortcomings of the traditional approach is no guaranteed consistency. Another issue is that, discrepancies between approaches of the various regulators

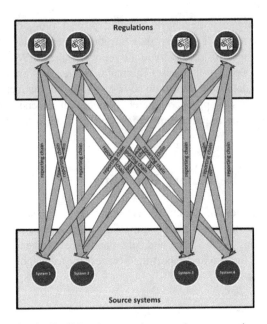

Fig. 1. Traditional approach to regulatory reporting.

involved in the regulatory initiatives can lead to discrepancies, leaving financial institutions with no clear picture of what course to take. In case there is no communication between the different reporting chains of the financial organization, this leads to complete chaos.

Compliance with multiple regulatory initiatives with similar intentions but nuanced data requirements suggests the need for a standardized data model for regulatory data. This is exactly the scope of the BIRD project [1], which aims to foster cooperation in the field of regulatory reporting by developing a harmonized technical data model. This initiative, however, is in its infancy. In particular, at the time of writing, only the ECB regulation EU 2016/687 [2] and EU regulation 1011/2012 [3] as amended by Regulation EU 2016/1384 [4] are combined during a pilot project (Fig. 2).

Similar initiatives take place at financial organizations. Financial organizations unify their data by developing or adopting a "universal data model" that serves as a central data store connecting to the different reporting chains. This ensures that data is sourced from a single consistent data model (Fig. 3).

Although this consistent data model is a good step towards overall consistency, it is no guarantee for correctness. In particular, the central data store, be it adopted or own development, is only as valid as the interpretation of the underlying data structures. That is, mapping of the *meaning* of the data structures in the data store to the *meaning*

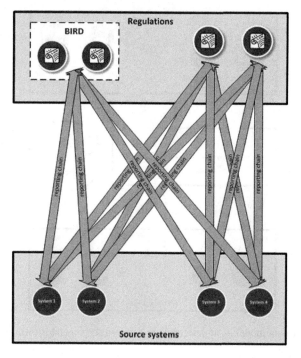

Fig. 2. Unifying the regulatory data model reduces complexity in reporting chains.

International organisations	INTRNTNL_ORGNSTN	Observation	Pseudo-ISO code for international organisations of the Eurostat's 'Balance of Payments Vademecum'.
Is derived enterprise size	IS_DRVD_ENTRPRS_SZ	Observation	Pure boolean (true and false values)
Is pulling effect	IS_PLLNG_EFFCT	Observation	Pure boolean (true and false values)
Is short-term credit assessment	IS_SHRT_TRM_CRDT_ASSSSMNT	Observation	Pure boolean (true and false values)
LEI code	LEI	Observation	String with strictly 20 characters

Fig. 3. The BIRD initiative – a fragment of the harmonized data model [1].

of the data elements in the different regulations as well as the different source systems is a prerequisite for a successful implementation of such a central data store. Therefore, a semantic enterprise model is a prerequisite for success (Fig. 4).

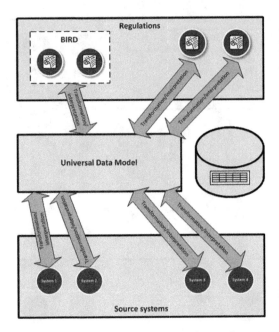

Fig. 4. Universal data model as an intermediate between the regulatory world and the internal world.

3 Supporting the Overall Process

The overall process consists of the following steps:

1. Identification of the requirements in the regulation
2. Analysis of the requirements
3. Definition of configuration-specific information for developing the universal data model.
4. Generating the sourcing format on the basis of the relational structure of the universal data model (Fig. 5).

3.1 Step 1: Identification of the Requirements in the Regulation

The first step of the process consists of identifying the relevant requirements in the regulation. Fortunately, regulatory requirements is, because of necessity, well structured. Unfortunately, clarity about the meaning of the regulatory requirements is not always the case. This because of (1) unclear terminology, (2) lacking definitions and/or (3) distribution of all relevant information with respect to one requirement over several articles of one or more regulations. For example, in the Anacredit regulation EU 2016/687 [1], the term "annual turnover" is defined as "annual sales volume net of all discounts and sale taxes of the counterparty in accordance with Recommendation 2003/361/EC, equivalent to the concept of 'total annual sales' in Article 153(4) of Regulation (EU) No 575/2013". In other words, in order to get a grasp on the definition

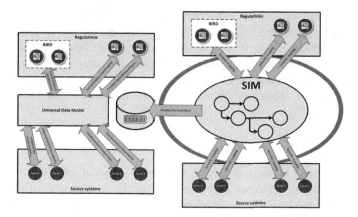

Fig. 5. Proposed approach: the semantic information model as leading for the mapping: ensuring correct interpretation.

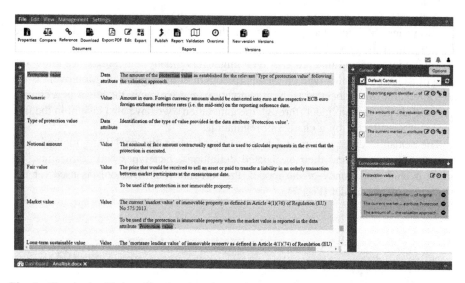

Fig. 6. Cognitatie aids in annotating the relevant fragments in legislation, and combine them to have all required insight about a requirement in one look.

of annual turnover, at least two other regulations have to be consulted. To support this identification, the software tool "Cognitatie" is used. With Cognitatie, we are capable to "annotate" a piece of text in a regulation, identify it (in this case: give it a requirement identifier), and relate it to pieces of text in other regulations, combining them in one context. This one context contains all relevant information for step 2 in the process: "analysis of the requirements". Also, it forms the starting point for the data lineage throughout the organization (Fig. 6).

Note that, with Cognitatie, we not only have the means to create annotations and relate annotations associated with each other, even though the text fragments that are annotated are distributed over several documents, Cognitatie has the unique feature to provide insight in the effect of changed regulations on the annotations. For example, if an annotated concept is changed in a regulation, the difference is made insightful. As such, the effect of a change of regulation on the identified requirements becomes insightful.

3.2 Step 2: Analysis of the Requirements

In [5], we elaborated on an approach to develop a semantic enterprise model. This semantic enterprise model is not only the basis for the development of the common language but also the basis for the development of the central data store, and provides the means to ensure lineage. That is, once requirements are identified, they are analyzed against the semantic enterprise model. In particular, each requirement is mapped to one or more existing fact types or, in case the concept and associated fact types do not yet exist, new fact types are introduced.

With each fact type, the requirements to which the fact type maps, is registered. This way, insight is created in the use of the fact types, and traceability from the semantic enterprise model to the legislation is maintained.

Taking into account that one fact type might serve many regulations, we know the effect of a change to a fact type on the interpretation of the regulation. Moreover, as we have a requirement associated with an annotation, and we know the effect of a change in regulation on a requirement (through the annotation), we have also insight in the fact types that are affected by a change in regulation.

The semantic enterprise model is constructed using the cogNIAM method, and consists of concepts and their associated definitions, fact types and constraints. To ensure overall consistency of the model, the software tool "Doctool" is used for the registration of the model (Fig. 7).

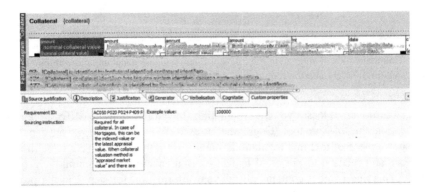

Fig. 7. The semantic enterprise model is modelled using the cogNIAM method and captured in Doctool, whereby for each fact type is specified to which regulatory requirements it maps.

3.3   Step 3: Definition of Configuration-Specific Information

The chosen approach follows the ANSI 3-layer data model approach as described in [6]. That is, as described in [6], three levels of data models exist, namely:

1. The conceptual data model which describes the semantics of the data relevant to the domain, independently of any possible means of implementation.
2. The logical data model, which anticipates the implementation of the data model on a specific computing system. That is, the content of the logical data model is adjusted to achieve certain practical efficiencies in comparison with the conceptual data model.
3. The physical data model, which represents the domain taking into account the facilities and restrictions that are part of a given storage system.

Mapping a conceptual data model to a logical data model requires choices to be made. For example, the handling of absorption for subtypes and the mapping of conceptual data types to logical data types needs to be specified. This mapping is done by the "cogNIAM exporter", which takes a cogNIAM model as input and provides the means to generate a logical data model, taking into account the configuration choices (Fig. 8).

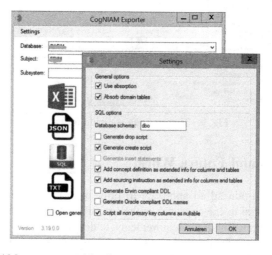

Fig. 8. The cogNIAM exporter provides the means to map a conceptual model developed using cogNIAM to a logical model.

By using the cogNIAM exporter, we are assured of traceability of the requirements as we know for each element in the logical model (be it an excel logical representation, a relational representation, or a .JSON or textual representation), on which fact type in the model it is based. And, since for each fact type we know to which regulatory requirements it contributes, we maintain traceability from regulation to logical.

In the current process, we generate a relational logical model on the basis of the conceptual model. This relational logical model forms the universal data model as introduced in Sect. 2.2. On this level, implementation specific data is added, like file metadata, in order to generate the physical level. This is only done for implementation-specific data than cannot be generated based on the conceptual model or can be set by parameters when generating the logical model.

3.4 Step 4: Generating the Sourcing Format on the Basis of the Relational Structure of the Universal Data Model

Once the universal data model is generated, this data model is used as the basis for the sourcing format. The sourcing format is the interchange format that is used by the different sources to transfer their data to the universal data model. For this purpose, the logical data model is first loaded into SQL Server as a relational database model in order to generate the physical model. The ultimate sourcing format is an XSD generated on the basis of the universal data model. By using specific tooling, the parameters are set for generating the physical model based on the logical model. The result is a fully generated XSD, without the need of any manual interventions, which implies that no additional steps have to be undertaken to ensure lineage (Fig. 9).

```
110    <xs:element name="CollateralType" minOccurs="0">
111      <xs:simpleType>
112        |   <xs:restriction base="xs:string">
153      </xs:simpleType>
154    </xs:element>
155    <xs:element name="NominalCollateralValue" type="ssf:Amount_Type" minOccurs="0"/>
156    <xs:element name="               " type="ssf:Amount_Type" minOccurs="0"/>
157    <xs:element name="               " type="ssf:Amount_Type" minOccurs="0"/>
158    <xs:element name="               " type="ssf:Amount_Type" minOccurs="0"/>
159    <xs:element name="               " minOccurs="0">
160      <xs:simpleType>
161        |   <xs:restriction base="xs:date"/>
162      </xs:simpleType>
163    </xs:element>
```

Fig. 9. The resulting sourcing format.

4 Conclusions and Future Work

In this paper, we introduced an approach to fulfil regulatory requirements in a consistent manner. Central to the approach is the use of a semantic information model to ensure correct interpretation of the requirements, to define a universal data model that is used as means to collect the data required for fulfilling the requirements, and to define the exchange format for different sources. This approach is used in practice and shows major advantages over the traditional approach of only mapping report by report or only through a logical model, as not only consistent reporting is achieved but also correct interpretation of the reporting requirements.

Future work includes further integration of the different tool to support the overall process and to implement the lessons learned with respect to analysis and modelling.

References

1. Banks' Integrated Reporting Dictionary. http://banks-integrated-reporting-dictionary.eu/
2. ECB: Regulation (EU) 2016/867 of the European Central Bank of 18 May 2016 on the collection of granular credit and credit risk data (ECB/2016/13) (2016)
3. ECB: Regulation (EU) No 1011/2013 of the European Central Bank of 17 October 2012 concerning statistics on holdings of securities (ECB/2012/24) (2012)
4. ECB: Regulation (EU) 2016/1384 of the European Central Bank of 2 August 2016 amending regulation (EU) No 1011/2012 (ECB/2012/24) concerning statistics on holdings of securities (ECB/2016/22) (2016)
5. Lemmens, I., Pleijsant, J.M., Arntz, R.: Using fact-based modelling to develop a common language. In: Ciuciu, I., Panetto, H., Debruyne, C., Aubry, A., Bollen, P., Valencia-García, R., Mishra, A., Fensel, A., Ferri, F. (eds.) OTM 2015. LNCS, vol. 9416, pp. 197–205. Springer, Cham (2015). https://doi.org/10.1007/978-3-319-26138-6_23
6. ANSI/X3/SPARC Study Group on Data Base Management Systems, Interim report. FDT. ACM SIGMOD Bull. 1, vol. 7, No. 2 (1975)

An Evaluation of a Design Science Research Artefact in the Field of Agile Enterprise Design

Klaas Meijer[✉], Maurice Nijssen, and John Bulles

Radboud University, Nijmegen, The Netherlands
klaas.meijer@gmx.com

Abstract. This paper describes a research approach to an evaluation of a Design Science Research (DSR) Artefact in the field of Agile Enterprise Design. The Artefact, the result of a program which engineered and combined three methodologies, is developed on the basis of an emerging concept since 2009 and recently (in 2016) implemented in several information systems. Because of the availability of several implementations of the artefact, a post evaluation based on hypothesis testing of the real artefacts is a feasible and necessary next research step, on which will we elaborate in this paper. Rather than a research question, three hypotheses are proposed in this research.

Keywords: Information system · Enterprise Design · Enterprise Ontology
Enterprise Architecture · DEMO · IS Architecture · Fact Based Modelling
CogNIAM · IT Architecture · Normalised Systems Theory · Hypothesis testing
Experimental research

1 Introduction

This paper is part of a larger Design Science Research [1] in the field of Enterprise Design and Information Systems Development.

2 Research Approach

The research started by an extensive literature study, collecting and capturing literature on Enterprise Design and Information Systems Development. The reviewed literature comprised the following domains:

1. Enterprise Ontology and Enterprise Architecture. The methodology under investigation in this research is DEMO of prof. Dietz.
2. Information and rules requirements specification, namely Fact Based Modelling according to the methodology of CogNIAM of prof. Nijssen.
3. IT Architecture, based on the Normalised Systems Theory of prof. Verelst and prof. Mannaert.

© Springer International Publishing AG 2018
C. Debruyne et al. (Eds.): OTM 2017 Workshops, LNCS 10697, pp. 212–219, 2018.
https://doi.org/10.1007/978-3-319-73805-5_22

As mentioned, for building the artefact the methodologies were used, these methodologies are also needed for creating information systems as they deliver the basis for the requirements phase.

So this research is not only about testing an artefact but also about the capability of an organization to accept and use these theories or parts of them. Identifying useable methodologies to improve the development of Information Systems and creating artefacts to support them is not practical if the IT staff is not able to adopt them.

In order to position the three methodologies in an overall architecture, we used an architecture developed by a co-creation in the Netherlands, the Blue Chamber [8], for IT-supported, interactive, regulation based services.

In this so called Blue Chamber architecture there is a distinction between 5 actor groups. The first actor group specifies the regulations, or in case of information systems not based on or based on only a few regulations, this group produces the initial requirements, from a business perspective.

The second actor group takes as input the regulations, or the initial specifications, and produces as output the complete, consistent and formal specifications including all the relevant test cases, all from the perspective of the business. These specifications could also be considered as the formal logical model from the business perspective of the new system. These specifications are durable and thus independent of the often changing IT. The third actor group transforms the complete and formal specifications into IT-dependent descriptions.

The fourth actor group consists of the users of the system.

The fifth actor group is concerned with jurisprudence. In the case of systems not primarily based on regulation, one could consider skipping this fifth group, although it could also be seen as a kind of regular feedback on the system.

The architecture is diagrammatically represented in the next figure (Fig. 1).

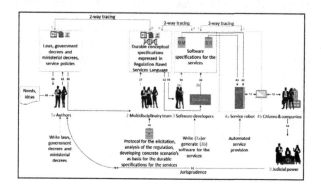

Fig. 1. Blue Chamber architecture [8]

The information systems mentioned have a typical lifespan between 20 and 30 years.

2.1 Enterprise Ontology

This paper focusses on the theoretical foundations of the DEMO methodology, namely its particular system concept and corresponding white-box model. These notions provide a constructional understanding, as opposed to the traditional functional understanding, of business processes.

Dietz claims the system concept to be a crucial success factor in redesign and re-engineering projects [2].

An example of constructional understanding is that a racing car driver is perfectly well able to drive a racing car on the basis of his functional knowledge of cars, i.e. on the basis of knowing the effects of manipulating the controls, taking into account various external conditions.

A racing car mechanic is perfectly well able to repair and tune a car for optimal performance. He does so on the basis of his constructional knowledge, i.e. on the basis of knowing how the constituent parts, like the engine, the gears, and the transmission chains, collectively realize the car's function, and how this is influenced by various external conditions.

Functional knowledge and constructional knowledge are of a very different nature.

In this paper we distinguish two general kinds of system definitions: ontological definitions and teleological ones. Ontological definitions are based on empirical observation of what a system is, distinct from other observable things. Teleological definitions are based on the interpretation of observed behaviour of a system.

Enterprise, Information and IT Systems

The system definition provided hereafter is derived from the very general and very exact ontological definition of the notion of system as provided by Bunge [3]. It defines the class of discrete dynamic systems.

Something is a (discrete dynamic) system if and only if it has all of the next properties:

- It has composition, i.e. there is a set of constituent elements. The nature of these elements determine the category to which the system belongs.
- It has structure, i.e. the elements influence each other's behaviour, such that every element influences or is influenced by at least one other element, and such that there are no 'isolated parts'.
- It has boundary, i.e. the composition is divided in two subsets: the kernel and the environment. Every element in the environment only influences or is influenced by one or more elements in the kernel of the system.
- It has activity, i.e. the elements cause changes in the state of some world. The number of changes in any finite interval of time is finite.

The notion of subsystem is very exactly defined as follows. A system A is a subsystem of a system B if and only if the kernel of A is a subset of the kernel of B, the environment of A is a subset of the composition of B, and the structure of A is a subset of the structure of B.

2.2   Fact Based Modelling

Fact Based Modelling has been used applied in industry for over 35 years, and is taught in universities around the world. The University of Maastricht has introduced a FBM Course in 2017 in the department Data Science & Knowledge Engineering[1]. The fact based modelling approach comprises a family of closely related languages and methods, the oldest being NIAM (Natural language Information Analysis Method), followed by Object-Role Modelling (ORM), Cognition enhanced NIAM (CogNIAM), Fully Communication Oriented Information Modelling (FCO-IM), Deploying Ontology-Grounded Methods and Applications (DOGMA) and Grounding Ontologies in Social Process by Language (GOSPL). An early version of FBM was the basis for ISO Technical Report 9007 (ISO TR9007) [7]. An important addition to the family of fact based approaches was the adoption in 2007 of the well-known Semantics of Business Vocabulary and Rules (SBVR) proposal by the Object Management Group (OMG). For this research CogNIAM will be used as the basis of Fact Based Modelling. CogNIAM is primarily used by the actor group 2.

What is the essence of CogNIAM? To accept the communication of a specific domain by the members of one or more communities as a solid basis to be used in a multidisciplinary team to specify the durable, hence IT independent specification of a new system. And in the case of IT supported, interactive, regulation based systems, CogNIAM fully accepts the legality principle that states that a system providing the regulation based services must fully adhere to the intent of the people that specified the laws and the regulations.

CogNIAM accepts the given laws and regulations and has an extensive protocol how to develop the complete set of test cases, how to communicate in a multidisciplinary group about the test cases and based on the consensus, or decision by the service and legal expert, formulate the durable legally and logically formal specifications.

CogNIAM works under the assumption that all (or most?) communication between members of one or more communities about a specific domain can best be taken as a starting point. Such communication is in the form of declarative facts. Of course such declarative facts can have any number of instantiated placeholders or variables. Hence CogNIAM assumes that the most often form of communication used is the exchange of declarative n-ary facts. That level is called level I in the CogNIAM knowledge triangle of three levels [6]. This is the most familiar level to most people in this world.

For communication purposes about a certain domain, certainly when more than one sub community is involved, it is strongly recommended to use Fact Communication Patterns and Rule Communication Patterns. Fact and Rule communication patterns can be used to guarantee the communication that a specific sub community prefers, while at the same time relating the Fact Communication Patterns to the Fact types, and the Rule Communication Patterns to the Integrity or Derivation Rules.

Most people prefer to have the construct called Event to start a derivation rule or make a change in a fact population.

---

[1] Fact based modelling as mandatory subject in the first year of a Knowledge Engineering program, Peter Bollen.

With the aim to make the communication about a domain as best as possible understood, CogNIAM describes any term for which there is the slightest assumption it may be misunderstood, a complete and understandable definition.

Hence a domain specific model in CogNIAM consists of:

1. Fact Types,
2. Object Types (nominalized Fact Types) and subtypes,
3. The Integrity Rules on the Fact Populations and Fact Population Transitions,
4. The Derivation Rules, that produce new Fact Instances from available Fact Populations,
5. Exchange Rules to add, remove, or modify (in case of combined facts) facts in the Fact Populations,
6. Event Rules to either start a Derivation Rule or an Exchange Rule,
7. Fact Communication Patterns to make sub community communication well understood, while maintaining the overall integrity of the system,
8. Rule Communication Patterns to express rules in a community preferred format and
9. Definitions for all terms to foster the highest degree on understand-ability among the various members of the sub communities.

The elements of these 9 different categories are strongly related to each other. These relationships can also be expressed as Fact Types, but then these fact types apply to any domain, and hence make up the domain agnostic specification, or domain agnostic conceptual schema, sometimes called meta conceptual schema.

In CogNIAM a unique aspect is that the meta conceptual schema is not postulated, but is *derived* using the CogNIAM protocol starting from concrete facts, derive the domain specific constructs, and from these derive the domain agnostic constructs.

The FBM community has set a research agenda for: *sustainable integrated methodologies based on Fact Based Modelling where stakeholders' individual perspectives are respected, while at the same time becoming part of an integrated model that provides bridges to a stakeholder's "legacy" systems.* This agenda is in line with the research, as described in this paper.

As CogNIAM has realized that a substantial number of persons prefer to think in processes as this is how they experience a system, CogNIAM provides that perspective on the entire conceptual model by providing a BPMN view.

2.3 Normalised Systems Theory

Normalized Systems studies evolvability of software architectures independent of a specific software language or framework. It uses the concept of entropy from thermodynamics and stability from systems theory to explain that a certain bounded input always leads to bounded output, even when the size of a system increases. As can be read in Mannaert and Verelst [4], Normalized Systems theory acts upon the postulate that an information system needs to be stable with respect to a defined set of anticipated changes such as: additional data attribute or field, additional data entity, additional action entity and additional version of a task.

They, Verelst and Mannaert [4] state the scientific claim that Normalised Systems Theory, if recognized and understood, can counteract the laws of Professor Meir "Manny" Lehman, who was the chairman of the Department of Computing at the Imperial College London. From 1974 on Lehman worked on eight laws of software evolution. Lehman suggests there will be continuing applications and systems growth in order to maintain user satisfaction. Applications and systems growth will cause a decline in quality as well as increase complexity.

This increasing complexity is a result of combinatorial effects (CE). Normalized Systems theory uses the next theorems to avoid these effects and ensure stability:

- Separation of Concerns (SOC): an action entity can only contain a single task in Normalized systems.
- Data Version Transparency (DVT): Data entities that are received as an input or produced as output by action entities need to exhibit version transparency in Normalized Systems.
- Action version transparency: Action entities that are called by other actions, need to exhibit version transparency in Normalized Systems.
- Separation of States: The calling of an action entity by another action entity needs to exhibit state keeping in Normalized Systems.

Normalised Systems Theory claims to support the ability to successfully analyse business and technical changes and realize Information Systems without disruption or technical debt and therefore resulting Normalised Systems are agile in design.

3   Three Hypotheses for Testing the Artefact[2]

The system and construct in this paper is the Enterprise Design of Information Systems of an organization.

The DSR Artefact Comprises of a methodology for Agile Enterprise Design and Information Systems Development and an implementation of a construct to accelerate information systems development. This concept emerged since 2009 and was recently in 2016 implemented in several information systems.

In this phase of the research the formulation of hypotheses is leading (Fig. 2).

Following Recker [5, p. 21]: *"A hypothesis is the empirical formulation of a proposition that is characterised as a testable relationship between two or more variables"*. In this research hypotheses are formulated such that they are empirically testable and allow for precise reasoning about the underlying proposition they represent.

---

[2] A hypothesis must contain a justified theoretical argument for why you expect a certain phenomenon to occur (or not). simply put, there is no such thing as a self-evident hypothesis or a hypothesis that you explore "because you can".
The hypotheses have to be connected to existing research, including references to key literature in building the argument and scientific claims.

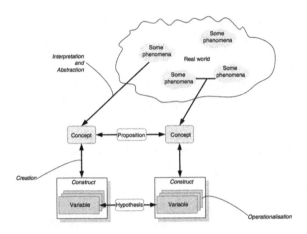

Fig. 2. Hypothesis testing [5]

- *Hypothesis 1 (EO⇒ISD): Application of Enterprise ontology with a function-construction perspective towards business processes increases the agility of Information Systems Development.*

Agility is in this research defined by "pre-determined change drivers and design constraints in the process of Information Systems Development" [4].

- *Hypothesis 2 (FBM⇒ISD): Application of Fact and Rule based specification of business processes increases the agility of Information Systems Development.*

Fact based specifications offers software patterns which reduces the complexity of functional software requirement analysis.

- *Hypothesis 3 (NS⇒ISD): Application of Normalization of software increases the agility of Information Systems Development.*

The operationalization of the hypotheses on *the agility of Information Systems Development* comprises two variables, namely Continuous Change and Stability of Complexity.

Continuous Change: helps to keep software modern and useful, reducing the need for large mass absorption. Continuous change means adding new functionality and/or changing current functionality.

Stability of Complexity: provides for not increasing complexity as much as possible in the face of more complex requirements. This counteracts the law of Lehman, who states that software does not age with use, but deteriorates by the need to adapt it to the changing technology and business requirements.

3.1 Further Research

The last phase will be the testing of the hypothesis on artefacts in several experiments over a longer period of time. This experimental research is considered [5, p. 82]: *"the gold standard in research as it is one of the most rigorous forms of collecting and analysing data, but it is also one of the most difficult research methods"*. Experimental research relies on very strong theory to guide construct definition, hypothesis specification and testing. Testing will be done in several case studies by adding – more and more - new requirements to the information system under research, which has to be adjusted to the changing environment, new legislation and technology.

References

1. Hevner, A.R.: Design science research in information systems. Manag. Inf. Syst. Q. **28**(1), 75–105 (2004)
2. Dietz, J.L.G., Mulder, J.B.F.: Organisational transformation requires constructional knowledge of business systems. In: HICCS (1998)
3. Bunge, M.A.: Treatise on Basic Philosophy, vol. 4. Reidel Publishing, Dordrecht (1979)
4. Mannaert, H., Verelst, J., De Bruyn, P.: Normalized Systems Theory: From Foundations for Evolvable Software Toward a General Theory for Evolvable Design. Koppa, Hasselt (2016)
5. Recker, J.: Scientific Research in Information Systems. Springer, New York (2013). https://doi.org/10.1007/978-3-642-30048-6
6. Nijssen, S., Valera, S.: An architecture ecosystem for the whole systems perspective, including system dynamics, based on logic & set theory and controlled natural languages. Working paper for the OMG Architecture Ecosystem SIG (2012)
7. ISO TR9007, Concepts and terminology for the Conceptual Schema and the Information Base, ISO Technical Report (1987)
8. Nijssen, S., Dulfer, D., Rozendaal, J.: Een duurzame Architectuur voor op regelgeving gebaseerde dienstverlening Versie 2.0 (2016)

Industry Case Studies Program (ICSP) 2017

ICSP 2017 PC Chair's Message

Cloud computing, service-oriented architecture, business process modelling, enterprise architecture, enterprise integration, semantic interoperability—what is an enterprise systems administrator to do with the constant stream of industry hype surrounding him, constantly bathing him with (apparently) new ideas and new "technologies"? It is nearly impossible, and the academic literature does not help solving the problem, with hyped "technologies" catching on in the academic world just as easily as the industrial world. The most unfortunate thing is that these technologies are actually useful, and the press hype only hides that value. What the enterprise information manager really cares about is integrated, interoperable infrastructures, industrial IoT, that support interoperable information systems, so he can deliver valuable information to management in time to make correct decisions about the use and delivery of enterprise resources, whether those are raw materials for manufacturing, people to carry out key business processes, or the management of shipping choices for correct delivery to customers.

The OTM conference series have established itself as a major international forum for exchanging ideas and results on scientific research for practitioners in fields such as computer supported cooperative work, middleware, Internet/Web data management, electronic commerce, workflow management, knowledge flow, agent technologies and software architectures, Cyber Physical Systems and IoT, to name a few. The recent popularity and interest in service-oriented architectures & domains require capabilities for on-demand composition of services. These emerging technologies represent a significant need for highly interoperable systems.

As a part of OnTheMove 2017, the Industry Case Studies Program on "Industry Applications and Standard initiatives for Cooperative Information Systems - The future for the Cyber Physical Systems", supported by OMG, IIC (Industrial Internet Consortium), IFAC TC 5.3 "Enterprise Integration and Networking", IFAC TC 9.3 on "Control for Smart cities" and the SIG INTEROP Grande-Région, emphasized Research/Industry cooperation on these future trends. The focus of the program is on a discussion of ideas where research areas address interoperable information systems and infrastructure. Four short papers have been presented, focusing on industry leaders, standardization initiatives, European and international projects consortiums and discussing how projects within their organizations addressed software, systems and architecture interoperability. Each paper has been reviewed by an international Programme Committee composed of representatives of Academia, Industry and Standardisation initiatives. We thank them for their dedication and interest.

We hope that you find this industry-focused part of the program valuable as feedback from industry practitioners, and we thank the authors for the time and effort taken to contribute to the program.

The OTM Industry Case Studies Program chair

September 2017   Hervé Panetto

The Recent AIPLA Meeting's New Trend as to Nationwide §101-Guidelines and the "Invention Description Language, IDL" — Trivializing Using ETCIs' FSTP-Tests

Sigram Schindler[1,2(✉)]

[1] TU Berlin, Berlin, Germany
[2] TELES Patent Rights International GmbH, Berlin, Germany
Sigram.Schindler@teles.de

Abstract. AIPLA 2017 Spring Conference turned out to be the most interesting event by AIPLA's standing, especially as to the IDL. This paper upfront confirms the truth of this assumption: The event provided the best survey/comment up to now concerning the recent nationwide §101/*Alice*-guidelines and similar international developments. Section 2 namely reports that the AIPLA 2017 Spring Conference was the first internationally attended meeting of the large expert community of 35 USC Substantive Patent Law ("SPL") that in several panels

- showed the by now vastly stabilized understanding of the Supreme Court's *Alice* decision
- complained of the still total helplessness as to an urgently needed key to — or, to the point: 'clou' of — the Supreme Court's *Alice* analysis, i.e. its *MBA*-framework, which would clearly/convincingly, totally robustly, and broadly acceptably separate patent-eligible ("PE") from nPE inventions.

But this 'clou' exists, even a 'big clou', as the latter enables by IDL for any ETCI to prove rationally & mathematically •trivially and •semi-automatically its totally robust SPL satisfaction (comprising its PE).

Keywords: Invention Description Language – IDL · FSTP-Test
Alice-guidelines · MBA framework · Solomonic clou
Limited preemptive · Rational · Knowledge Representation – KR
Refined rational/Mathematical claiming

© Springer International Publishing AG 2018
C. Debruyne et al. (Eds.): OTM 2017 Workshops, LNCS 10697, pp. 223–231, 2018.
https://doi.org/10.1007/978-3-319-73805-5_23

1   The AIPLA 2017 Spring Conference and the §101/Framework Issue

By targeting the AIPLA 2017 Spring Conference the [21] assumed already that it would become — as to the 35 USC §101 problem, its Supreme Court's framework, and the CAFC's actual precedents — the most interesting event by AIPLA's standing, especially as to the IDL [21]. This continuation of [21] upfront confirms the truth of this assumption: This event provided the best survey/comment up to now concerning the recent nationwide §101/*Alice*-guidelines and similar international developments, e.g. by [27].

Section 2 namely reports that the AIPLA 2017 Spring Conference was the first internationally attended meeting of the large expert community of 35 USC Substantive Patent Law ("SPL") that in several panels

- showed the by now vastly stabilized understanding of the Supreme Court's *Alice* decision[1(a), (b)] — as socioeconomically indeed being of groundbreaking importance for the US innovation economies and their role in warranting the wealth of US society — and, on the other hand,

---

[1] [(a)]**FSTP** = 'Facts Screening/Transforming/Presenting' (Several versions of it were published already after the Supreme Court's *KSR* decision, as initial drafts and then incomplete as without PE checks, yet notionally with 'E-crCs' already). **ETCI** = 'Emerging Technologies Claimed Invention'.

The §101 position papers of the here involved large IPR associations/organizations/consortia resp. dominating innovation-economies in the US came until the end of 2016 solely from the USPTO [10, 14, 15], in 2017 (vastly US election caused) from the IPO [23], the ABA [25], the AIPLA [22], and in between from such important consortia as e.g. the EFF [28] and the Internet Association [19] — importantly also the SIPO [26]. None of these statements still steers the formerly often openly confrontative course of •bashing the Supreme Court's framework[(d)] or •just misinterpreting it — both earlier pursued by a thin but resilient resistance net of broadly known veterans of leading the 'old school of the NPS', e.g. by a seemingly smaller part of the CAFC, in total by today being a small minority, clearly shrinking yet residual for a potentially long time.

But this change does not mean the Supreme Court's short term interception potential is no longer needed, e.g. for enforcing its *Teva* decision ('upgrading' of district courts v. CAFC & USPTO in SPL precedents about ETCIs [29, 30]) and/or the it supporting *Heartland* decision [30].

[(b)]except in part of this resistance net[(a)] with its belief in an US patent system, •reconciling itself after the many CAFC, district courts, and PTO in- and external clashes [1, 30], that •in the future would consistently/predictably decide the large number of ETCI-based cases •without adjusting the SPL interpretation to what the Supreme Court's framework requires — being as stable as 'the earth is flat', 'electrons are of wood', ...

[(c)]The Supreme Court left this "**clou**" to be derived by the patent community's experts and the CAFC from the direction pointing hints provided by what it called [18/ftn2.b.2] its [*MBA*-] "**framework**"[(d)]. Meanwhile it is expected that this new notion of the *Alice* analysis, "**clou**", is exactly to the point.

[(d)]— known since [17, 18, 21] at the latest and now trivialized by the IDL. Thereby "*MBA*", standing for "*KSR/Bilski/Mayo/Myriad/Biosig/Alice*", indicates that all 6 Supreme Court decisions are needed for deriving from them this '**clou**'[(C)]. Its highlighting is omitted from here on.

[(e)] according to the definition for an ETCI to be "PE", provided by the *MBA*-framework[(c)].

[(f)]The nontrivial reason being: [17, 21] proved rationally and even mathematically: "**An ETCI satisfies SPL iff it passes the FSTP-Test**".

- complained of the still total helplessness as to an urgently needed key to — or, to the point: **'clou'** of — the Supreme Court's *Alice* analysis[1(c)], i.e. its *MBA*-framework[1(d)], which would clearly/convincingly, totally robustly, and broadly acceptably separate patent-eligible ("PE") from nPE inventions[1(e)].

But this **'clou'** exists[1(d)], even a **'big clou'**, as the latter enables by IDL for any ETCI to prove rationally & mathematically •trivially and •semi-automatically its totally robust SPL satisfaction (comprising its PE)[1(f)].

[31] A.1/.2 explains — by derivatives of the below Fig. 1. from [21] — the [IDL]FSTP-Test's and an abstract [IDL]ETCI's triviality.

Fig. 1. At a first glance, the ETCI's FSTP-Test looks complex — in this [IDL]KR [21] — yet trivial at a second look [31][1(a)]

2   The §101/*Alice* Decision About ETCIs Is by IDL Trivialized — Its Solomonic Clou

By now there are broadly accepted[2(a)] basic truths as to all ETCIs of the Supreme Court's §101/*Alice* decision: "The Supreme Court indicated by its *Mayo* opinion the need of a socioeconomically broadly acceptable way[2(b)] to avoid disincentivizing investing much money and/or time for creating ETCIs — just because any ETCI is preemptive [12ftn 3(a), 11ftn 10(b)]. This disincentivation would inevitably occur if the Supreme Court a priori took on one of the two extreme positions: Declaring all ETCIs •PE though many ETCIs are unlimited preemptive (any one threatening to put into jeopardy the entire US NPS, see below), or •nPE though many ETCIs are limited preemptive — being indispensable for generating this incentive."

Given this 'basic SPL-testing dilemma' for ETCIs, the fundamental question is whether a Solomonic[2(c)] test exists that is capable of solving this dilemma for any ETCI according to 35 USC/SPL and the Alice analysis, i.e. of deciding this ETCI's being PE or nPE[2(d)].

This question is equivalent to asking for more (ETCI embedded) details: whether there is a test that is

---

2 (a) — except by the residual resistance groups[1(b)] —

    (b)— which it thereafter in principle found by its 'Solomonic' *Alice* analysis —

    (c)A way — alternativeless/trivially being a test — to avoiding this disincentivation is called **"Solomonic"** if it finds any ETCI to be PE iff it is rationalizably/mathematizably provably 'limited preemptive', which is equivalent to a conjunction of tests not referring to preemptivity.

    This follows from the FSTP-Test as having, for any ETCI that passes it — because of test1 — for any COM(ETCI) a rational/mathematizable refined claim interpretation proven correct. Moreover then holds: test1–test10 are rationally and mathematically proven as comprising any ETCI's PE-criterion (test4–test7) [17] — with test7 redundant to test5∧test6 (i.e., its test4∧test7 = test4∧test5∧test6) — and PA-criterion (test8–test10), each depending on ETCI-individual and potentially also RS-specific "***MBA*-framework knowledge, *MBA*-FK**", by the Supreme Court required to be disclosed for the purpose by the ETCI's specification and potentially also RS-specific TTi's specifications [31].

    (d)A side remark: Due to the socioeconomic trends in patenting ETCIs [6(a)/(b)/(c)] these are socially affordable only iff SPL-satisfiability test is vastly automatable. Because of the future socioeconomic predominance of ETCIs, refraining from automating it also puts the NPS into jeopardy.

    (e)— which comprises guiding the tester by questions to disaggregate the ETCI's A-crCs into its E-crCs and to adjust the potential TTi's to this E-KR.

    (f)The USPTO's IEG starts the *Alice* analysis — instead from these basic §101/*Alice*-truths and using therein the rational [31] *MBA*-FK, as the Supreme Court requires[2(c)] — by its "2-step-test" simplifying the *Alice* analysis, which rationally totally ignores the individual *MBA*-FK about this ETCI[2(c)] and instead uses highly metaphysical 'pseudo-rationales' as to the being PE of the ETCI's subject matter. This *MBA*-FK is inevitably needed for refining the basic dilemma as required by the *Alice* analysis for rationally deriving for this ETCI its individual PE decision. Thus, for the USPTO's "2-step-test" it is rationally impossible to rationally deliver the same PE decision as the *Alice* analysis — which leaves the user without any guidance how to rationally decide an ETCI's being. **NOTE:** This legal error applies also to CAFC decisions proceeding as the USPTO.

1. known & for any ETCI applicable & finite & rational & today already vastly automatically executable &
2. capable of guiding the tester of an ETCI to a KR of it that enables testing it for SPL-satisfiability[2(e)] &
3. Solomonic.

These questions' answers[3(b), 2(c)] cannot yet be the "**big clou**" — as not yet solving the SPL-problem[3(b)].

Finding this big clou of the Supreme Court's Alice Decision — hidden in its philosophical/metaphoric language, as now implicitly confirmed by some parties — without the FSTP-Test would have been extremely unlikely: As then there wouldn't have been the for this 'clou finding' absolutely necessary guidance of the FSTP-Test's 'SPL-logic questions asking system' (on the IES [16]), thus showing how to find the nonevident way to this big clou. And also the FSTP-Test by itself is for patent practitioners nonevident.

First, in brevity, what at all the big clou is: **IDL trivializes for anybody FSTP-Testing of ETCIs**.

Next 10 guideline[1(a)] comments from this AIPLA conference, indicating key points (of the basic thinking about the *MBA*-framework) underlying these comments[2(f)]: •The hitherto underestimation of ETCIs' preemptivities is broadly recognized but not yet clear, just as •CAFC's recent PE decisions, some requiring reconsideration, their trend is ok, •powerful groups not understanding this issue and hence this trend — including famous names of really honorable men, •"virtually all parties dropped novelty" (being a specific statement as to the preceding issue), •the need of one and only one PE criterion, •no need of separation of SW-Tech from Bio-Tech ETCIs, •doubts about feasibility of Congressional intervention, •the need to keep the Judicial Committee informed, •several Innovation Economies being in great troubles due to investment disincentivation, •nobody joined or only seemed to appreciate an appeal to Supreme Court bashing. All these commentators and observers seemed to enjoy these univocal agreements.

A common denominator of these 10 comments on exemplary 101/*Alice* issues is that classical claiming encounters for ETCIs fundamentally disastrous blind SPL-spots causing that the parties[1(a)] meanwhile agree[1(b)]: **ETCIs' classical claiming must be refined — as by the Supreme Court required.**

But, now they disagree about the *MBA*-framework specific way of refining claiming of ETCIs — hoping there were better such ways that had nothing to do with the allegedly incomprehensible *Alice* notions "nature of an application" and its transformation's result being "significantly more"[3(a)]. But this hope is in vain again, as the *Alice* analysis is improvable — by a clou — only within the *MBA* framework[3(b)].

Moreover, today this clou must be considered insufficient — in spite of scientifically resolving all the §101/*Alice* problems — as it does not resolve, for any ETCI given, •also its SPL-problem, i.e. its additional §§102/103-problem, in a way •for anybody usable. Thereby the second bullet point is socioeconomically more important than the first one. This holds in particular as now[3(b)] ETCIs' SPL-problems are no longer caused by sophisticated 35 USC §§112/101/102/103 requirements (as resolved

---

[3] [(a)]Two clarifications, not yet hitting the "clou point", are in place here:

• none of the parties[1(a)] provide a suggestion alternative to the *MBA*-framework for how to exclude unlimited preemptive ETCIs from being patented — the latter politically threaten to put the entire US NPS into jeopardy as socioeconomically untenable, unless fair sublicensing of preempted ETCIs is legally enforced (whereby the notion of 'fair' is known to be indefinable, and thus creates another source of inconsistency and unpredictability of patent precedents about ETCIs) — and

• the FSTP-Technology, basically the FSTP-Test — induced by the *MBA*-framework's thought, by FSTP-Technology brought into line with AIT [2] thinking — shows that none of the suggested modifications[1(a)] of the *MBA*-framework comprises a hint that it has fully recognized this Solomonic cognition of the Supreme Court (disclosed by its *Alice's* PE analysis and transformed into FSTP-Test, i.e. into purely mathematical thinking as envisioned by Kant [24]). This statement holds also for the USPTO's IEG interpretation of the Supreme Court's *Alice* analysis, its '2-step-test', and for any of the current CAFC PE precedents (even in *DDR*, though it is correct in the AI

[(b)]and evidently none of the parties[1(a)] has attempted[(c)] anything alike. This *Alice* analysis refinement is scientifically/notionally/semiotically rationally clarified since years [3–5] and published for the US patent community. I.e., hence since then it is available — this **"clou"** it now asks for. This delay is due to the legal bodies[1(a)] are scholastics minded, not analytics/cognitions driven — otherwise they also might have recognized the FSTP-Test's charm as already embodying the "clou" and now as directly guiding to trivializing an ETCI's SPL-satisfaction testing (provided they had also invented the IDL needed to this end), i.e. embodying the "big clou".

[(c)]— barring rationality to penetrate into this intricate realm of the SPL. This has been enabled by all time interest driven pretentions that patent law is insolubly interwoven with the mystery of successful constructive creativity (indispensable for creating ETCIs). But since the revitalization of (decent) AI, in the 70s/80s, it is known how in principle to separate the •transcendence of this mystery from •rational/mathematical thinking about it [7, 13]. Namely: By creating inventive concepts, encapsulating their increments of transcendence into individual axioms, and tying these transcendences' effects into rationality, predominantly by lowest semantic/rational effort required to this end, e.g. by their applications/specifications/systems/incarnations/instantiations/declaration/objectivation/.... This then revolutionary knowledge and the meanwhile incredible increase of the power of so structured IT systems (alias general purpose computers) enabled those familiar with both areas of human cognition to practice this thinking of advanced system design — here for designing and implementing FSTP-Technology and the IES prototype for it [16] in the FSTP-Project.

Similar paradigm shifts, as caused by this FSTP-Project — induced by the Supreme Court created SPL-precedents about ETCIs — occurred during the last 3 millennia in any technology. The time that any such paradigm shift needed from its technology's creation to the latter's full use shrunk from originally dozens of centuries (e.g. the change-over from Ptolemaic to Copernican navigation), to few centuries (e.g. high-voltage technology from Lincoln to Tesla), to few dozens of years (e.g. in rocketry), and now to few years (e.g. in IT, FSTP-Technique).

by the above clou), but by another well-known innovation blocker existing in all emerging technologies.

This innovation blocker is hitherto caused by the ubiquitous but today unavoidable incapability of all expert communities to cooperate with each other — here about ETs' issues[3(c)], due to the today high pace of development of any ET. This disastrous innovation barrier is eliminated by IDL [20]: By expanding the above common denominator of all ETCI-/SPL-problems, for enabling all members of all such communities to communicate with and thereby precisely understanding each other. This is the above big clou.

This short paper terminates by 5 **'ETCI creation boosting potentials'** of this big clou — explained in 3:

1. **IDL is so trivial that it need not be learned — it may be used by just 'copying' it!** This resolves the patent practitioners qualification problem as enabling them to instantly perform ETCIs' FSTP-drafting&testing.
2. **The tester is by QA in IDL semi-automatically guided, for any ETCI, to all its rational COM(ETCI)s and through their rational FSTP-Tests** — whereby his/her only vague 35 USC/SPL knowledge is needed.
3. **The tester is by QA in IDL guided to any ETCI's all mathematical COM (ETCI)s and through their mathematical correct FSTP-Tests** — starting from 2., his/her precise 35 USC/SPL knowledge is now needed.
4. **Broad & fast knowhow dissemination in IDL** — of all SPL-precedents about ETCIs and potential impacts.
5. **Automatically assessing that none of the many facts to be input by the tester is forgotten** [32] (as all prompted & reminded by the IES [16]) — excluding already the most likely as hardly detectable errors.

In total: IDL trivializes nothing of the ETCIs' FSTP-Test — but just using it, thus dramatically increasing the efficiency of working with patents as to all its aspects, including qualifying for it. And: IDL warrants the total robustness of its FSTP-Test-proof ETCIs, thus dramatically increasing also the qualities of •patents for ETCIs, of •incentives to invest into creating them, and of •SPL-drafting&-testing them.

References

FSTP = Facts Screening/Transforming/Presenting (Version of 14.06.2017 (*This paper is available at www.fstp-expert-system.com under the number given in the square bracket.)); Most of the FSTP-Project papers below are written in preparation of the textbook [9] – i.e. are not intended to be fully self-explanatory independent of their predecessors.

1. Schindler, S.: US Highest Courts' Patent Precedents in Mayo/Myriad/CLS/Ultramercial/LBC: 'Inventive Concepts' Accepted, – 'Abstract Ideas' Next? Patenting Emerging Technologies'. Inventions Now without Intricacies.[*[1]]
2. AIT: "Advanced Information Technology" alias "Artificial Intelligence Technology" denotes cutting edge IT areas, e.g. Knowledge Representation (KR)/Description Logic (DL)/Natural Language (NL)/Semantics/Semiotics/System Design, just as MAI: "Mathematical Artificial Intelligence", the resilient fundament of AIT and "Facts Screening/Transforming/Presenting, FSTP"-Technology, developed in this FSTP-Project
3. Schindler, S.: Math. Model. Substantive. Patent Law (SPL) Top-Down vs. Bottom-Up. Yokohama (2012). JURISIN 20[*[5]]
4. Schindler, S.: "FSTP" pat. appl.: THE FSTP EXPERT SYSTEM (2012)[*[6]]
5. Schindler, S.: "DS" pat. appl.: AN INNOVATION EXPERT SYSTEM, IES, & ITS PTR-DS (2013)[*[7]]
6. (a) Schindler, S.: Patent Business – Before Shake-up (2013)[*[9]]. (b) Schindler, S.: Patent Business – Before Shake-up (2015)[*[9]]. (c) Schindler, S.: Patent Business – Before Shake-up (2017)
7. SSBG's Amicus Brief to the CAFC in case CLS, 12 June 2012[*[42]]
8. Schindler, S.: The CAFC's Rebellion is Over – The USSC, by Mayo/Biosig/Alice, ... published 07 August 2014[*[113]]
9. Schindler, S.: Basics of Innovation-Theory and Substantive Patent Law Technology. Textbook (in prep.)
10. (a) USPTO: July 2015 Update on Subj. Matter Eligibility, 30 July 2015[*[235]] (b) USPTO: May 2016 Update: Memorandum - Recent Subj. Matter Eligibility Decisions, 19 May 2016[*[235]]
11. Schindler, S.: The IEG's 2015 Update & the 'Patent-Eligibility Granteding, PEG' Test. publ., 18 December 2015[*[244]]
12. Schindler, S.: Patent-Eligibility and the "Patent-Eligibility Granteding, PEG" Test, resp. the CAFC Object. Counters the Supreme Court's MBA Framework, by its DDR vs. Myriad/Cuozzo Decisions, 05 January 2016[*[251]]
13. Parnas, D.: Software Fundamentals. Addison-Wesley (2001)
14. Bahr, R.: USPTO: MEMORANDUM as to Recent Subject Matter Eligibility Decisions ...., 19 May 2016[*[292]]
15. Bahr, R.: USPTO: MEMORANDUM as to Recent Subject Matter Eligibility Decisions ...., 02 November 2016[*[345]]
16. Schoenberg, D.: The IES Prototype Qualification Machine. GIPC, New Delhi, 11–13 January 2017[*[352]]

17. Schindler, S.: An Amazing SPL Cognition: Any Patent Application is Draftable Totally Robust, Memo A. Published on 31 January 2017[*354]

18. Schindler, S.: An Amazing SPL Cognition: Any Patent Application is Draftable Totally Robust, Memo B. Published by 07 March 2017[*355]

19. IA ("Internet Association"): Letter to the President-elect Trump, 14 December 2016[*360]

20. Schindler, S.: "IDL" pat. appl.: An 'Innovation Description Language, IDL' & its IES Interpreter (2017)[*350]

21. Schindler, S.: "Innovation Description Languages, IDLs" & Knowledge Representations, KRs, and Easily Drafting & Testing Patents for Their Total Robustness. Publ., 16 May 2017[*372]

22. AIPLA: Legislative Proposal and Report on Patent Eligible Subject Matter, 12 May 2017[*376]

23. IPO: Proposed Amendments to Patent Eligible Subject Matter, 07 February 2017[*377]

24. See the correct reference in the V.27 of the [21] at the below URL, in a few days

25. ABA: Letter by D. Suchy to the USPTO, 28 March 2017[*379]

26. SIPO: Message by H.-M. Tso, J. Yi, 31 March 2017[*380]

27. Stoll, B.: 101 in the Future. AIPLA, 17 May 2017[*383]

28. EFF: Comments Regarding ... Subject Matter Eligibility, 18 January 2017[*385]

29. Duffy, J., Bays, C., Sichelman, T.: The future of patent venue. In: AIPLA 2017 Spring Conference, 18 May 2017[*387]

30. USSC, Decision in Heartland v. Kraft, 22 May 2017[*388]

31. Schindler, S.: ANNEX of the Solomonic Clou of the §101/*Alice* Decision about ETCIs — by IDL Trivialized, 20 June 2017[*391]

32. Schindler, S.: The FSTP-Test and the *DDR's* ETCI Reconsidered — as Model Case (in prep.)

User Experience and Agile Software Practices – An Industry Perspective

Prabal Mahanta[✉] and Bhavneet Kaur

SAP Labs Pvt. Ltd., No. 138, EPIP Area, Whitefield, Bangalore 560076, Karnataka, India
{p.mahanta,bhavneet.kaur}@sap.com

Abstract. User Experience and Agile Software Development are both user-focused iterative methods. Usually they both are difficult to realize as per the theoretical concepts in real world development. The challenge is how to integrate them in the development process.

There is a need for gaining perspective from all the stakeholders which includes not only customers but internal teams involved in development. This approach will lay the foundation of taking care of the requirements from both the product and human perspective so that the development and expectations are consistent.

The paper will present the framework for managing the design of processes for each stake holders – Developer, QA, Customer and Management. The framework tries to resolve the complexity that evolves through collaboration between self-organizing, cross-functional teams.

Keywords: User experience · Development · Agile · Process

1 Co-existence of User Experience and Agile

The two disciplines of Agile Development and User Experience often come to a debate when we apply the concepts to the real-world product development. With the misconception of using User Experience as a tool to package and renew products with front end design is a myth which needs to be addressed. Agile on the other hand if not applied in a seamless manner will create deliverable of lesser quality.

UX [1] and Agile [2] have two different objectives which are product interaction with user and code creation for a product respectively. The challenge is where to merge them and how to merge them so that there is a genuine interaction between the two components. This doesn't mean that developers will be on the side of agile and designers will be on the UX front. As per the current literature and methodologies available there are very few concepts or tools that solves the problem of interaction between a developer's workflow and designer's workflow.

The UX workflow typically comprises of:

a. Assessing the problem
b. Research
c. Ideation

© Springer International Publishing AG 2018
C. Debruyne et al. (Eds.): OTM 2017 Workshops, LNCS 10697, pp. 232–235, 2018.
https://doi.org/10.1007/978-3-319-73805-5_24

    d. Prototyping
    e. Testing
    f. Collaboration to Development process

    The Agile workflow typically comprises of:

a. Hypothesis
b. Research
c. Estimation
d. Development
e. QA
f. Release
g. Support

As we see that the two workflows are diverse and need to merge which itself is a daunting task. There are lot of theories which presents concepts around this problem but they all lack practical implementation.

The need of the hour is not to apply the theoretical concepts for teams to become productive but to facilitate a framework for the perspective change in the organization mindset [3].

2   Perspective of Stakeholders

As a Developer

There should be:
- A clear requirement and technical feasibility study
- Design ready with User acceptance of design
- Detailed development activities

As a QA

There should be:
- A clear definition of features
- Design of corner cases and feedback loop for developers

As a Designer

There should be:
- A clear understanding of user requirements
- Complete the design of the workflow of the application

As a Sponsor

There should be:
- A holistic understanding of the requirements
- Customer acceptance of the approved plan
- On time delivery of quality artifacts

As a Customer

There should be:
- Proper understanding of the requirements in the delivery
- Application with complete features on time
- No Bugs

With all the perspectives in place, we need a framework which ties them together for an effective result or an outcome. Sometimes agile or user experience methodologies alone cannot achieve the requirement of a seamless integration or a collaboration. In the next section we will present the framework that will help overcoming this problem [4].

3 DesEdge = Design Framework with Agile Workflow

We come up with a framework for enabling the teams to share their workshop outcomes in form of designs which are easy to comprehend from each of the stakeholders.

So the idea is as follows:

a. Before formal development starts, we need every stakeholder to share and agree on the development outcomes. This can only be possible when all of them share their expectation and a developer in this mode can also have a clear understanding what a business team wants to deliver to the customer. This way customer's tech team also understands what is being delivered and if it is not the expected delivery then they have a way to provide the feedback before the expected delivery date arrives to prevent any delays.

b. After Development ends the design and design artifacts are shared with QA and continuous feedback cycles are managed between the teams. This way bugs are prevented (to some extend) from reaching a production environment where customer is affected.

c. Post the Cycle, All the teams are aware of the deliverable and all the artifacts are available review.

d. Agile methods like SCRUM/KANBAN [5, 6] can help managing the expected time to delivery. But the most effective way is to keep lesser stand-ups and flexible to reduce stress on the development-design-testing teams to preserve the quality.

e. The workshops at every phase of the design of each stake-holders holds a significance where all the stakeholders are to participate to provide a holistic overview to the workshop objectives (Fig. 1).

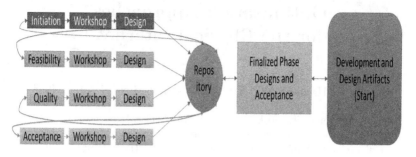

Fig. 1. DesEdge workflow

4   Conclusion

There are various ways to attain a seamless integration but the problem is with the change of mindset that is required to adopt the change. The teams must adopt a subset of design thinking methods [7, 8] which involves observation to discover non-delivered expectations with the context of set constraints. This will frame the scope of innovation and refine the existing solution in a coordinated fashion without stressing the teams.

References

1. Hassenzahl, M.: User experience (UX): towards an experiential perspective on product quality. In: Proceedings of the 20th Conference on l'Interaction Homme-Machine. ACM (2008)
2. Highsmith, J., Cockburn, A.: Agile software development: The business of innovation. Computer **34**(9), 120–127 (2001)
3. Rajkumar, M., Pole, A.K., Adige, V.S., Mahanta, P.: DevOps culture and its impact on cloud delivery and software development. In: International Conference on Advances in Computing, Communication, and Automation (ICACCA) (Spring), pp. 1–6. IEEE, April 2016
4. Plattner, H., Meinel, C., Leifer, L. (eds.): Design Thinking Research. Springer, Heidelberg (2012). https://doi.org/10.1007/978-3-642-21643-5
5. Sutherland, J., et al.: Distributed scrum: Agile project management with outsourced development teams. In: 2007 40th Annual Hawaii International Conference on System Sciences, HICSS 2007. IEEE (2007)
6. Ikonen, M., et al.: On the impact of kanban on software project work: An empirical case study investigation. In: 2011 16th IEEE International Conference on Engineering of Complex Computer Systems (ICECCS). IEEE (2011)
7. Plattner, H., Meinel, C., Leifer, L. (eds.): Design Thinking: Understand–Improve–Apply. Springer, Heidelberg (2011). https://doi.org/10.1007/978-3-642-13757-0
8. Lindberg, T., Meinel, C., Wagner, R.: Design thinking: A fruitful concept for IT development? In: Meinel, C., Leifer, L., Plattner, H. (eds.) Design Thinking. Understanding Innovation, pp. 3–18. Springer, Heidelberg (2011). https://doi.org/10.1007/978-3-642-13757-0_1

Optimization Approaches
for the Physical Internet

Viktoria A. Hauder[1,2(✉)], Erik Pitzer[1], and Michael Affenzeller[1,3]

[1] Heuristic and Evolutionary Algorithms Laboratory,
School of Informatics, Communications and Media,
University of Applied Sciences Upper Austria, Hagenberg Campus,
Hagenberg im Mühlkreis, Austria
{viktoria.hauder,erik.pitzer,michael.affenzeller}@fh-hagenberg.at
[2] Institute for Production and Logistics Management,
Johannes Kepler University Linz, Linz, Austria
[3] Institute for Formal Models and Verification,
Johannes Kepler University Linz, Linz, Austria

Abstract. With the Physical Internet (PI), a global economic transformation towards a more holistic consideration and collaboration of different agents is promoted. Its goal is the implementation of global sustainable logistics by increasing the utilization of available resources. This should be reached by developing a network in which goods of different organizations are transported, stored and handled. One aspect of the PI is the optimization of the transport procedure. In this paper, potential optimization models for a subset of three key elements of the PI, the containers, movers (all kinds of transportation means), and nodes (all kinds of locations), are presented. Moreover, corresponding algorithmic approaches are proposed. The novel modeling approach of optimization networks (ON) with the objective of finding an overall optimized solution considering the involved interrelated subtasks in a holistic sense is compared to highly reactive solution methods based on rules that are learned offline. With the proposed approaches, interoperability between different (economic) agents and (software) systems is supported. The goal of multidisciplinary collaboration of different participants and their integration into one PI network should be approached.

Keywords: Physical internet · Optimization network · Integration
Interoperability · Sustainable logistics

1 Introduction

With the development of the so-called Physical Internet (PI or π), a novel type of transportation of goods is suggested, in which the interoperability of software systems, humans, and organizations is supported [10]. The current way how physical objects such as containers are transported and handled is associated with a loss of optimization potential and thus considered to be unsustainable [10].

© Springer International Publishing AG 2018
C. Debruyne et al. (Eds.): OTM 2017 Workshops, LNCS 10697, pp. 236–245, 2018.
https://doi.org/10.1007/978-3-319-73805-5_25

Therefore, a network which is based on the idea of the digital internet is proposed by Montreuil et al. [10,11]. With the support of software systems, standardized containers find their way through a transportation network in which vehicles and locations of different organizations are connected [10]. Thus, the goal of the PI is a change from the current globally existing fragmented transportation network to an interconnected one, which can be seen in Fig. 1.

One aspect of the PI which has to be investigated is the design of the transportation flow of containers [10]. It has to be decided which containers are transported in which vehicles and in which sequence containers are packed into one vehicle [10]. As the PI aims at a novel type of interconnection of transportation, including vehicles and locations of different enterprises, it has to be deliberated if so far used optimization approaches in the area of production and logistics are adequately applyable or new, alternative methods have to be developed.

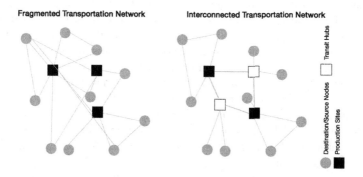

Fig. 1. Fragmented versus interconnected transportation.

The goal of this paper is to give an overview of different possible optimization approaches for the transportation of containers within the PI. The novel approach of an optimization network (ON) is compared to a multi-agent optimization method. Within an ON, production and logistics processes are connected and optimized simultaneously. In contrary to that, a multi-agent system consists of a decentralized decision process where incomplete and only local available information is used for optimization and therefore is highly reactive. With the presentation of both approaches, it is demonstrated, which possibilities concerning logistics optimization in the PI, and therefore supporting interoperability, exist.

The remainder of this article is organized as follows. Related work concerning the Physical Internet is discussed in Sect. 2. This part is followed by the presentation of an optimization network and a multi-agent optimization system for the PI in Sect. 3. Finally, Sect. 4 provides concluding remarks and gives directions for further research.

2   Literature Review

With the proposal of the Physical Internet, Montreauil et al. [10,11] suggest a paradigm shift in the transportation of goods. Its necessity is argued with the existing grand challenge concerning the sustainability of global logistics in an economic, environmental and societal way [10]. This challenge is based on 13 unsustainability symptoms such as the current existing under-utilization of warehouses or long home absence periods of truck drivers due to their current route schedules [10]. The three physical elements of the PI are

- π-movers (PI transportation means, for example trucks or conveyors),
- π-nodes (PI locations, for example distribution centers or warehouses), and
- π-containers which are standardized transport boxes [11].

Montreauil et al. [10,11] suggest a multi-segment intermodal transportation network where π-containers are dynamically routed through a global open supply web in the same manner as digital internet data packets are transmitted. π-containers are equipped with a smart tag, inter alia, to be able to route themselves through the PI network. Depending on transport order specifications and not predictable environmental influences, the routing can be dynamically changed. π-containers can be moved by different π-movers and through different π-nodes on their way from their source to their destination node. With this holistic consideration, so far unseen opportunity costs for participating organizations are revealed. The afore mentioned unsustainability symptoms are conquered and interoperability efforts between different software, human and organizational agents are supported [10,11].

As the PI is a new approach in the area of production and logistics, several possibilities of research exist, for example the development of necessary new business models or the design of standardized containers [10,11]. Considering operations research (OR), one research focus is on the design of transportation protocols [4,10,11]. Algorithms have to be developed which route the π-containers through the PI network, from its source to its destination, if feasible with several transshipments at intermediate stations (π-nodes). Sarraj et al. [13] describe in their work the advantages of the PI in contrary to a fragmented logistics network. They propose a point to point routing without loops and a subsequent Bin Backing Packing Problem (BPP) [9] formulation for the assignment of π-containers to transportation means (π-movers) and use a discrete-event simulation modeling approach, the AnyLogic multi-agent based system. Fazili et al. [4] suggest a sequential optimization and simulation consisting of three phases. After solving a BPP, a Vehicle Routing Problem (VRP) [14] is optimized, followed by a scheduling optimization, where trucks are assigned to not yet performed jobs. It is shown that in transportation networks where the ratio of packing costs is lower than driving costs, the PI is advantageous. They suggest further research activities concerning the PI with a special focus on integrated modeling approaches and dynamic and multi-agent optimization and simulation. Based on these suggestions, the integrated approach of an optimization network and a multi-agent based optimization approach for the PI are proposed in this paper.

3   Optimization Approaches for the Physical Internet

The traditional way of transporting goods consists of a fragmented logistics network, in which organizations move their own or third-party goods and, with few exceptions such as cross docking platforms [15], usually do not share their resources with other organizations. Thus, until now research efforts in the area of operations research have been focused on the consideration of single optimization problems. In contrast, with the concept of the Physical Internet, a holistic, integrative transportation network is demanded [10,11]. Resources of organizations should be used collaboratively and goods should be transported in standardized π-containers [10,11]. To accomodate these requirements, new developments concerning the optimization of the proposed transportation network are necessary. Hereinafter, three potential optimization models which can be taken into account for optimizations within the PI are pointed out. Moreover, two algorithmic solution approaches for a holistic optimization of the PI network, an optimization network and a multi-agent optimization approach, are proposed.

3.1   Optimization Models

As already stated in Sect. 2, the three physical elements within the Physical Internet are π-movers, π-nodes, and π-containers [11]. For the consideration of the routing of containers through the PI in this work, for π-movers, all kinds of vehicles and carriers, such as trucks, locomotives, trailors, or wagons are addressed. Concerning the π-nodes, all possible source, destination, and intermediate stop nodes of goods which have to be transported are included.

Network Flow Problem. With the optimization of network flows, supply and demand nodes and routes which connect them are modeled and solved [1]. Differentiations can for example be made concerning single- or multi-commodities, static and dynamic flows, where values of flow change over time and time and capacity constraints [1,6]. A real-world approach for the network of the PI could be a dynamic multi commodity capacitated network flow model [12]. The objective of minimizing storage corresponds to aimed minimal storage costs at π-nodes. The minimization of processing and transportation costs coincides with the routing of π-containers between π-nodes and within π-nodes from unloading to loading platforms, where π-movers are already waiting for further transportation at minimal costs. Moreover, specific customer requests, such as forbidden commodity flows, for example due to legal requirements, can be considered, as depicted in Fig. 2.

Vehicle Routing Problem. For the routing of π-containers through the PI network, one possibility is the consideration of a Vehicle Routing Problem [14]. The VRP is designed to optimize round trips and no point to point transportations as proposed for the PI [10,11,13]. However, one of the goals of the PI is a reduction of working times and an increased amount of possible daily home return journeys for truck drivers [4,13]. Therefore, the optimization of round trips within the PI is at least worth looking at to have possibilities of comparison with other

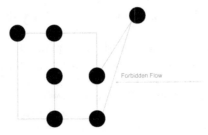

Fig. 2. Network flow connection.

(point to point) modeling approaches. The VRP is a very well studied optimization problem with a lot of works on real-world applications [14]. Its objective is very often the minimization of costs, respectively distance traveled, or time needed [14] which corresponds to minimal transportation costs of π-containers routed through the PI network. Associated constraints are for example customer demand and vehicle capacity constraints, and customer delivery and depot opening time constraints [14].

Bin Packing Problem. For loading π-containers into π-movers, the already well-known Bin Packing Problem [9] can be applied. The BPP consists of a number of objects (π-containers), which have to be assigned to bins (π-movers). The objective commonly is the minimization of used bins, respectively π-movers, subject to capacity constraints of bins and transportation demand requests of objects [9]. Depending on the complexity of the problem, one-, two- or three-dimensional bins can be considered [9]. In terms of the Physical Internet, three-dimensional π-containers have to be taken into account to be able to implement valid real-world results.

3.2   Algorithmic Solution Approaches

Previous works concerning transportation optimization of the Physical Internet show that with a combination of existing, for the PI adopted problem models and already tested algorithmic approaches, valid solutions can be achieved [4,13]. Subsequently, two further solution approaches are proposed for the transportation optimization within the Physical Internet.

An Optimization Network for the Physical Internet

In the field of operations research, single production and logistics problems are often mathematically modeled and solved with an individually developed heuristic approach or an exact algorithm. In contrary to that, with an optimization network, multiple optimization problems are connected and solved simultaneously. For the here proposed ON, the loading of the π-movers with the π-containers and the routing of the π-containers between the π-nodes is considered. With regard to Sect. 3.1, the Network Flow Problem (NFP) and the Bin Packing Problem are considered within the here suggested ON for the PI.

The conventional optimization case would be a sequential optimization of both problem models. After one problem has been solved with one algorithm, its solution is considered for the optimization of the second optimization problem. Next, the results are sumed up and the optimization process is finished. However, with the here proposed ON for the PI, all problem models and solution approaches are interconnected and several optimization runs are carried out within one optimization framework. The optimization network's parts, the problem solvers, the orchestrator, and the meta solver and its operating procedure is explained in detail consecutively. Moreover, the here explained procedure of an ON for the Physical Internet is also presented in Fig. 3.

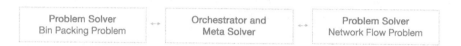

Fig. 3. Functionality of an optimization network for the physical internet.

Problem Solver: For every problem model considered in the ON, one problem solver is designed. Depending on the problem size, exact or heuristic methods can be used. The BPP can for example be solved by applying a Genetic Algorithm (GA), and the NFP can be modeled exactly and solved by a connection with an existing exact solver, such as the IBM ILOG CPLEX Optimization Studio[1].

Orchestrator: The orchestrator considers the solution of the first problem solver, for example the NFP, takes necessary input data out of this solution and gives it to the second problem solver. In this specific case, the orchestrator picks the information of which π-containers are assigned to which π-movers from the first problem solver's solution and gives this information to the BPP problem solver. Next, the second problem solver is started and the BPP per necessary π-mover is optimized. After that, the solution of both problem solvers are merged. The loading costs of the BPP and the storage, transportation and process costs of the NFP are sumed up to one overall result. This overall result is given to the third part of the ON, the meta solver.

Meta Solver: The meta solver is responsible for the optimization of the calculated overall result of the orchestrator. With this optimization, an algorithm finds new parameter configurations for the problem instances of the problem solvers, for example based on a black box optimization of the overall result of the ON. The new parameter configurations are given to the problem solvers, which find better solutions within the next optimization run of the whole ON. It may be noted that changed parameter configurations of a problem instance are accompanied with a change of real world data. However, after every optimization of one problem solver, the solution, respectively the optimized costs are taken into account and transmitted to the other parts of the ON with original problem instance data.

---

[1] https://www.ibm.com/at-en/marketplace/ibm-ilog-cplex.

The exact functionality of this variegation and return transfer of parameter configurations with the guarantee of valid real world solutions has been already proved and can be read in [2,7,8].

After the meta solver has optimized the overall result, the orchestrator starts a new optimization run of the whole optimization network, which means that the here described procedure of problem solvers, orchestrator and meta solver starts again. The amount of optimization runs depends on the optimization algorithm chosen for the meta solver. For example, applying a GA for the meta solver, the amount of generations would correspond to the amount of allowed optimization runs of the ON.

As the ON for the Physical Internet is a novel optimization approach, investigations concerning algorithmic parameter configurations and real world applications on a Physical Internet test bed are necessary to be able to implement this new method. However, first results where an ON is tested on production and logistics problems out of the OR literature have shown the potential of this approach [2,7,8].

A Multi-agent Optimization System for the Physical Internet

In contrary to the proposal of an optimization network for the PI, where there are central and decentral decision mechanisms (meta solver and problem solvers), the multi-agent optimization is built upon local solving strategies. In other areas of production and logistics optimization, where multiple nodes and complex decision support is demanded, multi-agent optimization is presented to be a reasonable solution approach [16,17]. As the Physical Internet is suggested to be a global and thus complex network, subsequently, a multi-agent optimization approach for the PI is suggested. With this approach, single optimization agents, problem dependent parameter information, and complex combined dispatching rules are considered.

- Within the multi-agent optimization for the PI, so-called agents have to be defined, which act autonomously, not considering any central decision mechanism. Agents are determined as π-containers with the objective of the minimization of their lead time within the PI system. Thus, the time needed for one π-container from the first appearance in the network to its total completion, respectively the arrival at the destination node, is minimized. Only considering one future step within the optimization, it has to be decided which (intermediate stop) π-node is chosen next.
- The fundament for the decision of the next (intermediate stop) π-node is the problem-specific parameter information, which has to be defined for the optimization [16,17]. Examples are the start date or the due date of one π-container or the number of π-containers which want to go the the same π-node.
- Based on the available parameter information, dispatching rules have to be designed for the overall agent function. The result of this overall function is a value which prioritizes every request, respectively every π-container which demands a routing through the network. As normally many different

π-containers are competing for a route, the agent with the highest priority function gets the best prioritization value.

Instead of using simple dispatching rules, it is possible to develop and apply complex combined rules. Especially when complex decision systems with loads of data request an optimized solution, combined dispatching rules can bring better solutions than for example very simple and well-known rules, such as the 'First Come First Serve' approach [3]. The basic parameter information is combined and synthesized by applying a tree representation [16, 17]. Dispatching rules are evolved using Genetic Programming [17]. With simulation optimization, in a training phase rules are evolved and in a test phase they are adapted and applied to so far not included test instances [3, 5, 17].

In contrary to the work of Sarraj et al. [13], the here proposed multi-agent approach is not based on a simulation environment such as their used AnyLogic multi-agent based system. The multi-agent optimization system has to be implemeneted into a specially designed optimization framework for the Physical Internet, the optimization framework HeuristicLab[3], and considers the above described complex combined dispatching rule optimization and simulation.

4   Conclusion

In this work, two possible optimization approaches for the Physical Internet have been proposed. Within an optimization network, there are central and decentral decision points. All participating agents and problem models are integrated into one system and the optimization processes of all single optimization nodes are interconnected. In contrary to that, the multi-agent optimization system only works with a decentralized optimization and tries to find optimized solutions by evolving complex combined dispatching rules. With these two presented approaches for the PI, interoperability efforts are supported due to their solution method inherent interconnection of software systems, humans and organizations.

The two presented optimization approaches for the Physical Internet have been developed within a PI project to be able to get further insights into the possibilities of transforming the current fragmented logistics network to an interconnected network. At the moment, it is tried to implement both proposals under consideration of artificial and real world data. Moreover, it is planned to test the proposed optimization network not only with a Network Flow Problem but also with a Vehicle Routing Problem. For the multi-agent based optimization, also variations concerning the agent are planned. Besides the here proposed π-containers, also π-movers will be test objects for the multi-agent based optimization. With these considerations, extensive comparison opportunities concerning optimization possibilities within the PI are aimed.

In general, for future work especially interoperability concerns, such as the intended cooperation of the different agents within the Physical Internet will be an important research subject. Not only for the examination and development

---

[3] http://dev.heuristiclab.com/

of potential business models, but also for the optimization of the Physical Internet transportation network, such considerations are crucial regarding an actual implementation and realisation of a global, interconnected network.

Acknowledgments. The work described in this paper was done within the project 'A Fast Track to the Physical Internet' (Atropine), within the funding program 'Strategic Economy and Research Program Innovative Upper Austria 2020', funded by the Government of Upper Austria (Land OOE).

References

1. Ahuja, R.K., Magnanti, T.L., Orlin, J.B.: Network Flows: Theory, Algorithms, and Applications. Prentice Hall, Upper Saddle River (1993)
2. Beham, A., Fechter, J., Kommenda, M., Wagner, S., Winkler, S.M., Affenzeller, M.: Optimization strategies for integrated knapsack and traveling salesman problems. In: Moreno-Díaz, R., Pichler, F., Quesada-Arencibia, A. (eds.) EUROCAST 2015. LNCS, vol. 9520, pp. 359–366. Springer, Cham (2015). https://doi.org/10.1007/978-3-319-27340-2_45
3. Beham, A., Kofler, M., Wagner, S., Affenzeller, M.: Agent-based simulation of dispatching rules in dynamic pickup and delivery problems. In: 2009 2nd International Logistics and Industrial Informatics, LINDI 2009, pp. 1–6. IEEE (2009)
4. Fazili, M., Venkatadri, U., Cyrus, P., Tajbakhsh, M.: Physical internet, conventional and hybrid logistic systems: a routing optimisation-based comparison using the eastern canada road network case study. Int. J. Prod. Res. **55**(9), 2703–2730 (2017)
5. Fu, M.C., Glover, F.W., April, J.: Simulation optimization: a review, new developments, and applications. In: 2005 Proceedings of the winter Simulation Conference, p. 13. IEEE (2005)
6. Hall, A., Hippler, S., Skutella, M.: Multicommodity flows over time: Efficient algorithms and complexity. Theoret. Comput. Sci. **379**(3), 387–404 (2007)
7. Hauder, V.A., Karder, J., Beham, A., Affenzeller, M.: A general solution approach for the location routing problem. In: EUROCAST (2017)
8. Karder, J., Beham, A., Wagner, S., Affenzeller, M.: Solving the traveling thief problem using orchestration in optimization networks. In: EUROCAST (2017)
9. Korte, B., Vygen, J.: Combinatorial Optimization. Springer, Heidelberg (2012)
10. Montreuil, B.: Toward a physical internet: meeting the global logistics sustainability grand challenge. Logistics Res. **3**(2–3), 71–87 (2011)
11. Montreuil, B., Meller, R.D., Ballot, E.: Towards a physical internet: the impact on logistics facilities and material handling systems design and innovation. In: Progress in Material Handling Research, pp. 305–327 (2010)
12. Raggl, S., Fechter, J., Beham, A.: A dynamic multicommodity network flow problem for logistic networks (2015)
13. Sarraj, R., Ballot, E., Pan, S., Hakimi, D., Montreuil, B.: Interconnected logistic networks and protocols: simulation-based efficiency assessment. Int. J. Prod. Res. **52**(11), 3185–3208 (2014)
14. Toth, P., Vigo, D.: Vehicle Routing: Problems, Methods, and Applications. SIAM, Philadelphia (2014)
15. Van Belle, J., Valckenaers, P., Cattrysse, D.: Cross-docking: State of the art. Omega **40**(6), 827–846 (2012)

16. Van Lon, R.R., Holvoet, T., Vanden Berghe, G., Wenseleers, T., Branke, J.: Evolutionary synthesis of multi-agent systems for dynamic dial-a-ride problems. In: Proceedings of the 14th Annual Conference Companion on Genetic and Evolutionary Computation, pp. 331–336. ACM (2012)
17. Vonolfen, S., Beham, A., Kommenda, M., Affenzeller, M.: Structural synthesis of dispatching rules for dynamic dial-a-ride problems. In: Moreno-Díaz, R., Pichler, F., Quesada-Arencibia, A. (eds.) EUROCAST 2013. LNCS, vol. 8111, pp. 276–283. Springer, Heidelberg (2013). https://doi.org/10.1007/978-3-642-53856-8_35

Manufacturing Intelligence in Furniture Product-Service Design

Evmorfia Biliri[1(✉)], Fenareti Lampathaki[1], Angelos Arvanitakis[1],
Ariadni Michalitsi-Psarrou[1], Javier Martin[2], Fernando Gigante[2], Vicente Sales[2],
and Maria Jose Nunez[2]

[1] National Technical University of Athens, Athens, Greece
{ebiliri,flamp,agg.arvanitakis,amichal}@epu.ntua.com
[2] AIDIMME Technology Institute, Valencia, Spain
{jmartin,fgigante,vsales,mjnunez}@aidimme.es

Abstract. Today, the Industry 4.0 paradigm has penetrated the everyday processes and operations of manufacturers, reframing traditional value chains and delivering novel products and services. Products and services need to be appropriately blended in the path to servitisation, yet manufacturers still struggle with gaining insights and collaborating with all involved stakeholders in the most effective way in order to design smart and connected products-services. In this context, this paper presents how smart furniture product-service bundles have been designed according to the needs of the furniture industry. Such bundles provide value added services during the whole Product Life Cycle of the furniture and range from IoT-enabled workplace monitoring to collaborative ideation and sentiment analysis in order to deliver manufacturing intelligence.

Keywords: Product-service · Product-service system · Manufacturing
Sentiment analysis · Knowledge management · Workplace monitoring

1 Introduction

In the Industry 4.0 era we currently live in, the massive deployment of Cyber-Physical Systems (CPS), the unparalleled power of advanced analytics and the exponential technology growth have breached the walls of manufacturing, accelerating the digital transformation of the traditional manufacturing industry.

The present paper presents a set of diverse, yet symbiotic, manufacturing intelligence solutions in furniture product-service design that materialize in the form of smart furniture product-service bundles. Such bundles encapsulate value added services in the concurrent Product-Service Life Cycle of the furniture and range from usage monitoring of the furniture in the working environment and analysis of postural hygiene of the office employees detecting wrong habits through sensors, to collaborative ideation for the renovation of specific offices and analysis of social media resources to understand the crowd sentiment, the market trends, and how they relate to the previous defined ideas. The product-service bundles that have been developed in accordance with the needs of

© Springer International Publishing AG 2018
C. Debruyne et al. (Eds.): OTM 2017 Workshops, LNCS 10697, pp. 246–250, 2018.
https://doi.org/10.1007/978-3-319-73805-5_26

the furniture industry have been tested in an office renovation case study implemented in Spain.

2 Product-Service Design in Furniture

2.1 P-S Workers Sentiment and Brand Value Assessment

Workers Sentiment Assessment. Surveys regarding the effect of the office environment to employees' job satisfaction and productivity have consistently proven throughout the years the strong dependency between them [1]. Hence, a worker sentiment component was developed to collect and process the opinions of workers at the office about their workplace, considering individual characteristics of their environment. This tool offers a formal and efficient way for grasping the feelings and opinion of the employees who operate in a specific workspace, regarding the different characteristics of the working environment and how they affect physical perceptions as well as emotional and behavioural responses.

The component is implemented in Python and includes an engine providing sets of questions to specified employees together with a management platform through which the questionnaires can be built based on predefined templates, while the assignment of questionnaires to employees also takes place, as employees who work in a specific workspace can anonymously provide their opinion for the workspace. The component includes a monitoring tool for checking the participation of employees, an alert/notification system and an intuitive analytics interface useful for extracting conclusions in a visualised way regarding the sentiment of the workers for each workspace under examination.

Brand Value Assessment. Brand value is defined as "consumer perceptions of a brand as reflected by the brand associations held in consumers' memory" and is usually measured either through an existing list of brand associations or through eliciting associations from scratch [2]. In PSYMBIOSYS, a brand value analysis component is created which leverages Aaker's brand personality list [3] and properly extends it to model brand associations in the furniture manufacturing domain. This component is used to collect and process the perspective that employees and visitors of the manufacturer's customer company have about the brand value transmitted through the office environment. The point of view collected from users is compared to the perspective of the company management in order to evaluate the deviation between both. The analysis results can be later combined with other types of input, indicatively including the brand image as perceived by the general discussions from social media.

The component is implemented in Python and includes two parts: an interface to the management and/or the marketing department through which the firm's brand value objectives are analysed and an online questionnaire for collecting customers' and visitors' opinions regarding the defined brand values.

2.2 P-S Workplace Monitoring

The IoT era has brought advancements in the "Smart Office" concept, ranging from improving ambient comfort and energy saving [4] to monitoring posture [5]. To leverage the potential of this new technology, a workplace monitoring component was developed. This component is in charge of capturing and processing data about the ambience in the office environment and the ergonomics of the employees at their workplaces.

Sensors at the different office workplaces send data wirelessly through xBee transfer to a central node which redirects it to a web server that collects and stores all the received measurements about ambient (such as temperature, humidity, noise and luminosity) and ergonomics values. Data is internally identified by user, workplace and timestamp. An event detection system is used to detect not recommended situations in any workplace, such as unpleasant high temperatures or incorrect sitting postures. Workers are able to receive notifications about these events through a mobile app that communicates with the web server application via a cloud push messaging system. Data collected from workplaces are compared to proper standards and regulations to identify the situations related to inadequate ambient conditions and postures that may result in discomfort or even eventual pain and worker injuries.

2.3 P-S Ideation

Open innovation has two main different scopes for a company: the broader of involving large external crowds to the brainstorming and decision-making processes and the less wide alternative of internal co-innovation where employees are invited to participate in the ideation and design processes, regardless of their department and main activities.

The PSY-Idea Generation Platform is an open source and light-weight ideation platform, designed to be easily used without any preconditions, in order to increase the adoption likelihood by the traditional manufacturing domain. It is implemented using the popular CMS Drupal and the Openideadapp module and its functionalities include: creation and management of ideation challenges, commenting and voting, gamification elements such as scores and prizes and domain-dependent idea categories, participation of internal and external stakeholders depending on the current company needs. Main driver of the platform is the collaboration among employees on expressing and continuously improving ideas, which is encouraged by the horizontal structure of the platform that by-design dismisses hierarchy biases among employees.

2.4 P-S Social Insights

Research on the field of social media remains active and recent findings validate the potential benefits from gaining insights into the collective sentiment encrypted in Web 2.0 channels offering a competitive advantage to any company willing to mine social data. However, the notion of product-service bundles is not yet mature enough and the traditional manufacturing domain lacks tools to provide social media analysis and insights regarding promising new P-S bundles.

The PSY-Crowd Innovation Platform was therefore created in order to extract knowledge from unstructured online conversations and sentiment expressions and further enrich and validate the insights gained from the ideation process. To that end, it supports data retrieval from various social networks, blogs and other online sources and extracts sentiment and, where possible, performs more fine-grained emotion analysis. This platform aspires to turn casual online discussions into product-service recommendations and unveil hidden relations among P-S bundles or specific product/service features, guiding the design team towards better and more innovative decisions. It is primarily addressed at P-S designers, providing them with intuitive (not requiring technical background) interfaces in order to support them through configuring the sources to include, filtering of information and finally interacting with the results in dashboards which will help them quickly understand the crowd sentiment, as well as the market trends, and also, potentially how they relate these insights to other sources, like the input collected through ideation and the brand value assessment results. To this end, the platform is an open source tool, built on various Python and Javascript frameworks and libraries, and open source tools, like Couchbase Server, Elasticsearch [6].

3 Conclusions

In order to facilitate such the servitization journey for manufacturers, this paper elaborates on concrete product-service bundles that aim at preserving the specific characteristics of office furniture products while building novel services in a symbiotic and harmonized manner. The P-S bundles that have been implemented through state-of-the art technical solutions leverage IoT, analytics, and eventually virtual reality technologies in order to achieve furniture manufacturing intelligence. The proposed P-S bundles comply with the needs of the furniture industry (that have been confirmed through focus groups and brainstorming sessions with furniture stakeholders) and have been validated in an office renovation case study implemented in Spain.

Acknowledgment. This work has been funded by the European Commission through the Horizon 2020 FoF Project PSYMBIOSYS: Product-Service sYMBIOtic SYStems (Grant No. 636804). The authors wish to acknowledge the Commission and all the PSYMBIOSYS project partners for their contribution.

References

1. Leder, S., Newsham, G.R., Veitch, J.A., Mancini, S., Charles, K.E.: Effects of office environment on employee satisfaction: a new analysis. Build. Res. Inf. **44**(1), 34–50 (2016)
2. Chandon, P.: Note on measuring brand awareness, brand image, brand equity and brand value, pp. 1–12. Insead, Fontainebleau (2003)
3. Aaker, J.L.: Dimensions of brand personality. J. Mark. Res. **34**(3), 347–356 (1997)
4. Jazizadeh, F., Ghahramani, A., Becerik-Gerber, B., Kichkaylo, T., Orosz, M.: User-led decentralized thermal comfort driven HVAC operations for improved efficiency in office buildings. Energy Build. **70**, 398–410 (2014)

5. Liang, G., Cao, J., Liu, X., Han, X.: Cushionware: a practical sitting posture-based interaction system. In: CHI 2014 Extended Abstracts on Human Factors in Computing Systems, pp. 591–594. ACM (2014)
6. Biliri, E., Petychakis, M., Alvertis, I., Lampathaki, F., Koussouris, S., Askounis, D.: Infusing social data analytics into future internet applications for manufacturing. In: 2014 IEEE/ACS 11th International Conference on Computer Systems and Applications (AICCSA), pp. 515–522. IEEE (2014)

DESDEVOPS - A New Paradigm for Dev-Ops: Rethinking Transition of Quality from Dev to Production

Prabal Mahanta[(✉)], Pavendra Maurya, and Akhilesh Kumar

SAP Labs Pvt. Ltd., No-138 EPIP Area, Bangalore 560066, Karnataka, India
{p.mahanta,pavendra.maurya,akhilesh.kumar02}@sap.com

Abstract. The dev-ops era has taken the IT world by storm and it has redefined the way the code is deployed into production environments. There are many tools which facilitates the standardization of flow of the artifacts onto the nodes. These workflows are certainly a great way of managing what goes into which environments but there is a lack of consideration of design and planning in the way it is done leading to more frequent patches. Many a times we firefight to keep the environments stable but we tend to ignore the considerations of a new feature to be designed. These scenarios are common in most of the cloud applications so there is a need to design the workflows, the code, the acceptance criteria and the preventive conditioning. The methods which are effective for scenarios are explored in this paper and concepts are presented to work towards a dynamic development environment.

Keywords: Design · DevOps · Standardization

1 DevOps and Design

Design is mostly ignored in DEVOPS and this leads to discrepancy and confusion during deployment across various environments. So, to avoid the missing link we will go through the design science concept. Design science consists of build evaluate and rebuild. Build - process of implementing an artifact for an objective and evaluate - process of discovering the corner cases. Just like natural science understanding an environment is very critical [1].

Similarly, the most over used concept DevOps or say it is a rushed perspective in the information technology domain. Everyone either confuses the concept with the same as a phenomenon, philosophy, mindset, toolset but at the end it is the approach which we need change to solve a problem and revoke the age old saying during an issue during production issues - "It works in my dev environment". The approach requires a proper design so that seamless and frequent delivery is possible. This should also lead to various service innovation [2, 3].

Evaluation is evolved into progress when design meets not only the expectations but also deals with the corner cases of unknown unknowns. This calls for a framework and associate tools per the need of the organization. The aim should be achieving a stable DevOps or a Continuous Delivery which can achieved by asking the right design aspects such as

© Springer International Publishing AG 2018
C. Debruyne et al. (Eds.): OTM 2017 Workshops, LNCS 10697, pp. 251–255, 2018.
https://doi.org/10.1007/978-3-319-73805-5_27

- Are the products open and responsive to DevOps?
- How the redesign of architecture impact the performance of the product?

If we can get the consensus about the questions in a right manner, then it will enable rolling deliveries and lesser patches. This will not only reduce human errors but also reduce manual efforts for overcoming the standardization problems in the environments and in turn bringing it closer to development.

2   Designing Phases of the Dev-Ops Lifecycle

When we start with any project we seldom jump into the coding aspect and leave very few scope for detailed planning. The idea should be to optimize communication between the teams and so starting with the first best practice concept where we adopt the framework to adopt dynamics between the organization teams.

2.1   Requirements and Planning

The requirements and planning phase be it waterfall model approach or agile methods both require a framework to optimize the outcomes and this can be done using the following design of the phase [4].

Here using this method, we can refine the technical requirements with accurate prerequisites and priority per the consensus score of the stakeholders. The outcomes of this phase should not be considered for productive release and always be considered for prototypes. This way we can get into the scenario of unknown unknowns and decipher a feasible solution for the same (Fig. 1).

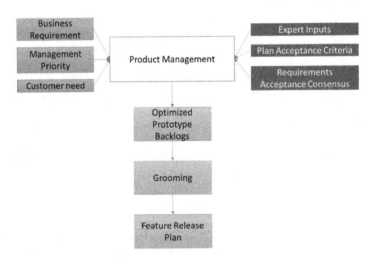

Fig. 1. Workflow for feature development

The main objective here is to assessment of requirements and performing a gap assessments. Performing a "AS IS" analysis on the deliverables should be done with the environment in scope like processes, tools and workflows with a proper communication bridge design in place [5].

2.2   Development

Before we start developing for production there should always be a pre-qa prototype to make it feasible for developers and operations to transition into production like environments. So, the start point should be a prototype even if there are well defined processes and requirements gathering is established. The way it works is to provide a validation option to find the known unknowns for any change or patch or a new feature before it is deployed to stage or production. The process also establishes the workflows to understand the tools and processes and the communication between the individual workflow sets (Fig. 2).

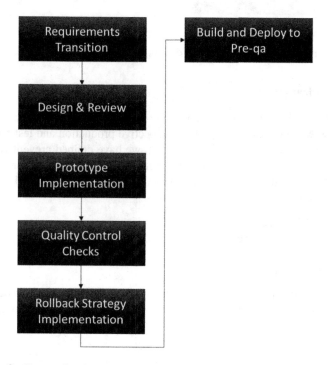

Fig. 2.   Feature development workflow for seamless production deployment

2.3   Quality Assurance

To have a quality assured it is very important to have deliverables verified for complete development lifecycle in a devops mode and this should be done stringently in a pre-qa environment so that there are no environment down time or consecutive deployments to patch a release with bugs. The lifecycle phase here would force the user to define post and pre-deployment checks along with acceptable time to load for web features or data mining cases (Fig. 3).

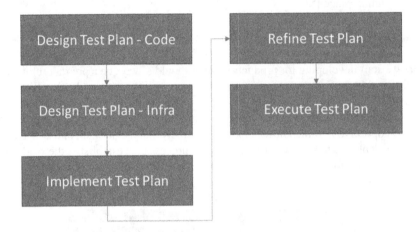

Fig. 3. Test plan for feature development and quality assurance

2.4 Standardization

To achieve the standardized environments, it is required to achieve single configurability for the whole DevOps workflows and the respective production and test bed environments. This phase can only be successful when we have defined preventive phases of the Dev-Ops lifecycle. The preventive measures should be designed for not only the features of an application but also for the workflow related tools and the environments [6].

Design User Driven Tests
Design User Acceptance Tests
Design Environment Tests
Design Management Acceptance Tests

Automating the activities for defining the tests will enable teams to deliver more frequent releases to customers and the user base without breaking the environments in question.

3 Conclusion

DevOps is often characterized by third-party tools, and more emphasis is given for configurations as infrastructure, product bear different sets of unique parameters. Emphasis on design and consensus acceptance for solution will provide stability to the overall development process.

Product based activities should not only be looked from the features perspective but also from the environment perspective. This way we can bring the operational or production environment closer to the developers. It means not to package and deliver packages via Docker like technology but preventive measures can follow the same suite of events [7]. It is not easy to mitigate the fact that monolithic software would take time to adopt next gen devops model with seamless production level deployments.

References

1. Babar, Z., Lapouchnian, A., Yu, E.: Modeling DevOps deployment choices using process architecture design dimensions. In: Ralyté, J., España, S., Pastor, Ó. (eds.) PoEM 2015. LNBIP, vol. 235, pp. 322–337. Springer, Cham (2015). https://doi.org/10.1007/978-3-319-25897-3_21

2. March, S.T., Smith, G.F.: Design and natural science research on information technology. Decis. Support Syst. **15**(4), 251–266 (1995)

3. Vassallo, C., et al.: Continuous delivery practices in a large financial organization. In: 2016 IEEE International Conference on Software Maintenance and Evolution (ICSME). IEEE (2016)

4. Mohamed, S.I.: DevOps shifting software engineering strategy-value based perspective. Int. J. Comput. Eng. **17**(2), 51–57 (2015)

5. Farroha, B.S., Farroha, D.L.: A framework for managing mission needs, compliance, and trust in the DevOps environment. In: 2014 IEEE Military Communications Conference (MILCOM). IEEE (2014)

6. Soni, M.: End to end automation on cloud with build pipeline: the case for DevOps in insurance industry, continuous integration, continuous testing, and continuous delivery. In: 2015 IEEE International Conference on Cloud Computing in Emerging Markets (CCEM). IEEE (2015)

7. Boettiger, C.: An introduction to Docker for reproducible research. ACM SIGOPS Oper. Syst. Rev. **49**(1), 71–79 (2015)

OnTheMove Academy (OTMA) 2017

The 14th OnTheMove Academy Chairs' Message

The 14th OnTheMove Academy Chairs' Message

Crucial for the success of OTM Academy is the commitment of our other OTMA faculty members whom we sincerely thank:

- Josefa Kumpfmüller (Vienna, Austria), Student Communication Seminar
- Erich J. Neuhold (University of Vienna, Austria), OTMA Dean

The OTMA submissions were reviewed by an international programme committee of well-respected experts. We gratefully thank them for their effort and time:

- Galia Angelova (Bulgarian Academy of Science, Sofia, Bulgaria)
- Christoph Bussler (Tropo Inc., USA)
- Paolo Ceravolo (Università degli Studi di Milano, Italy)
- Claudia d'Amato (Università degli Studi di Bari, Italy)
- Manu De Backer (University of Ghent, Belgium)
- Rik Eshuis (Technical University Eindhoven, The Netherlands)
- Claudia Jiménez (Universidad de los Andes, Chile)
- Frédéric Le Mouël (University of Lyon, France)
- Hervé Panetto (University of Lorraine, France)
- Erik Proper (Public Research Centre - Henri Tudor, Luxembourg)
- Rudi Studer (Karlsruhe Institute of Technology, Germany)
- Georg Weichhart (Profactor GmbH, Austria)

We also express our thanks to Christophe Debruyne (Vrije Universiteit Brussel) who again volunteered to be the OTMA 2017 "social media master".

The OTM Academy 2017 organising chairs:

September 2017

Peter Spyns
Maria Esther Vidal

Developing a Modelling and Mining Framework for Integrated Processes and Decisions

Faruk Hasić[1(✉)], Johannes De Smedt[2], and Jan Vanthienen[1]

[1] Leuven Institute for Research on Information Systems (LIRIS),
KU Leuven, Leuven, Belgium
{faruk.hasic,jan.vanthienen}@kuleuven.be
[2] Management Science and Business Economics Group,
University of Edinburgh Business School, Edinburgh, UK
johannes.desmedt@ed.ac.uk

Abstract. With increasing automation of business processes, the possibilities for the automation of routine business decisions grow: granting a loan, insurance or energy premium; simple diagnosis; sensor control systems in manufacturing; etc. are not uncommon automated decisions anymore, deployed and supported by systems and processes. Although each decision is relatively small and operational, they come in large numbers so that they eventually represent a large value for organizations. Reconciling and integrating processes and decisions is therefore of paramount importance, both when it comes to modelling the two concerns consistently, as well as in terms of automated discovery of process-decision models. This paper outlines a research proposal for the development of a framework allowing a sound integration of processes and decisions both for modelling and mining, relying on the newly developed Decision Model and Notation (DMN) standard.

Keywords: Decision modelling · Process modelling
Integrated modelling · Hybrid modelling · Decision mining
Integrated mining · DMN · BPMN · Separation of concerns
Service-oriented architecture

1 Introduction

There is a strong need for automation, since decision-making (in e.g. online and mobile applications) needs to be executed less costly and more efficiently. Therefore, it is important that the decision logic can be formulated in a correct, flexible and maintainable way. Sound decision modelling and mining techniques are required that allow to unambiguously describe and implement the decisions deployed in business processes and systems. Recently, decision modelling and notation approaches have emerged. Although a lot of research has already been devoted to process modelling and mining, there is still a lot of research to be done on the decision side, and on the integration between decisions and processes, both in modelling and automated discovery or mining.

C. Debruyne et al. (Eds.): OTM 2017 Workshops, LNCS 10697, pp. 259–269, 2018.
https://doi.org/10.1007/978-3-319-73805-5_28

The new *Decision Model and Notation (DMN)* standard [1] is a big step in modelling routine business decisions, next to business processes and business data. But fundamental research is needed in order to build a framework for the integration of business processes and decision, both from a modelling and a mining perspective. Automating and maintaining even small business decisions requires good modelling techniques. This proposal aims at providing a sound theoretical basis for **integrated decision modelling and mining** in terms an integration approaches between decisions and processes. The results of the project will be applicable in a large number of domains, such as standard operating procedures, credit and loan decisions, pricing and discount policies, marketing decisions, insurance claims, legal decisions and advice, and so on.

This paper is structured as follows. In Sect. 2, the necessity for integrated process-decision modelling and mining is elaborated upon and in Sect. 3 the objectives of this research project are elucidated. Section 4 outlines the methodology and work plan for each of the objectives, followed by Sect. 5 which discusses the preliminary results. Finally, Sect. 6 discusses the future work and concludes.

2   Context

Process modelling captures the all-encompassing task of setting up, analyzing, and maintaining process-aware information systems. Business process management and business process improvement and reengineering are essential in business nowadays to increase efficiency in a more competitive world [2]. Typically, the focus is put on both the **control flow** perspective, i.e., the routing and scheduling of activities, as well as the **data** and **resource** perspective, but **decisions are often neglected**. Especially in knowledge-intensive processes, such as healthcare, where expert decisions have to be made based on the staggering amount of research and patient data, it becomes hard to express good process models that account for all the flexibility that is needed along all the different perspectives, without referring to the key issue: the structure and content of the decisions to be made.

The term decision modelling refers to the various ways to represent decision rules, constraints, and conditional statements that describe the premises and outcomes of a specific situation and govern the actions that take place in applications and systems. Decision representations are used in many domains, e.g., business process management [3,4], credit risk [5,6], and medical diagnosis [7]. But they are often tailored towards specific use-cases (one specific decision type), and not standardised. In this context, Decision Model and Notation (DMN) comes into play as an **application-independent** modelling language for business decisions. Driven by an expanding need for decision support and automation, the Object Management Group (OMG) has developed this new standard [1]. A first version of the standard has been made available in September 2015. Many vendors, such as Oracle, IBM, Signavio, Camunda, Decision Management Solutions and FICO, already offer tooling, and industry users are starting to adapt the standard. DMN is built around two layers, i.e., the decision requirements layer, which encompasses all input data, business knowledge models, and sub-decisions, and the decision logic layer, which captures the logic to make each decision in the requirements model. This is illustrated in Fig. 1. DMN has proven to gain rapid adoption in literature for decision modelling in general [8,9] and for the integration with business process models [10,11]. The focus of the research is the need for incorporating decision models into dynamic environments, where a chain of decisions is often the driver of a business process and decisions should not be hard-coded into processes.

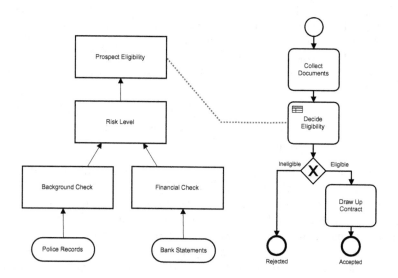

Fig. 1. Prospect acceptance decision model linked to a process model.

While each of these paradigms provide well-rounded solutions for processes and decisions respectively, they **neglect the interplay that exists between them**. Most processes are state- or data-driven, i.e., they transform inputs into outputs by using (data) resources that need to be structured and reasoned over in activities. But, in knowledge-intensive business processes, they often just represent the steps that have to be taken when making a decision, without modelling the underlying decision logic. Modelling the execution steps is not the same as modelling the logic, because a decision model can be executed in multiple ways, depending on criteria such as efficiency, customer centrality, etc. Both models should be considered when devising a decision-making process, which makes the case for an **integrated modelling and mining approach**. Otherwise processes are hard-coded, inflexible and not very suited to deal with change and variability.

3   Research Objectives

Decision modelling, and especially DMN, provide an apt paradigm for representing knowledge-intensive and complex decisions that are based on multiple inputs and stages. Hence, they form a strong declarative backdrop for enriching current process modelling approaches towards achieving fully flexible modelling, execution, and verification environments. Literature is converging towards this mixed-paradigm approach [8,9,12,13], but there is still a wide array of problems to address. First of all, a **decision-first** approach for **integrated process-decision modelling** needs to be constructed in conjunction with DMN. This needs to be done both for **procedural** and **declarative** process modelling languages. Secondly, a **discovery approach** for obtaining **holistic** and **process-independent** decision models from historical and real-time data needs to be devised as well.

3.1   Objective 1: Devise an Integrated Decision-Driven Procedural Process Modelling Approach

The importance of the interplay of decisions and processes has been illustrated in previous works [4,8]. Up until now, most studies focus on the loose combination of modelling constructs, i.e., process workflow models and decision models, mostly by establishing proof-of-concept languages built out of prevalent process modelling languages and DMN. However, to truly obtain a rigorous connection between processes and their surrounding decisions, a fundamental basis of the dynamic behavior of such decisions must be performed in integration. Processes provide the dynamic aspect, but neglect the decision requirements and logic layer, and decisions do not capture the dynamics that are tied to the requirements and logic. An integrated approach will ensure the synchronization of both.

Therefore, in an initial stage, it has to be researched how complex the construct base for dynamic decisions needs to be, and to what extent they overlap with current procedural process modelling languages, such as Business Process Model and Notation (BPMN) [14] and Petri nets [15]. Consequently, an integrated and consistent process-decision modelling framework will be devised in the form of modelling rules, principles and guidelines.

The following sub-objectives will be examined for Objective 1:

- **O1.1:** A comparative study of the existing **decision-driven process modelling** approaches to establish a baseline of modelling constructs needed to support decisions in process-aware information systems.
- **O1.2:** Develop a set of integrated modelling **principles** and **guidelines** in order to ensure consistent integration between **procedural** processes and decisions, hence adhering to the *Separation of Concerns* paradigm and ensuring flexibility and verification possibilities.

3.2   Objective 2: Devise an Integrated Decision-Driven Declarative Process Modelling Approach

Declarative approaches such as Declare [16] are of particular importance for knowledge-intensive processes given their flexibility in execution. Hence, declarative approaches form an interesting subject group, as they rely on a rule-based specification which corresponds to constraints. **Rule-based specifications** are typically compatible with decisions, as decisions are often expressed as a set of rules, decision tables and structures [3,17,18].

In analogy with Objective 1, an approach will be constructed for consistent modelling of decisions and declarative processes by providing rules, principles, and guidelines for integrated process-decision modelling.

- **O2:** Develop a set of integrated modelling **principles** and **guidelines** in order to ensure consistent integration between **declarative** processes and decisions, hence adhering to the Separation of Concerns paradigm.

3.3   Objective 3: Design a Control Flow-Independent Automated Decision Discovery Mechanism

In the third part of the research, the link with existing execution systems will be made. A plethora of data exists provided by numerous data sources that contain decisions that have a dynamic aspect to them. In numerous domains, such as claim handling and patient diagnostics, the decision is made in multiple stages and records are updated with observations, intermediate decisions, to finally get to a decision regarding insurance or a diagnosis respectively. This is the perfect breeding ground to lose track of the different variables and factors that are in play, and can benefit greatly from automatic discovery to streamline the evocation of the problem towards the decision maker. Hence, this research objective will address how the **intertwined process** and its underlying **decisions** can be retrieved from existing information systems logs, as a combination of **process mining** and **data mining**. Objective 3 is therefore defined as follows:

- **O3:** Build a discovery algorithm for obtaining **control flow-independent**, **holistic**, yet **process discovery compatible decision models** from logs.

4   Methods and Work Plan

In this part of the paper, we present the methodology and the work plan on how to achieve the objectives specified in the previous section.

4.1   For Objective 1

A comparative study of the existing decision-driven process modelling approaches will be conducted to establish a baseline of modelling constructs needed to support decisions. The emphasis will be put on what type of interactions with the parts of the decision process are made, i.e., how different activities within a process influence a decision and its variables, and how they relate to other activities as well. A typology will be proposed for classifying how different activities in the process contribute to the decision-making. Currently this typology is missing and leads to a lack of detail concerning how the decision requirements layer is represented within a process. This objective will be reached in the following steps:

1. Obtain a clear overview of all the **existing techniques** using decision-making in process models.
2. Classify techniques into **decision-first** and **process-first** approaches.
3. **Classify activities** according to their influence on the decision-making, allow for relating both the decision requirements level and the control flow level over the activity set in an integrated model.
4. Establish **modelling guidelines** and **principles** to ensure the **integration** between the decisions in the decision model and the decision activities in the process model.

4.2   For Objective 2

In analogy with Objective 1, a declarative process construct lexicon for use with DMN will be established. Based on the overview constituted in the first objective, the most ratified relations needed to model dynamic decisions in process models are withheld to form an expressive modelling language geared towards understandability as well as execution. The emphasis will be put on finding the most basic relations necessary, and combining them into simple, but expressive modelling constructs, such as atomic activity decisions, composite activity decisions for single outputs, next to general sequencing constructs that illustrate their place in the decision process. They should be modular in order to obtain a flexible and declarative approach towards building an execution and verification environment. An ideal declarative process modelling candidate seems to be **Declare** [16] as it has proven to be an adequate choice for knowledge-intensive processes given its flexibility in execution. Furthermore, Declare relies on a rule-based specification which corresponds to constraints, making it compatible with decisions, as decisions are often expressed as a set of rules. This objective will be conducted as follows:

1. Connect the **decision activity classification** obtained in Objective 1 with modelling constructs of the **Declare** language.
2. Integrate Declare constraints with **data-aware Declare** [19] relating to decision outcomes of the decision activities.
3. **Formalise** the the **integration** of data-aware Declare and DMN in order to consolidate the **execution flexibility** and the **verification** of the integrated declarative process-decision model.
4. A **subset** of the defined **construct lexicon** can be used in order to reduce overall modelling complexity. The defined construct lexicon should be **modular** in order to obtain a truly flexible and declarative approach.

4.3   For Objective 3

A discovery algorithm for obtaining holistic decision and process models from recorded data is the final objective of this project. Currently, mining decisions in processes boils down to finding decision points in processes and constructing decision models in these points separately, rather than combining the information that resides in multiple data-entry locations of the process into one model [8,20,21]. This objective investigates how to retrieve a full decision model by either integrating the decision models of separate decision point tasks, or by providing a **pre-process mining** step that delineates the **impact** of the **data structure** to make the activities decision-aware. Better algorithms can be constructed due to the structuring of the decision model-setup: by recognising both the time dimension and the data dimension as two integral parts, discovering models from data can better pinpoint which behavior corresponds to which modelling constructs to create a **holistic** view of both the decisions made and their evolution over time.

The discovery algorithm will be based on the principles of Objective 1 and 2, most notably on the activity classification in Step 2 of Objective 1. In order to do so, a mapping of the different constructs needs to be made. First of all, the data constructs need to be linked with the **decision variables** and the reasoning that is required in the **decision activities** themselves. Next, the dynamic aspects need to be formalised in terms of control flow and data flow dependencies. By using insights from process mining [21–24], the correct composition of decision- or process-first approaches will be selected. This objective contains the following steps:

1. Build a discovery algorithm that is able to retrieve the activity modelling construct lexicon by retrieving **data dependencies** from the historical or real-time data that determine the **decision activity** types.
2. Extend the algorithm with **relational data** between these decision activities. Where no decision information is found, standard process mining techniques for control flow can be applied. Where no control flow information is found, standard data mining techniques can be applied.
3. Extend the algorithm with the decision logic over the relational activities. As the **structure** of the **decisions** is mined, it is possible to obtain the way they are related from a reasoning point of view.
4. Find a suitable **representation** form for convoluted models that are retrieved from big data sets by designing appropriate **filters** for size, noise, and particular parts of the data set.

Most approaches display strong abilities to extract the **control flow** and relating data variables to its routing elements. Other approaches provide a strong **decision model** output, but do not focus on how the decision is established throughout the process [8]. Hence, there is a gap between strong **control flow-driven** and **decision model-driven** approaches, and the challenge is to develop a decision mining approach that is driven by the decision model, rather than by the control flow containing decision points. Therefore, an integrated way of capturing the **decisions** that are **embedded** in the **process**, while providing a decision model which **encompasses** the **full process** execution span, is of paramount importance.

5   Preliminary Results

Seminal work was already conducted for this research project. For **Objective 1** some preliminary studies were carried out. In [25], we assessed the syntactical **complexity** of the **DMN** standard in order to motivate the need for integration between DMN and BPMN. It was shown that DMN has a relatively low meta model-based complexity and that an integration with BPMN would not necessarily lead to a drastic increase in modelling complexity. Building further on this idea, potential **integration scenarios** for BPMN/DMN integration were enumerated in [26], ranging from a *process only* to a *decision only* occurrence in the **process-decision continuum**. Additionally, possible **incompatibilities** between the process and decision model were specified [26,27]. These inconsistencies must be remedied to achieve a consistent process-decision integration [28]. The work in [26] further confers opportunities and challenges in achieving this integration. A first attempt to remedy these inconsistencies was carried out in [28,29]. Finally, in [30] the role of decisions in supporting process flexibility and scalability was discussed.

For **Objective 3**, significant progress has been made in [31], where a **holistic decision-first framework** for integrated mining was proposed based on the classification of activities into **operational, administrative**, and **decision activities**. This is achieved by retrieving data dependencies from the event log representing the process, obtaining the way the decisions are related and consequently representing them in a DMN format. This approach shows to be **control flow-independent**, yet it is **compatible** with **process discovery** techniques. Furthermore, the proposed framework is better able to represent the underlying decision layer of a process than existing decision point mining techniques, as the proposed technique does not solely rely on control flow information. Rather, it provides insights on how data variables and underlying decisions are related to process activities, incorporating both **long distance dependencies** among process constructs, as well as **loops** in the process.

6   Conclusion and Future Work

This work discusses insights and research for an integrated modelling and mining approach of processes and decisions. Most existing literature approaches the matter from a simplistic point of view by merely dealing with decisions embedded in a single place in the process, hence making the decisions process-dependent. That way, the Separation of Concerns paradigm is breached and issues regarding maintainability, understandability and flexibility of both processes and decisions arise. Since the introduction of the Decision Model and Notation (DMN) standard, a suitable way of representing decisions within processes has become available. The framework to support this decision representation must provide a holistic approach to decision modelling and mining that is control flow-agnostic, i.e. a decision-first rather than a process-first approach.

In future work, we will further investigate the integration and interaction of processes and decisions, both in terms of modelling and mining. The focus will remain on developing a framework for integrated modelling of decisions with both procedural and declarative process modelling languages. Furthermore, attention will be given to control flow-agnostic discovery of holistic decisions spanning over entire processes.

References

1. OMG: Decision Model and Notation 1.1 (2016)
2. Dumas, M., La Rosa, M., Mendling, J., Reijers, H.A.: Fundamentals of Business Process Management. Springer, Heidelberg (2013). https://doi.org/10.1007/978-3-642-33143-5
3. Vanthienen, J.: What business rules and tables can do for regulations. Bus. Rules J. **8**(7) (2007)
4. Vanthienen, J., Caron, F., De Smedt, J.: Business rules, decisions and processes: five reflections upon living apart together. In: Proceedings of the SIGBPS Workshop on Business Processes and Services (BPS 2013), pp. 76–81 (2013)
5. Kim, D.J., Ferrin, D.L., Rao, H.R.: A trust-based consumer decision-making model in electronic commerce: the role of trust, perceived risk, and their antecedents. Decis. Support Syst. **44**(2), 544–564 (2008)
6. Li, H., Zhou, X.: Risk decision making based on decision-theoretic rough set: a three-way view decision model. Int. J. Comput. Intell. Syst. **4**(1), 1–11 (2011)
7. Sun, X., Faunce, T.: Decision-analytical modelling in health-care economic evaluations. Eur. J. Health Econ. **9**(4), 313–323 (2008)
8. De Smedt, J., vanden Broucke, S.K.L.M., Obregon, J., Kim, A., Jung, J.-Y., Vanthienen, J.: Decision mining in a broader context: an overview of the current landscape and future directions. In: Dumas, M., Fantinato, M. (eds.) BPM 2016. LNBIP, vol. 281, pp. 197–207. Springer, Cham (2017). https://doi.org/10.1007/978-3-319-58457-7_15
9. Calvanese, D., Dumas, M., Laurson, Ü., Maggi, F.M., Montali, M., Teinemaa, I.: Semantics and analysis of DMN decision tables. In: La Rosa, M., Loos, P., Pastor, O. (eds.) BPM 2016. LNCS, vol. 9850, pp. 217–233. Springer, Cham (2016). https://doi.org/10.1007/978-3-319-45348-4_13
10. Biard, T., Le Mauff, A., Bigand, M., Bourey, J.-P.: Separation of decision modeling from business process modeling using new "Decision Model and Notation" (DMN) for automating operational decision-making. In: Camarinha-Matos, L.M., Bénaben, F., Picard, W. (eds.) PRO-VE 2015. IFIP AICT, vol. 463, pp. 489–496. Springer, Cham (2015). https://doi.org/10.1007/978-3-319-24141-8_45
11. Horita, F.E., de Albuquerque, J.P., Marchezini, V., Mendiondo, E.M.: Bridging the gap between decision-making and emerging big data sources: an application of a model-based framework to disaster management in brazil. Decis. Support Syst. **97**, 12–22 (2017)
12. Batoulis, K., Meyer, A., Bazhenova, E., Decker, G., Weske, M.: Extracting decision logic from process models. In: Zdravkovic, J., Kirikova, M., Johannesson, P. (eds.) CAiSE 2015. LNCS, vol. 9097, pp. 349–366. Springer, Cham (2015). https://doi.org/10.1007/978-3-319-19069-3_22

13. Bazhenova, E., Weske, M.: Deriving decision models from process models by enhanced decision mining. In: Reichert, M., Reijers, H.A. (eds.) BPM 2015. LNBIP, vol. 256, pp. 444–457. Springer, Cham (2016). https://doi.org/10.1007/978-3-319-42887-1_36

14. OMG: Business process model and notation (BPMN) 2.0 (2011)

15. Murata, T.: Petri nets: properties, analysis and applications. Proc. IEEE **77**(4), 541–580 (1989)

16. Maggi, F.M., Mooij, A.J., van der Aalst, W.M.P.: User-guided discovery of declarative process models. In: 2011 IEEE Symposium on Computational Intelligence and Data Mining (CIDM), pp. 192–199. IEEE (2011)

17. Kumar, A., Liu, R.: A rule-based framework using role patterns for business process compliance. In: Bassiliades, N., Governatori, G., Paschke, A. (eds.) RuleML 2008. LNCS, vol. 5321, pp. 58–72. Springer, Heidelberg (2008). https://doi.org/10.1007/978-3-540-88808-6_9

18. Ligeza, A., Nalepa, G.J.: A study of methodological issues in design and development of rule-based systems: proposal of a new approach. Wiley Interdiscipl. Rev. Data Mining Knowl. Discov. **1**(2), 117–137 (2011)

19. Montali, M., Chesani, F., Mello, P., Maggi, F.M.: Towards data-aware constraints in declare. In: Proceedings of the 28th Annual ACM Symposium on Applied Computing, pp. 1391–1396. ACM (2013)

20. Rozinat, A., van der Aalst, W.M.P.: Decision mining in ProM. In: Dustdar, S., Fiadeiro, J.L., Sheth, A.P. (eds.) BPM 2006. LNCS, vol. 4102, pp. 420–425. Springer, Heidelberg (2006). https://doi.org/10.1007/11841760_33

21. de Leoni, M., van der Aalst, W.M.P.: Data-aware process mining: discovering decisions in processes using alignments. In: Proceedings of the 28th Annual ACM Symposium on Applied Computing, pp. 1454–1461. ACM (2013)

22. De Smedt, J., De Weerdt, J., Vanthienen, J.: Fusion miner: process discovery for mixed-paradigm models. Decis. Support Syst. **77**, 123–136 (2015)

23. Caron, F., Vanthienen, J., Vanhaecht, K., Van Limbergen, E., Deweerdt, J., Baesens, B.: A process mining-based investigation of adverse events in care processes. Health Inf. Manag. J. **43**(1), 16–25 (2014)

24. Kalenkova, A.A., van der Aalst, W.M.P., Lomazova, I.A., Rubin, V.A.: Process mining using BPMN: relating event logs and process models. In: Proceedings of the ACM/IEEE 19th International Conference on Model Driven Engineering Languages and Systems, p. 123. ACM (2016)

25. Hasić, F., De Smedt, J., Vanthienen, J.: Towards assessing the theoretical complexity of the decision model and notation (DMN). In: Enterprise, Business-Process and Information Systems Modeling, pp. 64–71. CEUR (2017)

26. Hasić, F., Devadder, L., Dochez, M., Hanot, J., De Smedt, J., Vanthienen, J.: Challenges in refactoring processes to include decision modelling. In: Business Process Management Workshops. LNBIP, vol. 308. Springer (2017)

27. Hasić, F., Vanwijck, L., Vanthienen, J.: Integrating processes, cases, and decisions for knowledge-intensive process modelling. In: International Workshop on Practicing Open Enterprise Modeling. CEUR (2017)

28. Hasić, F., De Smedt, J., Vanthienen, J.: Five Principles for Integrated Process and Decision Modelling (5PDM): an Illustration. Technical report, KU Leuven (2017)

29. Hasić, F., De Smedt, J., Vanthienen, J.: A service-oriented architecture design of decision-aware information systems: decision as a service. In: Panetto, H., Debruyne, C., Gaaloul, W., Papazoglou, M., Paschke, A., Ardagna, C.A. (eds.) OTM 2017 Conferences, Part I. LNCS, vol. 10573, pp. 353–361. Springer, Cham (2017). https://doi.org/10.1007/978-3-319-69462-7_23

30. Hu, J., Aghakhani, G., Hasić, F., Serral, E.: An evaluation framework for design-time context-adaptation of process modelling languages. In: Poels, G., Gailly, F., Serral, A.E., Snoeck, M. (eds.) PoEM 2017. LNBIP, vol. 305, pp. 112–125. Springer, Cham (2017). https://doi.org/10.1007/978-3-319-70241-4_8

31. De Smedt, J., Hasić, F., vanden Broucke, S.K.L.M., Vanthienen, J.: Towards a holistic discovery of decisions in process-aware information systems. In: Carmona, J., Engels, G., Kumar, A. (eds.) BPM 2017. LNCS, vol. 10445, pp. 183–199. Springer, Cham (2017). https://doi.org/10.1007/978-3-319-65000-5_11

An Overview of Challenges and Research Avenues for Green Business Process Management

Exploring the Concept of a Circular Economy

Dries Couckuyt[(✉)] 🆔

Department of Business Informatics and Operations Management,
Faculty of Economics and Business Administration,
Ghent University, Tweekerkenstraat 2, 9000 Ghent, Belgium
dries.couckuyt@ugent.be

Abstract. Business organizations acknowledge the importance of Information Systems (IS) to cope with their responsibility in environmental degradation. The problem with current IS contributions is that the crucial role of process-centered techniques is often ignored. Moreover, a common understanding of environmental sustainability is missing. In response, this paper introduces Green Business Process Management (BPM) which focuses on the ecological impact of business processes. The concept of a circular economy is introduced to concretize environmental sustainability at the organizational level. Following the design-science paradigm, this paper provides a work plan to examine the theoretical and practical evidence on Green BPM instruments. The research methods we propose are a systematic literature review (SLR), expert panels, case studies and field-testing.

Keywords: Green business process management · Green information systems
Environmental sustainability · Circular economy · Design-Science paradigm

1 Introduction

The deterioration of the natural environment is a preeminent issue for the global society. Resource depletion and environmental pollution are results from household and industry activities. Therefore, business organizations are often directly addressed to implement environmental sustainability targets [1]. As part of a comprehensive strategy, companies have developed a growing interest in the application of Information Systems (IS) to cope with their responsibility in environmental degradation. Green IS, a specialization of the IS discipline, examines the possibilities of IT-based systems in order to encounter environmental problems [32]. Based on a survey of 143 organizations, [21] concluded that businesses invest in IS as part of the solution to pursue both eco-efficiency and eco-sustainability objectives. Another survey, conducted among 508 senior managers, showed several motivations for Green IS adoption [13]. Finally, [4] found that both the practitioner and academic community have a strong interest in the benefits of Green IS initiatives.

© Springer International Publishing AG 2018
C. Debruyne et al. (Eds.): OTM 2017 Workshops, LNCS 10697, pp. 270–279, 2018.
https://doi.org/10.1007/978-3-319-73805-5_29

The problem with current Green IS contributions is that the crucial role of process-oriented techniques is often ignored [19, 24, 27]. Process improvement is the central topic in Business Process Management (BPM), which refers to a body of methods, techniques and tools to discover, analyze, redesign, execute and monitor business processes [8]. The optimization objectives of BPM typically refer to cost, quality, time, and flexibility aspects of business processes, the so-called "devil's quadrangle" [25]. However, in recent years, more and more researchers advocate to extend the scope of BPM with an environmental sustainability dimension [27]. This new approach, Green BPM, copes with the environmental impact of business processes [15, 23, 24, 28]. Although both research fields are closely related, Green BPM, as opposed to Green IS, has a main focus on process change that goes beyond solely IT applications. From academic and practitioner literature, it can be concluded that the importance of process-centered techniques is acknowledged but that the research field of Green BPM is currently dominated by Green IS [19, 24, 27]. In a literature review it is stated: "although the technical aspects of Green IT are certainly important, we as IS researchers should go beyond IT infrastructure and focus on other aspects of Green IS, such as business processes" [4, p. 35]. Similarly, several other authors claim that only through process change, the transformative power of IS can be fully leveraged [19, 24, 27].

There are two main challenges that need to be addressed to develop process-centered techniques that act upon the upcoming environmental needs. First, some clarification is required on the environmental sustainability dimension. Especially, the integration with the economic sustainability dimension and traditional optimization objectives such as cost, quality, time and flexibility is relevant. As the focus is on business organizations, the integration of the environmental sustainability dimension should be economically beneficial. Secondly, as practitioners show a deep interest in environmental sustainability initiatives, the process-centered techniques should be developed in the form of concrete applications. This will allow practitioners to identify appropriate Green BPM instruments for their domain.

The current research on Green BPM has some limitations. Although the importance of ecological process-centered techniques is acknowledged, incertitude still exists about the scope of the environmental sustainability dimension. Some researchers solely focus on the reduction of carbon emissions in business processes [14] while others aim to reduce all environmentally harmful effects of organizational activities [27]. Moreover, concerning resource utilization, only energy consumption is discussed so far [5]. These different attitudes are not contributing to a durable development of the research field. As indicated by [3], the research community should first have a common understanding of the discipline for successful development. Moreover, another problem in the field of Green BPM is the lack of concrete applications. So far, Green BPM research has mainly focused on initial thoughts and basic concepts [15, 23, 24, 28].

To clarify the environmental sustainability dimension we will first rely on the Triple Bottom Line [9] which defines three dimensions of sustainability (i.e. economic, social and environmental). According to [9], organizations should focus on all three interdependent dimensions in order to succeed in the long run. Secondly, we will go beyond the current Green BPM contributions and make the environmental sustainability dimension more concrete on an organizational level by introducing the concept of the circular economy. This emerging sustainability notion recently gained importance in policy, academics and business organizations. In contrast to the holistic idea of environmental sustainability, most authors conceptually simplify the circular economy to individual economic benefits through input reduction, efficiency gains, and waste avoidance with relatively immediate results. Finally, we propose an approach with the aim to explicitly contribute to concrete applications. The organization of our research follows the design-science paradigm which focuses on the development of instruments with the explicit aim of improving their functional performance [16].

Following the design-science paradigm [16], we propose a work plan with three research questions. RQ1 aims at identifying the current state of Green BPM that provides the applicable knowledge. The objective of RQ2 is to integrate environmental sustainability, concretized by the concept of the circular economy, into conventional BPM techniques. Finally RQ3 aims at testing the developed Green BPM instruments by returning the output of RQ2 into the business organizations for study and evaluation in practice. Our research will add new knowledge to the Green BPM discipline by providing a research framework that helps researchers identifying and completing gaps. Furthermore, we aim to develop (novel or adapted) validated instruments to analyze environmental sustainability in business processes. Finally, we plan to provide evidence of successful Green BPM instruments in a business context.

The remainder of this article is structured as follows. Section 2 summarizes related work. Then, Sect. 3 identifies the research questions and proposes our design and methods. Section 4 discusses some preliminary findings. Finally, concluding remarks will be highlighted in Sect. 5.

2   Related Work

2.1   Sustainability in Information Systems Research

The Brundtland report issued by the World Commission on Environment and Development [29] introduced the concept of sustainability in economic sciences. In this EU report it is stated that sustainable development "meets the needs of the present world, without compromising the ability of future generations to meet their own needs" [29, p. 41]. Later, [9] defined three dimensions of sustainability. The Triple Bottom Line consists of economic sustainability (profit), social sustainability (people) and environmental sustainability (planet). Organizations should focus on all three interdependent dimensions in order to succeed in the long run. In a single-minded focus on economic sustainability (profit), future generations and the society at large have not been considered as stakeholders for a long time (people). Moreover, in this narrow economic perspective (profit), natural resources have long been taken for granted (planet). This single-minded focus can only lead to short-term success [9]. Although challenging, the three sustainability dimensions should be integrated and not represented as opposing. For instance, reducing waste from packaging can also reduce costs.

Although sustainability has three dimensions, it seems that within the BPM discipline authors focus on economic and environmental sustainability. It could be argued that the economic dimension of sustainability is already included in conventional BPM as it optimizes processes in light of time, cost, quality, and flexibility. An extended approach, referred as Green BPM, focuses on the ecological impact of business processes [24]. Literature reviews mention several contributions to this emerging discipline [15, 23, 24, 28]. Consequently, a full integration of the sustainability concept as defined by [9] in the BPM discipline would also require research and practice on the social dimension. However, the existing approaches are often overlooking this dimension [20, 28]. Further research is required but it seems that the Triple Bottom Line [9] could be a valid starting point for a new foundation theory of sustainability-aware BPM. This could clarify the role of BPM for economic, environmental, and social responsibility as a theoretical contribution. To narrow our scope and to be in line with earlier work, for the present research, sustainability in business processes will also be interpreted as environmental sustainability implemented in an economically beneficial way.

The reason that sustainability in the BPM discipline is interpreted from an environmental perspective is probably due to the close link with Green IS. Many Green IS scholars contributed to the field of Green BPM [15, 23, 24, 28]. Some definitions of Green BPM mention an inevitable role for IS by stating that Green BPM is the intersection of both BPM and Green IS [19, 27]. Although we agree on the close link, one should be careful to assume IS as inevitable. Green BPM (and BPM in general) does not inherently require IS- and IT-applications. Moreover, the problem with current Green IS initiatives is that the crucial role of process-centered techniques is often ignored [19, 24, 27].

2.2   The Circular Economy and the BPM Lifecycle

BPM involves different iterative phases and activities. These are often referred to as capability areas. The traditional business process lifecycle is based on the established Plan-Do-Check-Act (PDCA) cycle [7]. In early BPM, research attention was focused on technical capabilities such as modelling, deployment and optimization [8]. As the research field evolved, management capabilities gained importance [33] and authors started also investigating the role of organizational capabilities such as culture and structure in order to support process improvements [30, 31].

The activities presented in the business process lifecycle will differ if a specific form of environmental sustainability is introduced. It can even lead to completely different outcomes [19]. For instance, process optimization with the aim to eliminate carbon emissions will differ from process optimization solely focusing on reducing costs. In the process discovery phase it will be necessary to include sustainability-related concepts that identify carbon emissions. This, in turn, will allow for analysis and redesign that not only consider cost reduction but also the ecological target of being CO_2 neutral. Then the redesigned sustainable process needs to be implemented. Therefore, organizations are required to provide training to employees with respect to the environmental targets, and put the ecological measures into action. This will again be different from traditional process implementation.

In recent years, several authors attempted to integrate environmental sustainability in particular capability areas. For instance, [14] introduced a framework that models the relationship between resources and activities to inform the business process with its carbon emission impact. In [19], ecological workflow patterns are proposed for environmental optimization of processes. Other authors attempted to be more holistic by proposing ecologically sustainable variants of the business process lifecycle. For instance, [2] presented a sustainable business transformation cycle with five steps: 'monitor and control', 'discover and learn', 'strategize', 'design', 'transform'. In [26] the BPM capability areas framework of [6] is used to integrate sustainability topics into an organization's management system. Sustainability is applied to a company's vision, strategy and management.

Our research aims to go beyond the current Green BPM contributions by focusing on the concept of the circular economy. This emerging sustainability notion recently gained importance. This is apparent from policies such as the comprehensive European Circular Economy package [11] and the Chinese Circular Economy Promotion Law [18]. The circular economy has also become an important field of academic research [12]. Likewise, companies are increasingly aware of the opportunities promised by the circular economy and have started to realize its value potential for themselves and their stakeholders [10]. Based on different contributions in the field, [12] defined the circular economy as: "a regenerative system in which resource input and waste, emission, and energy leakage are minimized by slowing, closing, and narrowing material and energy loops. This can be achieved through long-lasting design, maintenance, repair, reuse, remanufacturing, refurbishing, and recycling" (p. 759). In contrast to the holistic idea of environmental sustainability, most authors conceptually simplify the circular economy to individual economic benefits through input reduction, efficiency gains, and waste avoidance with relatively immediate results. This more narrowly framed concept provides clearer directions for its implementation. For the present research, the concept of the circular economy should help clarifying how the idea of environmental sustainability can be concretized at the organizational level, namely when outputs of business processes can become new inputs for the same or other business processes.

3   Research Questions, Design and Methods

The primary goal of our research is to investigate how environmental sustainability, concretized by the concept of the circular economy, can be integrated in conventional BPM techniques [22] in order to develop valid Green BPM instruments. We intend to examine the theoretical and practical evidence on Green BPM techniques. Subsequently we aim to develop and test Green BPM instruments that could help organizations to incorporate environmental sustainability into the BPM lifecycle. Our work will be organized in three work packages (WP) that each have a main research question. Following concrete research methods we aim to provide a specific output. An overview is shown in Table 1.

Business organizations are demanding problem-solving instruments to cope with their responsibility in environmental degradation. So far, Green BPM research has mainly focused on initial thoughts and basic concepts, concrete applications are rather limited [15, 23, 24, 28]. Therefore, we propose a different approach with the aim to explicitly contribute to concrete applications. The organization of our research follows

Table 1. Overview of work packages, research questions, methods and output

WP	Research questions	Methods	Output
1. Research identification	RQ1. What is the current state of Green BPM practices and research?	SLR	Research gaps
2. Instrument development	RQ2. How can environmental sustainability, concretized by the circular economy, be integrated into conventional BPM?	Expert panels, case studies	Preliminary instruments
3. Instrument testing	RQ3. Which Green BPM instruments enhance principles of the circular economy in a business context?	Field-testing	Validated instruments

the design-science paradigm which focuses on the development of instruments with the explicit aim of improving the functional performance of the instruments. In order to develop and evaluate the instruments, research relies on the environment to identify business needs and on a set of foundations and methodologies to extract applicable knowledge [16].

RQ1 aims at identifying the current state of Green BPM that provides the applicable knowledge of our design-science research. We conducted a SLR to study all relevant articles and to give insights in current Green BPM contributions. Furthermore, we presented an appropriate definition to avoid misinterpretation about the field of Green BPM. Finally, a framework for further research was provided by identifying deviations with conventional BPM instruments. This framework can help researchers to identify and complete gaps in Green BPM research. More details about the SLR are presented in Sect. 4.

The objective of RQ2 is to integrate environmental sustainability, concretized by the concept of the circular economy, into conventional BPM techniques. In this work package, the current state of Green BPM will be evaluated in organizations to identify business needs. Here, an application context is required that not only provides the conditions for the research (e.g., the opportunity/problem to be addressed) but also defines acceptance criteria for the evaluation of the research results. Expert panels in sustainability-aware companies is a suggested research method to detect valid Green BPM practices. Subsequently, case studies will be used as intermediate evaluation methods for these practices. BPM offers both qualitative (e.g. value-added analysis, root cause analysis and issue documentation) and quantitative (e.g. performance measures) techniques to improve business processes. Work package two will focus on the inclusion of an environmental sustainability dimension by developing best practices and adaptations to conventional BPM techniques. To further narrow our scope, the choice for specific BPM techniques will be based on the outcome of the expert panels and case studies.

Finally, RQ3 aims at testing the developed Green BPM instruments. Here, the output of RQ2 will be returned into the business environment for study and evaluation in the application context. This will result in validated instruments. As our research progresses, we will decide which qualitative or quantitative techniques are most appropriate to test the developed instruments.

4   Preliminary Results

The SLR (currently under review) presented the first research maturity assessment of the Green BPM field. We focused on a bibliometric analysis, a definition for the discipline and a content analysis of the literature in the research field. The research questions aimed at generating a comprehensive overview about application domains and research topics. The answers to these questions deliver potential benefits for both research and practitioner-related communities. Researchers may use the classification framework as a research agenda in Green BPM. Simultaneously, the study may be a good starting point for practitioners too, e.g. to identify appropriate Green BPM instruments for their domain.

Following [17] we defined a review protocol, specifying and documenting a search strategy with explicit inclusion and exclusion criteria. The structured approach allowed us to collect a comprehensive sample of 43 articles focusing on Green BPM. Other reviews discussed a smaller sample or broadened their scope to Green IS. Inclusion of the term "circular economy", as a concept to make environmental sustainability more concrete at the organizational level, did not generate any additional results. This underlines the potential of the concept in BPM research.

By means of a bibliometric analysis we provided insights in the research field. We found that the current contributions are mainly conference proceedings, with a significant part related to IS conferences. In order to further develop Green BPM, more research attention is needed on BPM platforms. Concerning geographical distribution of authorship, it was concluded that European research groups are leading the discipline.

We also screened our sample on Green BPM definitions. We analyzed ten unique definitions and found that a significant majority of authors agrees on the term "Green BPM", which can be seen as an extension of conventional BPM techniques in light of general environmental objectives. Based on these results, and inspired by other findings in the SLR, we proposed a definition. In our opinion, Green BPM concerns the modelling, deployment, optimization and management of business processes with dedicated consideration paid to their environmental consequences. In our definition we also stated the importance of facilitating capability areas as culture and structure for successful Green BPM implementation.

Finally, the sampled articles were screened to identify BPM-related capability areas and mapped on three possible categories evolving from rather technical to organizational capabilities: (1) business process lifecycle, (2) business process management and (3) business process orientation. We found that Green BPM research so far mainly focuses on the first category, to a lesser extent on the second category and the third category is hardly not discussed. These findings show that Green BPM follows a similar development as BPM, namely from a more technical perspective to also including the managerial perspective. Based on the identified gaps, possible research avenues were presented in order to further develop Green BPM towards a more mature discipline. Moreover, our results also stressed the need for Green BPM research in organizations and the introduction of concrete applications. This supports the approach presented in the present paper; the design-science paradigm focuses on the development of instruments with the explicit aim of improving their functional performance.

5   Conclusion

The integration of environmental sustainability into conventional BPM techniques is concretized by the concept of the circular economy. Therefore, our research goes beyond the current Green BPM contributions. This emerging sustainability notion recently gained importance in policy, academics and business organizations. Our preliminary results showed that the concept of circular economy did not yet find its way in Green BPM. However, as the circular economy is defined as a closed loop of inputs and outputs, BPM seems a suitable approach to contribute on this topic. As the Green BPM discipline provides preliminary work with a focus on environmental sustainability, it is a valid starting point.

The research responds to two calls from the practitioner and academic community. First, there is a focus on process-centered techniques instead of solely IT-applications as provided by the Green IS discipline. Secondly, a different approach is proposed with the aim to explicitly contribute to concrete applications. So far, Green BPM research has mainly focused on initial thoughts and basic concepts. This will be achieved by following the design-science paradigm which focuses on the development of instruments. Successful completion of this research will add new knowledge to the Green BPM discipline and will provide validated instruments to analyze environmental sustainability in concrete business processes.

Acknowledgements. This PhD project will be funded by Ghent University (Belgium) under the supervision of Prof. dr. Manu De Backer (administrative promotor) and Prof. dr. Amy Van Looy (daily supervisor).

References

1. Adger, W.N., Arnell, N.W., Tompkins, E.L.: Successful adaptation to climate change across scales. Glob. Environ. Change **15**(2), 77–86 (2005)
2. Ahmed, M.D., Sundaram, D.: Sustainability modelling and reporting: from roadmap to implementation. Decis. Support Syst. **53**(3), 611–624 (2012)
3. Baskerville, R.L., Myers, M.D.: Informations systems as a reference discipline. MIS Q. **26**(1), 1–14 (2002)
4. Brooks, S., Wang, X., Sarker, S.: Unpacking green IS: a review of the existing literature and directions for the future. In: vom Brocke J., Seidel S., Recker J. (eds.) Green Business Process Management: Towards the Sustainable Enterprise, 1st edn., pp. 15–37. Springer, Heidelberg (2012). https://doi.org/10.1007/978-3-642-27488-6_2
5. Cappiello, C., Plebani, P., Vitali, M.: Energy-aware process design optimization. In: International Conference on Cloud and Green Computing. Workshop on European Actions Towards Eco-Friendly Data Centers, pp. 451–458. Institute of Electrical and Electronics Engineers (IEEE), Karlsruhe (2013)
6. de Bruin, T., Rosemann, M.: Using the delphi technique to identify BPM capability areas. In: Proceedings of the 18th Australasian Conference on Information Systems (ACIS), Toowoomba, vol. 42, pp. 642–653 (2007)
7. Deming, W.E.: Out of the Crisis, 1st edn. Massachusetts Institute of Technology, Center for Advanced Engineering Study, Cambridge (1986)

8. Dumas, M., La Rosa, M., Mendling, J., Reijners, H.A.: Fundamentals of Business Process Management, 1st edn. Springer, Heidelberg (1998). https://doi.org/10.1007/978-3-642-33143-5

9. Elkington, J.: Cannibals with Forks: the Triple Bottom Line of Sustainable Development, 1st edn. Capstone Publishing, Oxford (1997)

10. EMF: Towards the Circular Economy. Ellen MacArthur Foundation (2013). https://www.ellenmacarthurfoundation.org/assets/downloads/publications/Ellen-MacArthur-Foundation-Towards-the-Circular-Economy-vol.1.pdf. Accessed 15 Nov 2017

11. European Commission: Closing the Loop - an EU Action Plan for the Circular Economy, Brussels (2015). https://ec.europa.eu/transparency/regdoc/rep/1/2015/EN/1-2015-614-EN-F1-1.PDF. Accessed 15 Nov 2015

12. Geissdoerfer, M., Savaget, P., Bocken, N.M.P., Hultink, E.J.: The circular economy – a vew sustainability paradigm? J. Clean. Prod. **143**, 757–768 (2017)

13. Gholami, R., Sulaiman, A.B., Ramayah, T., Molla, A.: Senior managers' perception on green information systems (IS) adoption and environmental performance: results from a field survey. Inf. Manage. **50**(7), 431–438 (2013)

14. Ghose, A., Hoesch-Klohe, K., Hinsche, L., Le, L.-S.: Green business process management: a research agenda. Australas. J. Inf. Syst. **16**(2), 103–117 (2009)

15. Gohar, S.R., Indulska, M.: Business process management: saving the planet? In: Australasian Conference on Information Systems, Adelaide, pp. 1–14 (2015)

16. Hevner, A.R., March, S.T., Park, J., Ram, S.: Design science in information systems research. MIS Q. **28**(1), 75–105 (2004)

17. Kitchenham, B.: Procedures for performing systematic reviews. Keele University Technical Report, TR/SE-04, Keele (2004)

18. Lieder, M., Rashid, A.: Towards circular economy implementation: a comprehensive review in context of manufacturing industry. J. Cleaner Prod. **115**, 36–51 (2016)

19. Lübbecke, P., Fettke, P., Loos, P.: Towards ecological workflow patterns as an instrument to optimize business processes with respect to ecological goals. In: Hawaii International Conference on System Sciences Proceedings, pp. 1049–1058. IEEE, Waikoloa (2016)

20. Magdaleno, A.M., Duboc, L., Betz, S.: How to incorporate sustainability into business process management lifecycle? In: Dumas, M., Fantinato, M. (eds.) BPM 2016. LNBIP, vol. 281, pp. 440–443. Springer, Cham (2017). https://doi.org/10.1007/978-3-319-58457-7_32

21. Molla, A., Pittayachawan, S., Corbitt, B.: Green IT diffusion: an international comparison. In: Green IT Working Paper Series, vol. 1, pp. 1–15 (2009)

22. Nowak, A., Leymann, F., Schumm, D.: The differences and commonalities between green and conventional business process management. In: International Conference on Dependable, Autonomic and Secure Computing Proceedings, pp. 569–576. IEEE, Sydney (2011)

23. Opitz, N., Krüp, H., Kolbe, L.M.: Environmentally sustainable business process management – developing a green BPM readiness model. In: Pacific Asia Conference on Information Systems Proceedings, Chengdu, pp. 1–12 (2014)

24. Opitz, N., Krüp, H., Kolbe, L.M.: Green business process management - a definition and research framework. In: Hawaii International Conference on System Sciences Proceedings, pp. 3808–3817. IEEE, Waikoloa (2014)

25. Reijers, H.A., Liman Mansar, S.: Best practices in business process redesign: an overview and qualitative evaluation of successful redesign heuristics. Omega **33**(4), 283–306 (2005)

26. Rozman, T., Draghici, A., Riel, A.: Achieving sustainable development by integrating it into the business process management system. In: O'Connor, V.R., Umay Akkaya, M., Kemaneci, K., Yilmaz, M., Poth, A., Messnarz, R. (eds.) European Conference on Systems, Software and Services Process Improvement. Communications in Computer and Information Science, vol. 543, pp. 247–259. Springer, Cham (2015). https://doi.org/10.1007/978-3-319-24647-5_20

27. Seidel, S., vom Brocke, J., Recker, J.: Call for action: investigating the role of business process management in green IS. In: All sprouts content, pp. 1–6. AISeL (2011)

28. Stolze, C., Semmler, G., Thomas, O.: Sustainability in business process management research - a literature review. In: Americas Conference on Information Systems Proceedings, pp. 1–10. AISeL, Seattle (2012)

29. UN World Commission on Environment and Development: Report of the World Commission on Environment and Development: Our Common Future. Oxford University Press, Oxford, New York (1987)

30. Van Looy, A., De Backer, M., Poels, G.: A conceptual framework and classification of capability areas for business process maturity. Enterp. Inf. Syst. 8(2), 188–224 (2014)

31. vom Brocke, J., Rosemann, M.: Handbook on Business Process Management 1&2, 2nd edn. Springer, Heidelberg (2014)

32. vom Brocke, J., Watson, R.T., Dwyer, C., Elliot, S., Melville, N.: Green information systems: directives for the IS discipline. Commun. Assoc. Inf. Syst. 33(1), 509–520 (2013)

33. Weske, M.: Business Process Management: Concepts, Languages, Architectures, 2nd edn. Springer, Berlin (2012). https://doi.org/10.1007/978-3-642-28616-2

Real-Time Business Process Model Tailoring: The Effect of Domain Knowledge on Reading Strategy

Sven Vermeulen[✉] [iD]

Department of Business Informatics and Operations Management,
Ghent University, Ghent, Belgium
Sven.Vermeulen@UGent.be

Abstract. Due to the use of thousands of often very complex process models, having them immediately usable towards their purpose is of great economic benefit. In order to maximize usability, process models must be intuitive and easily understandable. In other words, processing the information contained within the process models must enable a successful completion of the task for which the model is being used. Recently, research efforts into the effects of user characteristics on understandability have increased. However, current limitations create promising research possibilities, particularly with regard to the use of realistic process models and direct data collection techniques. This thesis will contribute to the existing body of knowledge by investigating domain knowledge as a fundamental user characteristic and utilizing eye-tracking as a direct data collection method while using realistic, complex process models. The end goal of this research is to propose an automatic process model tailoring technique, with the aim of enhancing a user's understanding and thus their performance. As of now a pilot study has indicated the existence of distinct reading strategies, which establishes the viability of the proposed future work.

Keywords: Business process modeling · Process model understandability
Process model visualization · Domain knowledge · Process model tailoring
Reading strategy

1 Introduction

The performance of a business is in large part achieved by modeling the business processes on which the enterprise relies [1]. Due to their communicative and supportive function for knowledge transfer, quality control and regulation [2], they are required to be intuitive and easily understandable [3]. Process model understandability is a field investigating the factors that influence this comprehension. Uncovering these effects facilitates a common understanding of processes and helps improve the quality of models [1]. Recently, studies on the cognitive aspects of process models have increased, establishing the importance of the effects of user characteristics (e.g. [4, 5]). We follow the reasoning that the way an individual receives, selects, organizes and uses the information visualized in a process model is an example of intrapersonal information behavior [6].

© Springer International Publishing AG 2018
C. Debruyne et al. (Eds.): OTM 2017 Workshops, LNCS 10697, pp. 280–286, 2018.
https://doi.org/10.1007/978-3-319-73805-5_30

Process models are used and must therefore be understood by a variety of people whose user characters' can have an even bigger influence compared to model factors [7].

In our work we will contribute to current research in three studies. First, we will study the effects of domain knowledge on reading strategy and process model understandability. Efforts into uncovering how users read models are very limited and recent although it has been established that looking at model elements is highly correlated with the individual's thinking process and performance [8]. Our work is innovative as it improves upon existing research by investigating the reading process, using a realistically complex model and applying eye-tracking as a direct data collection technique. Given the stadium at which our research currently stands, the metrics' thresholds (e.g. CFC) are yet to be determined, based on which a model will be deemed "complex".

In our second study, we intend to investigate and apply these factors to the idea of tailoring process models [9]. The static way in which processes are currently visualized is a major shortcoming as it prevents individual and customized perspectives on business processes [1, 10], hampering performance. Based on the results of this second study, we will work towards a fully automatic approach that will tailor process models to specific user characteristics as a third contribution.

2 Related Work

2.1 Process Model Reading

In the domain of process model reading, Figl and Strembeck [11] focus on modeling direction and the effect on process model comprehension. The authors remarked a lack of complexity in the models used in the experiment. We intend to improve upon this by using a realistic, complex model. We further argue that since the experiment did not contain a direct data gathering method with regard to reading a model, such as eye-tracking, the deeper cognitive principles remained unknown. Specifically aimed at model inspection for quality issues, Haisjackl et al. [12] investigated the strategies undertaken by model readers in search of errors. In this study, data collection was done using a think-aloud protocol for which we argue the same limitations apply.

2.2 Investigating Domain Knowledge

Only four studies could be identified investigating domain knowledge in the context of process model understandability. These findings are supported by a very recent literature review [1]. None of these studies reported an effect of domain knowledge on model comprehension. Either researchers have kept domain knowledge constant (as a control variable) (e.g. [5, 13]), have used homogenous groups of participants [14] or domain knowledge was measured using a self-reported scale [15]. The key problem is that when the extent of knowledge in a domain is itself unknown, no basis exists for a person to estimate what they don't know. In other words, an individual is unable to assess their own level of domain knowledge as their understanding of the domain affects their understanding of their own knowledge level [16].

For all studies mentioned in this chapter, we argue that the data collection method does not allow a direct observation and registration of the reading strategy and underlying cognitive processes. Furthermore, as explained by Figl et al., domain knowledge has as of yet not been a factor under study in the process modeling domain even though relations with performance are well established in other fields [17]. Therefore, utilizing eye-tracking as a data collection method would be our fourth contribution, next to our study of domain knowledge, reading strategy and the use of realistic models.

2.3 Process Model Tailoring

Configuring process models so they only provide relevant information for a particular user is not a new idea (e.g. [18]). Within this field of study, however, the effects of different configurations of the process on a user's understanding have received less attention. More specifically, in line with our work, the idea of tailoring the model to personal factors [9] has not yet been empirically assessed. In [1], potential future work on tailoring process models is limited towards variables for which interaction effects with various forms of representation have been found. Given the limitations of research regarding the use of domain knowledge as a factor, we aim to contribute to both areas (i.e. determining the effect of domain knowledge on comprehension and tailoring process models to personal factors such as learning style or personality).

3   Research Questions and Methodology

Our end goal is to develop a technique for dynamically visualizing process models based on user characteristics. Specifically, we intend to personalize these models based on domain knowledge and reading strategy. To this end, we first need to establish an understanding of the effects of domain knowledge on process model reading and understandability. Experts and novices acquire and integrate information in different ways [19]. The extent of tacit knowledge – general and domain specific skills acquired over time – separates experts from novices [20]. As experience and ability form an individual's internal state of knowledge, they determine performance.

A preliminary experiment will determine the presence of different reading strategies and their potential relation with domain knowledge [21]. A process model reading strategy can be defined as "the set and sequence of reading actions performed to translate the model into meaning". Eye-tracking will be used as a direct data collection method. It uncovers the mental processes underlying task behavior as eye movement paths, eye fixations and pupil dilations reflect the internal processing of information [22]. The actions that will be recorded are: *fixations,* where the eye stops for a brief moment on a model element; *saccades,* where the eye is quickly positioned on a new model element, *regression,* where the eye returns to an already visited element and *perceptual span,* which refers to the size of the visual window processed at each fixation. These actions will be analyzed individually (e.g. total number and average duration of fixations). Furthermore, recording the sequence of the elements themselves as read by each participant, a reading strategy will be interpretable as a sentence, on which text reading analysis techniques can be applied. Research that employs eye-tracking has high external validity as it is a non-invasive process tracing technique. This is also supported by [1] who consider the use of eye-tracking as the one neurophysiological tool that has been successfully applied in the area of process model comprehension.

Two process models will be used in the form of BPMN-diagrams, each a realistic representation of a process in a distinct domain: one on complaint handling and one on the treatment of stroke in healthcare. Both models were created in collaboration with employees active in the process. A set of domain related questions will be presented to each participant determining their level of domain knowledge. This set will be the result of discussions with longtime process participants, who, given their experience with the domain, will serve as proxies for domain experts. This approximation is necessary because a user can only be deemed an expert by other experts, for which we would also need the set of questions, causing a vicious cycle to start. The set will be deemed complete if no further questions are provided by new proxies. By creating a set that is as representative and long as possible, the risk of choosing a sample which includes "a preponderance of questions to which the subject happens to know the answers" [16] is avoided.

Participants will be domain experts in exactly one of the domains depicted by one of the models. By that logic, participants can be treated as novices for the model depicting the domain they are not an expert in. In order to determine reading strategies and differences between domain knowledge, each participant will receive both models. Whichever model they see first will be randomized to avoid bias. We will collect data on a sample of at least 70 participants (i.e. around 35 per domain) to maximize significance (following [23]). These are still to be determined, but will most likely be employees currently active in the used processes.

We focus on comprehension and problem solving measured by questions on semantics and pragmatics. This study does not aim to investigate differences in modeling knowledge and thus has no need to include syntax related questions. Performance will be determined by the results on these tests. We except domain experts to outperform novices. Therefore we hypothesize:

H1a: Domain experts will have higher performance on comprehension than novices.
H1b: Domain experts will spend less time reading the process model than novices.

Experts will rely on their prior knowledge to build an understanding of the model. Therefore we expect them to require less time, resulting in lower fixation rates and longer saccades. This is supported by the information-reduction hypothesis, which proposes that expertise optimizes the amount of processed information by neglecting task-irrelevant information and actively focusing on task-relevant information [24]. This effect is also expected to result in a different reading strategy and performance.

H2: Domain experts will exhibit a different reading strategy from novices.
H3: A correlation can be found between reading strategy and performance.

Participants will be required to read the entire model without a questionnaire. We argue that the specificity of the reading process is too much dependent on question choice [8] and therefore does not fully represent the cognitive processes that would otherwise unfold. The majority of research on process model understandability provides a questionnaire adapted to the factors under study. Consequently, those model elements not included require separate research and might fragment the body of knowledge. Since there will be no question list provided, participants will likely adopt a certain reading strategy to process the model in a way that best fits their learning style without being directed through the model as they are given the liberty to explore and process the model as they chose. This is in line with research on reading strategies of data models where participants were "simply asked to give a complete specification of each data model" [25].

The second stage starts after participants are convinced of understanding the model. They are only then provided with the aforementioned questionnaire. To avoid memorization in stage one, the model will be kept in view while solving questions. That way, participants will not feel the need to memorize for short-term recollection, but will instead use this first reading as an initial step of a learning process. Again, eye-tracking will be used to collect data in terms of fixation rates, saccades and reading strategies. In line with research on data models [25] and process models [12] we expect to be able to identify distinct reading strategies in both stages and differences in performance based on those strategies.

In the following phase, based on the findings of the experiment, we will develop a solution in the form of a collection of propositions towards personalized visualizations of process models. These will include guidelines and patterns to optimize process models with regards to a user's domain knowledge and reading strategy in order to enhance understandability. We aim to study the results of certain model manipulations on understandability for different users and reading strategies to conclude on a set of guidelines for each. Further in the thesis, we will work towards an automatic approach that will adapt models in real-time based on a user's domain knowledge, reading strategy and the corresponding set of modeling guidelines. To determine the success of a process configuration, a user's performance will be monitored with the use of intermediate questions.

4   Exploratory Study Preliminary Results

A pilot study was conducted with the single goal of determining the existence of distinct reading strategies. In case none of the participants exhibited dissimilar reading behaviour on the same process model understanding task, there would have been need to adjust our hypotheses and/or research track of future experiments as these rely on this initial assumption. A small set of users (10) was invited by the researcher to participate. These were chosen to ensure adequate variance in the user characteristics (i.e. modelling expert and modelling novice, abstract learner and structured learner,..). Using the SMI Red250Mobile eye-tracker (binocular mode at 250 Hz sampling rate with average operating distance of 65 cm) data was collected on reading sequence and characteristics (e.g. saccades, fixations, regressions, dwell time,..). Both types of data were used to define a user's reading strategy. At the point of writing, this data has only been inspected visually by comparing scan paths and fixation sequences side by side on dual monitors. This visual analysis already made evident the existence of differences in reading strategy.

However, we plan on continuing the analysis by converting fixation sequence data into strings on which string similarity measures (e.g. Jaccard index,..) will be applied.

5 Conclusion

Within the large body of knowledge on process model understandability, the growing importance of the effects of user characteristics is evident [1], establishing the need for further study. As an answer to current research opportunities, this thesis will contribute by investigating the effects of domain knowledge on reading strategy and process model understandability. This work will provide an innovative addition to research on four aspects: (1) using eye-tracking as a direct data gathering method in order to uncover participants' cognitive processes; (2) using realistically, complex process models so as to recreate as much of a realistic setting as possible; (3) investigating domain knowledge as the independent variable and (4) studying differences in reading strategy. These findings will ultimately lead to an automatic tailoring solution, which would personalize process models depending on the user, thus enhancing their performance.

Acknowledgements. This Ph.D. project will be funded by Ghent University (Belgium) under the supervision of Prof. Dr. Manu De Backer (administrative promoter) and Prof. Dr. Amy Van Looy (daily supervisor).

References

1. Figl, K.: Comprehension of procedural visual business process models. Bus. Inf. Syst. Eng. **59**, 41–67 (2017). https://doi.org/10.1007/s12599-016-0460-2
2. de Oca, I.M.M., Snoeck, M., Reijers, H.A., Rodríguez-Morffi, A.: A systematic literature review of studies on business process modeling quality. Inf. Softw. Technol. **58**, 187–205 (2015). https://doi.org/10.1016/j.infsof.2014.07.011
3. Dehnert, J., Van Der Aalst, W.M.P.: Bridging the gap between business models and workflow specifications. Int. J. Coop. Inf. Syst. **13**, 289–332 (2004)
4. Mendling, J., Strembeck, M., Recker, J.: Factors of process model comprehension-Findings from a series of experiments. Decis. Support Syst. **53**, 195–206 (2012). https://doi.org/10.1016/j.dss.2011.12.013
5. Turetken, O., Rompen, T., Vanderfeesten, I., Dikici, A., van Moll, J.: The effect of modularity representation and presentation medium on the understandability of business process models in BPMN. In: La Rosa, M., Loos, P., Pastor, O. (eds.) BPM 2016. LNCS, vol. 9850, pp. 289–307. Springer, Cham (2016). https://doi.org/10.1007/978-3-319-45348-4_17
6. Heinrich, L.J., Riedl, R., Stelzer, D., Sikora, H.: Informationsmanagement: Grundlagen, Aufgaben, Methoden. De Gruyter, München (2014)
7. Reijers, H.A., Mendling, J.: A study into the factors that influence the understandability of business process models. IEEE Trans. Syst. Man Cybern. **41**, 449–462 (2011). https://doi.org/10.1109/TSMCA.2010.2087017
8. Petrusel, R., Mendling, J.: Eye-tracking the factors of process model comprehension tasks. In: Salinesi, C., Norrie, M.C., Pastor, Ó. (eds.) CAiSE 2013. LNCS, vol. 7908, pp. 224–239. Springer, Heidelberg (2013). https://doi.org/10.1007/978-3-642-38709-8_15

9. Aysolmaz, B., Reijers, H.A.: Towards an integrated framework for invigorating process models: a research agenda. In: Reichert, M., Reijers, H.A. (eds.) BPM 2015. LNBIP, vol. 256, pp. 552–558. Springer, Cham (2016). https://doi.org/10.1007/978-3-319-42887-1_44

10. Kolb, J.: Abstraction, Visualization, and Evolution of Process Models. Ulm University (2015)

11. Figl, K., Strembeck, M.: On the importance of flow direction in business process models. In: Proceedings of the 9th International Conference on Software Engineering and Applications (ICSOFT-EA 2014), pp. 132–136 (2014)

12. Haisjackl, C., Soffer, P., Lim, S.Y., Weber, B.: How do humans inspect BPMN models: an exploratory study. Softw. Syst. Model 1–19 (2016). https://doi.org/10.1007/s10270-016-0563-8

13. Bera, P.: Does cognitive overload matter in understanding BPMN models? J. Comput. Inf. Syst. **52**, 59–69 (2012)

14. Recker, J., Dreiling, A.: Does it matter which process modelling language we teach or use? An experimental study on understanding process modelling languages without formal education, pp. 356–366 (2007)

15. Recker, J., Reijers, H.A., van de Wouw, S.G.: Process model comprehension: the effects of cognitive abilities, learning style, and strategy. Commun. Assoc. Inf. Syst. **34**, 199–222 (2014)

16. Borgatti, S.P., Carboni, I.: On measuring individual knowledge in organizations. Organ Res. Methods **10**, 449–462 (2007)

17. Hambrick, D.Z., Engle, R.W.: Effects of domain knowledge, working memory capacity, and age on cognitive performance: An investigation of the knowledge-is-power hypothesis. Cogn. Psychol. **44**, 339–387 (2002)

18. Santos, E., Pimentel, J., Castro, J., Finkelstein, A.: On the dynamic configuration of business process models. In: Bider, I., Halpin, T., Krogstie, J., Nurcan, S., Proper, E., Schmidt, R., Soffer, P., Wrycza, S. (eds.) BPMDS/EMMSAD -2012. LNBIP, vol. 113, pp. 331–346. Springer, Heidelberg (2012). https://doi.org/10.1007/978-3-642-31072-0_23

19. Libby, R., Luft, J.: Determinants of judgment performance in accounting settings: Ability, knowledge, motivation, and environment. Acc. Organ. Soc. **18**, 425–450 (1993)

20. Schmidt, F.L., Hunter, J.E.: Tacit knowledge, practical intelligence, general mental ability, and job knowledge. Curr. Dir. Psychol. Sci. **2**, 8–9 (1993)

21. Patig, S.: A practical guide to testing the understandability of notations. In: Proceedings of the Fifth Asia-Pacific Conference on Conceptual Modelling, vol. 79, pp. 49–58. Australian Computer Society, Inc. (2008)

22. Weber, B., Pinggera, J., Neurauter, M., et al.: Fixation patterns during process model creation: Initial steps toward neuro-adaptive process modeling environments. In: 49th Hawaii International Conference on System Sciences, pp. 600–609 (2016)

23. Petrusel, R., Mendling, J., Reijers, H.A.: How visual cognition influences process model comprehension. Decis. Support Syst. **96**, 1–16 (2017). https://doi.org/10.1016/j.dss.2017.01.005

24. Haider, H., Frensch, P.A.: Eye movement during skill acquisition: More evidence for the information-reduction hypothesis. J. Exp. Psychol. Learn. Mem. Cogn. **25**, 172 (1999)

25. Nordbotten, J.C., Crosby, M.E.: The effect of graphic style on data model interpretation. Inf. Syst. J. **9**, 139–155 (1999). https://doi.org/10.1046/j.1365-2575.1999.00052.x

International Conference on Ontologies, DataBases, and Applications of Semantics (ODBASE) 2017 – Posters

ODBASE 2017 PC Co-chairs' Message

We are delighted to present the proceedings of the 16th International Conference on Ontologies, DataBases, and Applications of Semantics (ODBASE) which was held in Rhodes (Greece) 24–25 October 2017. The ODBASE Conference series provides a forum for research and practitioners on the use of ontologies and data semantics in novel applications, and continues to draw a highly diverse body of researchers and practitioners. ODBASE is part of the OnTheMove (OTM 2017) federated event composed of three interrelated yet complementary scientific conferences that together attempt to span a relevant range of the advanced research on, and cutting-edge development and application of, information handling and systems in the wider current context of ubiquitous distributed computing. The other two co-located conferences are CoopIS'17 (Cooperative Information Systems) and C&TC'17 (Cloud and Trusted Computing). Of particular relevance to ODBASE 2017 are papers that bridge traditional boundaries between disciplines such as artificial intelligence and Semantic Web, databases, data analytics and machine learning, social networks, distributed and mobile systems, information retrieval, knowledge discovery, and computational linguistics.

This year, we received 46 paper submissions and had a program committee of 48 dedicated colleagues, including researchers and practitioners from diverse research areas. Special arrangements were made during the review process to ensure that each paper was reviewed by 3–4 members of different research areas. The result of this effort is the selection of high quality papers: twenty regular papers, six short papers, and four posters. Their themes included studies and solutions to a number of modern challenges such as querying, cleaning, publishing, benchmarking and visualizing linked data, RDF documents and graph databases, ontology engineering, semantic mapping, social network analysis, and semantics-based applications to various domains, such as health, tourism, smart cities, law, etc. The scientific program is complemented with a very interesting keynote speech by Markus Lanthaler on Pragmatic Semantics at Web Scale.

We would like to thank all the members of the Program Committee for their hard work in selecting the papers and for helping to make this conference a success. We would also like to thank all the researchers who submitted their work. Last but not least, special thanks go to the members of the OTM team for their support and guidance.

We hope that you enjoy ODBASE 2017 and have a wonderful time in Rhodes!

September 2017

Adrian Paschke
Nick Bassiliades
Hans Weigand

District-Scale Data Integration by Leveraging Semantic Web Technologies: A Case in Smart Cities

Kiril Tonev, Simon Kappe$^{(\boxtimes)}$, Preslava Krahtova, Hendro Wicaksono,
and Jivka Ovtcharova

Karlsruhe Institute of Technology, Institute for Information Management
in Engineering, Zirkel 2, Karlsruhe, Germany
{kiril.tonev,simon.kappe,preslava.krahtova,hendro.wicaksono,
jivka.ovtcharova}@kit.edu
http://www.imi.kit.edu

Abstract. Technologies of the Semantic Web stack promise to alleviate some of the challenges related to data integration on a massive scale and high level of heterogeneity. This paper explores their application in the smart cities domain with a focus on energy efficient districts. We develop an ontology grounded in several well-established vocabularies to leverage their shared semantics and facilitate data interoperability and we apply the developed ontology to integrate state-of-the-art energy simulation facilities into a general district-level monitoring framework.

Keywords: Smart cities · Building energy simulation
Semantic data integration · Ontology alignment

1 Introduction

The energy management at a city or district level requires a synergetic participation of multiple stakeholders, for instance citizens, utility companies, policy makers or municipalities, and companies providing services related to energy efficiency e.g. energy consultants, building energy management providers, software companies. Multiple tools or services are also utilized to help the stakeholders to perform energy management activities. The multiple stakeholders and services consume and produce data resulting in heterogeneous data formats and sources. The data often come from multiple and unrelated domains, for example building geometry and topology data, sensor data, occupant behavior data, regulations, weather and geospatial data [1].

In order to accomplish accurate and efficient energy management activities involving multiple stakeholders, it requires access and efficient processing of up-to-date and comprehensive information coming from the heterogeneous data [2]. The interoperability issue is still the main challenge in achieving it. Semantic Web technologies promise to alleviate some of the challenges related to data integration on a massive scale and high level of heterogeneity. This paper introduces

© Springer International Publishing AG 2018
C. Debruyne et al. (Eds.): OTM 2017 Workshops, LNCS 10697, pp. 289–292, 2018.
https://doi.org/10.1007/978-3-319-73805-5

an approach to develop an ontology that reuses well-established vocabularies to leverage their shared semantics and facilitate data interoperability in the smart city context.

The energy consumption analysis on district or city level requires an aggregation of energy consumption data of buildings located in the district. Since not all buildings are equipped with energy metering infrastructure, building energy simulations are performed to predict the energy consumption of a building based on building envelope profile, occupant profile, and surrounding factors.

2   Ontology Development

In DAREED project, we have followed the principle of ontology reuse and grounded the main concepts within the frameworks of other, well-established ontologies. Figure 1 summarizes the main concept of the ontology.

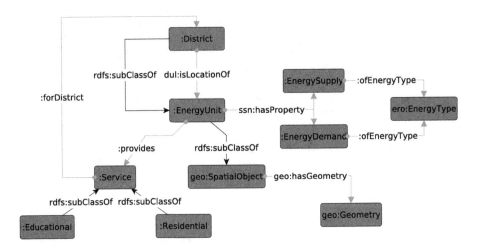

Fig. 1. Main concepts of DAREED district ontology.

In our model, a district is described by a region encompassing a set of energy units. The demand and supply of the district are dependent on the energetic behavior of the energy units within. To further distinguish energy units, we describe the main services they fulfil as members of the district: for example, houses provide residential services, schools provide educational services, parks provide open spaces, and office buildings provide industrial services and so on. An energy unit can demand and supply energy, and we distinguish the types of energy involved in the balance.

The computational platform uses the aggregated area usages for each service category and estimates the demand and response curves of the district in 15-min steps. Since the spatial characteristics of the energy units have such a central role within the district model, we have opted to model these dimensions against the GeoSPARQL ontologys Spatial Object and Geometry concepts.

Other aspects of the upper district ontology are the Key Performance Indicators and metrics that describe the services and districts themselves. To that end, we have followed the suggestions outlined by Fox [3]. We derive the service and district metrics from the Quantity and Measurement concepts of the Ontology of units of measure [4].

3   Integrating Simulation Data Within the District Knowledge Graph

Smart meters are becoming increasingly available in districts as electrical networks are moving towards implementing smart grids for meeting the environmental challenges. Despite that, monitoring a significant portion of the districts energy usage with sensors or smart metering devices remains unviable. We maintain that without addressing the privacy issues, the district-wide coverage of the energy consumption will unlikely penetrate the household segment.

To cope with that challenge, we have developed a framework for integrating simulation data directly into the district knowledge graph. Thereby, we have leveraged EnergyPlus simulation package since its availability as open source and text-based IO formats.

Our approach bases on [5], in that it leverages a mapping specification for providing a linked-data view of the simulation results. The mapping specification is XML-based and offers two distinct operators not available in existing packages: the aggregation operator building a single value from a range of fields and the list operator exporting a range of fields as `rdfs:List`.

The mapping specification facilitates the extraction of RDF graphs from table-based sources. It proposes a way for specifying the URLs of resources and their property assignments in an XML file. Once a specification is written, a graph can be extracted by processing the input schemas or tables with an implementation of two interfaces which instruct how to access the data items and their properties.

Given an input and an output file, we proceed to extract a linked-data graph describing the energy unit and its energetic behavior. The mapping file we developed for the purposes of the DAREED project can be logically subdivided into three categories: building structure (or product model), the resources model and the sensing model.

The resources model describes the energy producers and consumers represented in the simulation input/output data. From the EnergyPlus data dictionary, we extract Simulation Resources entities expressing different level of aggregation of the calculated energetic behavior. These range from the Zone to the Plant level. We extend the Semantic Sensor Network Ontology [6] with the special EnergySupply and EnergyDemand concepts expressing which side of the energetic balance the calculations should be related to. Lastly, we further describe the type of energy involved in the energetic balance of the building by drawing from the Energy Resources Ontology.

With the resources model, we are able to describe the energetic behavior of the simulated building or individual zones thereof only qualitatively. The actual estimated measurements are the subject of the Sensing Model. The Sensing Model leverages several ontologies and linked data vocabularies to provide a tabular view of the data encoded within the EnergyPlus simulation output without sacrificing the rich metadata model we have described thus far.

This concludes our overview of the conceptualization of a simulated building and the related output data as used in the DAREED project. It allows us to answer the key question required for the functioning of the monitoring platform, namely how the consumption and production of the building and its zones are behaving over time. By selecting appropriate ontologies and vocabularies from semantic web repositories and the literature, we are capable of building a semantically rich model that can be interpreted and processed by third-party systems with very little effort. We emphasize that our model has been primarily informed by the requirements of the project and, more importantly, the simulation input files developed therein.

Acknowledgments. The DAREED project has received funding from the Seventh framework programme of the European Union (EU) under grant agreement 609082.

References

1. McGlinn, K., Wicaksono, H., Lawton, W., Weise, M., Kaklanis, N., Petri, I., Tzovaras, D.: Identifying use cases and data requirements for BIM based energy management processes. In: CIBSE Technical Symposium (2016)
2. Wicaksono, H., Dobreva, P., Häfner, P., Rogalski, S.: Methodology to develop ontological building information model for energy management system in building operational phase. In: Fred, A., Dietz, J., Liu, K., Filipe, J. (eds.) IC3K 2013. CCIS, vol. 454, pp. 168–181. Springer, Berlin, Heidelberg (2015)
3. Fox, M. S.: City data: Big, open and linked. Municipal Interfaces, 19–25 (2013)
4. Rijgersberg, H., van Assem, M., Top, J.: Ontology of units of measure and related concepts. Semant. Web 4.1, 3–13 (2013)
5. Skjveland, M. G., Giese, M., Hovland, D., Lian, E.H., Waaler, A.: Engineering ontology-based access to real-world data sources. Web Semant.: Sci., Serv. Agents World Wide Web, **33**, 112–140 (2015)
6. Compton, M., Barnaghi, P., Bermudez, L., García-Castro, R., Corcho, O., Cox, S., Graybeal, J., Hauswirth, M., Henson, C., Herzog, A., Huang, V., Janowicz, K., Kelsey, W.D., Phuoc, D.L., Lefort, L., Leggieri, M., Neuhaus, H., Nikolov, A., Page, K., Passant, A., Sheth, A., Taylor, K.: The SSN ontology of the W3C semantic sensor network incubator group. Web Semant.: Sci., Serv. Agents World Wide Web **17**, 25–32 (2012)

Digital Assistance Based on an Ontology Driven Model of the IT-Systems Along the Product Lifecycle

Klemens Haas[✉], Simon Kappe, Martin Siebert, Hendro Wicaksono, and Jivka Ovtcharova

Karlsruhe Institute of Technology, Institute for Information Management in Engineering, Zirkel 2, 76131 Karlsruhe, Germany
{klemens.haas,simon.kappe,hendro.wicaksono,jivka.ovtcharova}@kit.edu
http://www.imi.kit.edu

Abstract. The market of Product Lifecycle Management (PLM) applications has changed into a complex landscape of heterogeneous systems in recent years. Consequently, it has become increasingly challenging for enterprises to identify a PLM application that meets their requirements and that can be successfully integrated into their existing IT systems. The approach presented in this paper aims at developing a decision-supporting model of the IT system landscape that provides different analysis tools based on existing IT systems. The model which is expressed by an ontology is intended to represent data flows between the different IT applications in order to provide relevant information through requests and rules in further proceedings.

Keywords: Digitization · Ontology · Product lifecycle management

1 Introduction

The digitization dominates the current trends. It is responsible for profound changes in all areas of life and it opens up new potentials for the industry. According to a study by McKinsey Global Institute, European Countries exploit only 12% of their digital potential on average. If for example Germany used its entire potential it would be possible to achieve an annual GDP growth of 1% until 2025, which corresponds to a monetary potential of 500 billion Euro. According to this study, Europe is rather a consumer than a producer of digital services. [3]. Digitization aims at the development of working processes that are faster, more dynamic and more interconnected. This leads to an increasing complexity of processes as well as to a higher demand for automation. The interconnection of systems is a major challenge. Another issue is the integration of new IT-systems into existing IT-system environments. Furthermore, it is necessary to examine legacy systems concerning their potentials. Based on this challenges this paper develops an approach to a digital assistance system. The methodology is based on a Product Lifecycle Management (PLM) ontology, which contains the IT systems of an enterprise as well as the corresponding information that is being processed.

© Springer International Publishing AG 2018
C. Debruyne et al. (Eds.): OTM 2017 Workshops, LNCS 10697, pp. 293–296, 2018.
https://doi.org/10.1007/978-3-319-73805-5

2   Related Work

Through the past years, the supply of PLM applications has increased rapidly and has caused the emergence of very heterogeneous system landscapes. This leads to growing challenges for the integration process of new applications into existing system landscapes. To solve this problem several papers have used methods of semantic annotation aiming at rebuilding the interconnection of PLM systems. Providing a survey and a literature collection, Liao et al. present an overview over semantic modelling in the context of PLM [4].

Matsokis and Kirtisis describe the specific modelling of a generalized PLM system with an ontology. They focus on the transformation of existing PLM models into an ontology with a detailed description of the technical realization in OWL DL. Their ontology is built around the physical product without referring to the separate PLM applications or taking into account the generated data [5].

Bruno and Villa refine this idea by considering data flows between the separate concepts of a PLM solution. These flows are interconnected using object relations to present the direction and the type of the data stream [2]. In a further paper with Antonelli, they jointly develop a generalized model of the PLM applications [1].

The EU project amePLM works on a reference ontology to support the product lifecycle. The emphases are the product model, meta data, documents, resources. The model is generalized and can be specified depending on different applications [1].

Wicaksono et al. develop an ontology that represents the correlations between properties of customized products, the involved production processes, and the corresponding resource and energy consumptions [7]. The correlations are discovered from data sets coming from different IT systems with the help of machine learning algorithms [6]. The knowledge model covers the whole product lifecycle. However, it lacks a model representing the involved IT systems.

3   OntoPLM - Digital Assistance

The emphasis of this paper is the conception of a data model, implemented through a corresponding ontology that models different inputs and outputs between PLM applications. The main components of the model are: (i) PLM applications; (ii) Data types; (iii) Data input and output flows; (iv) stages of the product lifecycle. The model considers a selection of IT systems for which the relevant data input and output flows are determined. The selection of the applications has been limited to main PLM applications (e.g. Product Data Management, Enterprise Resource Planing, Manufacturing Execution, Computer Aided design, Computer Aided Manufacturing, Office Systems, Supply Chain Management, Customer Information System). This selection can be extended by an arbitrary number of systems and builds the basic structure of an integrated approach. Based on the data input and output flows of the PLM applications, similar data types are aggregated under distinct terms and then structured into five data classes: (i) Construction data; (ii) Simulation data; (iii) Production Data; (iv) Commercial Data; (v) Customer Data.

The ontology is designed in two steps. In the first step, the taxonomy is created. It consists of the previously selected IT applications as well as of the data model and the stages of the Product Lifecycle Management. In the second step the class hierarchy and relations are implemented. They describe the relationships of the different classes within the ontology on a file type level and represent the data flows between the PLM applications. For a basic framework each PLM application was analyzed and the belonging data inputs and outputs were added in the ontology.

Based on the ontology and the additional subdivision into development steps or departments, existing workflows can be created and analyzed in companies. For this instance, rules determine which information and corresponding development steps are required and processed by the individual IT system. In line with the ontology, it can be checked whether this workflow is possible with the installed IT systems and which interfaces are implemented.

The developed ontology addresses on the one hand providers of PLM software and suppliers of tools of the Digital Factory which intend to present their systems and tools vividly to their prospect customers. On the other hand, present and future end customers of IT applications also belong to the potential target group of this ontology. The ontology has to be instantiated individually in accordance with company-specific IT system environment. On the basis of this ontology different analysis mechanisms can be triggered (Fig. 1). They have the opportunity to proof how a new tool can be successfully implemented in their already existing system landscape as data flows are made transparent by the model. Existing and required interfaces can be thereby identified with less effort and the product that has the maximum compatibility can be selected. Furthermore, Lifecycle Analytics methods are intended to be applied to the ontology.

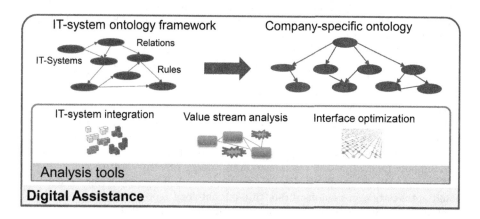

Fig. 1. Concept of Digital Assistance.

The developed model covers a selection of PLM applications, data types and the stages of the product lifecycle. Each of these elements can be extended by adding an arbitrary number of new classes and thus generating further benefits.

It seems reasonable to add additional PLM applications to the model to extend the scope of the requests within the application. The same applies to the tools of the Digital Factory which can be implemented analogously to the conception in this paper. Suppliers of these applications and tools can present the data input and output flows of the product to their prospect customers. An end user will be enabled to make better decisions concerning investments and to choose a product which can be integrated optimally into the existing system landscape.

4   Conclusions

In this paper a basic framework of the data input and output flows of PLM applications has been developed. Through company individual adaptions and extensions analysis regarding the IT-Systems can be made. Areas of applications are the selection and integration of new IT applications based on existing systems and tools for enterprises. Furthermore the existing connections between the IT-Systems along the product lifecyle can be analysed. The next steps will be further evaluations and identifications of analysis scenarios.

References

1. Bruno, G., Antonelli, D., Villa, A.: A reference ontology to support product lifecycle management. Procedia CIRP **33**, 41–46 (2015)
2. Bruno, G., Villa, A.: The exploitation of an ontology-based model of PLM from a SME point of view. In: IFAC Proceedings, vol. 9, issue 46, pp. 1447–1452 (2013)
3. Bughin, J., Hazan, E., Labaye, E., Manyika, J., Dahlström, P., Ramaswamy, S., de Billy, C.C.: Digital europe: Pushing the frontier, capturing the benefits. Technical report, McKinsey Global Institute (2016)
4. Liao, Y., Lezoche, M., Panetto, H., Boudjlida, N., Loures, E.R.: Semantic annotation for knowledge explicitation in a product lifecycle management context: a survey. Comput. Ind. **71**, 24–34 (2015)
5. Matsokis, A., Kiritsis, D.: An ontology-based approach for product lifecycle management. Comput. Ind. **61**(8), 787–797 (2010)
6. Wicaksono, H.: An Integrated Method for Information and Communication Technology (ICT) Supported Energy Efficiency Evaluation and Optimization in Manufacturing: Knowledge-based Approach and Energy Performance Indicators (EnPI) to Support Evaluation and Optimization of Energy Efficiency (2016)
7. Wicaksono, H., Rogalski, S., Jost, F., Ovtcharova, J.: Energy efficiency evaluation and optimization in manufacturing through ontology represented knowledge base. Int. J. Intell. Syst. Account., Finance Manage. 1099–1174 (2014)

Systematical Representation of RDF-to-Relational Mappings for Ontology-Based Data Access

Lars Runge, Sebastian Schrage, and Wolfgang May[✉]

Institute of Computer Science, Georg-August Universität Göttingen,
Göttingen, Germany

Abstract. This paper presents a representation for storing OBDA mapping information in an easily understandable, user-accessible, and extensible format in dedicated metadata tables in the relational database.

1 Introduction and Motivation

Ontology-based Data Access (OBDA) systems aim to allow users to state queries based on the vocabulary of an ontology against data stored in a relational database. The core of OBDA tools is a mapping between both formats. Such mappings can be created manually, or by (semi)automatic alignment tools. When evaluating such (semi)automatic database alignment approaches through the evaluation of query translation (SPARQL to SQL), it was found that the generated alignments are often incomplete or partially incorrect [1]. Most systems do not allow the user to check and modify the mapping directly because it is only stored internally in the system. Making the mappings available to the user by storing them in a well-defined and accessible format in metadata tables inside the relational database overcomes this limitation. This paper introduces the "RDF2SQL" approach, which defines a framework for storing RDF↔relational mappings in a *Semantical Data Dictionary* (SDD) consisting of generic metadata tables. The full paper and more information can be found at [2].

2 Generic Metadata: Semantical Data Dictionary

We illustrate the approach by a fragment of the MONDIAL [3] database whose ER diagram is shown below that contains examples for typical patterns in conceptual modeling. In an OBDA setting, the OWL ontology of the application contains the same information; the MONDIAL ontology can also be found at [3]. Some modeling details deserve some attention (cf. ER diagram below):

LocatedAt is an $n{:}m$ relationship between cities and waters. The locatedOn relationship is also $n{:}m$ between cities and islands, while between mountains and islands, it is $n{:}1$. The attributed $n{:}m$ isMember relationship between countries and organizations includes a type attribute. This leads to reification, which in the relational model means an $n{:}m$ table with an aditional type column. In RDF

© Springer International Publishing AG 2018
C. Debruyne et al. (Eds.): OTM 2017 Workshops, LNCS 10697, pp. 297–301, 2018.
https://doi.org/10.1007/978-3-319-73805-5

(or UML) modeling, there is an artificial reified **Membership** class with reference properties ofCountry and inOrganization.

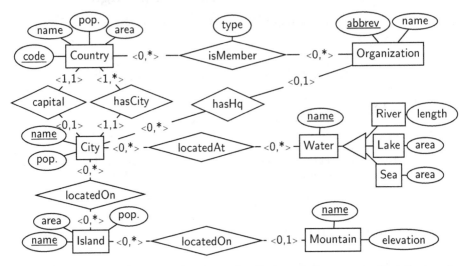

The OWL ontology fragment for these details is as follows; note that it already represents the modeling *after* reification.

```
:locatedOn a owl:ObjectProperty;
    rdfs:domain [ owl:unionOf ( :City :Mountain ) ]; rdfs:range :Island.
:Mountain rdfs:subClassOf [a owl:Restriction;
    owl:onProperty :locatedOn; owl:maxCardinality 1].
:ofMember a owl:ObjectProperty; a owl:FunctionalProperty;
    rdfs:domain :Membership; owl:inverseOf :inMembership; rdfs:range :Country.
:inOrganization a owl:ObjectProperty; a owl:FunctionalProperty;
    rdfs:domain :Membership; owl:inverseOf :hasMembership; rdfs:range :Organization.
```

For illustration of the SDD, we apply the standard design of a relational database schema according to [4, Ch. 7]. In the OBDA case, the required information is extracted from the OWL ontology. (Alternatively, the SDD can e.g. based on an existing relational database and canonically deriving a ontology from it, or from an R2RML mapping [5]).

The *Class Tables* contain all functional properties as columns; and a uri column acts as the primary key. $n{:}m$-relationships are mapped to binary $n{:}m$ tables:

```
Country(uri, name, code, population, area, capital).
City(uri, name, population, hasCity_inv).
Organization(uri, abbrev, name, hasHq).
Membership(uri, ofCountry, inOrganization, type).
River(uri, name, length).      Lake(uri, name, area).    Sea(uri, name, area).
Mountain(uri, name, locatedOn).    Island(uri, name, area, population).
locatedAt(city, water).        locatedOn(city, island).
```

The SDD Tables. The *Mapping Dictionary (MD)* represents where a property p of a class c is stored/looked up, i.e., in which table, and in which column of it. For properties like Country.hasCity that are inverse-functional, a lookup in the inverse direction is required. The range *class* of every property is also stored: MD : (Class × Property) → (Class × Table × Column × inv?):

MappingDict					
Class	Property	RangeClass	Table	LookupAttr	inv
Country	name	xsd:string	Country	name	false
Country	code	xsd:string	Country	code	false
City	name	xsd:string	City	name	false
all functional literal-valued properties:					
(class, property, range-datatype, Class=tablename, column=propertyname, false)					
Country	capital	City	Country	capital	false
Country	hasCity	City	City	hasCity_inv	true
Country	inMembership	Membership	Membership	ofCountry	true
City	hasCity_inv	Country	City	hasCity_inv	false
City	locatedAt	Water	locatedAt	Water	false
City	locatedOn	Island	locatedOn	Island	false
Organization	hasHq	City	Organization	hasHq	false
Organization	hasMembership	Membership	Membership	inOrganization	true
Membership	inOrganization	Organization	Membership	inOrganization	false
Membership	ofCountry	Country	Membership	ofCountry	false
Membership	type	xsd:string	Membership	type	false
River	locatedAt_inv	City	locatedAt	city	false
Lake	locatedAt_inv	City	locatedAt	city	false
Sea	locatedAt_inv	City	locatedAt	city	false
Mountain	locatedOn	Island	Mountain	locatedOn	false
Island	locatedOn_inv	City	locatedOn	city	false
Island	locatedOn_inv	Mountain	Mountain	locatedOn	true
Water	name	xsd:string	River	name	false
Water	name	xsd:string	Lake	name	false
Water	name	xsd:string	Sea	name	false
Water	locatedAt_inv	City	locatedAt	city	false

For the $n:m$ tables, e.g., locatedAt, the entries tell that the (URIs of the) waters where a city is located can be found in the Water column of the locatedAt table. Note the different handling of locatedOn for Cities ($n:m$) and mountains (functional). In case of relationships, the lookup yields the URI of an object, which then must be joined appropriately; in case of $n{:}m$ tables, also the "back-wards" join to the domain side is needed:

The *Range Tables Table* (RTTab) gives for each pair (table, column) the ClassTables where the referenced URIs can be found. The *NM Join Table (NMJ)* table yields the column name to be used for the "back" join with the domain: NMJoinTab : (Class × Table × (LookUp)Attribute) → (FKJoin)Attribute; where $(c, t, l) \mapsto f$ means that, for an instance of class c, to look up the attribute l in the ($n{:}m$-)table t, the attribute f of t must be matched with the URI column of ClassTable c. Note that a lookup in the NMJ always follows a lookup for (c, p) yielding (t, l) in the MD.

Example. Consider the following SPARQL query pattern:
  { ?C :name ?CN; :locatedAt ?L . ?L a :Lake; :name ?LN }

RTTab

Table	LookupAttr	RangeTable
Country	capital	City
City	hasCity_inv	Country
Organization	hasHq	City
Membership	inOrganization	Organization
Membership	ofCountry	Country
locatedAt	City	City
locatedAt	Water	River
locatedAt	Water	Lake
locatedAt	Water	Sea
locatedOn	City	City
locatedOn	Island	Island
Mountain	locatedOn	Island

NMJoinTab

Class	Table	Lookup	FKJA.
City	locatedAt	Water	City
Water	locatedAt	City	Water
River	locatedAt	City	Water
Lake	locatedAt	City	Water
Sea	locatedAt	City	Water
Island	locatedOn	City	Island
City	locatedOn	Island	City

First, the classes of the variables are determined: either given by an *is-a-*pattern, or as the intersection of the domains of the properties used in the query. Thus, ?C can be identified to range over cities. The MD tells to look up ?C.locatedAt in locatedAt.Water whose range tables (for ?L) are according to the RTTab River, Lake, and Sea. ?L is restricted in the query to lakes whose names are looked up in Lake.name. The NMJ tells to join City.URI with locatedAt.City:

    SELECT city.name, lake.name FROM country, locatedAt, lake
    WHERE locatedAt.Water = lake.uri AND city.uri = locatedAt.city

Additional SDD Tables and Coverage. The SDD also contains information about the inverses and about the class hierarchy. Further, the following modeling aspects are also covered (see [2]): renaming, abstract subclasses, shortcut for reified properties, symmetric non-functional properties, vertical partitioning.

3   Current Functionality of RDF2SQL

The current prototype of RDF2SQL can be found at [2]. The central functional-ity is the transformation of an OWL ontology (optionally with additional anno-tations about concrete and abstract classes, reification etc.) into a relational schema and the generation of the SDD tables. The analysis of the ontology is done as described in [6]. RDF data can be inserted either from a file, or triplewise. SPARQL queries can be translated into SQL queries and can be evaluated.

References

1. Pinkel, C., et al.: RODI: Benchmarking relational-to-ontology mapping generation quality. Semant. Web J. (to appear)
2. RDF2SQL Demo (2017). http://www.semwebtech.org/rdf2sql/
3. Mondial database. http://dbis.informatik.uni-goettingen.de/Mondial/
4. Elmasri, R., Navathe, S.B.: Fundamentals of Database Systems. Addison-Wesley
5. W3C: R2RML: RDB to RDF Mapping Language. https://www.w3.org/TR/r2rml/
6. Hornung, T., May, W.: Experiences from a TBox reasoning application: deriving a relational model by OWL schema analysis. In: OWLED 2013. CEUR Workshop Proceedings, vol. 1080 (2013). CEUR-WS.org

Towards a Core Ontology for Financial Reporting Information Systems (COFRIS)

Ivars Blums[1](✉) and Hans Weigand[2]

[1] SIA ODO, Riga, Latvia
Ivars.Blums@odo.lv
[2] University of Tilburg, Tilburg, The Netherlands

Abstract. Among models and information about economic phenomena that help to understand how enterprises produce value, Accounting and Financial Reporting still play a leading and regulative role. The regulative role is established by enforceable International Financial Reporting (FR) Standards. Ontology engineering methods, which have proven to cope with difficult standardization issues, are seldom used in developing these standards. Furthermore, no widely accepted computational ontology, covering the concepts and relations of FR, and the Information Systems supporting FR, exists. This paper proposes an initial version of the Core Ontology of Financial Reporting Information Systems (COFRIS) grounded on the Unified Foundational Ontology (UFO).

Keywords: UFO · COFRIS · IASB · IFRS · Shared ledger

1 Introduction

Ontology engineering methods, which have proven to cope with difficult standardization issues [5], are seldom used in developing standards of international financial reporting (IFRS). Consistency, completeness and clarity of recent editions of Conceptual Framework for FR [1] and reworked standards [2] by the International Accounting Standards Board (IASB) still need to be improved [12]. Additionally, we see the following deficiencies of this framework and standards:

- absence of ontology engineering tools used for standard setting;
- limited, inconsistent and not generalized conceptualization of economic contracts and their progression events [11];
- repetitions and inconsistency among IFRS standards;
- inconsistency with other enterprise standards and enterprise ontologies;
- limited account for the impact of modern information technologies, such as data analytics and shared ledger [10].

The main contribution of this paper is the initial version of the Core Ontology of Financial Reporting Information Systems (COFRIS) grounded on the Unified Foundational Ontology (UFO) [5] network. Section 2 depicts an essential fragment of COFRIS presented in OntoUML [5] diagram in Fig. 1 and definitions of the main concepts and relations with references to the UFO patterns [3–9] and IASB conceptual framework [1] and IFRS standards [2] in Fig. 2.

© Springer International Publishing AG 2018
C. Debruyne et al. (Eds.): OTM 2017 Workshops, LNCS 10697, pp. 302–306, 2018.
https://doi.org/10.1007/978-3-319-73805-5

2   COFRIS OntoUML Diagram, and Concept Definitions

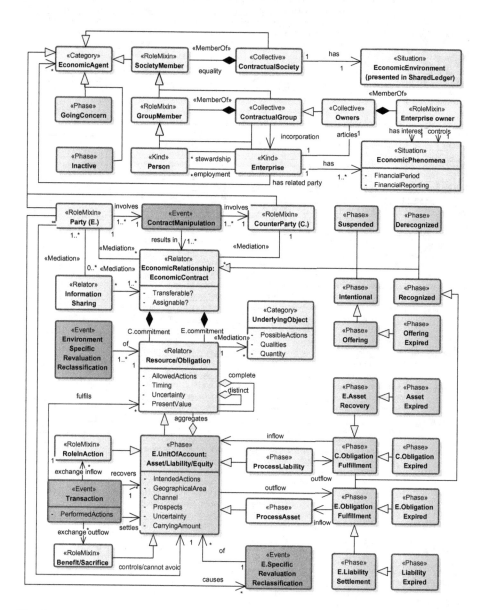

Fig. 1. An OntoUML diagram of COFRIS economic agents (in yellow), relations (in beige), phases (in pink), and events (in blue).

COFRIS term	COFRIS concept and relation definitions	UFO pattern	IASB[2]
Financial reporting (FR)	provides information relevant to investors about the reporting enterprise's economic phenomena - relationships with economic agents and the changes of those relationships.	Normative description [3]	CF[1]
Reporting period	is used to decompose the changes of the whole as separate one-period flows.	Time period [9]	CF[1]
Economic agent:	is a category of persons and enterprises, contractual groups of people and enterprises, or the society at large. Economic agents are capable of committing and fulfilling economic actions.	Social, Human agent [3]	CF[1]
Enterprise	(subject of FR), is an incorporated contractual group with some inherent goals, An enterprise has control to actions upon economic resources to attain its goals and fulfill its obligations.	Institutional agent [3]	CF[1] IFRS 3
Enterprise owner	controls or has a non-controlling interest in an enterprise as per the articles contract.	Social role [3]	IAS 1
Economic relationship:	is a relational entity existentially dependent on economic agents playing the roles of the party and the counterparty and having commitments/claims quantified in monetary terms, regarding some underlying object. These commitments/claims are: individual/mutual intentions; or enforceable by society: obligations [duties]/rights of a party against a counterparty; or rights of a party against all economic agents [permissions].	Social, Legal relator, Entitlement and Burden/Lack [3, 4]	CF[1]
Timing	is a condition indicating when the resources are to be used/obligations fulfilled.	Events [7]	IAS 39
Present value	is a price that exists independent from the enterprise, and is used as a measurement unit for FR	Value [6]	IFRS13
Resource	is a right that has the disposition to produce economic benefits. The allowed (by law, contract or nature) rights prescribe permissions of economic agents to use economic resources.	Resource, Disposition [5]	CF[1]
Obligation:	is an action to which an economic agent is legally or constructively bound.	Duty [4]	CF[1]
Distinct obligation	fulfillment creates a distinct liability of the counterpary and revenue recognition for the party.		IFRS
Complete obligation	fulfillment creates an unconditional right of the party, a complete liability of the counterparty.		
Underlying object	is a physical or intellectual object; or amount of matter, including human and natural environment energy; or an obligation/right/both (eg, to exchange) for another underlying object.	Endurant [5]	CF[1]
Unit of account:	is a group of recognized by an enterprise enforceable/constructive [net] rights/obligations/both, classified by their intended use and valuation, with assessed uncertainty and impairment.	Resource [5]	CF[1]
Carrying amount	depicts account value after deducting any accumulated depreciation and impairment losses	Value [6]	CF[1]
Uncertainty	of receiving economic benefits. Assessed through provisions and mitigated by hedging.	Disposition [5]	IFRS 9
Intended actions (Function)	refers to the primary actions and assets and liabilities used in those actions in which an enterprise is engaged and capable, eg, selling goods/services, manufacturing, or administration.	Resource, Capability [5]	CF[1]
Role in an action (Nature)	refers to the economic characteristics or attributes that distinguish assets and liabilities used in actions that do not respond similarly to similar economic events, e.g., raw materials, labour.		CF[1]
Benefit/Sacrifice	refers to the outcome form of intended or performed action, which increases/decreases equity.		
Asset	is a present economic resource controlled by the enterprise as a result of past events.		
Liability/Equity	is a present obligation of the enterprise to transfer a resource as a result of past events.	Duty [4]	
Correlative association	If one party has an obligation to transfer an economic resource (a liability), it follows that another party (or parties) has a right to receive that economic resource (an asset).	Correlative association [4]	
Economic event:	is an economic exchange (manifestation of disposition that inhere in economic relationship) or other event in environment and society, that affects economic relationships.	Events [7]	CF[1]
Contract manipulation	includes offer, inception, modification, [un]suspension and cancellation events.	Communicative act [7]	IFRS 15
Revaluation	of economic relationship due to changes in the environment or enterprise		IFRS 9
Reclassification	of economic relationship due to changes in the environment or enterprise intended actions.		
Economic exchange	deploys one economic relationship to obtain another for a gain in value for an enterprise. Contains two opposite processes of partial, distinct and complete transfer.	Interaction [7] Exchange [11]	IFRS 9, 15-17
Impairment [loss]	is a condition that exists when the carrying amount exceeds the present value.		IAS 36
Economic contract	establishes a right and an obligation to exchange economic resources. In a contract, a party has a commitment to transfer some resource/obligation to the counterparty in exchange for a claim to receive another resource/obligation. The contract progresses in phases manifested by economic events and the effects of these events become parts of the contract.	Service contract relator [4], [11]	IFRS 9, 15-17
Relator Phase	models the evolution of an instance's membership in a type along its lifecycle and generally includes four phases: *intended* (scheduled), *recognized* (active), *suspended*, *derecognized*	Social Phase [3] Relation Stat.[8]	CF[1]
Contract phases:			
Offering phase	is formed by a contract offer event as a meta-commitment by a provider to a customer, to exchange. The offering may further enter into the *negotiation* phase or become *expired*.	Offering [7], [11]	IFRS 15
Obligation fulfillment phase	starts with the inception of the contract, includes enterprise/counterparty transfers creating process assets/liabilities and ends with the fulfillment of their respective obligations.	Delivery [7], [11]	
Liability settlement phase	starts when the enterprise/counterparty/obligations are fulfilled and reciprocal liability is accrued and ends when liability is settled or expired.		
Asset recovery phase	starts when the enterprise/counterparty obligations/liabilities are fulfilled/settled and assets are received and ends when asset is recovered or expired.		

Fig. 2. COFRIS terms and definitions with related UFO patterns and IFRS standards.

3   Conclusions

Financial reporting standard setting, implementation and the corresponding information system development at present is a partially informal and long process and, as exemplified by other domains, may be improved using ontological conceptual modeling approaches. Existing foundational and core ontologies, as showed by UFO ontology network usage, provide upper level patterns for representing FR concepts and relationships.

Contract economic relationships as dispositions of economic exchange events, creating new or progressing existing contract lifecycle, is a fundamental and reuse facilitating pattern of capturing economic phenomena for FR. Based on this exchange pattern it is possible to extract patterns from particular standards to facilitate reuse. Ontological analysis allows for explication of the core contract phases and exchange types to capture full partition of the economic phenomena usable for FR. Introducing event reification per [9] should release income/expenses elements of FR from semantic overloading and unify FR concepts for performance statements and notes.

Aligning FR concepts with UFO allows for understanding the FR concepts meaning and classification in the enterprise domain, as for instance, the economic resource and asset definitions. Elaboration of correlative associations between enterprise and counterparty may lay a foundation for consensus based accounting in shared ledger environment.

Further, a full validation of COFRIS by modeling all IFRS standards is needed, including solving the ontology version transition problem.

References

1. IASB ED/2015/3. Conceptual Framework for Financial Reporting, IASB (2015)
2. IASB homepage. IASB (2017). http://www.ifrs.org/issued-standards/list-of-standards
3. Almeida, J.P.A., Guizzardi, G.: An ontological analysis of the notion of community in the RM-ODP enterprise language. Comput. Stand. Interfaces **34**, 1 (2013)
4. Criffo, C., Almeida, J.P.A., Guizzardi, G.: From an ontology of service contracts to contract modeling in enterprise architecture. In: EDOC 2017, Québec City, Canada (2017)
5. Azevedo, C., et al.: An ontology-based well-founded proposal for modeling resources and capabilities in ArchiMate. In: EDOC 2013, Vancouver (2013)
6. Sales, T.P., et al: An ontological analysis of value propositions. In: EDOC 2017, pp. 1–10 (2017)
7. Nardi, J., et al.: Towards a commitment-based reference ontology for services. In: EDOC 2013, Vancouver (2013)
8. Artale, A., Guarino, N., Keet, C.M.: Formalising temporal constraints on part-whole relations. In: KR 2008, pp. 673–683 (2008)
9. Guizzardi, G., Guarino, N., Almeida, J.P.A.: Ontological considerations about the representation of events and endurants in business models. In: La Rosa, M., Loos, P., Pastor, O. (eds.) BPM 2016. LNCS, vol. 9850, pp. 20–36. Springer, Cham (2016). https://doi.org/10.1007/978-3-319-45348-4_2

10. de Kruijff, J., Weigand, H.: Understanding the blockchain using enterprise ontology. In: Dubois, E., Pohl, K. (eds.) CAiSE 2017. LNCS, vol. 10253, pp. 29–43. Springer, Cham (2017). https://doi.org/10.1007/978-3-319-59536-8_3

11. Blums, I., Weigand, H.: Towards a reference ontology of complex economic exchanges for accounting information systems. In: EDOC 2016, pp. 119–128 (2016)

12. Gerber, M.C., Gerber, A.J., van der Merwe, A.: The conceptual framework for financial reporting as a domain ontology. In: 21st Americas Conference on IS, Puerto Rico (2015)

Author Index

Affenzeller, Michael 236
Aires, Ana Paula 56
Åkerman, Magnus 76
Arvanitakis, Angelos 246

Bassiliades, Nick 120
Ben Halima, Riadh 36
Biliri, Evmorfia 246
Bjeković, Marija 141
Blums, Ivars 302
Bollen, Peter 133, 163, 173, 183, 193
Bulles, John 163, 202, 212

Cartigny, Bas 163
Chan, Iotong 46
Chimienti, Michela 5
Ciuciu, Ioana 98, 114
Coşofreţ, Gheorghe 98
Couckuyt, Dries 270

Dassisti, Michele 5
De Smedt, Johannes 259
Dulfer, Diederik 173, 183, 193

Eidelloth, Christina 87
Eppelein, Martin 16
Ermer, Andreas 56

Fast-Berglund, Åsa 76

Gigante, Fernando 246
Giovannini, Antonio 5
Guedria, Wided 36

Haas, Klemens 293
Hasić, Faruk 259
Hauder, Viktoria A. 236
Hepp, Martin 103
Hoppenbrouwers, Stijn J. B. A. 141

Jablonski, Stefan 56
Jaekel, Frank-Walter 16

Kaar, Claudia 66
Kappe, Simon 289, 293
Kaur, Bhavneet 232
Knothe, Thomas 16
Krahtova, Preslava 289
Kumar, Akhilesh 251

Lampathaki, Fenareti 246
Lemmens, Inge 202
Li, Qing 46

Mahanta, Prabal 232, 251
Maier, Andreas 87
Martin, Javier 246
Maurya, Pavendra 251
May, Wolfgang 297
Meijer, Klaas 212
Merla, Pasquale 5
Michalitsi-Psarrou, Ariadni 246

Nazarian, David 120
Nijssen, Maurice 212
Nijssen, Sjir 173, 183, 193
Nunez, Maria Jose 246

Ovtcharova, Jivka 289, 293

Panetto, Hervé 5
Piprani, Baba 152
Pitzer, Erik 236
Proper, Henderik A. 141
Pu, Yudi 46

Rozendaal, Jos 173, 183, 193
Runge, Lars 297

Sales, Vicente 246
Saton, Johan 202
Schindler, Sigram 223
Schliephack, Wolf 16
Schmidt, Rainer 87

Schönig, Stefan 56
Schrage, Sebastian 297
Servadei, Lorenzo 87
Siebert, Martin 293
Stary, Christian 26, 66
Stolz, Alex 103

Tang, Qianlin 46
Teoca, Mihaela 114
Tonev, Kiril 289
Torka, Jan 16

van de Laar, Bas 202
van Gils, Bas 141
Vanthienen, Jan 259
Vermeulen, Sven 280

Wei, Hailong 46
Weichhart, Georg 26
Weigand, Hans 302
Wicaksono, Hendro 289, 293

Zouch, Mahdi 36

Printed in the United States
By Bookmasters